TRANSFORM EMOTIONS IN A LEADER'S HEART

by Anita Carman
Founder & President of Inspire Women
Foreword by Jill Briscoe

A Personalized Curriculum to Transform Loneliness, Rejection, and Fear into Passionate Purpose
According to God's Word and to Build a Community of Authentic Friendships

Anita Grace Lie Carman
Founder and President of
Inspire Women

Dedication

This book is dedicated to
Robert Carman
Robbie and Thomas
the Mighty Men in my life
and my spiritual daughter
Mia Yoo

At the age of 17, Anita Carman arrived in the free land of America after the tragic suicide of her mother. By God's grace, He carried Anita on an incredible journey from bondage and fear to physical, emotional and spiritual freedom. Today, Anita is the Founder and President of Inspire Women, a 501(c) 3 non profit organization that inspires women across ethnicities, denominations, and economic levels to connect their lives to God's purpose and funds biblical resources and scholarships to train women for missions and ministry.

After receiving her M.B.A. from the State University of New York, Anita pursued a successful management consulting career at Exxon and Booz, Allen, and Hamilton. In 1986, God called Anita out of corporate America to serve His purpose. She served as a leader in Beth Moore's Sunday School class for seven years and prepared for ministry at Dallas Theological Seminary where she graduated at the top of her class. She also rose from Director of Women's Ministry to Vice President of Special Programs and Special Assistant to the President at the largest multi-ethnic Bible College in the country. To answer God's call, she walked away from an executive position that few women have attained at an established institution, to birth Inspire Women.

Anita's leadership is recognized by the business community and ministry leaders. She was given the Professional Women's Fellowship Community award, the Chinese Community Center "Asian American All-Star" award, the Daughters of the American Revolution "Americanism" award for leadership and community impact. She is on the Gifted for Leadership advisory panel for Christianity Today International. Her leadership was highlighted in front cover stories of Inspire Women in the Houston Chronicle religious section, Just Between Us magazine, Houston Woman's Magazine and stories in the Memorial Villages newspaper, the Memorial Buzz, and on WB-39 and Fox 26 television. She writes a regular devotion and a Christian "Ann Landers" column that reaches thousands through the Houston Chronicle website. She is married to Robert Carman and has two sons who both tower over her at 6' 3". They encourage their mother in supporting the ministry of Inspire Women.

About the Ministry of Inspire Women

Inspire Women is a 501 (c) 3 organization which exists to inspire women across ethnicities, denominations and economic levels to connect their lives with God's purpose and funds biblical resources and scholarships to train women to serve at their God-given potential.

Inspire Women began as an independent non-profit organization in May, 2003 and by November, 2006, the ministry was established as a perpetual part of the infrastructure of Houston, Texas, to inspire and to equip women to change the world with the power of God's Word in action. Inspire Women invested over $1 million in the first three years in the training of those called to missions and ministry. As God's miracle story in establishing Inspire Women spreads, the ministry continues to trust God to invite His friends to name Inspire Women as a beneficiary in their estate planning. In addition, Inspire Women welcomes those who join the Dream Society, a united sisterhood of women who stand with those beyond their church walls and denominations, who are committed to the study of God's Word and to the training of those who serve God's dreams.

Inspire Women produces citywide conferences as simply the beginning. From the events, the ministry then offers more intensive leadership training and mentoring through Inspire Women's Leadership Institute. The ministry searches for those set apart for missions and ministry and funds biblical resources and scholarships for biblical training in accredited Bible colleges, seminaries and specialized programs to best prepare those called to serve in abuse centers, prisons, homeless shelters, youth centers, veterans hospitals, orphanages, women's ministry and missions around the world.

Through invitations to national leader's conferences, the story of Inspire Women is traveling from Houston, Texas to inspire women throughout the world to fulfill God's dreams.

Foreword by Jill Briscoe

I was on a flight last month and the air stewardess was trying to get people's attention as she went through the pre-flight procedures. I am a million mile flyer and the temptation for me is to switch off knowing the drill by heart. I have learned however to put my book down and listen as I should, if for no other reason than to be a good example. As she demonstrated the use of the masks in case oxygen was a problem in an emergency, I heard with new ears, "Put your own mask on first before you assist a child."

I thought about that. Everything in me would want to get life sustaining oxygen to that child sitting next to me. But the application is obvious. If I'm unconscious I can't help my own child or any one else's. I can't even help myself!

This material that Anita Carman has written (coming from long experience based in the bedrock of the Word of God) helps you as a leader to put on your own mask first. It is life giving air. It will help you to get the spiritual oxygen that it is going to take to keep you healthy and thinking clearly in a crisis, acting on scripture and not responding only to your emotions. And this not only in crisis but in life service to Christ.

I remember hearing some bad news that literally took my breath away. In fact for days I was in such an emotional turmoil I could hardly breathe. I certainly had no breath for words that would comfort and encourage others around me in the same pain I was in. I had to use my will to review the facts. I knew the safety drill I had heard over and over again. Then I began to function as a leader whatever my emotions were doing to me.

As you work through these principles your heart rate should quiet and your faith should be able to "turn your eyes to the hills, from whence comes your help". Happy studying then go out to be the blessing the world is waiting for.

In His life,

Jill Briscoe

Jill Briscoe
Author, Bible teacher and international women's leader

NOTE: The materials on "Transforming Emotions in a Leader's Heart" are available in bound format for your personal use or in a loose leaf binder format so you can personalize the material and use it as a tool to build authentic friendships and community. The loose leaf binder format allows you to easily insert pages with your own testimony and with testimonies from those in your community.

Introduction

When I began my journey to serve God, I was not alone in my enthusiasm. Yet when I look around me today, I see only a few of the zealous friends who began with me. I did some research on the attrition of Christian leaders and the statistics indicated one third will abandon the dream before their time on earth is over. As I reflected on the torpedoes that came my way during the establishment of Inspire Women, I saw that the biggest challenge I had to overcome was ME!!! When my emotions defeated me, I could not get out of bed. I wonder today if you have ever found yourself in a place where you have given up before the battle was won.

Whether God has given you dreams for yourself, a family, a business, a church, a ministry, a community, a nation, or the world, you are a leader in whatever small or large group God has given you to influence. Your emotions can either fuel a passion to keep you on God's eternal timeline or they can shut you down and disperse your focus all over the map. **When a leader craters and starts grasping for straws to feel whole, the wandering from God's purpose begins.** Instead of acting like a sharpened arrow heading toward a target, our hearts look more like fragments that exploded from a landmine. In this state of disarray, you will abandon any dream that had a chance to make an eternal difference. Has God entrusted you with employees, children, and/or audiences in a family, business, church, ministry, community, nation, or the world to lead them towards goals with lasting significance? Then you must learn to fortify your heart as God's keeper of the vision, the one entrusted to fulfill God's dreams.

When you step into God's dreams for you, you are not living in neutral territory. You are living in enemy territory. The devil doesn't care what you do when you are unfocused. But once you get focused, you show up on Satan's radar and you can almost hear him say to his angels "Vessel in motion. Engage and destroy." His goal is to put you out of commission. One way I have seen the devil do this is through our emotions. This is especially true with women because we tend to be more emotional. The strategy is simply to get you to crater on the inside so you either won't care enough anymore to make a difference in the world or you're totally defeated and don't care at all. In training leaders, I asked the Lord what I could teach them that could be of help. He said, "Teach them the importance of guarding their hearts and show them how my Word transformed your emotions before you were ready to establish Inspire Women."

How God Transforms Emotions to Accomplish His Purpose

"Transforming Emotions in a Leader's Heart" was written to focus on how God transforms the emotions of loneliness, rejection and fear into a passionate purpose to accomplish His dreams. I chose these emotions because they were the top three God helped me overcome in my life with His Word as He shaped me into a suitable vessel for His purpose.

The way God transformed my emotions was through the practicing of God's Word, not just the quoting of it. This curriculum is divided into three modules, each focusing on an emotion. Module One covers loneliness, Module Two covers rejection and Module Three covers fear.

The format I have used to cover each emotion is to begin with a section of personal journal entries capturing the situations and emotions I felt. This is followed by a Bible Study with instruction from God's Word on dealing with those same situations and emotions. The goal is to give you a tangible way to apply God's Word in your life so that you can respond to your situations in a way that fulfills God's purpose. With our study on transforming emotions, I have included additional testimonies from those who have experienced and overcome the same emotions with the power of God's Word.

You will learn that a life of faith is not some mystical feeling but the concrete application of God's Word in the following ways:

- No matter what family background you came from and how things were done in your earthly family, all believers belong to God's royal family and are therefore expected to act according to the customs of the royal family.

- Whenever I experienced an emotion because of a challenge or a decision I needed to make, God taught me to do the following:

  o I ask myself, "What am I feeling? What exactly is the emotion I am dealing with?"

  o I ask myself, "Is the level of the emotion I am feeling in proportion to what just happened? If not, what wound did it open from my past to cause me to over react?"

  o I ask myself, "Is there a teaching in God's Word that parallels the situation I just encountered? Are there verses that speak to the situation that will give me guidance on how to respond?"

  o If I cannot find specific verses, then I look for biblical examples of someone who dealt with a parallel situation. Since I am to act as a member of God's royal family, I ask myself, "What is the custom of God's royal family and how would God expect me to act?" A tangible way to learn the customs of the royal family is to study the lives of God's faith heroes and how they responded in a parallel situation. I was then able to imitate how the faith heroes responded. There are times I learned from the mistake of a biblical character as described in my concluding thoughts which shares a situation that almost made me abandon the dream.

    A life of faith then is a concrete way to respond based on what God has revealed in His Word. A person who lives by faith is one who intentionally models behavior after the right choices of the faith heroes in the Bible and trusts that making such a choice is the best choice, no matter what the outcome. The result is a life that moves with conviction and confidence by making choices that are anchored in truths from God's Word and learning from the responses of those who are part of our spiritual heritage.

My niece, Rachel, wrote a devotion titled, **"Do you belong in the palace?"** I thought it was a beautiful application of how God wants us to act like royalty. So I have included it below:

Think about a time when you felt totally out of place. How did you react? Were you so uncomfortable that all you wanted to do was leave and hope no one noticed? Or did you take everything in thinking, "This is great!"?

When I was living in Dallas, a friend of mine married a man whose family was close personal friends with Jerry Jones, owner of the Dallas Cowboys. Mr. Jones was a very successful, wealthy business man who had a "larger than life" persona. As the owner of a legendary football team in sports-crazy Texas, he enjoyed a fair amount of celebrity in the area. Imagine my surprise when one day I received an invitation to dinner at the Jones home in celebration of Laura and Jeff's recent engagement. I was giddy with excitement.

*When the day arrived, my friend Kristy and I carpooled together. Decked out in recently purchased attire acquired for just this event, we humbly drove through the gates to the estate in Kristy's 1997 Honda Accord. Dallas police were directing traffic and checking invitations before allowing entry. As soon as we drove inside, I lost my composure entirely. "Look at that!" I'd exclaimed, pointing. "I've got to take notes for my mother! The house is HUGE! It's gorgeous! The grounds are AMAZING!" Finally, Kristy grabbed my arm and said sternly, **"Would you act like we belong here?"** "Oh, right," I thought. "I need to get a hold of myself."*

*The truth of the matter was that **I did** belong there as an **invited guest** who had received an invitation by virtue of my relationship to Laura and Jeff. That relationship gave me access to a place that I would never otherwise have been able to enter on my own. But once I entered the gates, I belonged there. I just had to remember that and then **act like it**.*

*In the same way, we have access to the throne room of God's Heavenly palace by virtue of our relationship with Jesus Christ. Read what Revelation 22 has to say about the throne room: **"Then the angel showed me the river of the water of life, as clear as crystal, flowing from the throne of God and of the Lamb...On each side of the river stood the tree of life... And the leaves of the tree are for the healing of the nation...and his servants will serve him...They will not need the light of a lamp or the light of the sun, for the Lord God will give them light. And they will reign for ever and ever."** NIV.*

*The Lamb who sits on the throne at the right hand of God the Father is the same Lamb who has given you access to the Father's Heavenly palace. If you have a relationship with Him, you not only have access to the palace, **you belong there**. Do you act like it? Do you approach God's throne with confidence or do you stand in the shadows, hoping to go* *unnoticed? Remember, Jesus **died** to give you access to the palace. He gave his very life in order to give you a Heavenly inheritance.*

Notice, though, that not only do you belong in the palace, but you have a role to play within the palace. You are not to stand in the shadows. You are expected to serve; to fulfill a heavenly calling. Your service begins today from this side of eternity and will continue to its fullest as we enter into God's presence. Are you ready to take your place as a daughter in God's royal palace? May you embrace your inauguration and begin your divine appointment today!

How does a child of the King act? Are you ready to learn the royal family code as it relates to transforming our emotions for God's purpose? Let me give you an example of how God transformed the painful emotions in my heart into passionate purpose through a greater understanding of the Bible and the application of God's Word in my life. There were times when I felt there was either someone missing in my life or someone missing on the team. It was like waking up to a huge obvious void that stared at me every day. So I asked God if there was a situation in the Bible when someone felt they were missing another individual in their lives. Then I asked God to teach me from this situation how to discover truths that apply to my life.

God showed me in the first pages of the Bible which records the creation of the world where it states He surveyed what He created and declared "**It is good.**" The first mention of the concept of "**It is not good**" was connected with the lack of relationship. God said in Genesis 2:18, "**It is not good for the man to be alone. I will make a helper suitable for him.**" NIV

What I missed, however, until I studied the Bible more carefully was the sequence of events. Genesis chapter 2, verse 15 said, "**The LORD God took the man and put him in the Garden of Eden to work it and take care of it.**" NIV. It was when Adam was clear on his mission "**to work**" and to "**take care of**" the garden that we find God saying in verse 18, "**It is not good for the man to be alone. I will make a helper suitable for him.**" NIV. The concept of "**it is not good for the man to be alone**" was in the context of the mission we have been assigned. The forming of relationships, therefore, was in the context of God's greater mission.

Through this parallel situation from the Bible of having someone missing in one's life, God taught me that He was the one who was first aware that someone was missing on the team. Moreover, He then proceeded to shape the person to fit what was missing. In this truth I learned that in my personal quest for relationships, I was short sighted when I pursued relationships just for relationship sake. Relationships were not meant for my self fulfillment or to avoid being by myself. God views relationships in the greater context of fulfilling His mission. Therefore, to even know what relationship is missing in my life, I must first be settled on my mission in life. In the context of my mission, I can trust God to put someone in my path to fulfill His purpose. If God delays in sending a person into my life who I feel is missing, then perhaps I need to ask if I am focused on the wrong mission. Perhaps the statement God wants to make in my life isn't what I thought it was. Perhaps for the mission God intended I actually do not need the relationship I thought I needed. Perhaps God is delaying because I am unclear on the mission. I would not recognize the relationship as the one needed even if God puts it right in front of me.

God may delay in sending you who you think you need because it takes time for God to shape the person who will serve as the missing relationship in your life. That person might be resisting the shaping or it may just take time for someone to grow into the vessel God is shaping them to be.

When God placed Eve in Adam's plain view, he said in Genesis 2:23, **"This is now bone of my bones and flesh of my flesh; she shall be called 'woman,' for she was taken out of man."** What Adam expressed was a "Wow! You are it!" comment! He recognized Eve as being the one to complete him for the purpose of finishing what God had assigned him to do. It was because of Eve's utmost perfection for the assignment that the Bible then instructed us in Genesis 2:24, **"For this reason a man will leave his father and mother and be united to his wife, and they will become one flesh."** He is to leave and cleave because she is the perfect completion for what is needed for his God appointed mission.

Although in Adam's and Eve's case, they were husband and wife, the principle God showed me through this passage was the fact that God established the mission first and then He brings together the relationships that will best fulfill His mission. It was in God's Word that I found the counsel for my life and the healing of my heartaches. How incredible to learn in this biblical example that if there is a relationship I need in order to fulfill my purpose on this earth, God Himself will be first to be aware of the need and He is the one who will shape the person to meet the need. More than that, He is the one who will put that person right in front of me. However, it is only when I understand the mission that I will then recognize the perfect fit!

The Bible is how God has chosen to speak to us and to reveal His character and purpose. The life of faith is not some mystical feeling. It is a tangible choice to do exactly what God said to do. In the Bible, I found my lifeline. It has been and continues to be my compass.

As you turn each page, I pray to serve you as a faith friend. I have poured myself out in my writing to you so that you would never feel alone in your emotions. As you learn more about me through my personal journal entries, I pray too that you will conclude that the ministry of Inspire Women could not possibly have been built by someone as weak as me. God gets all the credit, praise, and honor. More than that, I pray you will be in awe of a great God who works through earthen vessels. If you let Him, He will transform your emotions to empower you with passionate purpose as His leader who will fulfill His dreams for yourself, your family, business, church, ministry, community, nation, or the world.

Personalize this Curriculum to Build Authentic Friendships and Community

In addition to giving you a tangible way to follow the example of God's faith heroes to transform your emotions into passionate purpose thus enabling you to fulfill God's dreams, this curriculum is also designed to give you a tool to build authentic friendships and community. Whether you are fostering an atmosphere of mutual support and encouragement in your family, business, church, ministry, or a community, this personalized leadership curriculum will help you to form lasting and special relationships. This personalized curriculum is your tool to help those you are leading start seeing themselves as God's instruments to minister to those around them through transparency and sharing of personal victories. The format of this personalized leadership curriculum is as follows:

- This curriculum has three modules, each focusing on a different emotion. Depending on the amount of time you have to meet with those you wish to bond together in friendship and community, you may lead a group in this curriculum using the following schedule:

  - Cover the three modules over a calendar year, meeting four weeks in the Spring, four weeks in the Summer, and four weeks in the Fall. This is the schedule we follow at the Inspire Women's Leadership Institute. The duration of each of our meeting times at the Institute is 2 hours. We spend the first fifteen minutes meeting and greeting, the next hour teaching, and the remaining time in the class for group discussion and inviting individuals to share their responses to the reflection questions.

  - If you do not have two hours and need to condense your meeting time, you may cover each module over a ten week period. Each module covers ten situations that evoked a particular emotion. So you could meet every week for forty five minutes to an hour to focus to discuss one situation per week. Be sure to give yourself ten minutes to meet and greet, then divide the time between teaching and inviting your group to share their answers to the reflection questions.

  - Because the material involves emotions and personal details of your life, try not to rush through the modules. I would not recommend covering all modules at the same time because it takes time to assimilate the material and to learn a new way to respond to life. Moreover, it takes time to build authentic friendships and community. So enjoy the journey as you grow together in the understanding and the application of God's Word.

- Each module begins with my personal journal entries from periods in my life when I was consumed with a particular emotion. I separated these personal journal entries so you can easily replace my personal journal entries with your own. Your transparency to share your personal journey is what will bond you to the ones you are leading. They need to see your heart and your pain before they can trust you to lead them to God's victory. In writing your journal entries, begin as I did with a timeline of key events in your life to give your journal entries context. If you did not keep a journal, then relive in your mind the times in your life when you experienced the emotion being addressed. Then, write a journal entry as if you were living through that emotion today.

- Following the personal journal entries is a Bible study with God's words on how to transform the emotion into a positive energy for His purpose. This study includes reflection questions to help examine your heart and apply God's truths to transform the painful emotions of loneliness, rejection, or fear into God's passionate purpose.

- In the Appendix are additional testimonies by friends who experienced the described emotion discussed in this curriculum, with their insights from God's Word. I included the testimonies of friends of Inspire Women. As you personalize the curriculum for your community, replace the testimonies of my friends with friends from your community.

I have included a sample letter of invitation for you to invite your friends to write their testimonies describing a situation where they experienced a particular emotion. You may invite them to pick one of the emotions covered in this curriculum that is most relevant to their lives.

By drawing them in to be a part of your personalized leadership curriculum, you are affirming their presence in your community and helping other Believers see themselves as ministers of God's hope in their communities. When all the segments of your personalized curriculum are assembled, you will have created a personalized keepsake that captures the lives of those God sent into your midst for a time of mutual growth and encouragement.

Other Ideas to Build Friendships/Community

Below are additional ideas to personalize your curriculum and to help bond those you are leading:

1. The materials of this book can be purchased for insert in a loose leaf binder. This way, you can easily add to my journal entries or even replace mine with your own. You can also add to or replace the personal testimonies of my friends with the testimonies of the women in your community. If you choose to keep my journal entries or the testimonies of my friends with your own personalized testimonies, you would use the content for illustration purposes of yet another testimony of a sister's journey with God and the victories we have from God's Word.

2. If you wish to personalize the front cover of your binder with photographs of your group, we can email you a template where you can insert photos and create your own personalized cover.

3. The butterfly on the front cover is available as a beautiful butterfly pin. If you think your women would enjoy wearing this pin when you get together every week, you can order the pin from Inspire Women for $15. Then as you teach this curriculum to different groups over time, think about creating an annual "Transforming Emotions Day" and have everyone who has been part of the curriculum wear their butterfly pin and attend a tea or a desert fellowship to share with each other the latest stories in their lives of how they responded with royal character to a situation in their lives.

Letter of Invitation to Invite a Friend to Share Personal Testimony

Dear _____,

   When God entrusts you with a dream for yourself, your family, your church, your workplace, your ministry or community, your emotions can either empower you or they can cause you to crater on the inside. When the protector of the dream craters, you can kiss goodbye any dream that was meant to make a difference.

   I am writing you because I am embarking on an exciting journey to share God's truths to transform the emotions in our minds and hearts into a positive energy for His purpose. Unlike other curriculums, I am so excited to be working with a "personalized" leadership curriculum. Because this is a personalized effort, I will need your help to make this adventure a success. The personalized curriculum I will be teaching has the following format:

- The curriculum is divided into 3 modules, each focused on an emotion. The three emotions we will cover are loneliness, rejection, and fear. I begin the discussion of each emotion by transparently sharing my personal journal entries or testimony from times in my life when I experienced the emotion being discussed.

- A Bible study with God's truths to transform each emotion into His passionate divine purpose follows my personal entries or testimony.

- Included in our study are additional testimonies from friends such as yourself. If you did not keep a journal you can draw from, I invite you to relive those times in your mind when you experienced either loneliness, rejection, or fear and write a personal testimony describing your situation and what you felt as if you were currently experiencing it. Then, add any truths God taught you in the midst reliving your emotions.

   I am inviting you to be a special part of this personalized curriculum to affirm your presence in our community and to help you to see that you have a message of hope to share with the community God has placed you in. I pray, too, that in this personalized curriculum, you will celebrate your divine appointment to contribute to the assembling of a personalized keepsake that will build the bond between us and create a lasting teaching instrument that will bless the members of our community for generations to come.

   Please let me know if you will join me in creating this personalized teaching material for our _____ (church, workplace, ministry, family, etc.). If you choose to participate, specify which emotion you wish to write about and what God taught you about it through His Word. Please keep your testimony under 3 typewritten 8.5 x 11 pages.

Grateful for your special friendship,

Worksheet to Help You Write Your Testimony

Please feel free to follow the flow below in writing your testimony. Just follow the flow and fill in the blanks.

Provide some information about yourself

- My name is _____

- I am _____ (married, single).

- If applicable, say I have _____ (kids, ages _____).

- If applicable, say I work as a _____ or I am currently retired but used to work as a _____ or I do not work outside the home.

- I would like to share with you a situation where I experienced the emotion of _____

Describe your situation
- What was happening?
- Where were you?
- When did this happen?
- What were you feeling as you were going through your situation?
- Describe how God's truths helped you to get through your situation.

Ending words to your testimony
If there was one thing you could say to others to help them through similar emotions you were feeling, what would it be? What did God teach you through His Word?

Chronological Listings of my Life

To give my personal journal entries context, I included a chronological listing and chart showing highlights of my life. In order to personalize your curriculum, you have the option of developing a list or to filling out a chart with key events of your life. This information will help your audience connect the events in your life as you share the emotions you experienced through your personal journal entries or testimony.

Below is a chronological listing of the highlights of my life. This information is repeated in chart form on the following page. I also included a blank chart you may use to develop a list of the key events in your life.

- I was born and raised in Hong Kong.

- My mother killed herself in 1974 when I was 17.

- Six months later, I left my country and went to college in Mississippi. I graduated from a four year program in two years in 1976.

- During my undergraduate studies, while away from home, I was sexually molested by a Christian leader.

- My father remarried shortly before I graduated. I did not attend my graduation since I had no family who knew me in the audience.

- I left for New York in 1977 and received my MBA in 1979.

- I fell in love with someone who wanted to change the world through politics and the government. I failed him totally because I could not handle his experiences with prejudice and the seemingly impossible mission to change the world.

- I accepted my first job in Washington D.C. in 1979 and started work alone in a new city.

- I left my job in search of myself in another city and moved to New Jersey in 1980 and joined Exxon.

- I met my current husband who I dated for six weeks and married in 1981. We moved to Brussels Belgium.

- I could not handle the loneliness in a country where I did not fit in and moved back to New Jersey in 1982 where I joined Booz, Allen and Hamilton, one of the largest management consulting companies in the world.

- My husband was offered a promotion in Houston in 1985 and I left my opportunity for a promotion at Booz, Allen and Hamilton to move to Houston.

- I had my first son in 1986 thinking the answer to my life will be in my kids.

- I went to Beth Moore's Sunday School class and Bible Study Fellowship in 1987.

- My second son was born in 1988.

- In 1995, Beth told me God had a ministry for me that was beyond the umbrella of what she was doing. I enrolled at Dallas Seminary as my way to prepare for God's service.

- In 1998 I joined the staff at the College of Biblical Studies where I began as Director of Women's ministry and became VP of Special Programs and Special Assistant to the President.

- In 2001 God led me to organize the first Inspire Women's conference. The conference was a huge success, drawing nearly 3,000 women across ethnic groups and denominations from across the city.

- In May 2003 Inspire Women separated from the Bible College to begin on its own with zero in the bank, no office space and one person on contract that I had no idea how I would pay. That same month, I attended Dallas Seminary's graduation ceremony to get my diploma and was surprised to discover I had won an award for top academic achievement. In God's most incredible grace, He encouraged me by allowing me to graduate top of the class before I entered a most incredible faith journey with Him to establish Inspire Women.

- By December of 2003, Inspire Women organized a citywide conference and luncheon that drew nearly 4000 women. That same month, Inspire Women deposited $100,000 in the Inspire Women's scholarship fund.

- My two sons left for college in 2005 leaving me with Inspire Women as the third child God entrusted me to raise.

- By 2006 Inspire Women invested over $1 million to train God's servant leaders for missions and ministry and seeded an endowment as God's trust fund for His daughters to be trained to serve at their God-given potential.

Below is a chart of the highlights of my life followed by a chart for you to fill on your life. Please feel free to adjust the columns of your chart to fit the number of key events in your life.

Year	Place	Activity
1974	Hong Kong	I was born and raised in Hong Kong. 1974, my Mom committed suicide when I was 17
1974	Mississippi	Undergraduate studies. Father remarried.
1977	New York	Entered Master's program
1979	Washington DC	First job in management consulting
1980	New Jersey	Second job in management consulting
1981	Brussels, Belgium	Married, relocated to different country
1982	New Jersey	Returned to USA. Third job in management consulting
1985	Houston	Husband's job transfer relocated us
1986	Houston	First son, Robbie was born
1987	Houston	Beth Moore's Sunday School. Also, Bible Study Fellowship
1988	Houston	Second son, Thomas was born
1995	Houston	Dallas Theological Seminary studies
1998	Houston	Moved up from Director to VP level at College of Biblical Studies
2001	Houston	God birthed the first Inspire conference
2003	Houston	Founder and President of Inspire Women
2005	Both sons left home to go out of state	Both sons out of nest in college
2006	Houston	Inspire Women seeded endowment and invested over $1M to train women for missions and ministry

Personalized Option: Use this Chart to fill in Key Events of Your Life

Year	Place	Activity

Transforming Loneliness to Fulfill God's Purpose

My two sons are nineteen months apart. I remember holding each of them in my arms when they were born and being filled with awe that God entrusted me with the raising of a human life for a God designed purpose. During my time in corporate America and in my ministry life, I was entrusted with different team members and given an overarching marching order from senior leadership to overcome challenges and to reach daunting goals. Could I unite the diversity of unique talents and personalities towards a common mission?

On the threshold of potential greatness hides a quiet loneliness in the heart of a leader entrusted with a vision for the future. Whether the vision you have is for yourself, your family, business, church, ministry, community, nation, or the world, there exists a loneliness within when the leader first sees what no one else sees and must guide others to the same vision.

When the shepherds saw the angels in the sky singing the birth of the Savior, they rushed to share the vision of the glorious scene with Mary and Joseph. Luke 2:19 recorded Mary's response as follows, **"But Mary treasured up all these things and pondered them in her heart."** NIV. Did she catch a glimpse of her son's future kingship?

The Apostle Paul said to Timothy in 2 Timothy 1:5-6, **"I have been reminded of your sincere faith, which first lived in your grandmother Lois and in your mother Eunice and, I am persuaded, now lives in you also."** NIV

Did Paul catch a glimpse of Timothy's potential as a future leader?

When King David was entrusted to build a kingdom, God's word tells us in 1 Samuel 22:2, **"All those who were in distress or in debt or discontented gathered around him, and he became their leader. About four hundred men were with him."** NIV. Unlike how corporate America screens for top performing candidates, God's vision for David's army included those God valued beyond what appeared pleasing to the physical human eye. Some of these same men were later described in 1 Chronicles 11:10 as **"These were the chiefs of David's mighty men -they, together with all Israel, gave his kingship strong support to extend it over the whole land, as the LORD had promised."**

I wonder today if you have ever caught glimpses of the future which seized your heart and compelled you towards a future that is yet to be birthed.

In the midst of God's intended design are the attacks of God's enemy to destroy the dream. God's vision for the future does not develop in friendly territory. Have you ever considered the possibility that Joseph may have died prematurely and left Mary alone for much of Jesus' life? It is a common belief that Joseph, who was with Mary at the time of the shepherds' glorious report, was no longer living. He was mentioned last when Jesus was twelve years old and was not present with Mary at the cross when Jesus' mission on earth was completed.

Neither was Jesus' brothers, who seemed to have abandoned him and turned away from his ministry before his resurrection.

Are you in a situation where the person who was with you at the beginning of a journey is no longer with you? There is no one who can take the place of the one who was with you from the start. Oh can you feel the loneliness of traveling on your own until the vision of what you saw at the beginning becomes a reality? Perhaps you have lost a husband who was present at the birth of your child and you must now witness alone your children reaching milestones such as graduation, landing their first job, getting married, having their first child, reaching a pinnacle of success which you first envisioned many years ago. Perhaps you have lost a founding member of your team. Now you must lead the mission forward knowing that when you reach your destination, no one will truly feel the significance in the same way as the ones who were there at the beginning. Do you know that God has been with you from the very beginning of whatever glimpses of the future He allowed you to see?

Whether you have dreams for yourself, your family, business, church, ministry, community, nation, or the world, loneliness is an emotion that can cause you to wither on the vine. However, you can allow God to transform your loneliness to fuel a greater passion to reach the finish line. In Module One of this curriculum, I will share with you what God taught me from His Word that transformed those times of loneliness into opportunities for greater focus and relationship with the God, who walks with me forever. In John 14:16-17, Jesus said, **"And I will ask the Father, and he will give you another Counselor to be with you forever - the Spirit of truth."** NIV.

The word "**forever**" is such a comforting word when promised by one who has the power to deliver on His promises.

As a leader, it is essential to learn how to guard your heart from emotions that can topple you. God's Word has been my protection. It has been and continues to be my compass and keeps me connected to the God who remains faithful no matter what other relationship or situation changes in my life. The doing of God's Word is a tangible way God allows me to be set apart as one belonging to His family tree. What sealed me in God's family tree is when I accepted the gift of Jesus' death on the cross as the full payment for my sins through His blood. However, what helps me experience my royal identity and connects my heart to my royal heritage is how I act, now that I am a member of the royal family. If you are feeling disconnected, could it be because you are acting out of character from one belonging to a royal family tree?

As the daughter of the King of Kings I am to exhibit royal emotions that are in submission to the teaching in God's Word. When I simply do what God shows me in the Bible, He protects my heart and transforms my emotions into positive energy to subdue the challenges in life as God leaves His fingerprints wherever I go. By obeying God's Word I allow myself to be molded in His image and connected to a family line of faith warriors. In my choices and behavior to follow God's instruction in the Bible, I find streams of living waters flowing through me when I feel what God feels and allow my heart to beat as one with my Creator's. I discover focused energy when my emotions align with God's emotions and compel me into action.

In the next pages, I will share with you what God taught me in His Word regarding transforming the following circumstances causing loneliness into opportunities to accomplish God's purposes:

- **When something is missing from your life**
- **When God releases you from a leader**
- **When you lose a co-laborer in ministry**
- **When you release your child to God**
- **When you accept God's decision to move on**
- **When God is silent in the storms of life**
- **When God delays**
- **When you feel no one is serving with you**
- **When you have totally let God down**
- **When God expects you to follow His voice**

When Something is Missing from Your Life

Situation: Are you in a situation where you are looking for someone or something to complete your life? Do you long for someone who is a soul mate and connects with your heart?

The purpose of the personal journal entries shown below is to capture the emotion of loneliness in situations where I felt someone was missing in my life. Some entries were taken from an actual journal, others were written more recently as I reflected on what I was feeling at the time. The dates of the entries are approximate and were included to give the reader some sense of chronological history. In teaching this material, feel free to use my personal journal entries as illustration or personalize your lesson with writing your own personal journal entries or testimony to capture the emotion of loneliness you felt in your own life. If you did not keep a journal, then try to relive the situation in your mind and write an entry today to capture what you felt at the time.

Feb 2, 1974

Dear God,
Today the ground from under my feet collapsed. Did you see it? How could it be that the one person on this earth that I trusted with all my heart would exit from my life without telling me? How many teenagers wake up to find that their mother, their best friend, chose to take her own life? There were so many dreams we dreamed together. As long as we were together, I felt I could conquer any challenge. What do I do now? She gave me my lines, and I read them diligently. My security was in her plan for my life. Did she give up on the dream? God, what do I do now? I don't know what my next line is.

March 12, 1974

Dear God,
I went back and forth between feeling like a spectator at Mom's funeral and feeling like it was just me and my Mom and everyone else was backdrop. Does anyone else feel the loss in my life the way I do? I heard someone say to my Dad, "Your daughter is 17. That's good. She's grown now." I don't feel grown God. Am I supposed to act grown? What does acting grown mean? I think it means acting all right on the outside even though you know you're not all right on the inside. It means putting on a big show because that's what is expected from you. I wonder how many people are putting on a show. How many people are crying on the inside?

God, I wrote this song for my Mom. Here are the lyrics:

Is that really you lying there?
A silent body all covered in white.
All the people around your coffin
But they'll never miss you like I will.
Can you hear me from where you are?
Can you hear me from where you are?
Let me tell you once again I love you.
Let me tell you once again I miss you.
Let me tell you once again I need you.

God, is she with you? If so, can you give her this song? I wonder if there is any one else on this whole planet who feels as alone as I do. It really doesn't matter how many people are around me. I have lost a part of my heart and I don't know where to find the missing piece. I feel like I'm in the middle of a storm and the waves are crashing down on me. I don't hear you God. Why do you seem so far away?

Nov 21, 1981

Dear God,
Did you send me a Prince Charming? Was he my rescue line? Well, he is everything a girl would want. There is absolutely nothing wrong with him. The problem is not him, the problem is me. He thought he could fill the loneliness in my heart but no human can fill it. He is giving me space to look for my answers. He thinks we should go to church. I don't really know where you live anymore. Am I just talking to myself?

April 30, 1989

Dear God,
I thought the answer was in having a family. The world sees me as having arrived. I have a perfect husband, I live in a grand house, and I have all the right degrees on my wall. Robbie was born in 1986 and Thomas was born nineteen months later in 1988. So I now have my two sons and two dogs. So what is missing?

What is this constant search I feel in my heart? Is it the loss of a relationship from years past that still haunts me? Is it because I repressed the grief instead of grieving the loss? Do I need counseling? What is this silence I feel inside me that is louder than all the activity around me?

I joined Beth Moore's class in 1987 the year after Robbie was born and my sister in law convinced me to be in Bible Study Fellowship at the same time. I feel like I'm inhaling your Word day and night. Why does it take so long to heal my heart? Is it me or is it you? I have decided to study your Word until whatever is supposed to happen, happens. But God, please hurry!

June 30, 1997

Dear God,
The British gave Hong Kong back to communist China. I always knew this would happen. Hong Kong was given to England in 1887 as part of a war treaty settlement, for a period of 100 years. I grew up in a country, knowing that it had a built-in expiration date. In a way, that sounds like planet earth. Didn't you say this earth will end one day? So in a way, all people live in a land that will one day no longer exist. Maybe you just had me experience it a little earlier. Is this your way to make your point that I am a citizen of your kingdom? I wonder how many people can even fathom what it feels like to be born in a country that doesn't exist anymore.

The corresponding truths God taught me from His Word to address my situation

Feel free to continue reading all my personal journals in Module One expressing feelings of loneliness before reading the Bible Study. Or you may wish to continue with the corresponding Bible study, which contains God's truths in addressing the situations described in the journal entries above. I have also included additional truths that God taught me to address situations that were not included in my journal entries. If you choose to personalize this curriculum as your way to bond with the group you are leading, feel free to use your own testimony and personal journal entries in the Bible study part as well as the journal entry section. Be sure to include what God taught you from His Word in your situations that evoked loneliness.

When Something is Missing from Your Life

Situation: Are you in a situation where you are looking for someone or something to complete your life? Do you long for someone who is a soul mate and connects with your heart?

Reminder: Let's learn the truths from God's Word that speak to our situations. Remember that as a member of God's royal family, we are to act according to the customs of the royal family. This means reinforcing our royal identity by living according to God's specific instructions in the Bible. When we cannot find specific instructions that speak to our situation, we are to search our spiritual heritage and model our lives after God's faith heroes who responded correctly to situations that parallel our own. We can also learn from their mistakes to avoid making the same mistakes in our lives.

In the movie "Message in a Bottle" released in 1999 with Kevin Costner, he played the role of Garret, a grieving widower. The story tells of how he wrote a note to his deceased wife and tossed it into the sea in a bottle. The beginning of his letter read, "I'm sorry I haven't talked to you in so long. I feel I've been lost. No bearings, no compass. I kept crashing into things, a little crazy I guess. I've never been lost before. **You were my true north. I could always steer for home when you were my home.**" Words like these paint a picture that when I find someone who completes my life, their absence destroys my sense of direction and sends my world into a tailspin. The idea that there is someone on this planet who is essential to complete us puts unrealistic pressure on another human who is mortal and cannot control either his life span or circumstances that might force him to change direction in mid course. The search for that perfect soul mate causes us to put our hopes in the wrong place.

Even when life does bring someone who is perfectly matched, the tragedy becomes even greater when death or other reasons separate the perfect duo. Could God possibly have designed life to work this way? It seems that you are either searching for that soul mate that is lost in action somewhere or you find someone you really connect with and you dread the day he might leave either by his own choice or forced by circumstances. So at the end of the day, what is the objective of life? Is it to find a soul mate for as many years as you can, knowing that the season will definitely end one day unless the two of you leave at the same time? How could this be a joyous picture of life?

"Before we know what relationship we need in our lives, we must first know our mission."

Yet, whether through a spouse, parent or best friend, there is something deep within us that longs to be connected with someone who feels our heartbeat. The fallacy, however, is to think that this connection is only for our personal fulfillment. In the context of Genesis, God first painted for Adam the grand destiny of subduing the earth. Genesis 2:15 tells us: **"The LORD God took the man and put him in the Garden of Eden to work it and take care of it."** NIV. It was in fulfillment of Adam's mission that God expressed the need for someone to complete him, in order for the mission to be fulfilled. It was after God clarified Adam's mission in the garden **"to work it and to care for it"** that God then said in verse 18, **"It is not good for the man to be alone. I will make a helper suitable for him."**

The incredible truth is to know that if there is anyone missing in our lives that God believes is necessary for His purpose to be fulfilled, God will provide that person. If that person is not on the scene, could it be that God is still clarifying our mission for us? Perhaps before we know what relationship we need in our lives, we must first know our mission. How can we know who will complete us if we are uncertain of our mission?

Even if God puts someone in my life to help me to complete the mission, my security comes from knowing that should I lose that person, God will send another. He will protect His own mission. Ultimately, God Himself is our anchor. He existed before we were ever born and will continue long after our time on earth is over. When God sends the perfect person for a marriage, a company, a ministry, a community, etc., he serves God's greater mission. If something should happen to him, God is the one who will shape and send the next perfect vessel into our lives for whatever new mission He has for us. In addition, could it be that one reason God allows someone to leave our lives is because their part is complete and either the vision is changing or it will take a different kind of person to take the vision higher?

My mother and I shared the dream of arriving in the Promise Land of America. Our focus was on reaching political freedom with opportunities to better our lives on earth. God redirected those dreams and gave me a passion for helping others reach God's eternal kingdom and make choices with their time, energy and resources while on earth to connect their lives with eternal significance.

Are you trying to relive yesterday's mission? What new information do you have that indicates God is reshaping the vision for your life?

Realize that though God reserves the right to reshape the mission, what is constant in our lives is the one who holds all missions in His hands. God is the <u>only</u> sure relationship we have on planet earth. The only time I will have solid ground beneath my feet is when my true North is someone who is unchangeable.

In the book of Psalm, chapter 144, verse 4, God tells us that **"Man is like a breath; his days are like a fleeting shadow."** NIV. How in the world could we find stability in a fleeting shadow? In contrast to human flesh which is mortal, God's Word tells us in the book of James, chapter 1, verse 17, **"Every good and perfect gift is from above, coming down from the Father of the heavenly lights, who does not change like shifting shadows."** NIV. Did you notice the words **"does not change like shifting shadows"**? No matter what mission God shapes or reshapes, the loneliness in my heart will dissipate when I cling to the unchanging God who will walk with me every day for the rest of my life.

Today, my older son is 21 and his brother is nineteen months younger. I wrote the story below which was published on Father's day in the Houston Chronicle when they were much younger. I am including this story to illustrate how our security in a Father's love can serve as the anchor in our lives.

Father's Relationship with Sons Helps to Shape Their Faith, Trust
Written by Anita Carman
Printed in the Houston Chronicle for Father's Day, June 18, 1995

It was late. I went in to check on my two boys, ages 6 and 5. Both were sleeping soundly. As I turned to leave the room, my eyes caught the tail end of a sheet of paper my 6 year old was clasping in his hands. I looked closer and knew it was the piece of paper on which he had written his Dad's phone number.

"This is where I'll be, Robbie," his Dad assured him before leaving on a business trip. "Call me if you need me."

The next morning, on the way to school, I saw Robbie fingering that paper nervously. "Why are you holding that number, Robbie?" I asked him.

"It makes me feel better."

"Why?" I asked.

"Because I know no matter what happens, if I can just get to my Dad, everything will be all right."

His words brought a lump to my throat. His words echoed in my mind all day. "If I can just get to my Dad…"

His Dad, the head of the family, his refuge, his hiding place, the heart through which he will learn his identity; the heart through which he will find rock for his feet and a place to soar into the future. How does a child develop that kind of safety, that kind of assurance? And then I knew. It came from only one thing. It came from relationship.

Robbie is my pensive child, my reflective child, my expressive child. At age 6, he wrote an essay on his Dad that read, "My Dad is the best Dad in the world…He plays with me even when he's tired. He works very hard so I can do a lot of fun stuff. He goes to work even when he's sick. I feel very happy about my Dad, and I love him a lot!" My other son, Thomas, is a man of few words. His Father's Day essay simply read, "I love my Dad because I just do."

Today, the boys are two years older. Robbie is 8 and Thomas just turned 7. They have encountered change in their lives as have so many of the children around them. They have moved, changed schools, lost friends and made new ones. They have prayed for Grandpa in the hospital and trusted God for the money to fix unexpected problems in a house that we bought. But through all the turns in the road, their world has remained solid because the leader in their home was solid. They always felt his umbrella of protection over their mother and over them. So much has changed and yet, for them, nothing has changed.

Recently, Robbie tried calling his Dad in Belgium but forgot about the time change. Fighting back the tears, he said, "The hotel said it's two in the morning. They won't put the call through." With a deep breath and trembling lips, Robbie walked silently into his room.

I did what I knew my husband would have wanted. I called Belgium.

"Bob," I said to my husband, "I'm sorry to wake you." Immediately he answered, "Is something wrong?" Before long, Bob was talking to his son. When he got off the phone, he said, "Daddy said I can call him anytime. He said not to worry about waking him. Whenever I need him or miss him, I can just call him."

Robbie walked away from that telephone with his shoulders held high. Once again, the message was clear. His feelings

mattered. Above anything else, he was important to his Dad. I was reminded of Psalm 121, verse 3: "**He will not let your foot slip – he who watches over you will not slumber**" and I was grateful that God had given Robbie an earthly father through whom he would one day learn to trust in his heavenly father.

Bob's job requires much travel as he plans and coordinates the company's computer technology. Bob's recent performance report described him as a "role model" in teamwork and competence. His secretary once said, "It is very unusual for someone at Bob's level to take the time he does for family. I really admire him for that." His peers also have remarked positively about his priorities.

I always knew Bob's priorities and yet, recently it brought tears to my eyes to have the evidence of his priorities stare me in the face. I was looking through the family album and for the first time realized that amid the flurry of daily activities, a story was being written. Through the photographs taken over the years, I saw a father who takes time to feed an infant, to bathe a toddler, to dress up as a clown, to teach math facts, to cheer a swim team, to coach basketball. More than that, a busy man who makes time to validate feelings and to repeat again and again, "I see you", "I hear you" and "I love you."

My husband's favorite game is golf but I watched him walk away from an opportunity for a company weekend golf excursion. He explained his reason with these words, "My boys look forward to being with me on weekends. When they are older and no longer want to be with me, then I'll play golf."

So much can happen in life, and my husband knows that as much as he wants to be there, a day will come when his time with the boys is over. So he gives his children the best gift he can, a foundation of trust through which they will learn to trust in a heavenly father. Only He can walk with them into the rest of their lives. And Bob prays that when that time comes, his boys will turn to their heavenly father and say as they do now, "If I can just get to my Dad, then everything will be all right."

I praise God for reminding me that His Word that has guided me in my life has the same power to guide my children's lives. I praise Him for the times of protection but I also know that when He allows a loss, His Word will carry us through our losses as well.

One of Inspire Women's scholarship recipients lost her children in a fire. She was so depressed she did not want to live anymore. What would be her purpose? But we have watched God's hand on her life and marveled at how He lifts us out of the miry pit. Today, God is training her in ministry to prepare her for His work with children from abuse backgrounds. In spite of our losses, God continues to show Himself as our hope. No matter what challenges lie ahead, we can be sure of one thing: **"Though He slay me, yet will I hope in Him**." In God, we will find protection, healing, recovery, and the passion to live His dreams.

When God Releases You from a Leader

Situation: Are you in a situation where God has called you out from a church, a workplace, or from under a specific authority figure in your life? Are you feeling the loneliness of leaving someone familiar?

The purpose of the personal journal entries shown below is to capture the emotion of loneliness in situations when God released me from a leader. Some entries were taken from an actual journal, others were written more recently as I reflected on what I was feeling at the time. The dates of the entries are approximate and were included to give the reader some sense of chronological history. In teaching this material, feel free to use my personal journal entries as illustration or personalize your lesson with writing your own personal journal entries or testimony to capture the emotion of loneliness you felt in your own life. If you did not keep a journal, then try to relive the situation in your mind and write an entry today to capture what you felt at the time.

December 19, 1974

Dear God,
My Dad came to visit me at Christmas. When we hugged at the airport it was like a missing piece of my life was put in place. But then I knew I should hold on lightly because he would be returning back to Hong Kong in ten days. Can't we just enjoy each day and not worry about the next? But I have to prepare my heart to let go. Is this what life will always be about? Is it learning to let go? God, why do I feel like you're about to make a change? Is my Dad going somewhere? Is he leaving my life too?

Jan 22, 1976

Dear God,
I had the goal of trying to get through college in two years thinking that when I got through, I could hurry back to Hong Kong to take care of my Dad. But he wrote me to tell me he would be getting married. It looks like he won't need me anymore. I

know this marriage is best for him because he told me that loneliness was killing him. His new bride will be good for him. I can see the sparkle return to his eyes. I want him to feel happy again. It will be so wonderful for him to return home and to have someone there to share his life with. This is his way to turn the page and to move on. I won't tell him God, he was all the family roots I had. Will he move on without me? What do I do now, God? I don't think he realizes how lost my sister and I feel. He was our anchor. Getting through school so I could take care of him gave me direction. He gave me the courage to keep going.

God, are you asking me to let go of my Dad to follow you? What will I do without him? I can't get up anymore. What happened to that girl who was voted by my teachers to be a future success? Didn't I win a full scholarship to college? Yet, with all the awards and talk of what I could amount to, I am shriveling on the inside. God, will all this potential you put in me just wither and die? If you don't rescue me soon, I fear it will be too late. God, if you are releasing me from my Dad, to what are you releasing me?

January 15, 1987

Dear God,
For the first time in my life, I went to a Sunday School class. I have never been to a Sunday School class. I never even knew such a thing existed. The teacher's name was Beth Moore. I don't know anything about her except that the words she speaks brings healing to my heart. The healing comes slowly. I wish it could be some quick fix but I feel the pain melting away a millimeter at a time. There are days when the healing feels so subtle that I want to rush out and try a faster solution. But she is there every Sunday like some sure balm. I feel like a wounded animal who laps living waters from her hands, goes away to watch her from a distance to see if she is safe, and then returns to lap some more. Is she safe God? I don't want to trust the wrong person. I don't think I can take another disappointment. Are you telling me that she is safe and represents your heart? And if she is safe God, how long will you let her stay in my life?

I started serving under Beth as a leader. I think I will serve her forever. God, why does the word "forever" feel like an illusion I'll never attain?

Feb 22, 1991

Dear God,
What happened? Why did Beth invite me to teach her class? She has nearly 300 women in her class! Is this the place you

have designed for me? Then let me be the best substitute teacher she has ever had. She said to me one day, "Anita, if it's not me then it's you." But something in my spirit tells me this won't last. She is not the answer to my loneliness. God, why is this happening? What role does she play in my life? Where are we going?

March 4, 1995

Dear God,
Beth told me today that she felt the ministry you had for me is not under the umbrella of what she is doing. She did not know where you were taking me but she encouraged me to trust you with my future. Is she telling me the truth? Sometimes I don't know what is true anymore. She became my safe place and it feels like I'm going to wander around in the desert again. I heard Dr. Swindoll on the radio today and he spoke of Dallas Seminary beginning a campus in Houston. If I am to cut the umbilical cord to go on a mission alone then perhaps I need to know more about you. Perhaps I have been trying to learn about you through someone else's experience. Perhaps you don't want me to live on fumes and want me to go to the source for my own supply. I don't know if this is where you are leading but Beth wrote a raving recommendation for my application to seminary. So is that the next stop? Maybe I should just live one day at a time.

Aug 2, 1998

Dear God,
My first professor in seminary just happens to be the President of the College

of Biblical Studies. He asked if I would help him in the ministry.

I really wasn't sure what he needed me to do but I would do whatever I could. I loved the stories he told in class about his relationship with his daughters. He said he raised them by himself after his wife left. It touched my heart. I let him into my heart as a godly leader I esteemed highly. God, please help me to serve him and the college well. One of the leaders at the college asked me if I joined the college for a lifetime or if I was just passing through. I feel like I could serve the college forever. They feel like the extended family I've always wanted. I've never had any grand parents. My siblings don't live in Houston. God, will you let the college be my family to fill what is missing in my life?

April 27, 2003

Dear God,
I drove away from the college with all my boxes in my car. Did you see the tears streaming down my face? I left on a weekend so it would not be so painful. The building in my rear mirror looked very substantial. I heard you say, "Are you more impressed with a building than with me?" I said, "Yes, I am! There is an office
in that building, there is a receptionist…You are a Spirit!" I'm sorry God but did you see how silly I felt driving away from something tangible to go to who knows where? I unloaded everything in my garage. So what's the next step? My last day at the college is officially May 1 of 2003. Did something end or did something just begin?

The President of the college wrote a letter to all supporters telling them that he is sad too but he knows this is right. It helped to hear that he felt this was the right thing to do. Still, I feel sad. How do I tell him and my friends at the college that I personally wanted to stay? But I feel like if I stayed, I'll never know what you wanted to finish. I feel like your dream will be a blessing to thousands. I sense that the platform you are building is bigger than what one institution can contain. It sounds silly though when I'm driving off with nothing but a mailing list the college gave me with their blessing. It is a wonderful gift because the list represents friends and relationships. I'll take friends and relationships any day. God, thank you for friends and relationships! Show me your friends, God. I know we can build your dream with your friends.

The corresponding truths God taught me from His Word to address my situation
Feel free to continue reading all my personal journals in Module One expressing feelings of loneliness before reading the Bible Study. Or you may continue with the corresponding Bible study which contains God's truths in addressing the situation described in the above journal entries with additional truths God taught me to address situations that were not included in my journal entries. If you choose to personalize this curriculum as your way to bond with the group you are leading, feel free not only to use your own testimony and personal journal entries. However, in the Bible study part, include what God taught you from His Word in your situations that evoked loneliness.

When God Releases You from a Leader

Situation: Are you in a situation where God has called you out from a church, a workplace, or from under a specific authority figure in your life? Are you feeling the loneliness of leaving someone familiar?

Reminder: Let's learn the truths from God's Word that speak to our situations. Remember that as a member of God's royal family, we are to act according to the customs of the royal family. This means reinforcing our royal identity by living according to God's specific instructions in the Bible. When we cannot find specific instructions that speak to our situation, we are to search our spiritual heritage and model our lives after God's faith heroes who responded correctly to situations that parallel our own. We can also learn from their mistakes to avoid making the same mistakes in our lives.

I served as a leader in Beth Moore's class for seven years. She used to call me to substitute teach her Sunday School class or at retreats. I thought my calling was to be the best substitute teacher she ever had. I never wanted her to worry about sending me anywhere to teach God's Word. Then one day, Beth told me that God had spoken to her heart and told her that my ministry would extend beyond the covering of her umbrella. She did not know where God was taking me but she encouraged me to follow His voice. I still remember the day she taught a lesson on Elijah and Elisha. She handed me an outline where she wrote at the top of the page, "Anita, this lesson is dedicated to you."

When God released me from Beth's class, I felt like a duck out of water. I had found my security in hiding under Beth's wings. I kept trying to run home to where I felt safe. I remember Beth saying to me, "Anita, I feel like you think you need something from me but you don't need anything from me. You have the cloak. Just dip it in the water." She told me I could call her any time. She had given me roots but now she wanted me to use my wings and fly.

For a season, I latched on to another leader not realizing that I was desperately trying to hide under the wings of someone else. Because I never envisioned myself as a leader, I operated as Timothy in search of a great Apostle Paul. I did not realize that God put me in Beth's class for a season in order to send me into the world as His royal ambassador. Although at one point in my life, God put teachers around me to lead me to Him, He was transitioning me into becoming a leader who would hear His heart for myself. Gone were the days when I could live off someone else's adventure with God. God wanted me to enter into an adventure of my own with Him.

If God has released you from being under the covering of a leader, could it be because He is taking you to a different level of maturity? What reasons could God have for allowing a separation in your life from someone you esteemed highly?

"Your ability to trust the changes God allows in your life comes from your confidence in God's character of goodness."

Our ability to flow with the changes in our lives comes from our belief in the Change Agent. Romans 8:28 tells us that **"all things God works for the good of those who love him, who have been called according to his purpose."** NIV. Your ability to trust the changes God allows in your life comes from your confidence in God's character of "goodness". Can you trust that God will work things out for "**the good**" because "goodness" is His very nature? In addition, the good God works out will be "**according to his purpose**" for those "**who have been called.**"

When you don't understand the changes in your life can you rest in saying, "But I know God is good and I know that whatever He has allowed to happen is an expression of His goodness to fulfill one of the reasons He called me." In order to accurately assess what is good in life you must first be in tune to what you were called to. If you were called to display God's power in a loss, then praise God for the loss which creates the stage for you to reveal God's power. If you were called to demonstrate victory in the midst of illness, then praise God for the illness which will showcase God's deliverance. When you don't understand what is happening in your life, try asking the question, "What statement is God making through my life? How will these changes in my life help fulfill my calling?" Connecting your situation with the purpose you were called will show you how God is working things out for your good.

I once heard a preacher invite his congregation to repeat the words "God is good" after each statement he made. He said, "I got a promotion" and they said, "God is good." He said, "I got married" and they said "God is good." He said, "I had a baby" and they said "God is good". He said, "My wife left me for another man" and all hesitated though some reluctantly said "God is good". He said, "My baby died" and no one said "God is good." The preacher made the point that we don't really trust God's goodness. In fact, we are constantly assessing God and evaluating His goodness. But how would life be different if we settled this question once and for all. Can you settle in your heart God is good and will work things out for your good no matter what is happening in your life?

King David tells us in Psalm 139:15-18, **"When I was woven together in the depths of the earth, your eyes saw my unformed body. All the days ordained for me were written in your book before one of them came to be. How precious to me are your thoughts, O God! How vast is the sum of them! Were I to count them, they would outnumber the grains of sand."** NIV.

Think of God as the leader who will lead you into the rest of your life. Do you truly believe that God has already counted all your days on earth before you were even born, that He thinks of you often, and that His thoughts towards you are for your good? How does knowing this about your leader change how you respond to the open doors God is prompting you to walk through?

"Could it be that we extend our own loneliness and stay in a sun scorched land because we rebel against God's instructions?"

How much do you trust God's goodness towards you? Do you trust God with re-assigning you to walk with different people in your life instead of demanding that your life be reserved for certain individuals? Psalm 68:4-6 tells us: **his name is the LORD — and rejoice before him. A father to the fatherless, a defender of widows, is God in his holy dwelling. God sets the lonely in families, he leads forth the prisoners with singing; but the rebellious live in a sun-scorched land.** NIV.

Did you see the words that tell us that God is the one who **"sets the lonely in families"**? Now, fast forward the tape from the Old Testament to a relationship in the New Testament. We see Mary the mother of Jesus at the cross with Jesus' most beloved disciple, John. Can you imagine how both of them were feeling as they watched Jesus slipping out of being physically present with them on this earth?

Now watch how Jesus, their spiritual leader sets the lonely in families. What Jesus said to Mary and John is an illustration of Psalm 68 in action. John 19:26-27 reads: **When Jesus saw his mother there, and the disciple whom he loved standing nearby, he said to his mother, "Dear woman, here is your son," and to the disciple, "Here is your mother." From that time on, this disciple took her into his home.** NIV.

Did you also observe in Psalm 68:6 that God said **"the rebellious live in a sun scorched land."** I wonder in your life if you have been resisting the new relationships God has put in your path. Will you trust God's decision and submit to the way He chooses to **"set the lonely in families"**? In Mary's case, Jesus invited her to adopt John as her son. In John's case, Jesus instructed him to take care of Mary. Could it be that we extend our own loneliness and stay in a sun scorched land because we rebel against God's instructions while demanding a restoration of the relationships we have lost or do we try to dictate to God the new relationships we prefer to have?

Has God connected your life with a new ministry with a new set of relationships to serve as your family? What new leader has God put you with?

When God led me from under the umbrella of the leaders I was privileged to serve, I did not understand. Why would God remove certain people from my life I personally would have chosen to cling to forever? In hindsight, I realize that God was not trying to take something from me but He was trying to give me so much more. It was in leaving that I was then free to build the community that God wanted.

Part of that community is the Dream Society that Inspire Women established. Sisters across ethnic groups, denominations and economic levels are offered the opportunity to join a society where they can stand together as a united sisterhood. This sisterhood represents one voice to the city expressing a common commitment to the study of God's Word and building communities on the foundation of biblical values. In my own plans, I would have stayed under the protective wings of the leaders I served. In God's plan, He pushed me out of the nest to rally thousands under the umbrella of God's greater family.

Are you still trying to relive relationships from your past? What greater impact could you have in the new family or relationships God has woven into your life?

I was in New York City one summer and was grieving that God had released me from my teacher, Beth Moore. Serving in her class for seven years had given me spiritual roots. I asked the Lord, "Will you weave my life back with Beth's ever again?" I asked this question with tear filled eyes while riding on a bus. I looked up and there in front of me was a billboard. It was a sign with big bold letters that read "The A.C. Moore company".

I had no idea what kind of company A.C. Moore was, but what caught my attention was the fact that "A.C." were my initials and "Moore" was Beth's last name. Was this just coincidence or was that God's answer that we would one day serve together? Then sure enough, when Inspire Women began with nothing in May of 2003, I asked the Lord if He would be so kind to allow the person who had meant so much to me spiritually to be the keynote speaker at the Inspire Women's conference. Beth had no idea what it meant to me emotionally to have her accept the invitation. I felt like I was attempting the impossible with my trusted friend by my side. She came to share a message and then left. I never got to tell her what was going on in my life because it really wasn't important. What was important was my discovery of how God works. He released me from under Beth for the expansion of His kingdom. We can do more holding on to Jesus' hand than holding on to each other's hands.

God sets the lonely in families and this includes the times I grieve the loss of my mother or the separation from a spiritual leader. Although God may put us under different authority figures, He is the King who does the "setting" and He chooses which family I will weave in and out of. No one could ever take Beth's place in my life because she took a spiritual orphan and put her in Jesus' arms. Although I am no longer physically serving along side Beth, some hellos do not end with goodbyes. In my heart, I carry what Beth has poured into me wherever I go.

When You Lose a Co-Laborer in Ministry

Situation: Are you in a situation where God has allowed the departure of someone you have worked closely with for many years? How do you keep going when an essential member of the team is no longer with you?

The purpose of the personal journal entries shown below is to capture the emotion of loneliness in situations when you lose a co-laborer. Some entries were taken from an actual journal, others were written more recently as I reflected on what I was feeling at the time. The dates of the entries are approximate and were included to give the reader some sense of chronological history. In teaching this material, feel free to use my personal journal entries as illustration or personalize your lesson with writing your own personal journal entries or testimony to capture the emotion of loneliness you felt in your own life. If you did not keep a journal, then try to relive the situation in your mind and write an entry today to capture what you felt at the time.

January 15, 1998

Dear God,
Seminary is going great. I am learning facts about you I never knew. More than that, you are no longer a fact book but a person with a history and dreams for the future. I am beginning to understand that this world isn't about my story, it's about yours. It never occurred to me that you have plans for this time and age and I exist to fulfill your plans. The strangest thing happened. My relationship with others doesn't feel so urgent anymore. What is essential is my relationship with you. As long as you and I are on the same page, I feel safe.

I really liked my professor who taught me about the role of women in the church. She wrote on my paper she felt she was standing in the presence of greatness. That sounded so funny, Lord. She must be dreaming. But I feel safe because when I look into her face, I see that she believes in me. I wish I could believe in something in

me. I don't know what's going on but she said she will no longer be teaching. Something has happened in her personal life. It looks like she will be leaving.

Why is it that every time I have someone in my life that I trust, you allow them to go away? Is everyone in my life for a season only? I feel like I'm in some kind of training program and I don't get to keep my coach for long. It's like you're moving me up some invisible ladder. Where in the world are we going? Why can't I just stay where I am?

Feb 24, 2001

Dear God,
There were over two thousand in the audience. My Mom always thought I would be on stage some day but I don't think she guessed it would be this kind of an event. What does she think of my service as a Christian women's speaker? I

know my friend Donna would have been sitting right there in the front row. It was her dream for me to speak in this auditorium but she died six months ago. So we keep going God. Why is it that those who dream the dream don't get to see it come true? Why is it that I find myself walking into the dream alone?

The corresponding truths God taught me from His Word to address my situation

Feel free to continue reading all my personal journals in Module One expressing feelings of loneliness before reading the Bible Study. Or you may continue with the corresponding Bible study which contains God's truths in addressing the situation described in the above journal entries with additional truths God taught me to address situations that were not included in my journal entries. If you choose to personalize this curriculum as your way to bond with the group you are leading, feel free not only to use your own testimony and personal journal entries but in the Bible study part, include what God taught you from His Word in your situations that evoked loneliness.

When You Lose a Co-Laborer in Ministry

Situation: Are you in a situation where God has allowed the departure of someone you have worked closely with for many years? How do you keep going when an essential member of the team is no longer with you?

Reminder: Let's learn the truths from God's Word that speak to our situations. Remember that as a member of God's royal family, we are to act according to the customs of the royal family. This means reinforcing our royal identity by living according to God's specific instructions in the Bible. When we cannot find specific instructions that speak to our situation, we are to search our spiritual heritage and model our lives after God's faith heroes who responded correctly to situations that parallel our own. We can also learn from their mistakes to avoid making the same mistakes in our own lives.

God's dreams cannot rest with another human vessel because we were not created to fulfill each other's dreams. Colossians 1:16-18 tells us, **"For by him all things were created: things in heaven and on earth, visible and invisible, whether thrones or powers or rulers or authorities; all things were created by him and for him. He is before all things, and in him all things hold together."** NIV. The good news is, God is our dream maker. In clinging to God's dreams for us, we will find the compass for our lives

"When everything changes, the one constant we can count on is the unchanging heart and mission of God."

When Jesus was alone on earth, Peter, James and John were the three Jesus drew closer to Him than the others. They were by themselves with Jesus when they saw a holy aura around the Savior. Matthew 17:1-2 tells us, **"...Jesus took with him Peter, James and John the brother of James, and led them up a high mountain by themselves. There he was transfigured before them."** NIV.

They were with Jesus when He raised Jairus' daughter from the dead. Mark 5:37 tells us, **"He did not let anyone follow him except Peter, James and John the brother of James."** NIV. They shared the most intimate moments of Jesus' agony at Gethsemane. Mark 14:33-34 tells us, **"He took Peter, James and John along with him, and he began to be deeply distressed and troubled."** NIV. Then after Jesus ascended into heaven, we are told in Acts 12:1-2, **"It was about this time that King Herod arrested some who belonged to the church, intending to persecute them. He had James, the brother of John, put to death with the sword."** NIV.

James is dead and the dynamic trio is no longer a trio. How did Peter and John deal with losing someone who was so much a part of their journey together? They focused on God's dreams for the world.

What greater mission do you serve in your life that transcends any earthly relationship in your life?

When I first started speaking at women's conferences, a women's leader at my church named Donna showed up at my house one day and asked for a list of my talks and a few audio tapes of my teaching. She had such a commanding presence that I gave her the materials she asked for and had no idea what she would do with them. I only found out a year and a half later when I was contacted to be the keynote speaker for the Great Hill's Women's Retreat in Austin, Texas.

By the time I was schedules to speak in Austin, my friend Donna who was the one who originally hand carried my materials to Austin had gone home to be with the Lord. I vividly remember the time she was in the hospital. I knew she had been ill but she always put on such a strong front, I had no idea how ill she was. I was surprised when I received a phone call from the hospital from another friend who said, "Donna would like to see you."

When I went to the hospital, I did not realize Donna only had a short time left. During our final moments together, she said to me, "What was that poem you recited when you were in elementary school?" I thought, "What poem? How did she remember?" She always remembered any time I had the opportunity to use my speaking gift because she was insistent

that I used my gift on a daily basis. She said, "Recite that poem to me." I felt it was her way to say, "Don't ever forget that God showed you your gift at a young age. Don't ever forget to use what God has put in you."

When I left the hospital, I knew I would not see Donna again. I clung to her last words to me, still not knowing what to do with them. I didn't know how I was supposed to use my gift. Then when the Great Hills Women's Retreat called, I walked into that auditorium in Austin, Texas, seeing Donna so clearly in my mind. I could hear her exhortation, I could hear her laughter. When I was on the stage, I knew exactly where she would be sitting on that front row. I could hear her say ever so proudly, "Look at my girl go!"

As I delivered my keynote, I watched the faces of the women in the audience as God's word flowed out of me and witnessed God's overflowing waters quench their thirst in parched souls so they would never thirst again. As I walked off the stage, I sensed an affirmation from God that I had come and I had finished what God intended. I whispered to myself, "Donna, that one was for you!" As soon as I said those words, I had a check in my spirit. From all that I remembered about Donna, I knew she was whispering back to me, "This one was for Jesus. It's all for Jesus!"

Years later, I found myself at another speaking engagement. Marge Caldwell, one of Inspire Women's cherished board members had gone to be with the Lord, and I attended her memorial service the day before my speaking engagement. As I walked in to deliver the keynote message, I was surprised to see a portrait of Marge displayed at the door. The women's ministry leaders said, "Marge was our speaker last year so we decided to remember her by displaying her photo." They had no idea Marge was on my Board and was someone I called often to guide me in the building of Inspire Women. I could not believe that the day after her memorial service I was stepping into the very place she had spoken the year before.

As I went on the stage, I felt a lump in my throat knowing I was stepping on the same grounds Marge previously stood on. I wanted to burst into tears because her presence in my life was so sorely missing. But God brought to my mind the scripture in Hebrews 12:1-2 which reads, **"Therefore, since we are surrounded by such a great cloud of witnesses, let us throw off everything that hinders and the sin that so easily entangles, and let us run with perseverance the race marked out for us.** NIV. In that moment I realized that Marge was not absent. It was not as if she had left me to walk alone on my journey. Instead she had simply gone ahead of me and she was waiting for me on God's mountaintop. My best way to honor her memory was to finish well.

What do you believe is God's mission on earth? What must you do to finish well?

God's mission is our stability. When everything changes, the one constant we can count on is the unchanging heart and mission of God. All authority has been given to Jesus. With that authority, He commanded us to go and make disciples of all nations. God has sounded His clarion call and He will not stop until every knee will bow and every tongue confess that Jesus Christ is Lord. Jesus said in John 5: 17, **"My Father is always at his work to this very day, and I, too, am working."** NIV. The question is, "Are you working with Him?"

When You Release Your Child to God

Situation: Are you in a situation where you must let go of a child who is leaving the nest, moving away, or who went home to be with the Lord? Whatever your situation, are you experiencing the loneliness of having to let go of part of your heart?

The purpose of the personal journal entries shown below is to capture the emotion of loneliness in situations when you must let go of a child. Some entries were taken from an actual journal, others were written more recently as I reflected on what I was feeling at the time. The dates of the entries are approximate and were included to give the reader some sense of chronological history. In teaching this material, feel free to use my personal journal entries as illustration or personalize your lesson with writing your own personal journal entries or testimony to capture the emotion of loneliness you felt in your own life. If you did not keep a journal, then try to relive the situation in your mind and write an entry today to capture what you felt at the time.

May 4, 1987

Dear God,
I never knew what pain was till I feared for my baby's life. He is only nine months old. I wish I could carry this suffering for him. Is this how you felt when your son went to the cross? You went with Him, God, didn't you? You heard His every cry from the cross.

The doctors think they have his asthma under control but they don't really know. His little hands are black and blue from all the IV's the nurses tried to put in him. Do we go home now and then wait to see if the medicine will work? I can't sleep at night. I am pacing within my heart and mind even though I am lying in bed. I feel like I am just waiting for the next shoe to drop. I live in fear that he might die during the night. God, I feel lonely just thinking about the possibility of losing my first born. I don't think I'll ever recover. God, when you gave me children, you opened my heart for love I never knew I was capable

of experiencing. I didn't realize that with more love I also opened myself up to more pain. God, how will I recover if I lose him? I feel like part of me is dying.

July 15, 2005

Dear God,
My oldest son is leaving the nest. He will be gone in a few days. I heard a little boy in the store today. He sounded just like Robbie used to sound when he was that age. How did time pass by so quickly? At least I'll still have Thomas at home for one year and then he will be gone too. When I came to this country my mother wasn't even alive but you carried me through my journey. You have proven yourself faithful in my life. I know that the same God who walked with me will walk with my children. Thank you God for being faithful in my life!

I feel like I have so many kids. Besides my sons, I have hundreds of daughters through Inspire Women. I don't think I will have time to think about the loss of my sons leaving the nest because there are so many daughters I have to take care of. I am relieved to know you will be leading my sons into the future. There is nothing more I can do for them. I remember Kay Arthur saying that when her children left, she was filled with anxiety thinking there was something she needed to do. Then you gave her peace by telling her that you will take care of the rest. Thank you for reminding me of that story, God. I know

there are probably a thousand things I could have done better but the great news is, you will cover me with your grace. Even with our imperfections, you can work out your perfect purpose.

Hold my sons God in your heart. While you walk with them in a new city, help me to raise all the daughters you have sent my way. There is so much work still to be done in the family.

The corresponding truths God taught me from His Word to address my situation
Feel free to continue reading all my personal journals in Module One expressing feelings of loneliness before reading the Bible Study. Or you may continue with the corresponding Bible study which contains God's truths in addressing the situation described in the above journal entries with additional truths God taught me to address situations that were not included in my journal entries. If you choose to personalize this curriculum as your way to bond with the group you are leading, feel free not only to use your own testimony and personal journal entries but in the Bible study part, include what God taught you from His Word in your situations that evoked loneliness.

When You Release Your Child to God

Situation: Are you in a situation where you must let go of a child who is leaving the nest, moving away, or who went home to be with the Lord? Whatever your situation, are you experiencing the loneliness of having to let go of part of your heart?

Reminder: Let's learn the truths from God's Word that speak to our situations. Remember that as a member of God's royal family, we are to act according to the customs of the royal family. This means reinforcing our royal identity by living according to God's specific instructions in the Bible. When we cannot find specific instructions that speak to our situation, we are to search our spiritual heritage and model our lives after God's faith heroes who responded correctly to situations that parallel our own. We can also learn from their mistakes to avoid making the same mistakes in our own lives.

When God's dreams become the reason for our lives, it will help us to hold on loosely to our earthly relationships. In the story of Hannah, she begged God for a son. After receiving this child who she wanted for years, we find her in a place where she willingly lets go of the child.

1 Samuel 1:24-28 reads, **"After he was weaned, she took the boy with her, young as he was, along with a three-year-old bull, an ephah of flour and a skin of wine, and brought him to the house of the LORD at Shiloh. When they had slaughtered the bull, they brought the boy to Eli, and she said to him, "As surely as you live, my lord, I am the woman who stood here beside you praying to the LORD. I prayed for this child, and the LORD has granted me what I asked of him. So now I give him to the LORD. For his whole life he will be given over to the LORD." And he worshiped the LORD there."** NIV. I wonder today if you trust God enough to put your child in His arms to serve His purpose.

Do you feel like God owes you children or a relationship you have waited for? How will life change if you can hold on to relationships loosely and trust God with His mission for you as well as His mission for those you love?

How incredible that God shows us examples in His Word of faith heroes in our spiritual family tree. Hannah is an example of a faith hero who chose to let go of Samuel for all the days of his life. Hannah's example taught me that I, too, can trust God with the future of my loved ones even if I am not physically present to protect them.

"God in His mercy wanted us to know the power of a mother's prayers."

Perhaps you are a parent who is agonizing over your biological or spiritual child living in an ungodly environment. Your child could be living with an ex-spouse who does not love God. Your child could be in a workplace or a ministry where the leadership is corrupt. If you are in a situation where you can remove your child from a harmful situation then do so with God's authority. However, if you are stuck in a commitment you made and are obligated to leave your child in a bad situation, then perhaps Hannah's example will encourage you.

In Hannah's case, we find that Samuel was in a household where Eli's sons disobeyed God. 1 Samuel 2:22-26 tells us, **"Now Eli, who was very old, heard about everything his sons were doing to all Israel and how they slept with the women who served at the entrance to the Tent of Meeting. So he said to them, "Why do you do such things? I hear from all the people about these wicked deeds of yours. No, my sons; it is not a good report that I hear spreading among the LORD's people. If a man sins against another man, God may mediate for him; but if a man sins against the LORD, who will intercede for him?" His sons, however, did not listen to their father's rebuke, for it was the LORD's will to put them to death. And the boy Samuel continued to grow in stature and in favor with the LORD and with men." NIV.**

How incredible that God in His mercy wanted us to know the power of a mother's prayers. Even in the midst of an imperfect environment, God is perfectly able to protect those who belong to Him. I have witnessed this in my own life. Though my mother was not here to see it, God answered her prayers to protect her children. Though her children came to this country for political freedom, all three of her children, through different paths, found their way to spiritual freedom.

If you find yourself in a place where evil has discouraged you, discover from God's Word that He sees all things and will avenge what is ungodly. His Word tells us that He allowed the wrong **"for it was the LORD's will to put them to death."** In God's Word we find that He sees all things, and He will bring justice to all situations. In God's Word, we also find that in the midst of blatant ungodliness, **"the boy Samuel continued to grow in stature and in favor with the LORD and with men." NIV.**

What imperfect situation are you facing with your children or those under your care? How does knowing about Samuel's growth in the midst of an imperfect environment encourage you?

I was teaching the materials on **"Transforming the Emotions in a Leader's Heart"** at the Inspire Women's Leadership Institute. During the course of the class, I invited the women from the class to feel free to email me directly. I wanted to hear what was going on in their lives so we could better assimilate the materials from the class with their personal situations. Below is an email exchange between me and one of the women whose son is in prison. With her permission, I have included this dialogue as an illustration of how we can apply the truths from God's Word to help us through the emotionally difficult situations in our lives.

Subject: **Read this when you have a little spare time.**
Date: 8/30/2007 3:37:46 A.M. Central Daylight Time
To: Anita@inspirewomen.org
From: Sallie

Sister Anita

I was glad to hear you announce in class that it is ok that we email you, that you are indeed available to speak with us concerning life, and that you actually want to know. That is so, so good for me. Before I start I want to ask you, "Anita, how are feeling today?" Hope that things are going well for you today. Have you heard from your sons lately? I sincerely pray that they are well. Honestly, when I communicate like that it makes me feel less selfish. It helps simply because you have boys that you have had to release and you are a Mommy too! I visited my son yesterday who is in prison. He was visibly nervous, a little shaken, which is a state that he is not usually in when he knows that I am coming to visit. I honestly believe that when he knows that I am coming to visit , he works to calm himself down. In other words when he knows that I am coming he has the opportunity to pull himself together.

However, it wasn't the case yesterday. In an attempt to be calm and cool he responded by asking for a hug which was so tight it could have broken me in two. We sat down and just said how glad we were to see each other. My last visit to him was in mid June. So it has been a month or so since I saw him last. He does not always tell me but he began to tell me about having to fight so much and how he is so absolutely tired of fighting these guys!!!! He began to tell me about a fight he had about 3 days ago, and how the guy outweighed him by at least 100 pounds. He said he kept telling the guy he didn't want to fight. The guy cursed him as well as he cursed the guy. He shared with me that the guy is a known bully, and if he could humiliate my son it would boost his reputation. My son said that he was afraid of him and the guy continued to approach him; in his fear my son threw the first punch and the guy's face began to bleed. During the struggle the guy ended up on top of him. He said at the time he thought his life was over. My son said he didn't remember how he got to his feet but he did. During the visit he showed me that his hand was swollen but he says that together they have concluded that the disagreement is over. All of this occurred because of a disagreement during a basket ball game!!!

Because the prison is an open prison, my son says he awakens every morning at six for safety reasons because he is most vulnerable to predators if he remains asleep in his bed beyond that time. Anita, I can look at him and tell he is a nervous wreck but as soon as he told me about the fight, he immediately said to me, "Awe, Mom, it really isn't that bad, I promise". He shouldn't concern himself about me worrying, because I can't. I must give all concerns over to the Lord. It is not that I don't love him but the burdens must go to the burden bearer, and that is Christ. I encouraged him to trust the Lord, to give his heart and all concerns to Christ. Of course I told him that I loved him but Christ loves him more. I told him that the protection he has received all these years is because of the mercies of God. I wasn't preaching to him but speaking words of encouragement to him. Anita, he was really glad to see me, as I was to see him. He prayed for me before I journeyed back to Houston. It did my heart good when I heard him pray for me!!!!!! When he said "Father God, I repent for my sins, in the name of Jesus." he continued his prayer for my safety. I then prayed for him. I thank God for his protection and restoration, and the renewing of his mind. I love my son. Please keep him in your prayers, his name is Kenneth, he is 27 years old. He has been in prison since he was 19 for selling drugs. Also keep my daughter and her family in your prayers as she balances her walk with God, her home, marriage, three kids and school. Thank you for hearing my heart. Love u Sister Anita.

Sister Sallie

Subject: **Re: Read this when you have a little spare time.**
Date: 8/30/2007 11:38:20 A.M. Central Daylight Time
From: Anita@inspirewomen.org
To: Sallie

Sallie,

I remember Jill Briscoe telling me how her son was devastated over going through a divorce. He was totally broken hearted and Jill found herself getting on planes to go to the ends of the earth to share the gospel. She wanted to be here to hold her son but God had a different assignment for her. As part of our class, what we try to do is to take our situations to God and say, "Show me someone in your Word who is going through what I am going through." Then as members of the royal family, we imitate what our faith heroes did because this is the royal custom. So we grow more and more into being the daughter of the King. It's a tangible way of living who you are by acting the way royalty responds to a cross!

So let's take your situation. Say to God, "God, I am here but my heart is there with my son who is in prison. Teach me how to function. Show me someone in your Word who was victorious in a similar situation." Then you search the Scripture for a parallel situation.

When I did this on your behalf, dear Sallie, God pointed me to Himself. He said, "My son took on the sins of the world. I sent him from his safe home in heaven to a prison on earth where he was bound by time and space. He was confined to the territory I placed him in and he sometimes slipped through the crowd of those who tried to hurt him but sometimes they were right in his face." Then the most incredible truth of all, Sallie, is this: He bore our stripes so we could be set free. So while your son is in prison, have the confidence to say "God, for the times my son suffers like you did, may he offer it to you as his form of worship. He is fellowshipping with you in what you encountered here on earth. But God, because Jesus came to take our stripes for us, I ask for Jesus' power to protect my son. May he not be beaten up because Jesus was already beaten up. May he not be bruised because Jesus was already bruised for our sakes. I ask for the gift of Jesus not only for salvation but for all the blows he suffered on our behalf. By His stripes we were healed. I receive this gift in Jesus' name. Amen."

Sallie, do you see what the class was designed to do? It was designed to give you something tangible to do as you step into your identity as God's daughter. We are part of a royal family that has a royal code as to how we act. When we act as God models for us through Himself and the saints before us, we are no longer alone in our journey. We are united as a family with a spiritual heritage and one day we will be part of that heritage as others learn from our choices.

Thank you for writing me dear one. Love, Anita

Subject: **Re: Read this when you have a little spare time.**
Date: 8/30/2007 7:38:10 P.M. Central Daylight Time
From: Sallie
To: Anita@inspirewomen.org

Thank God for such a powerful word from Him, through you my sister. Anita, you are right if it were not for God I would have fainted long ago.....but because I trust Him, I have lived on His Word Alone. One person God allowed me to look at is Hannah in the Book of 1 Samuel 1:21-24 reads, **"When the man Elkanah went up with all his family to offer the annual sacrifice to the LORD and to fulfill his vow, Hannah did not go. She said to her husband, "After the boy is weaned, I will take him and present him before the LORD, and he will live there always." "Do what seems best to you," Elkanah her husband told her. "Stay here until you have weaned him; only may the LORD make good his word." So the woman stayed at home and nursed her son until she had weaned him. After he was weaned, she took the boy with her, young as he was, along with a three-year-old bull, an ephah of flour and a skin of wine, and brought him to the house of the LORD at Shiloh.** NIV.

In this example, Hannah not only had to wean her son from her breast milk, she had to wean herself from her son. I believe that the maternal weaning process is extremely difficult. I looked at what the scripture says. Her intent was to leave him there. Oh, how I continue to ask God to help me leave him there, not so much as in the prison, but to leave him with God. As Hannah left Samuel, she left him to worship and serve in the temple. The temple however was filled with young men of corruption, Eli's sons were corrupt. The temple also had a high priest who was out of order as far as discipline was concerned. Hannah may have known those particular situations, but her confidence and commitment were in leaving her son with the LORD...and there he remained with the Lord after they both were weaned.

Love you Nita, Sallie

If you are in a situation where there is nothing you can do for your child but pray, is God asking you to wean yourself from worry in order to focus on His purpose for you where you are? What other needs has God brought to your attention? What has God put before you to do?

I remember when I held my first son in my arms. I could not imagine anyone taking care of him better than I could. I would hold him close and listen to him breathe. I could tell as soon as he was coming down with a cold. When I found out he had asthma, I was afraid to go to sleep at night, thinking that if I fell asleep I might not hear him if he was gasping for air in the middle of the night. I was an emotional basket case.

Then God showed me that I was the one who was putting myself under such intense pressure because I was not designed to be God. I had to let God be God. He was the one who created my baby and I had to put my baby back in God's arms. Freedom came when, like Hannah, I offered God my son for the rest of his days on earth. I thanked God for the privilege of having my son in my life for however long God chose for him to be in my life. From the minute I dedicated my son to God, the stress lifted and I never worried again about his life.

This summer I had the utmost joy of having both my sons serve with me at Inspire Women. Every day was pure bliss for me. At the same time, every day brought us closer to the end of the summer. I knew the day was arriving when both of them were leaving home to go to college out of state. When the day finally arrived, I busied myself to get my mind off the fact that they were leaving. Our family went out for our

farewell lunch. I was praising God for the opportunities He had given my sons for college while at the same time I knew the empty place they would leave in our home and in my heart. The last moments before their departure, I got in a panic and wanted some last minute photos. I made my husband retake the photo over and over again to try to get the perfect shot. I could tell my sons were humoring me because they knew this time was hard for

me and they were letting me do whatever I needed to do to get through the farewell scene. As I grew more frustrated over trying to capture the perfect shot, the Holy Spirit spoke to my heart and told me to let go. All those perfect Kodak moments have already been captured in my heart. There is no still photograph that could ever capture what my sons have meant to me.

So I gave them a final hug and let them go as they drove away. They were leaving with their father so the boys could have their time together as they drove to college. As soon as they left, I felt the Lord standing with me.

"I have them," He said.

"I know, Lord," I said.

"I carried you all these years, you can trust me with them," He said.

"I know, Lord." I said and fell on my knees to worship Him.

When You Accept God's Decision to Move On

Situation: Are you in a situation where you keep holding on to hopes for a relationship to work but you sense God has moved on? How do you move on with God?

The purpose of the personal journal entries shown below is to capture the emotion of loneliness in situations when you must accept God's decision to move on from someone you wanted in your life. Some entries were taken from an actual journal, others were written more recently as I reflected on what I was feeling at the time. The dates of the entries are approximate and were included to give the reader some sense of chronological history. In teaching this material, feel free to use my personal journal entries as illustration or personalize your lesson with writing your own personal journal entries or testimony to capture the emotion of loneliness you felt in your own life. If you did not keep a journal, then try to relive the situation in your mind and write an entry today to capture what you felt at the time.

March 21, 1976

Dear God,
He was a senior. He said he would always protect me. Perhaps I looked up to him because he was more mature and sure of himself. He was raised as a Christian. He knew his Bible. He could argue Scripture. I felt like a spiritual infant next to him. He was in Christian ministry. Did I trust him because I needed a friend? I had not felt safe for a long time but I felt safe with him. It was as if we were soul mates. We talked for hours and connected on so many things. But last night, I don't know what happened. Do things like this happen in places away from home and everyone just pretends like nothing happened? Where is my home? Where is my safe sanctuary? I was asleep when it happened. He came into my room and startled me from my sleep. Then I froze. So many thoughts raced through my head. What was I feeling? Was it confusion? Was it betrayal? Was it the utter loneliness of knowing that your best
friend was really an enemy? What do I do now, God? Did you see a Christian leader hurt one of your sheep? Why did you just stand there and let it happen? I am too embarrassed to tell anyone. So I guess this will be a secret the rest of my life! Do you expect me to write him off and just keep walking?

April 22, 1977

Dear God,
Why do I keep falling in love with the wrong person and getting my heart broken? How could it be that the relationship has ended? Surely, God, there must be a way to salvage the relationship?

I know he abused me. I know I should not want him in my life. Is it wrong to still love someone even though they hurt you? What are you saying, God? Are you saying you have someone better? But what if I want to stay? Is it wrong to be afraid of the unknown? It's like I'd rather have what's bad than have nothing at all. Are you saying I need to trust you to bring someone better?

Life feels so alone when I think of the relationship being over. Am I on my own again? Do we write off all the time we shared? Do I get to keep any part of the relationship or is it goodbye forever? God, it feels so strange to think that someone could be in your life and then we just walk away from each other and keep walking. What do you do with the memories? How do you get past what could have been?

God, if you could just take me now I would be grateful. But if you keep me on this earth, then can you stop my heart from bleeding? Can't you tell I'm sinking? If you don't reach out for me I'll sink to the bottom and I'll never rise to the surface again! Are you there, God? Why are you silent?

May 15, 1980

Dear God,
I thought things would be different with someone older, more mature and established in business. Could it really be true? Does he have someone in every city who thinks she is the only one? I should just walk away but why is it that I still long to rescue the relationship? I play over the scenes in my mind, I can still hear his words, and I can still see the look in his eyes. What happened to all that warmth? Was it just my imagination? God, how can I just walk away as if we never met? It feels so strange to go through so much with a person and then to walk away. How many times God must we walk away until we find truth? Are you tired of lies too God? Are there times when you walk away?

The corresponding truths God taught me from His Word to address my situation
Feel free to continue reading all my personal journals in Module One expressing feelings of loneliness before reading the Bible Study. Or you may continue with the corresponding Bible study which contains God's truths in addressing the situation described in the above journal entries with additional truths God taught me to address situations that were not included in my journal entries. If you choose to personalize this curriculum as your way to bond with the group you are leading, feel free not only to use your own testimony and personal journal entries but in the Bible study part, include what God taught you from His Word in your situations that evoked loneliness.

When You Accept God's Decision to Move On

Situation: Are you in a situation where you keep holding on to hopes for a relationship to work but you sense God has moved on? How do you move on with God?

Reminder: Let's learn the truths from God's Word that speak to our situations. Remember that as a member of God's royal family, we are to act according to the customs of the royal family. This means reinforcing our royal identity by living according to God's specific instructions in the Bible. When we cannot find specific instructions that speak to our situation, we are to search our spiritual heritage and model our lives after God's faith heroes who responded correctly to situations that parallel our own. We can also learn from their mistakes to avoid making the same mistakes in our own lives.

If you are a parent or someone in a role who is responsible for developing the potential of others, then one of the most difficult challenges in your life will be to move on to develop someone else when those under your care refuse to listen to your instruction. If you believed in the potential of your relationship with someone your heart is connected to, one of the hardest challenges is to accept that the relationship is over.

"Have you ever clung to the image of what someone could be no matter what facts are staring you in the face?"

We serve a God who gives us free will to make our choices. God also judges the choices that we make. When God decides that someone has had enough time to understand the truth but intentionally chooses against God, you will find that God will move on. Sometimes God will move on for a season. At other times, God will move on for the rest of that person's life on earth. The question you must settle is whether you are more loyal to God or if you have traded God for your

affection for those you have allowed into your heart.

In 1 Samuel 16:1, **The LORD said to Samuel, "How long will you mourn for Saul, since I have rejected him as king over Israel? Fill your horn with oil and be on your way; I am sending you to Jesse of Bethlehem. I have chosen one of his sons to be king."** NIV

God showed me through these words that Samuel was still mourning for Saul. In the same way, you may find yourself agonizing over someone's wrong decision. Perhaps you see their potential and you cannot bear to know that they will lose their blessing. In spite of their blatant rebellion, something in us holds on, clings to and continues to dream of the day when they will repent and return to God. Have you ever clung to the image of what someone could be no matter what facts are staring you in the face? Oh the loneliness of believing and not wanting to give up hope when everyone else has left!

Samuel had to get back on the same page with God. God told him to **"Fill your horn with oil and be on your way."** At some point in our lives, we will feel whole again when we get going with God's next plan. What God taught me was how the dream cannot be in a person, and God's dreams cannot be thwarted by human decision. God taught me that I am not called to help a person reach his or her personal dreams. I am called to support God's dreams. When someone refuses to get on the same page with God, they are fighting against God. God expects me to choose sides. He expects total loyalty.

In God's relationship with Saul, God made the decision to reject Saul because of Saul's blatant disobedience against God. Samuel had to make a choice. Does he continue alone in fighting for Saul or will he agree with God that Saul has had his chance and move on with God's plan of appointing the next person to take Saul's place?

Whether you are a leader over a family, business, church, ministry, community, or nation, there will be those you have allowed into your heart who you had high hopes for. When they continuously reject their calling and God's plans for their lives, you will find yourself in a place where God will require His plans to continue through someone else.

I tell my sons all the time that there is nothing magical about their being born in our family. They cannot expect my support just because they have the Carman name or blood. Although I may be their parent, my first allegiance is to God and the entire family exists to serve God's purpose. In fact, because they are in the Carman family, I will expect more allegiance from them to serve God's purpose. Should they at any point choose to put priority on goals that do not align with God's plans, they will not receive any support from my husband or me to reinforce their wrong choices. We, as a family, are committed to supporting God's plans with our time, energies, and resources. My prayer is that these values will continue in them and their families.

Is there someone in your life you are close to who does not share God's priorities? How will you show by your response that you are more loyal to God's agenda than in joining a loved one in their rebellion against God?

In the story of the relationship between the Apostle Paul and John Mark, we see Paul withdrawing for a season. Acts 13:13-14 tells us that **"From Paphos, Paul and his companions sailed to Perga in Pamphylia, where John left them to return to Jerusalem. "** NIV. In the middle of a mission with Paul, John Mark leaves.

Fast forward the tape and we find Paul and Barnabas in an argument as to whether John Mark gets to come along again. There are times when God leads His leader to let go of someone who is not mature enough for the mission. Acts 15:36-41 tells us: **Some time later Paul said to Barnabas, "Let us go back and visit the brothers in all the towns where we preached the word of the Lord and see how they are doing." Barnabas wanted to take John, also called Mark, with them, but Paul did not think it wise to take him, because he had deserted them in Pamphylia and had not continued with them in the work. They had such a sharp disagreement that they parted company. Barnabas took Mark and sailed for Cyprus, but Paul chose Silas and left, commended by the brothers to the grace of the Lord. He went through Syria and Cilicia, strengthening the churches.** NIV.

Some may judge Paul as being harsh. Barnabas was ready to give John Mark a second chance. Paul, on the other hand, was adamant that John Mark was not ready to join them because he had concerns over whether he understood the mission. Oh the loneliness in a leader who must make a decision to protect God's overall mission and let go of a disciple who is not mature enough to be on the team. I wonder what it was like for Paul to continue the journey with Silas. Oh the

incredible grace of God to affirm Paul's decision by showing him that his decision resulted in "**strengthening the churches**."

"The only way I was able to get through the week was to know that I made the decision to put God first."

I remember a time when I had to make a decision to remove someone from the team. The decision totally broke my heart. Everything in me wanted this person to come along. I was ready to carry the extra load. But at the end of the day, I knew that my allegiance was not to an earthly person but to God. If allowing someone to come along will jeopardize the mission, then I had to make the decision to let her go. It was a lonely day to set sail on a new project with a new face on the team. The only way I was able to get through the week was to know that I made the decision to put God first.

In Paul and Mark's case, 2 Timothy 4:11-12 reports Paul as saying, **"Get Mark and bring him with you, because he is helpful to me in my ministry."** NIV. Even as if we let go of someone for a season, if that individual truly has a heart to serve with us, we must trust that God will bring the person back in due time. If you are in a place where you had to remove someone from the team, will you allow this example in God's Word to fill your heart with hope? Will you trust that when you put God's purpose first, He will work things out in due time?

Have you had to let go of someone from the team? How has the team dynamics changed? How has God affirmed your decision was the right one?

Is there someone you need to remove from the team to protect God's mission? Why do you believe that their removal will prove your loyalty to God's plans above your personal interests?

I wish that I had always moved on with God but this was not the case. When I recall the choices I made in my twenties, I shudder to think of what God must have thought. I was involved in a relationship with someone who was emotionally abusive. Because of his anger towards his mother, he delighted in leading women to fall in love with him. He deliberately sets them up to fall apart as he sweeps them off their feet and then suddenly decides to leave them. He experienced satisfaction to watch them scramble as they desperately tried to win his love back thinking there was something they did wrong. Instead of running as fast as I could the other way, I tried to rescue this person. I had sympathy for his background and decided that I could save him. Instead of rescuing him, I almost lost myself in the process.

Over and over I heard God warn me that I was the daughter of a King and I was dishonoring my heavenly Father by allowing myself to be emotionally abused. I was driving to his house one day when the Holy Spirit's presence was so strong I literally felt Him take the wheel of my car and turn it around. I exercised my free will and made a U-turn to once again go in the direction of his house. God's Spirit took over again and turned the car around. I went up and down the same road for fifteen minutes doing six U-turns as God pulled one way and I pulled the other. I wish I could tell you that God won that battle but He finally allowed me to have my way. I walked into this man's house knowing that I was being blatantly disobedient to God's counsel. I justified my sin by saying, "God, I can't help it. I love him and I have this need to save this relationship." I thought that God would understand since I hid my disobedience under the disguise of love. It never occurred to me that I was telling God that I was more devoted to a person I wanted a relationship with than I was devoted to the God who created me.

Jesus said in Matthew 22:37-39: "'**Love the Lord your God with all your heart and with all your soul and with all your mind.' This is the first and greatest commandment. And the second is like it: 'Love your neighbor as yourself.'**" NIV. Any time when I love someone or something more than God, I have violated one of the first and greatest commandments of God. Did you observe that the second command is to love your neighbor as yourself? We cannot justify our disobedience to God by saying, "I did it because I loved him!"

Who or what have you loved more than God? What must you change to give God first place in your life?

Anytime we violate God's laws, we set ourselves up for pain. The relationship was doomed to fail. This man was a prolific liar. I was in his home one day when the phone rang. I don't know why I picked up the phone because I don't normally answer his phone. He immediately grabbed the phone from my hands. In that instant, I realized there was another woman on the other line and he did not want her to know about me. He hung up the phone and we stood there in silence.

Then I said, "She doesn't know about me, does she?"

He said, "No."

"Is she in this city?" I asked.

He said, "No."

"How many women do you have going at the same time in different cities?" I asked.

He hesitated and then he said, "Eight."

I said, "Do they all think they are the only one in your life?"

He said, "Yes."

Right in front of him, I felt my heart breaking into a thousand pieces. I picked up my bag, slowly walked out of the house and quietly shut the door behind me.

I wish I could tell you that I never wanted to turn back, but I would be lying. Despite the facts, every bone in my body wanted to go back to rescue the relationship. Then God showed me the image of a bird cage with the door open. There was a canary walking all around the cage but it did not fly away. "What's going on with that bird, Lord?" I asked.

He said, "That bird is like you. I have opened the cage door. The entire world is in front of that bird, but it's afraid to fly. "How long will you live in your cage with the door open?"

What about you? How long will you mourn and cling to a relationship that God has instructed you to leave? Today, I sometimes bring a few miniature bird cages to class when I teach. I tell the women in the class God has released someone in this room to walk away from a bad situation. I open the door of the cage to show them the door is open wide. I ask how many would like to come up and take home a cage with an unlatched door as a reminder that God has set them free.

What about you? Would you like one of the cages with the open door? You have a whole world waiting in front of you. Is today the day you will fly away?

When God is Silent in the Storms of Life

Situation: Were you sure you were in God's will only to find yourself in the midst of challenges greater than before? Do you find yourself accusing God?

The purpose of the personal journal entries shown below is to capture the emotion of loneliness in situations when God is silent during crisis times you found yourself in while following His will. Some entries were taken from an actual journal, others were written more recently as I reflected on what I was feeling at the time. The dates of the entries are approximate and were included to give the reader some sense of chronological history. In teaching this material, feel free to use my personal journal entries as illustration or personalize your lesson with writing your own personal journal entries or testimony to capture the emotion of loneliness you felt in your own life. If you did not keep a journal, then try to relive the situation in your mind and write an entry today to capture what you felt at the time.

Dec 15, 1981

Dear God,
I feel like I solved one problem and created another. I thought that getting married would remove the loneliness. Here I am a newly wed living in Brussels, Belgium. I live in one of those fairy tale cottages surrounded with beautiful flowers. How could life be depressing when it's publicly so good? How do I tell my Prince Charming that he can't fill the emptiness in my heart? Is it the shock of being in a different country the day after the wedding that is making me unravel on the inside? What is it that I am looking for? It eludes me.

It rains all the time in Brussels, Belgium but they tell me it's good for the flowers. All my life, the dream was to go to the Promise Land of America. My husband tells me it's exciting to live in Europe but I feel disconnected. It's hard to get connected when you don't speak the language. I wake up every morning and just stare at the walls. What do I do with myself? The other women who are expatriate wives are having a great time. They get their hair done in Paris. They have lunch in Germany. I don't feel like I have anything in common with anyone. What is wrong with me?

God, why did you let my dog Casper wander off? I forgot he was disoriented too. The police said he got lost and wandered onto the highway. They brought me his collar and tags. I can't believe I just lost the only friend I had to get me through the day. I used to walk with him into town just to have something to do in the day. We talked to each other. Well, actually, it was a one way conversation but he always looked like he understood. Now I will walk alone or maybe not at all.

God, you gave me my husband as an answer to prayer. He said we should go to church? Is that where I will find your will?

Nov 11, 2002

Dear God,
I told my sons you gave us this house. I told them you only give gifts that are good. They want to know, "If God's gift is so good then why does the house flood?" What do I tell my sons God? I found out the neighbors on this road have been fighting with the city for ten years to fix the drainage. God, we are the new kids on the block. How could we possibly rally the whole neighborhood? I don't understand why we are in this place. How could receiving a gift from you result in this place of total chaos? The house is under water. Surely you don't mean for us to be under water.

Nov 5, 2005

Dear God,
We threw a party to celebrate the repair of the road to solve the drainage problem. The week after the celebration it rained and no one else's house flooded but ours. How could you have allowed such a thing to happen? We look really silly, God. Here we are telling everyone how you delivered us from the storm and then no one else's house flooded but ours. I heard someone say, "God sent the rain. Why don't you talk to your God?" I feel like I'm trying to defend your reputation. But you don't seem to care.

The corresponding truths God taught me from His Word to address my situation
Feel free to continue reading all my personal journals in Module One expressing feelings of loneliness before reading the Bible Study. Or you may continue with the corresponding Bible study which contains God's truths in addressing the situation described in the above journal entries with additional truths God taught me to address situations that were not included in my journal entries. If you choose to personalize this curriculum as your way to bond with the group you are leading, feel free not only to use your own testimony and personal journal entries but in the Bible study part, include what God taught you from His Word in your situations that evoked loneliness.

When God is Silent in the Storms of Life

Situation: Were you sure you were in God's will only to find yourself in the midst of challenges greater than before? Do you find yourself accusing God?

Reminder: Let's learn the truths from God's Word that speak to our situations. Remember that as a member of God's royal family, we are to act according to the customs of the royal family. This means reinforcing our royal identity by living according to God's specific instructions in the Bible. When we cannot find specific instructions that speak to our situation, we are to search our spiritual heritage and model our lives after God's faith heroes who responded correctly to situations that parallel our own. We can also learn from their mistakes to avoid making the same mistakes in our own lives.

It would seem that when we are standing right beside God, we would not feel alone. How could we feel alone when God is in our midst? Yet, this is what the disciples experienced.

The book of Mark, chapter 4, verses 35-39 reads: **"That day when evening came, he said to his disciples, "Let us go over to the other side." Leaving the crowd behind, they took him along, just as he was, in the boat. There were also other boats with him. A furious squall came up, and the waves broke over the boat, so that it was nearly swamped. Jesus was in the stern, sleeping on a cushion. The disciples woke him and said to him, "Teacher, don't you care if we drown?" He got up, rebuked the wind and said to the waves, "Quiet! Be still!" Then the wind died down and it was completely calm."** NIV.

Observe that it was while the disciples were on a journey with Jesus that the storm arose. Don't miss the fact that it was Jesus who initiated the conversation and said, **"Let us go over to the other side."** So the fact that the disciples were even in a place where they were affected by the storm was because of an idea Jesus came up with. Have you ever found yourself in a pickle and knew it was not your decision that brought you to your predicament? Do you find yourself saying to God, "Wait a minute! This was your idea. So where are you in the middle of the storm?"

"It takes an intentional choice not to panic."

The fallacy is to think that when we are in the middle of God's will, we will feel secure. Although the safest place is in the middle of God's will, we may not feel safe. Our human tendency is to panic every time a storm arises. It takes an intentional choice not to panic. Like the disciples, our first human reaction when we face challenges is to accuse God and say, **"Don't you care if we drown?"** In other words, "Wake up, God! Where are you? Don't you see what's happening?" To this accusation that God does not care, God is offended but in His grace, He speaks the words **"Quiet! Be still!"** He calms the storm so we can discover once again that He will never forsake us. Then comes the additional lesson in the words as expressed in Mark chapter 4 verse 40,

"Why are you so afraid? Do you still have no faith?" NIV

Did you see the word "**still**" in the question "**Do you still have no faith**?" How many more miracles will we need to see before we will trust God? For us on this side of Calvary, God has shown us the undeniable evidence of His love by His death on the cross. How many more nails must be driven into Jesus' hands and feet before we believe He loves us? How much more suffering do we need Jesus to endure before we will believe that while He could have called the legions of angels to deliver Him, He chose to stay on the cross? He stayed to ensure the full payment of our sins so God could offer us the gift of eternal life. God sent us His Son to protect the dream He had for us to reign with Him forever. If God did not spare His one and only Son for us, surely we can count on Him to protect us along our earthly journey!

What else do we need God to do before we will trust Him? The next time we turn the corner to find that something has blown up in our lives, instead of accusing God, let us have the faith to trust in God's protection.

In spite of the storm, Jesus had no intentions of getting out of the boat or turning it around. He intended for the disciples to also keep going. In God's call for your life, do you find yourself being called into one ministry or one activity and then convincing yourself that you have been called out? If someone were to plot your life on a chart, would it show a lot of starts and stops? Do you hide your own lack of faith by covering your choices with spiritual jargon and using words like "My season has ended." I wonder if it's time for you to finish what you began instead of ending your seasons prematurely.

Jesus said he was going to the other side. When God makes statements He means it. He has every intention of reaching the other side. What mission did you begin with? Besides the challenges, what other indication do you have that God has changed His calling? Has it been your pattern of life to change your own calling? If so, why?

In the midst of the storm, we can be assured God is not in a panic. He knew about the storm even before it showed up on our radar screen. In due time, we will hear Him say, **"Quiet! Be still!"** Meanwhile, what God wants us to do is to stay on course. Don't throw out your calling every time you hit a challenge. Oh may we receive the counsel from God's Word and may the storm subside in us even before God quiets the turbulence around us!

A few years ago, I was getting ready to go out of town to speak at a women's conference with over two thousand women registered to attend. I heard there was a storm coming towards the city and because I had to prepare for this major speaking engagement I was sure God would not allow my house to flood. As I was listening to the rain, I realized that the louder the rain hit the roof, the faster my heart pounded. The softer the rain fell, the quieter my breathing as I started to relax. Then the thought occurred to me that I had attached my emotional peace of mind with the environment. I was going up and down an emotional roller coaster based on what was happening around me.

When I constantly adjust the thermostat in our house or the level of the radio in the car, my husband would say, "My wife is very environmentally sensitive." But it's one thing to have preferences for the conditions of your environment but it is sin when we trust our environment as the dictating factor to our sense of security as compared to putting our trust in God.

As soon as God redirected my trust to Him alone, the most amazing thing happened. He allowed our house to flood. I could not believe God was sending me to speak at an out of town conference when our house was under water. At the conference, I realized that God's priority was not in my convenience. His priority was to send me as His voice to share His hope with those who were seeking answers for their lives. He said, "The women are hurting. I cannot send a speaker who is untouched by life."

When I shared with the audience that my house was under water, I saw many were encouraged by my misery. It surprises me sometimes how we can be more of an encouragement in our misery than in our success. It is our power in the midst of our weakness that gets the world's attention. Was this what Paul discovered when he said in 2 Corinthians 12:8-9, **"Three times I pleaded with the Lord to take it away from me. But he said to me, "My grace is sufficient for you, for my power is made perfect in weakness."** NIV. Could it be that God allows the storms to display His power?

Are you in the middle of a storm in your life? Though God seems absent, will you trust that you are right in the midst of His perfect will to display His power? How will knowing this change how you respond to life?

**"This storm too shall pass.
All storms do."**

As I was writing this week, God reminded me that our house flooded four times. The first time, it took nine months to get everything repaired. When it happened the second time, I told the Lord I did not have the energy to deal with it. But I did deal with it. By the third time I was a pro. And by the fourth time, my goodness, it was a non-event! Through it all, I said to the Lord, "Why is it that after you part the Red Sea, I turn the corner and there's another Red Sea?" He said, "To see if you will panic this time." He said, "If you've gone through one Red Sea, your faith should be stronger for the next one." So I have learned that God watches how I will respond so I am determined to choose not to panic.

Over the years, God taught me to manage my environment instead of letting it manage me. I know that if our house floods, it always floods the week before the Inspire Women's conference. So I am no longer surprised. I know what the family routine is during a flood. The boys carry the furniture and rugs to the second level. Mom comes home and wades through knee deep water. There is usually a pizza on the kitchen counter. So Mom stands at the counter and eats pizza while the boys try to vacuum the water out of our house. I go in the

backyard and find the dog swimming and panting from exhaustion. So I rescue the dog, put him sitting on a crate and tell him to drip dry. It is not true that we have to be traumatized by our situations. We do what we can, we keep going, we produce the citywide conference to reach thousands, and we finish cleaning up our house when we can. So life goes on in the Carman family. It's just another day, and the most important thing is to finish God's mission.

The office called one day and told me the streets were flooded. The girls asked if they could go home. Mia, my Chief Operating Officer thought to have fun with the girls so she said, "Anita said to stay focused and keep working." She said their jaws just dropped because they thought Mia was serious. Then she burst out laughing and said, "Anita said to go home and stay dry." The point being, we don't volunteer for hardship. We avoid it when we can. But when you are in a storm and there is no escape, then instead of panicking and forgetting the mission you were on, just stay on course.

By the way, the city came in with a second phase to repair the drainage. The house doesn't flood anymore! The moral of the story is this: This storm too shall pass. All storms do.

When God Delays

Situation: Have you been waiting on God to act only to find life sitting at a dead stop? How do you stay encouraged when nothing seems to be happening?

The purpose of the personal journal entries shown below is to capture the emotion of loneliness in situations when God delays. Some entries were taken from an actual journal, others were written more recently as I reflected on what I was feeling at the time. The dates of the entries are approximate and were included to give the reader some sense of chronological history. In teaching this material, feel free to use my personal journal entries as illustration or personalize your lesson with writing your own personal journal entries or testimony to capture the emotion of loneliness you felt in your own life. If you did not keep a journal, then try to relive the situation in your mind and write an entry today to capture what you felt at the time.

Sept 1, 1977

Dear God,
I feel the weight of the whole world on my shoulders. What happens if I make the wrong choice? There is no fallback plan. What happens God if I accept the wrong job or go to the wrong city? Is there ever a way to know what happens down the road not taken? Why do you let me stumble? Where are you? How come there always seems to be a lag between the time I ask my questions and the time you answer. You don't ever seem to be in a hurry.

July 18, 1979

Dear God,
I received four job offers. I've moved to a new city. I have a great paying job. I'm in a company that will treat me well if I perform. People look at me and they see me as successful. God, I don't feel successful. What is it that I'm searching for on the inside? Is it having a home? Is it

having roots? Is it having a place to belong?

It's awfully quiet in the office on New Year's Eve. I don't know what everyone else is doing but I would rather be in the office than in the house all by myself. So here we are, God. Why does it take so long to connect the dots of my life? Would you like to help me figure out this problem?

June 5, 2003

Dear God,
I thank you for the miracle of donated office space. I feel guilty to say that in the midst of the miracle, I still feel the loss. Where are my spiritual children? I am no longer on campus. I no longer see the students who were so much a part of my life. I feel like a Mom who had to leave the nest because it was your way to ensure food for the family. In my country, the one who left did so to send help home. I feel like I am fighting a battle for my daughters but they are totally oblivious of the

sacrifice. People say this is a battle I chose to fight but they don't understand that I had no choice. This was not my idea. I wish you could shout from heaven so people could know this separation was not my idea. There is something you want to establish for your daughters. You must really believe in the potential of your daughters to complete your spiritual army.

I'm not really sure what just happened to me. How did I get myself in this script? What story are you writing? There is a greater story going on than what the physical eyes can see. As far as the students are concerned, I'm like the Mom who moved out and is never coming back. My photo came off the wall and the name plate on my office door was replaced with someone else's name plate. From all outward appearance, it looks like I abandoned my daughters. But the fact is, I am leaving with the college's blessing to do more for my daughters than has ever been done before. How do I tell the students this move will benefit them in the long run? God wants a ministry to inspire His daughters into service and to ensure the funds for women for biblical training. How can I assure them we will return stronger than ever and that this is your dream to protect the future of your daughters for generations to come?

God, your dream sounds like such a grandiose plan. It feels so absurd when my reality is that of walking into empty office space. There are no women here, no daughters in sight. Yet, I hear their voices. I see them in my mind's eye. But when God, when? How long will this desert experience last before you fill the place to overflowing? Are you asking me to trust you even when I have no idea how long this story will take to unfold?

Oct 15, 2006

Dear God,
You always finish what you begin. After twelve years, the city came in with a second phase to fix the drainage problem at my house. As I watched them put in the big drainage pipes, I knew you were giving me this tangible picture of how you come through for us even when no one else is looking. At the time when the challenges in the ministry were hardest, you solved the drainage problem and gave me visible evidence that you always finish what you begin. Even in the delay you fulfilled your purpose. The house was under water four times and the flood occurred each week before I was to do a keynote at the Inspire Women's conference. You wasted nothing. Even the suffering was used to inspire the women at the conference. And now to have the drainage fixed right before our endowment luncheon is a testimony that you always finish what you start. I know you will finish an endowment to protect your daughters.

When God Delays

Situation: Have you been waiting on God to act only to find life sitting at a dead stop? How do you stay encouraged when nothing seems to be happening?

Reminder: Let's learn the truths from God's Word that speak to our situations. Remember that as a member of God's royal family, we are to act according to the customs of the royal family. This means reinforcing our royal identity by living according to God's specific instructions in the Bible. When we cannot find specific instructions that speak to our situation, we are to search our spiritual heritage and model our lives after God's faith heroes who responded correctly to situations that parallel our own. We can also learn from their mistakes to avoid making the same mistakes in our own lives.

God's delay was something that always perplexed me. When I ask God for answers, why is He silent? It seems to me that since His goal is to reach the world for Him, then when I ask Him, "What do you want me to do with my life?" He should answer quickly and immediately so I can get on with life. Instead, there is often silence. Why would God be silent if He desired me to do His will?

"God was silent because He was showing grace! Once God speaks I am held accountable..."

I wonder how many people have said to God, "I surrender all!" or "Wherever you lead I'll go". Then they are left standing there with no further direction. Seems like such a waste for God to get us to the place of total surrender and then not give us further direction. Many times, I felt very alone while waiting for God to speak. I kept thinking the problem was God but one day God opened my eyes to see that the problem was me.

God was waiting because I was not ready. I had said the words "I surrender all" without understanding the cost. I had said "Wherever you lead I'll go" but I had my own ideas as to where I was going. My intention was for God to bless my plans. It never occurred to me that God had plans of His own and I existed for His purpose. To my total shock, I realized one day that God was silent because He was showing grace.

Once God speaks, I am held accountable for whether I obey or shrink away. So He waits. God was silent because I was still in preparation.

Mark 1:19-20 tells us: **When he had gone a little farther, he saw James son of Zebedee and his brother John in a boat, preparing their nets. Without delay he called them, and they left their father Zebedee in the boat with the hired men and followed him.** NIV. Observe that when God calls, it said "**without delay he called them**." Once God calls, He expects immediate obedience. Both James and John left their father in the boat to follow Jesus.

When God is ready to move, He expects us to follow even if it means losing our assets. Hebrews 10:34-39 says: **You sympathized with those in prison and joyfully accepted the confiscation of your property, because you knew that you yourselves had better and lasting possessions. So do not throw away your confidence; it will be richly rewarded. You need to persevere so that when you have done the will of God, you will receive what he has promised. For in just a very little while, "He who is coming will come and will not delay. But my righteous one will live by faith. And if he shrinks back, I will not be pleased with him." But we are not of those who shrink back and are destroyed, but of those who believe and are saved.** NIV.

Did you see the words "**joyfully accepted the confiscation of your property**"? So even in the case of believers losing their assets, God is clear that when He is coming, He "**will not delay.**" God expects us to adjust to His time table instead of us telling God when it will be most convenient for us to follow Him. He tells us not to "**throw away our confidence**" because "**it will be richly rewarded.**"

Observe how God differentiates those who live by human logic as compared to "**my righteous one will live by faith.**" Once God starts moving in a set direction, He does not change His mind mid course. He expects us to follow Him. He even says, "**And if he shrinks back, I will not be pleased with him.**" This choice to follow God's voice was what God expected from Jesus. It is also what He expects from us as we are being conformed to the image of Christ.

Luke 9:59-62 tells of several situations where those who professed their desire to follow Jesus then came up with all kinds of reasons to justify their delay. The situations included the following: **He said to another man, "Follow me." But the man replied, "Lord, first let me go and bury my father." Jesus said to him, "Let the dead bury their own dead, but you go and proclaim the kingdom of God." Still another said, "I will follow you, Lord; but first let me go back and say good-by to my family." Jesus replied, "No one who puts his hand to the plow and looks back is fit for service in the kingdom of God."** NIV

What excuse have you been giving God? Did you know that God considers all your excuses as sin? What must you do today to stop sinning?

The more I understand God's expectations, the more I stop fretting when I don't hear God's voice. He knows where I live. God does not waste His resources. If He has not spoken, it must be because I am not ready.

"Could it be that a prepared life that is totally obedient is who God uses to change the world?"

When God finally launched the ministry of Inspire Women, it was like He never took a breath. He just kept going. But it took years before God launched. As I look back at my life, I see how His delay was for my preparation. I was in Bible Study Fellowship for six years, I was in Beth Moore's class for seven years, I was in Dallas Theological Seminary for seven years. All the while I was feeling restless, I was not ready yet. The ministry required major sacrifice from my family and me. It required a reprioritization of our time, and energy, and resources.

I remember being so depressed one day over all the freedom I felt I had lost. I was up studying all night and envied those whose lives were easier. My son who was fifteen at the time said, "Mom, eagles fly alone." I think he heard that saying from a sports coach. I said to him, "I don't want to be an eagle. I want to be a chicken and cluck around with the pack." He said, "The only problem is, you don't get to choose. God is the one who has chosen."

When God delays it is to prepare us for the sacrifice and service He has planned for us. Luke 2:52 tells us, **"And Jesus grew in wisdom and stature, and in favor with God and men."** NIV. 1 Samuel 2:26 tells us, **"And the boy Samuel continued to grow in stature and in favor with the LORD and with men."** NIV.

In any great work God plans on doing, He takes the time to prepare the vessel. When Jesus showed up in the public eye at the age of 30, God did more through him in three years than He accomplished in any human form. Could it be that a prepared life that is totally obedient is who God uses to change the world?

If things are not progressing as quickly as you had hoped, what preparation do you think God might be doing in your life? Is there a knowledge base you need to take time to acquire before you are ready to launch? Do you need a deeper relationship with God before you will be ready to lay down your life in service?

"God designs the path to lead us to a place where we are able to say "Yes".

How does God prepare His vessels? Jesus said in John 6:44-45, "**No one can come to me unless the Father who sent me draws him, and I will raise him up at the last day.**" NIV. Did you notice the word "**draws**"? What events and circumstances does it take to draw someone who is heading one direction and redirect the person to where God wants her to go?

God told His disciples to be fishers of men. When I think of fishing, I remember putting bait on a hook and strategically tossing it to one side of the boat and then to the other. I would sit and wait and watch and change strategies till I could draw fish to the bait. In the same way, I find God strategically planting experiences in my life. Not only do those experiences draw me to understand His message of salvation, but also I find God continuously drawing me through my personal experiences as He walks me into understanding His plan for my life. When God calls, He is not random. God draws me by designing my path to lead me to the place where I will say "Yes". Jesus said in John 6:65, "…**no one can come to me unless the Father has enabled him**." NIV. When God delays He is making a deposit in us before He makes a withdrawal.

"My delay in following Jesus boils down to the question Jesus asked Peter, 'Do you love me?'"

How incredible to think that God in His mercy "**draws**" us and has deposited experiences in us that leads us to respond to His call. Yet, I have seen zealous disciples who professed to be totally surrendered, who started backpedaling as

fast as they can when things did not turn out the way they planned.

Peter told Jesus in Mark 10:28, "**We have left everything to follow you!**" NIV He saw himself as "sold out" and surrendered. But when Jesus turned his face towards Jerusalem and spoke of the persecution that was ahead of Him, Peter said in Matthew, chapter 16, verses 22-23, "**Never, Lord!...This shall never happen to you!**" NIV. To this, Jesus replied in verse 23, "**Get behind me, Satan! You are a stumbling block to me; you do not have in mind the things of God, but the things of men.**" NIV.

I inquired of the Lord, "What happened?" I know that you did not set Peter up to fail. You would not have drawn Peter to this moment where he declared he would follow you only to show he was unable to fulfill his commitment. What happened? What is it that causes us to shrink back?

God showed me that there are three stages to our understanding of our calling. The first is our ability to declare that we will follow. Then, we are confronted with the cost, and there are many times the cost surprises us. We find ourselves saying, "I didn't realize the calling would entail this! Oh if I had known…". What causes us to shrink back is the reality of the cost of fulfilling our calling.

Jesus explains the cost in Luke 14:28-30 which reads, "**Suppose one of you wants to build a tower. Will he not first sit down and estimate the cost to see if he has enough money to complete it? For if he lays the foundation and is not able to finish it, everyone who sees it will ridicule him, saying, 'This fellow began to build and was not able to finish.**" NIV.

The second stage to understanding the calling is to fully appreciate the cost. Some say we should have assessed the cost before declaring our commitment. In my experience, there are times when no matter how long I have taken to assess the cost, I did not fully appreciate the cost involved until I made my declaration. For example, I can imagine what it might be like to be in the mission field, but until I get there, I will not fully appreciate the cost of not having plumbing or a normal bed to sleep on, being exposed to illnesses, and being far from home and those I love.

What will compel us to not only declare our commitment to Christ, but also actually pay the cost of following Jesus? God showed me that my delay in following Jesus boils down to the question Jesus asked Peter, "Do you love me?"

John 21:17 reads: **The third time he said to him, "Simon son of John, do you love me?** NIV Could it really be that simple? Does my choice to follow God boil down to this one question I must answer, "Do I love Him?" Oh, the simplicity and yet the depth of God's Word!

Why is this the question God asks to help us settle in our hearts if we will follow Jesus? God showed me the answer through my own personal life. If I had someone I loved in my family who was ill, would I spare any expense to help them recover? Would I not reprioritize my schedule to get them to the hospital? Would I not cut expenses everywhere I could to be able to afford their medication? Would I spend one second analyzing whether I would pay the cost? Would I not feel privileged and blessed to be able to pay the cost? I would not resent the sacrifice. In my actions I am answering the question, "Do I love you?"

"…just because I want to be able to pay the cost is no guarantee that I will be able to do it in my human power!"

Few people question how much they will give their children or grandchildren. Few parents would hesitate to give their kidney if this was what would save their child. Yet when it comes to giving God what He longs for, what happens to us? Do we find ourselves setting a ceiling on our affections? Instead of the attitude, "Whatever it takes to do God's will", do we shrink back and backpedal?

The first stage of accepting God's call is to declare that we will follow. The second is to truly understand the cost and be able to say that we want to pay it. Then comes the third stage. I have found that just because I want to be able to pay the cost is no guarantee that I am able to do it in my human power. Was this the lesson Peter learned when he answered Jesus in John 21:17, "**Lord, you know all things; you know that I love you." NIV**.

So, how do we get to a place where we will no longer delay doing God's will because of our inability to pay the cost in our human power? Could it be that after we declare our commitment, after we understand the cost and want to pay the cost, comes the third stage of being humbled in realizing the only way we can give God what He desires is through leaning on and trusting in His power?

I had a woman who wrestled with God when He first called her to serve in the ministry. Then she accepted the calling to serve. Then she found herself understanding more clearly how much her calling would cost her. She made the next leap of faith to accept the cost. She was feeling very surrendered until God brought her to the next phase. He was calling her to leave corporate America to serve Him full time. She asked God to part the Red Sea by providing for her financially before she cut the umbilical cord. As I watched her wrestle with her decision, I knew from observing God's patterns that He was not going to provide the provision before she cut the umbilical cord. God had brought her to a place where He wanted her to see that she would not be able to pay the cost in her own power. In her human capability, she was not able to have that level of faith to walk away from corporate America to trust Him with her future. In the same way, Peter could not fathom loving Jesus to the point of going to the cross for Him. All Peter could do was to offer God his willingness to pay the cost but in humility confess to God that "**You know all things**." In other words, "God, I want to but I can't. Help my unbelief."

"…we began by thinking we were surrendered and willing to do great things for God, we arrive at knowing He knows all things, that we are totally incapable of loving Him the way we thought we could."

It is in this place of total humility that God then carries us to a level beyond our wildest imagination. When we are at stage three of our calling, we find God teaching us that we began by thinking we were surrendered and willing to do great things for God. He knows all things and knows that we are totally incapable of loving Him the way we thought we could. It is at this place that He then shows us how He will receive what we are able to give and He will do great things through us.

Let me show you this truth from God's Word. When Jesus asked Peter if he loved Him, he asked him the question three times. The first time Jesus said in John 21:15, "**Simon son of John, do you truly love me more than these?**" NIV. The word Jesus used for "**love**" was the Greek word "agapao" which is a decision to love, the same kind of love that led Jesus to finish His work on the cross. There are times we do not "feel" like loving but we do so as an act of our choice and will. To Jesus' question, Peter answered in John 21:15, "**you know that I love you**" but the word for love Peter used was the Greek word "phileo" which is a friendly friendship kind of love, clearly not one as intense as what Jesus was asking for. Don't miss the fact that what Peter was able to offer did not measure up to the love God was asking for.

Jesus asked Peter a second time in John 21:16, "**Simon son of John, do you truly love me?**" once again using the word "agapao". Peter answered in the same verse, "**Yes, Lord, you know that I love you**" using once again the word "phileo". Have you ever had a conversation when you clearly know that you are unable to do what someone is asking of you?

Jesus did not overlook what Peter was saying. Then the most incredible thing happened. Jesus said a third time in John 21:17, "**Simon son of John, do you love me?**" NIV. This time, however, Jesus substituted the Greek word "phileo" for the word "**love**". God confirms Peter's admission that he cannot in his own power do what God is asking of him. So God will begin with "phileo". God begins where we are and He is the one who will grow us into what He is asking of us. Jesus confirmed this truth by saying in John 21:18-19, "**I tell you the truth, when you were younger you dressed yourself and went where you wanted; but when you are old you will stretch out your hands, and someone else will dress you and lead you where you do not want to go**." He was saying, "Just as you are, Peter, I will take you just as you are. If you are willing to pay the cost but "phileo" is all you feel capable of, then offer me "phileo" and I will grow you from "phileo" to "agapao." Trust me, Peter. It might be hard for you to fathom it now. But one day, you will stretch out your hands and you will go where you do not want to go. You will serve out of "agapao" the kind of love that is a decision of your will, no matter how you feel."

Even if I want to pay the cost, I cannot give God what He wants in my own strength. I will only be able to pay the cost by drawing on His strength. When God delays, is it God who is delaying or could it be the vessel that needs more preparation?

Is God waiting for you to stop trying to pay the cost in your own power? How are you trusting God to pay the cost of the service He has asked of you?

If you have been trying to pay the cost in your own power, then expect to fall flat on your face and find yourself continuously frustrated. God never expected you to pay the cost in your own power. Jesus told Peter that one day he would be able to pay the ultimate cost to serve God. But when that day came, Peter's ability to follow through was not because of the great thing he could do for God, but it was because Peter learned to trust God's power to do a great thing through him.

"When you don't know how to fly without a parachute, you don't argue. You just follow directions!"

When God led me to walk away from an established institution to birth Inspire Women as an independent non-profit organization, I woke up every morning asking God what I was supposed to do next. I made a list of all that I needed for the ministry. The list included such items as office space, furniture, equipment, money to pay the one person I had on contract and an accountant to help file the papers to establish Inspire Women as a 501 (c) 3 organization. The list just kept growing. I took a pen to prioritize what needed to get done first and then I simply said to God, "This is your dream. Show me what to do next."

God brought me to a place where I knew that no human of sound mind would even imagine parting the Red Sea by himself. I knew the dream God had put on my platter could only be done in His power. So every day, I began by asking God for my to-do list. I did not argue since I did not come with my opinions on how to fulfill the dream. I came ready to listen and I clung to obedience as my safety net. When you don't know how to fly without a parachute, you don't argue. You just follow directions!

If you have been arguing with God, could it be because the dream is too small? Or perhaps you have reduced the dream to a goal you can handle. How have you redefined God's dream?

"God wanted to know if He could trust me to keep going even when He was silent!"

I wish I could tell you that God spoke clearly, but on many days, I could not hear Him. At the same time, I was sure He was there. Why was He choosing to keep silent? So I simply proceeded in any open door I could find. I called person after person. Every day was filled with people I had to see and details I had to research. In the midst of running from place to place, I found myself crashing on the couch and bursting into tears. It was a strange period in my life where on the one hand I was filled with energy to move forward, on the other hand I was ready to just crawl into bed and never wake up.

Sleep was a great escape for me. I clung to God as my sustenance knowing that only He could fill me up to get up again the next day.

Days rolled into each other but no doors were opening. Yet, all the while, I felt a strong conviction that I was doing exactly what God wanted. I was so sure what I was pursuing was God's dream because I knew that if left up to me I would never have volunteered for this mission. I felt like I was an immigrant, going from one place to another, in search of home. I have always hated being an immigrant. All my life I wanted roots. Therefore, I knew that all this wandering around in search of a place to land could not possibly be born from my heart.

As I look back at the time when Inspire Women began, I realize that God was watching over me the whole time. For some reason, God wanted to know if He could trust me to keep going even when He was silent. In God's silence, He was trusting me with a Calvary experience.

Jesus trusted God even when God was absent. In Mark 15:34, Jesus cried out, "**My God, my God, why have you forsaken me?**" NIV. Yet, Luke 23:46 tells us Jesus called out with a loud voice, "**Father, into your hands I commit my spirit.**" NIV. How could Jesus commit His spirit to a God who is absent, evidenced by His Words, "**Why have you forsaken me?**"

In God's Word, I learned that the more we walk with God, the greater faith He expects from us. As God conforms us to Jesus' image, He will walk us into times when He is intentionally silent and He watches to see if we will stay on course and keep doing the last thing we heard Him say. When I saw the biblical pattern, I knew what to do. As a member of God's royal family, He showed me the royal custom and how I was to respond.

Are you getting restless during the times God delays in giving you further direction? How will life change if you simply stayed on course?

Looking back, I realize God was testing my heart. He wanted to see if He could trust me before He could entrust me with His daughters. What kind of mother was I? Was I a Mom who would have a love that endured? Would I keep fighting to protect the dream for women from all ethnicities even when they did not know me? Would I do it just because I knew Inspire Women was a ministry God wanted for His daughters?

In less than six months after Inspire Women was established by God's power, the ministry reached nearly 4000 women and established the first Inspire Women's scholarship fund in the amount of $100,000. In three years time, the ministry invested over $1 million to train God's servant leaders for missions and ministry. After every Calvary experience is the resurrection. What scares me is to think that I might have ended the journey prematurely. What if I had thrown in the towel and gone home? What if I had gotten mad at God for being silent and had simply walked off? Oh what blessing would be lost when we do not trust God during the delays in our lives!

Describe a time you began a journey with God only to find Him silent. What blessings will be lost if you give up the mission before the battle is won?

"God delayed Paul for his protection"

There are times God delays for our protection. God delayed intentionally in Jesus' life. Matthew 2:19-20 tells us: **After Herod died, an angel of the Lord appeared in a dream to Joseph in Egypt and said, "Get up, take the child and his mother and go to the land of Israel, for those who were trying to take the child's life are dead."** NIV.

Notice that it was after Herod died that God instructed Joseph to come out of hiding from Egypt? It would seem to me that one way God could have protected Jesus immediately was to take Herod's life as soon as he became a threat. But God chose to delay and wait until Herod died before bringing Jesus out of Egypt. In God's perfect plan, He protects us from harm and during those times of being away from harm's way, He is growing us up for His purpose.

God delayed Paul for his protection as well. We are told that when Paul first started to preach the word boldly, his life was threatened. Acts 9:30 tells us, **"When the brothers learned of this, they took him down to Caesarea and sent him off to Tarsus."** NIV.

Recall when God confirmed Paul's calling we were told in Acts 9:11, God told Ananias, **"Go to the house of Judas on Straight Street and ask for a man from Tarsus named Saul, for he is praying."** NIV. God also told Ananias in **Acts 9:15-16, "Go! This man is my chosen instrument to carry my name before the Gentiles and their kings and before the people of Israel. I will show him how much he must suffer for my name."** NIV

Don't miss the fact that God's calling was specific and confirmed to Paul through Ananias. Notice too that God referred to Paul as **"a man from Tarsus"**. Recall that the city Paul was shipped to by the brothers was Tarsus, which was Paul's home town. So we have here a situation where a man from Tarsus whose calling was confirmed finds himself preaching boldly, only to be sent out of the public's eyes back to his own hometown in Tarsus. God's objective was to protect Paul but can you imagine what it feels like to begin with so much momentum only to find yourself sitting on a shelf at home when life is happening for everyone else?

What could God also be doing in Paul while he was being protected? As I reflected on Paul's life, I wondered if the time away from the public's eyes helped solidify his conviction which he stated in Philippians 3:8-10, **"I consider everything a loss compared to the surpassing greatness of knowing Christ Jesus my Lord, for whose sake I have lost all things. I consider them rubbish, that I may gain Christ…"** NIV. Could it be that before God can trust us with a ministry to thousands He must be sure we can handle success and not allow the accolades to cause us to think we must be something special? Instead, God must begin with a heart that is humbled and one that sees Jesus alone as the prize.

While Saul, later known as Paul, was in Tarsus, God was changing Him. He was also changing history and opened the door for His church to reach the Gentiles. In God's perfect timing, Saul stepped into the original calling God spoke to his heart, which was to be an instrument to the Gentiles. Acts 11:25-26, **"Then Barnabas went to Tarsus to look for Saul and when he found him, he brought him to Antioch"**. NIV.

Are you sitting on a shelf today? If so, how can you work in your open doors and trust God to know when you are ready to handle a ministry that is more public?

In my own life, I remember a time when I sat at home and I would hear of all the great things God was doing through someone else. Did God forget where I lived? I would hear of others being overloaded and I wondered why they did not let me pick up some of the load? It was the most frustrating experience to feel like you want to help and then realize no one is asking you. I praise God for this time of "sitting on the shelf" because it so clearly showed me that whatever I have accomplished is "**rubbish**". Christ is the one who has center stage. Whatever I can do is by His invitation and by His power. Before God can trust me to expand my territory He wanted to be sure I knew that at any moment, He can remove me from His ministry. Though He has chosen to work through human vessels at this time and invites me to join Him, He is not dependent on me. No human can thwart God's plans and He certainly would not need me to join Him for His plans to succeed. He will move on without me. If I get to be any part of what God is doing, it is an honor and a privilege.

As God continues to expand Inspire Women, I beg God to help me stay focused on His strength and not mine, on His dream and not mine. When God delays, I find myself saying, "God knows where He is going." If I think I'm ready and feel like God is lagging behind, I probably don't have the right vision in mind as to where God is going. I have seen how much God can do in a short time. I have seen how God used delays to refine me. When God delays, I know He is operating out of His grace and mercy. I don't ever want to rush God. I will wait and stay on course until He gives me the next green light.

I remember the time when our family went to pick a puppy. When we went to see the litter in their pen, each of those puppies jumped up towards us with the sweetest expression on their faces that said, "Please pick me!" When you get the green light from God, realize that He picked you. Be in awe that from all that He could have chosen, He chose to pick you!

Like that puppy who came home with us to enter into a lifetime friendship, I find myself in awe of my journey with God. We will get to experience the mountain top highs and the valley lows together. What kind of a friend will I be? When I get the green light from God, I just want to walk right next to Him the way my puppy stuck right next to me. The fact that I get to go along for the walk is an awesome privilege.

God has called me to walk with a Savior who gave His life for me. I remember a movie I saw where a little terrier followed His master around. Then his master became ill and died. He watched where the people buried the body. Then no matter what he was doing during the day, he came back at night, climbed onto the mound under which his master's body lay. And he slept on his master's grave. Men from the dog pound tried to catch him but he would evade them every time. All he wanted to do was to stay on the mound to be as close to his master as possible.

The Apostle Paul said in 2 Corinthians 4:10, "**We always carry around in our body the death of Jesus, so that the life of Jesus may also be revealed in our body**." NIV. It is in remembering His death that we will choose to pay the cost. It is in remembering His death that we will no longer hesitate. We will go where God goes even if He is heading for the cross. We will go just because there is nowhere else we would rather be than right next to our Lord and Savior. Like Peter said in John 6:68-69, "**Lord, to whom shall we go? You have the words of eternal life. We believe and know that you are the Holy One of God**." NIV

When You Feel No One is Serving with You

Situation: Do you feel like no one feels led to serve God's mission the way you do? Do you feel alone in your efforts?

The purpose of the personal journal entries shown below is to capture the emotion of loneliness in situations when you feel you are alone in your efforts to serve God's mission. Some entries were taken from an actual journal, others were written more recently as I reflected on what I was feeling at the time. The dates of the entries are approximate and were included to give the reader some sense of chronological history. In teaching this material, feel free to use my personal journal entries as illustration or personalize your lesson with writing your own personal journal entries or testimony to capture the emotion of loneliness you felt in your own life. If you did not keep a journal, then try to relive the situation in your mind and write an entry today to capture what you felt at the time.

May 15, 2003

Dear God,
Did you notice I'm crying a lot these days? People don't understand. They say to me, "What's your problem? You're the one who wanted to leave." How could following your call feel this lonely? No one will ever understand that it was your relentless voice that kept hounding me. Now that you have severed all ties between me and my past, will you pick me up? If you don't pick me up, I'm just going to stay down. You know where I live God. If you tell me what to do next I will do it no matter how ridiculous it sounds. Just don't leave me on my own. I won't make it on my own.

God, is there anyone else going on this journey with me? Please send help!

May 20, 2003

Dear God,
Sometimes I wonder if the devil plays games with my mind. When there is something you wish to accomplish in the city that is God-sized, I know that you have already chosen the ones you want to get involved. It's lunacy for me to think that I am the only one you spoke your vision to. So it must be a trick of the devil to cause me to feel utterly alone as if I am single handedly parting some Red Sea. In fact, it's arrogance to even think I can do anything alone. I wonder God if this is the lesson you are trying to teach me. When it feels like no one is around, could it be because you want me in my humility to know that no matter how the circumstances seem, the fact is, you already have your battalion lined up to take the hill? And if it was actually true that no one else was going on this journey but me then it must be because you are the only one who can take the hill with me.

And the only reason you are sending my earthly body into the battle is so that everyone can see your victory through my earthly tangible form.

It's so strange God that the way we think totally dictates how we feel which in turn changes how we act. It's what we believe that will determine our future. The challenge is, we must believe in what is true and not something we have conjured up in our own imagination. I guess that's why you say it's so important to read the Bible which is your love letter to us. In it I will discover your heart and your purpose. In getting to know you, I will get to know me. Since I was created in your image, the better I know you, the better I will know me. Now, that's backward logic but I think it is the way you designed this earth to work.

The corresponding truths God taught me from His Word to address my situation
Feel free to continue reading all my personal journals in Module One expressing feelings of loneliness before reading the Bible Study. Or you may continue with the corresponding Bible study which contains God's truths in addressing the situation described in the above journal entries with additional truths God taught me to address situations that were not included in my journal entries. If you choose to personalize this curriculum as your way to bond with the group you are leading, feel free not only to use your own testimony and personal journal entries but in the Bible study part, include what God taught you from His Word in your situations that evoked loneliness.

When You Feel No One is Serving with You

Situation: Do you feel like no one feels led to serve God's mission the way you do? Do you feel alone in your efforts?

Reminder: Let's learn the truths from God's Word that speak to our situations. Remember that as a member of God's royal family, we are to act according to the customs of the royal family. This means reinforcing our royal identity by living according to God's specific instructions in the Bible. When we cannot find specific instructions that speak to our situation, we are to search our spiritual heritage and model our lives after God's faith heroes who responded correctly to situations that parallel our own. We can also learn from their mistakes to avoid making the same mistakes in our own lives.

John the Baptist was described in Matthew 3:3 as "**A voice of one calling in the desert, 'Prepare the way for the Lord, make straight paths for him**." NIV. Did you notice the words "**a voice in the wilderness**"? The text did not say "voices in the wilderness", it says "**a voice of one**" and this "**voice of one**" is calling in the wilderness. I wonder today if you are the one who has been called to pave the way for God on grounds no one else has treaded. Have you been feeling alone in the wilderness?

How much time do you spend feeling sorry for yourself because of your calling?

As I read the life of John the Baptist, I saw how he did not express any feelings of loneliness. How did he stay focused in spite of his calling to be the one to represent "**a voice**"? Though no one shared his calling because it was unique to him, John embraced his calling and started serving. As a result, Matthew 3:5-6 tells us, "**People went out to him from Jerusalem and all Judea and the whole region of the Jordan. Confessing their sins, they were baptized by him in the Jordan River.**" NIV.

How much time have you spent justifying your calling to others because of its uniqueness? How much time have you spent feeling sorry for yourself because of your calling? How can you simply start serving?

Unlike John who never complained to God about being "**a voice**" in the wilderness, we find the story of Elijah in the Old Testament. Elijah is an example of a servant of God who felt alone in his mission. 1 Kings 18:22-23 records Elijah saying, "**I am the only one of the LORD's prophets left, but Baal has four hundred and fifty prophets.**" NIV.

In spite of his aloneness, Elijah succeeded in calling down fire from heaven to prove the power of God in front of the prophets of Baal. After such a display of God's presence, he evoked the wrath of Queen Jezebel. 1 Kings 19:1-2 reads: **Now Ahab told Jezebel everything Elijah had done and how he had killed all the prophets with the sword. So Jezebel sent a messenger to Elijah to say, "May the gods deal with me, be it ever so severely, if by this time tomorrow I do not make your life like that of one of them."** NIV In hearing this outcome, we see Elijah in a panic and running for his life.

"Don't be surprised if you feel depressed after a great victory."

No matter how grand the victory, any time you are in a battle for God against those who do not represent Him, you can be sure that it will take a toll on your physical body. Emotions will run high until any conflict is resolved. Even when you win the battle, you will feel totally drained emotionally. Don't be surprised if you feel depressed after a great victory.

When I was in corporate America, I found myself getting depressed after reaching insurmountable goals. The euphoria is even higher in God's work when we have been in a place where God worked mightily through us to conduct divine transactions with eternal consequences. Personally I block off days after a big spiritual event because I know I will start to experience a "let down" somewhat similar to after wedding blues or post partum depression. I surround myself with people who love me and I take the time to praise God and to let Him replenish me with His presence. There are times when my human flesh cannot handle being in another miracle. I just need to soak in the presence of God and enjoy Him for who He is and not for what He does.

Have you been feeling the blues lately? Are you living in the aftermath of a big success? How have you taken the time to simply enjoy God's presence?

Realize that we are especially vulnerable after a major spiritual high. Imagine, therefore, turning the corner to experience yet another conflict. This was the case with Elijah. After overcoming the prophets of Baal, Elijah hears of Queen Jezebel's wrath and he has had it. He starts to run but the problem is, we can never run from our calling. Do you find yourself saying to God, "What do you want from me?" Do you find yourself complaining? Do you find yourself making your case and showing God how unfair life is?

Elijah tells God in 1 Kings 19:10, "**I have been very zealous for the LORD God Almighty. The Israelites have rejected your covenant, broken down your altars, and put your prophets to death with the sword. I am the only one left, and now they are trying to kill me too.**" NIV.

God shares the beautiful truth of what the real personnel situation is in 1 Kings 19:15-18 when the LORD said to Elijah, "**Go back the way you came, and go to the Desert of Damascus. When you get there, anoint Hazael king over Aram. Also, anoint Jehu son of Nimshi king over Israel, and anoint Elisha son of Shaphat from Abel Meholah to succeed you as prophet. Jehu will put to death any who escape the sword of Hazael, and Elisha will put to death any who escape the sword of Jehu. Yet I reserve seven thousand in Israel-all whose knees have not bowed down to Baal and all whose mouths have not kissed him.**" NIV.

Not only did God name individuals who were part of God's mission but he said, "**Yet I reserve seven thousand in Israel all whose knees have not bowed down to Baal and all whose mouth**

have not kissed him." Oh, the incredible truth to know we are not the Lone Ranger who rides alone! Instead, we serve a commanding chief officer who has a whole platoon He has commissioned.

As God's undercover agent, commanding general or a pioneer entrusted with some kind of mission impossible, the devil tries to deceive us into thinking that no one is aware of or cares about our battle. To the contrary the battle belongs to God. David's confidence in battle came from knowing this truth. He said to the Philistines in 1 Samuel 17:47, "**All those gathered here will know that it is not by sword or spear that the LORD saves; for the battle is the LORD's, and he will give all of you into our hands.**" NIV. Zech 4:6 put it this way, '...**Not by might nor by power, but by my Spirit,**' says the LORD Almighty. NIV

God is the one who saves the day, not us!

We get overwhelmed when we start to think that we are the one to save the day. In reality, God saves the day, not us! We are part of His greater plan. In that plan, He has already reserved the ones who have been set apart to bring His plans to fulfillment.

When reinforcements do not come, it is not because you are alone in the battle. Rather, it is because God is doing something in you. Perhaps what God desires is the very encounter Elijah had with God. We grow from our times of wrestling with God. We must feel the panic in order to feel His relief. In His perfect timing, God sends reinforcements because He will never allow His own dreams to fail.

How does knowing you are not the one to save the day bring you relief? How does knowing God has already appointed your successor and/or comrades in arms change the way you respond to your challenges?

When God set me apart to begin Inspire Women, His Spirit had already stirred the hearts of those He had hand picked to join me. I did not know who these individuals were till God revealed their names to me. Some I had known for years, others I barely knew. Over time, God knitted our hearts together. God showed me that the battle belonged to Him and He is perfectly able to recruit for His own spiritual army. This does not mean I should just sit and wait for God to do the work. It means I step out in faith, I pour out my life in service as my form of worship unto a God who is worthy, I knock on every door I know to knock on, I speak boldly in God's name instead of fearing human disapproval. I do all of the above while serving without the stress of feeling like the whole world is resting on my shoulders.

In his service to God, Paul served with passion but he was never stressed. He was intentional, focused, diligent and consistent. In his farewell final words to the Ephesians he said in Acts 20:18-21, **"You know how I lived the whole time I was with you, from the first day I came into the province of Asia. I served the Lord with great humility and with tears, although I was severely tested by the plots of the Jews. You know that I have not hesitated to preach anything that would be helpful to you but have taught you publicly and from house to house**." NIV

Notice the words "**the whole time**". Paul did not have a season when he was distracted or unfocused. He set his hands to the plough and he kept on serving. The final statements of his life included "**I have not hesitated**".

If you had to sum up your life, could you say that you have not hesitated? If not, why not? Did you know that when God has spoken then every second of your delay is an act of disobedience? What must you do to get back in God's will?

"Paul did not strive to make life happen…"

Notice that in spite of Paul's focus and diligence, he did not strive to make life happen. Instead, he stepped into what was happening and went with the flow. He said in Philippians 4:12-13, "**I know what it is to be in need, and I know what it is to have plenty. I have learned the secret of being content in any and every situation, whether well fed or hungry, whether living in plenty or in want. I can do everything through him who gives me strength**." NIV. Could it be that the reason we strive is because we are still trying to control life. When we are willing to flow freely with God from plenty to sacrifice, then we are truly free to serve God. Notice too that our only hope of living this way is "**through him who gives me strength**." NIV.

God's dreams begin and end with Him. He invites us to go on the journey but ultimately, life is all about Him. Paul tells us in 1 Corinthians 3:7, "**So neither he who plants nor he who waters is anything, but only God, who makes things grow**." NIV.

Jesus was created to be Savior. We get to serve under Him in His strength. When we have given God our total surrender and all that we have to give, He is the one who takes the loaves and fish and multiplies them to feed the five thousand. If we try to feed five thousand with our loaves and fish, we will send ourselves to the asylum!!! God never intended for us to solve God sized problems with our human strength.

The next time you feel the pressure to save the world, stop and picture the following image of Jesus as described in Revelation 19:11-16, "**I saw heaven standing open and there before me was a white horse, whose rider is called Faithful and True. With justice he judges and makes war. His eyes are like blazing fire, and on his head are many crowns. He has a name written on him that no one knows but he himself. He is dressed in a robe dipped in blood, and his name is the Word of God. The armies of heaven were following him, riding on white horses and dressed in fine linen, white and clean. Out of his mouth comes a sharp sword with which to strike down the nations. "He will rule them with an iron scepter." He treads the winepress of the fury of the wrath of God Almighty. On his robe and on his thigh he has this name written: KING OF KINGS AND LORD OF LORDS.**" NIV

Jesus is the hero who will save the day. Like John the Baptist, may we serve to point others to Jesus but may we serve knowing that the stage belongs to Him.

We were designed to decrease so He will increase. John the Baptist said it so well when he said in John 3:29-30, "**The friend who attends the bridegroom waits and listens for him, and is full of joy when he hears the bridegroom's voice. That joy is mine, and it is now complete. He must become greater; I must become less.**" NIV.

Realize that the more God trusts us with success the more we can get ourselves in a place where we are our own worse enemy. Instead of laying our gift on the altar and giving God the limelight, we find ourselves trying to keep ourselves with a certain title or position or trying to top ourselves in performance. Then we get irritated when we don't make the goals. Then we complain that we have no one to help us and we are all alone. John the Baptist was "**a voice**" crying in the wilderness but he never felt overwhelmed. He never lost focus as to the purpose of his calling. He was not trying to be impressive. His role was to make a way for the crowds to see Jesus and to get out of the way so Jesus could have the limelight.

Are you wearing yourself out by trying to impress? What has it taken to protect your title or your promotion? How can you change the way you work so you can just serve where you are needed and let God take care of your role and place of service?

I remember being so overwhelmed one day that I just stayed home. Mia, my spiritual daughter and Chief Operating Officer at Inspire Women called me and immediately knew something was wrong. She said, "Are you crying?" I said, "Yes." She said, "I'm coming right over."

As soon as she arrived she wanted to know what was wrong. I told her I could not handle all that was on my platter. I had been writing and teaching and trying to raise the funds for the women who could not otherwise afford to pay their tuition for seminary. She said, "Why don't you let me help?" I told her I knew how much she hated to appeal for funds so I was trying to keep her from doing what she disliked to do. She said, "You don't like raising funds either but you do it to serve God. So why can't I do the same?" In that moment, I saw how we may not have the opportunity to lay down our lives the way the disciples did in Jesus' time but in our own way, we are laying down our lives for each other by taking off each other's platter what we dislike doing. I make appeals for women I don't even know. Mia was ready to do the same to keep me from carrying the burden alone.

We hugged each other and she left to return to the office.

When I recall those precious moments we shared, the fact that she offered touches my heart deeply. I felt like a Mom trying to work three jobs at the same time and my spiritual child offered to do a paper run or whatever she could do to help make ends meet. But oh how I would have missed out on the blessing had I not allowed myself to be vulnerable and to share my need. I did not require her to help as part of some job description. I simply shared my burden and found that she offered to help out of love. That is God's way. That is the royal way.

God never meant for us to serve alone. In carrying each other's burdens, He is the one who raises up co-laborers who serve in love. With all my heart, I believe the reason God has blessed Inspire Women is because of my spiritual children who have poured out their hearts to love me and the women in our city. They are living the teaching of 1 Timothy 1:5 which reads, "**The goal of this command is love, which comes from a pure heart and a good conscience and a sincere faith.**"

When You've Totally Let God Down

Situation: Do you feel like you have let God down? When once you were sure of yourself, do you feel like you have failed and don't know how to recover?

The purpose of the personal journal entries shown below is to capture the emotion of loneliness in situations when you've totally failed in doing the right thing. Some entries were taken from an actual journal, others were written more recently as I reflected on what I was feeling at the time. The dates of the entries are approximate and were included to give the reader some sense of chronological history. In teaching this material, feel free to use my personal journal entries as illustration or personalize your lesson with writing your own personal journal entries or testimony to capture the emotion of loneliness you felt in your own life. If you did not keep a journal, then try to relive the situation in your mind and write an entry today to capture what you felt at the time.

Jan 9, 1979

Dear God,
I made a big mistake. I fell in love with someone who I could never love the way he needs to be loved. I talked about being a Christian and how your love could overcome anything. I wasn't just representing me, I was representing you and I failed miserably. I made you look bad because I said you were powerful enough to handle any problem. Here I was representing your power and I could not handle the challenges in his world.

God, he experienced war in his home and war abroad. It was as if his entire life was some kind of combat zone. As a young boy, he defended his family in place of an absent father. He remembers holding a cleaver while someone tried to break into the house. What kind of memory is that for a young boy?

God, I did not know how to help him through the feelings of rejection that he felt when people judged him based on the color of his skin. I did not know how to help him through nightmares of his days in Vietnam. How do you live with the memory that your platoon was wiped out yet you lived? How do you act normal when you have been in a field full of land mines and watched limbs fly off the bodies of your comrades? I am so sorry God because I never meant to hurt anyone. How do you tell someone you are sorry because you don't have it in you to be what they need?

December 15, 1979

Dear God,
He said he would always love me. He told me not to feel bad. How can life feel so lonely when I am the one leaving? Do we just turn the page and keep going? He deserves better than me. One day, I might be half the person that he is. But today, I am too wounded to help the wounded.

God, how do you say goodbye to someone you love because you know there is someone else out there who will be better for him? How do you tell him that you really love him but you know you are wrong for him? How do you keep going as if you never met? Why was he in my life? How will these pages of my life fit into what my life is all about? God, I feel like I have given you a bad reputation. I am such a lame representation of your power. How can I even talk about your strength when I can't handle real life and real challenges? I talk about the Bible, I quote verses but what do I really know about your power? I should just keep my mouth shut!

July 5, 1997

Dear God,
I am so sorry I missed my divine appointment. I was afraid to accept the invitation to be the only keynote speaker at a three day women's retreat, so I said,

"No." I know I should have said "Yes" and trusted that you would show me how to fulfill the commitment. I know I made a wrong decision because I used my human logic and I was so sure I could not do what was needed. Since when did I trust in my own credentials? But today I did exactly that. I looked at what I was able to do in the past and concluded I could not possibly accept a goal that was so much higher than what I had ever done. Worse of all, I never even asked you if you wanted me to accept this invitation. I just said "No" and I didn't even care if there was anyone else to take care of the need. I know that just because no one else is willing to do it does not mean I'm supposed to do it. But there are times when no one has stepped up to the plate because you have already chosen but the one chosen refuses to go. I know I can't undo the past God but will you ever come back to trust me again with your assignment? Will you give me another chance?

The corresponding truths God taught me from His Word to address my situation
Feel free to continue reading all my personal journals in Module One expressing feelings of loneliness before reading the Bible Study. Or you may continue with the corresponding Bible study which contains God's truths in addressing the situation described in the above journal entries with additional truths God taught me to address situations that were not included in my journal entries. If you choose to personalize this curriculum as your way to bond with the group you are leading, feel free not only to use your own testimony and personal journal entries but in the Bible study part, include what God taught you from His Word in your situations that evoked loneliness.

When You've Totally Let God Down

Situation: Do you feel like you have let God down? When once you were sure of yourself, do you feel like you have failed and don't know how to recover?

Reminder: Let's learn the truths from God's Word that speak to our situations. Remember that as a member of God's royal family, we are to act according to the customs of the royal family. This means reinforcing our royal identity by living according to God's specific instructions in the Bible. When we cannot find specific instructions that speak to our situation, we are to search our spiritual heritage and model our lives after God's faith heroes who responded correctly to situations that parallel our own. We can also learn from their mistakes to avoid making the same mistakes in our own lives.

In the book of Luke, chapter 22, verses 56-62 we watch Peter stumble. The verses read: **A servant girl saw him seated there in the firelight. She looked closely at him and said, "This man was with him." But he denied it. "Woman, I don't know him," he said. A little later someone else saw him and said, "You also are one of them." "Man, I am not!" Peter replied. About an hour later nother asserted, "Certainly this fellow was with him, for he is a Galilean." Peter replied, "Man, I don't know what you're talking about!" Just as he was speaking, the rooster crowed. The Lord turned and looked straight at Peter. Then Peter remembered the word the Lord had spoken to him: "Before the rooster crow today, you will disown me three times." And he went outside and wept bitterly**. NIV

"How quickly we fall when we start to break our word"

Observe the time frame. It was not even 24 hours from the time Peter made his promise when he began to unravel. When the unraveling began, the second denial came **"a little later"** and the third denial came, **"About an hour later."** How quickly we fall when we start to break our word. I wonder today if you are breaking one promise after another. As you face your own failure, are you at a place where you are still justifying your behavior? As long as you are still defending yourself with thoughts such as "No one should expect anyone to be able to do this", you are not at a place where God can restore you because you are filled with self justification. Observe that Peter **"went outside and wept bitterly."** NIV.

Can you imagine the loneliness Peter felt? How could he even put into words how it felt to have Jesus look straight into his eyes and to remember the promise he made and the promise he broke? But oh to know that the recovery begins when those who have fallen will humble themselves to weep bitterly before God. When you are still defending yourself to God, He cannot begin the restoration. If you are the one who has broken a promise, is it time to make amends and keep your promise? If you are not in a position to make things right, then like Peter, will you trust God to cover your weakness and bring restoration despite what you have done? Realize that it is in your restoration that God is growing you up to be His future leader.

When Jesus was resurrected, He came back to look for Peter. He did not chastise him. He simply asked him in the book of John, chapter 21 verse 15, **"Simon son of John, do you truly love me more than these?"** Observe that Jesus included the words "**more than these**" because Simon was the one who said that he would stand by Jesus even if all abandoned Him. God does not forget our promises and so He reminds Peter of what was said. Then as the conversation progressed, Jesus asked Simon a second time in the book of John chapter 21:16, **"Simon son of John, do you truly love me?"** NIV Then Jesus asked Simon a third time in verse 17, **"Simon son of John, do you love me?"** Observe that in the second and third question, Jesus did not say "**do you love me more than these?**" God has already concluded that while Peter set himself up above the rest, he was no different than the rest in his imperfection. God was simply asking if Peter loved him, not above anyone else, but simply, **"Do you love me?"** To this, Peter replied with humility in verse 17,

"Lord, you know all things; you know that I love you." NIV.

"We cannot make any promises. All we can say is, "God, take me as I am."

I wonder today if you ever felt you were more surrendered than others only to realize you were not as sold out as you thought. Perhaps you made statements such as "I would never do that" only to find that you are doing the very thing you judged others for doing though you thought you were above them.

No matter how much we have failed, God returns to call us out of our lonely place of defeat. Once we have walked with God, there exists a part of our heart that will always be tender towards God. How can anyone meet Jesus and not be changed in some way? When we have failed, all we can do is to give God the soft part of our heart that still wants to be part of His purpose and trust Him to transform us from a timid soldier into a valiant warrior. We will not truly know the cost of what God has called us to do. We cannot make any promises. All we can say is, "God, take me as I am. I love you but you know all things. Help me with my unbelief and give me the strength to finish all that you have designed for me."

If you failed in an assignment, say what you learned about God and about yourself through the failure. What would you change if you could live the past all over again?

My son asked me once, "Mom, are there parts of your life you wish you could live all over again?" That question stopped me in my tracks. As I look back at my life, there are situations that still glare at me and remind me of my utmost failure. If I took the time to dwell on this question, I am sure I can name many incidents but the one incident that scarred me for many years was my Mom's suicide.

I was a seventeen year old when my mom came into my room and startled me the day before she died. I was doing my homework. She just stood there at the doorway. I was impatient with her and asked what she needed. She said, "Tell me you'll be fine without me." I did not know what she was referring to so just to get her to leave me alone, I said, "I'll be fine without you!"

The next day when I found she had taken her life, I realized she was in a state of desperation. Before her exit strategy she was saying to me, "You are my youngest, my baby. I just want to know that my baby will be fine if I am not here." And like a fool, I gave her permission to leave.

How many sleepless nights I have spent going over that scene in my mind's eyes! Oh how I wish I could rewind the tape and relive that moment. I would tell her it would take me years to recover. I would tell her no one would ever be able to take her place in my life.

I asked the Lord if there was someone in the Bible who wished they could turn the clock backwards. He showed me that Saul who later became Paul went around killing the Christians. When he later became a believer, he still had to face the families of those he had killed. How can he undo something so permanent? Paul's solution was to use his story to direct the attention to God's greater story. He said 1 Timothy 1:15-16, "**Christ Jesus came into the world to save sinners-of whom I am the worst. But for that very reason I was shown mercy so that in me, the worst of sinners, Christ Jesus might display his unlimited patience as an example for those who would believe on him and receive eternal life**." NIV.

Instead of focusing on his smaller story, Paul fully confessed to being a sinner and used his life as an example of God's mercy. All glory then goes to God and His greater story. In my own life, I found God taking my imperfections to "**display his unlimited patience**." What I failed to do for my mother in helping her to find her purpose, God then resurrected in me His new life to help thousands to find their purpose in Him.

I began my journey by failing my mother. I continued my journey by trying to fight for the political rights of all ethnicities to have equal opportunity and failed miserably. God transformed my human effort into a spiritual work to affect lives for eternity. Inspire Women does not exist for equal rights of women of all ethnic backgrounds. It exists for maximum service of God's daughters called to go to the ends of the earth to express our Father's mercy, love, and hope. God's dreams are so much bigger than our own. If we let Him, He can repair any dream. More than that, He transforms the desires of our heart and gives us over and exceeding all that we could have imagined for ourselves.

When God Expects You to Follow His Voice

Situation: Do you find yourself surprised by what God is calling you to do? Do you feel God's directions defy logic and is requiring more than you ever expected?

The purpose of the personal journal entries shown below is to capture the emotion of loneliness in situations when God expects you to follow Him no matter how foolish, hard or unexpected you feel the calling is. Some entries were taken from an actual journal, others were written more recently as I reflected on what I was feeling at the time. The dates of the entries are approximate and were included to give the reader some sense of chronological history. In teaching this material, feel free to use my personal journal entries as illustration or personalize your lesson with writing your own personal journal entries or testimony to capture the emotion of loneliness you felt in your own life. If you did not keep a journal, then try to relive the situation in your mind and write an entry today to capture what you felt at the time.

July 19, 1974

Dear God,
Are you telling me to keep going even when my Mom is no longer with me? I wrapped my arms around me when I boarded the plane and imagined them to be your arms. There are times when you feel very distant. Can you speak louder? I am leaving all that is familiar to me. I see my father standing alone at the airport waving goodbye to me. I know he will be going back to an empty home. He lost my Mom six months ago and now I am leaving. I can't imagine how he must be feeling. What will the ride be like as he drives himself home? I wish I could help him but my own world is unraveling.

This was supposed to be your answer to many years of prayer. This was supposed to be the beginning of a dream come true. This was the day our family had waited for. I did not expect the dream to be fulfilled in this way. So what am I supposed to be doing in America? God, do we keep going even the dream is not what we expected?

May 9, 1977

Dear God,
I finished a four year program in two years. I thought I was honoring my father by finishing as fast as I could so I could return home to take care of him. I'm not sure now why I was in such a hurry. Now my Dad is happily married and he doesn't need me at home anymore. I'm happy for my Dad but I did not expect life to turn out this way. I did not go to my graduation ceremony. There is no one in the audience who know me. Everyone else will have family around them. So I think the best thing to do is to pack my bags and head on for graduate school. I'm not sure I expected to be going to graduate school. God, I feel like you are filled with surprises? What's around the corner?

100

July 11, 1980

Dear God,
I thought you told me to find a Christian room mate. How could this situation turn out so strangely? I found a house to rent. I found a Christian room mate. Today was the day I moved into the house. The electric company forgot to turn on the electricity. My room mate who was supposed to bring the furniture is in the hospital. So I found myself sitting on the floor in an empty house. It got darker and I told myself this is like camping out in the dark. It's going to be all right. It was awfully quiet sitting in the dark in a house with no furniture. Is this how life begins in a new city when I'm following your will?

My room mate "to-be" said she wasn't moving in with me after all. What was it that happened? She broke up with her boyfriend and tried to slit her wrist. Was this the Christian room mate I was so excited about? Let me get this straight. She was in love with this guy that you didn't like. She split up with him because you told her to. She could not handle leaving him but could not handle not doing what you said. So when caught between a rock and a hard place, she decided to try an exit plan with her own life. Well, so much for having a Christian room mate. Maybe the answer is not in Christians. It's hard though to really get to know you when those who represent you lead such defeated lives. God, what is the way to get to know you? I wish I could hear you better.

How could following your voice lead to such a dead end? What are you trying to tell me?

June 22, 1985

Dear God,
Moving to Europe the day after the wedding seemed like such a fairytale thing to do. Who would have imagined that Brussels, Belgium would be such a depressing time in my life! So we returned to America after ten months. I thought perhaps it was the career I missed, so I joined a top management consulting company. I know you were the one who opened the door to that opportunity. I threw myself into my work and in three years I rose up the corporate ladder. The company even offered me the new position as manager over a whole department. The same day I received my long sought after appointment, my husband gets news that he has been promoted to a position in Houston! Was that a coincidence or was that your plan? It seems like every time I get settled in a community, it's time to move. God, why did you give me success in corporate America only to lead me where I am walking away? Do you like uprooting me? Why are we moving to Houston, Texas?

September 1, 1989

Dear God,
A year ago, my sister-in-law advised me to join Bible Study Fellowship. So I did. Was that you talking through her? I couldn't believe that Bible Study Fellowship was a six year program. I couldn't imagine anyone in a Bible study for that long. I am embarrassed to say that I signed up for Bible Study to find someone to have lunch with.

Alice, my discussion leader called me every week. She was really sweet. If she hadn't called me every week, I don't think I would have gone back to bible study. It's taking way too long. I need something quicker. God, don't you have a faster way to heal?

Alice told me her job was to put my hand in the hand of Jesus. She said Jesus was the only one we can trust in this world. I think through her help I will one day hear your voice clearly. It will be so loud it will be like you're breathing behind my neck. I know that day is around the corner! I wish it could be today! God, am I on the right track? Do I just do the last thing I heard you say and stay there till you speak again?

June 15, 1998

Dear God,
I was offered a job in corporate America. The pay was wonderful. The work hours fit perfectly. The company said I could have Fridays off to speak at women's retreats. I did not expect you to shut this door. How did all those green lights turn into a red light? When you shut the door to corporate America, I told you that if I had my choice I would work for a multi-ethnic ministry. I didn't tell anyone else what we talked about. I told you I would love to be in a ministry that reached women of all ethnic backgrounds. Then three days later, I received a call from a multi-ethnic ministry inviting me to join the staff.

God, I don't know where this will lead but my pastor said not to worry about that. He said ministry is not a career. He said to just do the next thing that will reach more people. So I'm just going to walk through this door God. And then I'll just walk through the next door that helps me tell more people about you. I guess that's the

way to choose what to do next. I should just serve in the best open door that will tell the most people about you.

I love serving at the Bible College. The other leaders are like my brothers. Their names are Buck and John. I think they were best friends in high school. I feel like the little sister who is pedaling as fast as she can to keep up with her big brothers. I love the campus, I love the students, I feel like I died and went to heaven. I hope I make my brothers proud. God, I'm following you to the college. Please lead me there one day at a time.

April 4, 2003

Dear God,
What happened? How could you be telling me to leave the Bible College? You know that having roots is something I desire with all my heart. You know that I have been wandering in a desert for many years in my life and there is nothing enticing about going off on my own. What do you mean when you tell me I am leaving? Why am I leaving? Where am I going?

I don't understand your ways, God. I was doing really well here. In a short time, I went from being Director of Women's Ministry to being Vice President of Special Programs and Special Assistant to the President. I am making a statement for women right where I am. I know you're not impressed with titles.

Are you testing my heart to see if I will walk away with nothing but your voice to lead me? The President of the Bible College gave me his blessings to go. They won't be able to help financially but I have their prayers. And I know they will always just be an email away. One of their Board members said to me, "You've jumped from a plane without a parachute before. You can do this!" I guess the question I asked was, "But why would I?" I can just go home. I don't have to do this. So what are you saying? Are you telling me you want this?

Nov 30, 2004

Dear God,
You were the one who said you wanted an endowment. Who else did you tell? How long will it take to raise an endowment for biblical training for your daughters? Who are the faith friends who will listen to your voice? You won't ask them for what is easy. You never do. You won't ask for what is logical. In fact, if they have things all figured out, it's probably not what you are asking for. What you want is a gift from the heart. What you want is a sacrifice. What you want is a statement that tells the world that you are worthy of all that we own. God, if someone could look into our financial records, would we be embarrassed? In our estate planning, who did we leave our assets to? Did we even think to return to you the wealth you trusted to us? God, it feels so lonely sometimes when we hear your voice because you lead us where few will go. Where will your voice lead? But more than that, how many will follow?

The corresponding truths God taught me from His Word to address my situation
Feel free to continue reading all my personal journals in Module One expressing feelings of loneliness before reading the Bible Study. Or you may continue with the corresponding Bible study which contains God's truths in addressing the situation described in the above journal entries with additional truths God taught me to address situations that were not included in my journal entries. If you choose to personalize this curriculum as your way to bond with the group you are leading, feel free not only to use your own testimony and personal journal entries but in the Bible study part, include what God taught you from His Word in your situations that evoked loneliness.

When God Expects You to Follow His Voice

Situation: Do you find yourself surprised by what God is calling you to do? Do you feel God's directions defy logic and is requiring more than you ever expected?

Reminder: Let's learn the truths from God's Word that speak to our situations. Remember that as a member of God's royal family, we are to act according to the customs of the royal family. This means reinforcing our royal identity by living according to God's specific instructions in the Bible. When we cannot find specific instructions that speak to our situation, we are to search our spiritual heritage and model our lives after God's faith heroes who responded correctly to situations that parallel our own. We can also learn from their mistakes to avoid making the same mistakes in our own lives.

God's greater vision for our lives often requires us to leave the comfort zone of familiar territory. Because I came to this country as an immigrant and was uprooted from family and friends, I have a deep emotional need to belong to a community. In my background lies my greatest strength but in it I also find my deepest weaknesses and vulnerabilities. When God's Spirit nudges me to uproot, I find myself telling God, "All this change is not good for me. I need to put down roots in my life!

"If you are a member of God's royal family, He expects you to fit your life to the family's schedule and plans for the world."

Thank God that He is not influenced by my drama and teary eyed theatrics. I have found that God will not be held hostage to my emotional baggage. He does not tend to stay in one place because His heart is for the world. I used to tell God that He and I were emotionally incompatible. My choice was always to stay and if I could possibly do it, I would build a fortress around me to secure the status quo. God's pattern is to go as His heart leads Him to other cities to offer more people His hope. I had to learn to allow God to be my true North and to realize that earth is not my home. As one made in God's image, He breathed eternity into me and my ultimate home is in heaven. While on earth, the closest thing to home on this planet is to attach myself to the person of Jesus and to what He wants to finish on earth.

I wonder today if God is growing you into a leader He can trust with His mission. If so, manage your expectations and learn from God's biblical patterns. As a member of God's royal family, be aware of the family's royal customs. Every family has its way of doing things. In God's family, He wants His family to leave its fingerprints on planet earth. His family is sent into different communities to bring His message. If you are in a company that is expanding, expect that if a project is being shaped in a different country, you may be invited to go and head up the project. In a similar way, those in God's royal family are part of a family whose mandate is to bring the product from where they live to the ends of the earth. The product that is the family's specialty is the gospel of salvation, the message of

God sending His one and only son to die for the sins of the world. This is the message that tells the world that salvation can be found in no other name. Acts 4:12 reads, **"Salvation is found in no one else, for there is no other name under heaven given to men by which we must be saved."** NIV. Those without the gift of Jesus to cover their sins will perish eternally.

In communicating this message, know that those in God's family live in a family culture where the Father of the household is urgent. He will not blink an eye to call you or to send you where He needs you to go. So if you have put down roots, built your dream house, decorated it perfectly, don't be surprised if God views your home as an encumbrance. Unless it serves the interest of your royal family for you to live in a palace on earth or to put down roots where you are, God will not bless a decision where you have declined a calling because of your reluctance to sell your home or to move your residence.

In the first book of the Bible, we read in Genesis 12:1: **The LORD had said to Abram, "Leave your country, your people and your father's household and go to the land I will show you.** NIV. God did not seem to be concerned that Abram was of an age where he would personally prefer to slow down and take it easy the rest of his life.

If you are part of God's royal family, then know that God expects you to fit your life to the family's schedule and plans for the world. If you are in a financially sound position, expect God to launch a new project. You may feel that all your life, you have been trying to get to a place of non-crisis so you can have some peace. You may be feeling like you have worked all your life and so you deserve to retire. Well, I hate to break the news to you but there is no biblical example of anyone who retired!

Interestingly enough, it is when we think we have created our place of stability on earth, that God stirs in our spirit to begin a new dream. If you have attained a level of financial security, you may think you can sail away into the sunset the rest of your life. Instead, did you know that you are strategically positioned to finish something major God has planned? The question is, will you listen to God's voice?

The book of 2 Samuel, chapter 7, verses 1-3 reads: **After the king was settled in his palace and the LORD had given him rest from all his enemies around him, he said to Nathan the prophet, "Here I am, living in a palace of cedar, while the ark of God remains in a tent." Nathan replied to the king, "Whatever you have in mind, go ahead and do it, for the LORD is with you."** NIV

King David could easily have said, "Given all the battles I have fought, I deserve this rest. There is no way I will oversee the finishing of a massive project. It will require both my time and resources. Besides, I am getting old." Instead, David obeyed the prompting of God's spirit to help his son Solomon to finish building the temple.

Is there someone God has called you to walk with? Will God require from you what He asked of David? Will you dig deep into your financial resources and experience base to help a younger leader succeed?

"When God speaks His vision to our hearts we become the protector of the dream."

Notice that the King was settled in his palace. Therefore one way the devil distracts us from God's plans is to keep our lives in a state of disarray. Don't be deceived if you feel the prompting to build another vacation home, to remodel your home or to accept a different job when your current job gives you more opportunity for ministry. Ask yourself, "Are these promptings from God or will all this change simply keep my life in a state of disarray?"

Unless we are settled, we are too busy with the details around us to notice the grand plan God is unfolding. We may be in the midst of a major spiritual movement and have no idea it is going on because we are unsettled with details that have no eternal significance. It is amazing how details can consume us if we are unaware of this intrusion.

What details have been consuming your life? Have you committed yourself for activities that carry no eternal significance? If so, why?

> **"When you disconnect yourself from your past, you then disconnect yourself from your future."**

It was when King David was settled that God revived the passion He had put in David's heart. David's passion had always been to worship God. He wrote numerous poems to express his relationship with God and God's relationship with him. In the book of Psalm, chapter 27, verse 4, King David said, **"One thing I ask of the LORD, this is what I seek: that I may dwell in the house of the LORD all the days of my life, to gaze upon the beauty of the LORD and to seek him in his temple."** NIV. Is it any wonder that when King

David was settled, the thing that stirred in his heart was to build the temple?

Realize that the dreams God gives us are often connected to the story God has been writing in our lives over the years. David spent a lot of time in the pasture. Spending time with God was something that was part of David's history. When God called me to establish Inspire Women, I thought God was coming from left field. Instead, what I have come to realize is that my background consisted of witnessing how women were belittled. I witnessed those who were physically abused. As a child, I had cried out, "When I grow up, I will…" Yet, due to all the changes in my life, I had forgotten my childhood passion to change the world with God's mercy for His daughters. God built on the background He had already given me to create a passion in me to encourage God's daughters to step into His purpose for their lives. Did you know that when you disconnect yourself from your past, you then disconnect yourself from your future? Is there a dream in you waiting to be born?

Imagine a time when all the details of your life are settled. What one thing have you always had a passion for?

I wonder if God is waiting for you to be settled so your life can be about the passion God has put in you. When God's Spirit begins to stir in you, realize that God expects you to fulfill the dream He is entrusting to you. What have you done with God's dream?

David tells Nathan the prophet about what was stirring in his heart. Observe that Nathan said, **"Whatever you have in mind, go ahead and do it, for the LORD is with you."** Nathan tells David to **"do it"**. What was David to do? He was to do "**whatever you have in mind.**" Notice Nathan was referring to what David had in David's mind, not what anyone else thought.

When God speaks His vision to our hearts, we become the protector of the dream. Even in the case that we don't get credit for the project (God told David his son Solomon was to build the temple),

David was still the one entrusted with the plan and invited to provide the counsel and the resources to build the temple.

Herein lays the loneliness of the calling. God speaks His plans to your ears. No one will understand the details like you will. No one can protect the dream like you can because God told you what the dream is supposed to look like. Nathan cannot provide the missing blanks for David. David had to go to God for the answers. David may talk about his calling with the world but in the end, he is responding to the audience of one. God is the only one who will know if David implemented the dream the way God intended.

If you are a leader to whom God has shown His vision, then stop asking someone else for the details of implementation. Don't insult God by having others vote on the plan. Instead, hear from God and proceed accordingly. If you are someone serving under a leader to whom God has entrusted a vision, then wait for your marching orders. To come up with another plan is usurping God's leader of a God given authority that God Himself granted. To offer ideas is one thing but to mumble under your breath that your plan is better is an act of rebellion where you have set yourself up against God's leader. God-birthed visions can only be finished in God's way because it is not possible for human logic to fulfill God-sized dreams.

"Have you traded your royal family's mission for your own personal agenda?"

In the New Testament, we see the biblical pattern of leaving a perfect environment in the example of Jesus. Philippians 2:3-8 reads: **Do nothing out of selfish ambition or vain conceit, but in humility consider others better than yourselves. Each of you should look not only to your own interests, but also to the interests of others. Your attitude should be the same as that of Christ Jesus: Who, being in very nature God, did not consider equality with God something to be grasped, but made himself nothing, taking the very nature of a servant, being made in human likeness. And being found in appearance as a man, he humbled himself and became obedient to death- even death on a cross!** NIV

Notice that the details of Christ leaving a perfect home to come to earth to die for our sins was given in a context where Paul was teaching his audience, **"Do nothing out of selfish ambition."** Notice also that Jesus' choice to let go was described as "**did not consider equality with God something to be**

grasped." When I put these two thoughts together, God's perfect counsel instructs me that when I am unwilling to let go of something familiar or perfect when God's mission needs me to let go of it, then I am acting out of "**selfish ambition.**" Have you traded your royal family's mission for your own personal agenda? Unlike Jesus who laid down his rights, are you filled with the attitude of "I deserve this. I worked for this. I paid for this. This is mine and I'm not letting go of it!"?

I have found God's calling in my life to be a lonely journey because there are times no one understands the calling. To the general public they may ask, "What are you doing? Why are you doing it?" In my own heart, I know I heard Him. It is my own immaturity when I hesitate when the Father has called. The way out of my loneliness is to stop having my feet in two worlds and to join God in what He is doing. I cannot represent the royal family while having my own agenda. If I know God has called but I stay where I am, is there any wonder I feel disconnected from God? Then I will also feel disconnected from those around me because I know I am an imposter. I am not like them. I have been set apart and called out and I am trying to fit in where God has already released me.

In the examples of my faith heroes, I find comfort. Abraham was in his retirement years when God called him out. David had spent a lifetime fighting battles and here's his chance to rest instead of being responsible for one more project, especially one so publicly visible and which needed the cooperation of hundreds. Jesus was in a perfect environment that He had every right to when God sent Him.

In my own life, when God asks me to leave the familiar to enter uncharted territory, instead of dreading it or resenting it, I know God wants me to receive it as confirmation that I am in the royal family. What is happening to me is reinforcement that I have a place in a royal family tree with its set of royal customs. It is not a curse but a blessing to be expected to respond differently than those who are not in God's family. I serve a Father whose eyes are on the world. He has a mission He wants to complete before the curtain falls on planet earth. This earth is temporary and my real home is in heaven. If I forget who my Father is, I will find myself disconnected from His purpose.

Is there something or someone familiar you must leave in order to fulfill God's calling? What is keeping you from letting go? How would one in God's royal family respond?

Before leaving all that is familiar, we need to settle in our heart, "What is the end goal? How will I know when I have finished?"

When I look back at my life, I realize that had I known God's Word better, I would have trusted God's biblical patterns more instead of expecting all the dots to connect immediately.

One pattern that would have helped me tremendously is to recognize that God's faith heroes may not have known the "how's" but they knew the "what." Before leaving all that is familiar, we need to settle in our heart "What is the end goal? How will I know when I have finished?" Some end goals are general, others are more specific but we still need to know what mission we are serving. Is it to make disciples, is it to secure the financial provision for a ministry, is it to create an infrastructure for God's purpose that will continue long after we are no longer on earth? What is it that we are aiming for?

When God called Abraham out, He told Abraham what he was to leave but He also told Abraham what the end goal was. He said in Genesis 12:2: **I will make you into a great nation and I will bless you; I will make your name great, and you will be a blessing. I will bless those who bless you, and whoever curses you I will curse; and all peoples on earth will be blessed through you.**

When God called Paul, he confirmed his calling through Ananias and said to him in Acts 9:15-16, **"Go! This man is my chosen instrument to carry my name before the Gentiles and their kings and before the people of Israel. I will show him how much he must suffer for my name."** NIV. Paul knew therefore that the goal was to reach the Gentiles as compared to a ministry to only the Jews. He was to bring God's salvation message to the world.

Before Jesus began his public ministry, he knew what the end goal was. In his first public address, Luke 4:16-21 tells us: **He went to Nazareth, where he had been brought up, and on the Sabbath day he went into the synagogue, as was his custom. And he stood up to read. The scroll of the prophet Isaiah was handed to him. Unrolling it, he found the place where it is written: "The Spirit of the Lord is on me, because he has anointed me to preach good news to the poor. He has sent me to proclaim freedom for the prisoners and recovery of sight for the blind, to release the oppressed, to proclaim the year of the Lord's favor." Then he rolled up the scroll, gave it back to the attendant and sat down. The eyes of everyone in the synagogue were fastened on him, and he began by saying to them, "Today this scripture is fulfilled in your hearing."** NIV.

Did you notice the words "**Today this scripture is fulfilled**"? Jesus also knew that the way He would bring freedom was to die on the cross for the sins of the world. By His death, He would conquer death. By His resurrection, He would give us His power to overcome and to live victorious lives in spite of our circumstances.

On the day you heard God's voice can you finish this sentence: Today God moved in mercy to set my life apart to_____. Can you feel the excitement in knowing there is a chosen day God set His plan into motion? Is today the day?

When I researched my spiritual heritage, I discovered that the heroes of the faith knew what they were to finish. Genesis 12:4 tells me, **"So Abram left, as the LORD had told him; and Lot went with him. Abram was seventy-five years old when he set out from Haran. He took his wife Sarai, his nephew Lot, all the possessions they had accumulated and the people they had acquired in Haran, and they set out for the land of Canaan, and they arrived there."** Did you see the words **"and they arrived there"**? Do you even know where you are supposed to arrive? If you don't know what the end goal is, then you will find yourself here, there, and everywhere. God never meant for us to allow circumstances to drive our life. We were created to subdue the earth. In the image of God and by the example of our faith heroes, we must settle the question, "What is my end goal? Where am I going and when will I know that I have arrived?"

In Jesus' life we read in John 19:30, **"When he had received the drink, Jesus said, "It is finished." With that, he bowed his head and gave up his spirit."** NIV. Did you see the words **"It is finished"**? Know therefore that no matter how many turns there are in the road and no matter how many people try to stop you and no matter how many obstacles you face, a life of faith is one where we don't lose track of our mission. Because Jesus knew the reason for His mission, He could say the words **"It is finished."** Unless you know what your mission is, you won't be able to assess if you have finished.

The Apostle Paul said in 2 Timothy 4:6-8, **"For I am already being poured out like a drink offering, and the time has come for my departure. I have fought the good fight, I have finished the race, I have kept the faith. Now**

there is in store for me the crown of righteousness, which the Lord, the righteous Judge, will award to me on that day-and not only to me, but also to all who have longed for his appearing." NIV

Did you see the words **"I have finished the race"**? Why did Paul conclude that he had finished? I discovered in studying Paul's life that his sense of completion came from three reasons: First Paul knew he had finished because he began with remembering the details that led him to hearing God's voice. Not only did Paul hear God's initial invitation to him to be an instrument to the Gentiles but He also heard the moment God was going full steam ahead to redirect Paul's focus from reaching Jews to reaching the Gentiles. From the moment Paul heard God's voice, he acted and kept going in what he heard God say.

Paul shared his story in Acts 22:6-21: **"About noon as I came near Damascus, suddenly a bright light from heaven flashed around me. I fell to the ground and heard a voice say to me, 'Saul! Saul! Why do you persecute me?' "'Who are you, Lord?' I asked. "'I am Jesus of Nazareth, whom you are persecuting,' he replied. My companions saw the light, but they did not understand the voice of him who was speaking to me. "'What shall I do, Lord?' I asked. "'Get up,' the Lord said, 'and go into Damascus. There you will be told all that you have been assigned to do. "My companions led me by the hand into Damascus, because the brilliance of the light had blinded me."** A man named Ananias came to see me. He was a devout observer of the law and highly respected by all the Jews living there. He stood beside me and said, 'Brother Saul, receive your sight!' And at that very moment I was able to see him. "Then he said: 'The God of our fathers has chosen you to know his will and to see the Righteous One and to hear words from his mouth. You will be his witness to all men of what you have seen and heard. And now what are you waiting for? Get up, be baptized and wash your sins away, calling on his name.' "When I returned to Jerusalem and was praying at the temple, I fell into a trance and saw the Lord speaking. 'Quick!' he said to me. 'Leave Jerusalem immediately, because they will not accept your testimony about me.' "'Lord,' I replied, 'these men know that I went from one synagogue to another to imprison and beat those who believe in you. And when the blood of your martyr Stephen was shed, I stood there giving my approval and guarding the clothes of those who were killing him.' "Then the Lord said to me, 'Go; I will send you far away to the Gentiles.'" NIV.

Don't miss the fact that sometimes God allows opposition to give you greater focus in your mission. The opposition of the Jews triggered God's timing to focus Paul on the Gentiles. Have you experienced opposition in your ministry? How could God be using the opposition you have experienced as His way to lead you to be more focused in what God wants to accomplish?

Once Paul heard God's voice, he obeyed. He did not forget the details of his divine encounter. Sadly, in ministry, I have found many who come to me with long details in their stories as to what brought them to Inspire Women. They will be in tears as they marveled at God's grace in setting them apart. And then a week or two later, they are nowhere to be seen. Then I get an email telling me that they don't believe this is their season. What I learned from studying the lives of the faith heroes in my royal family is how they were sure of the details that led to their calling and then they kept going in the direction of their calling.

Could you write the details that led to the first time God's Spirit set you apart for His purpose? What were the details in your circumstances and what did God ask you to do? Are you still on course?

The second reason Paul was sure he had finished was because once he heard God's voice, he did not waiver. He set his eyes towards the goal of reaching every living breathing Gentile he could in every open door that was open to him. He tells us in Acts 20:19-21, **"I served the Lord with great humility and with tears, although I was severely tested by the plots of the Jews. You know that I have not hesitated to preach anything that would be helpful to you but have taught you publicly and from house to house. I have declared to both Jews and Greeks that they must turn to God in repentance and have faith in our Lord Jesus."** NIV

Did you see the words "I have not hesitated"? In your life, when God opens the door for you for ministry, do you give up your calling for more wages in the corporate world? Do you go where you personally prefer a given lifestyle? What criteria do you use to make your decisions that show you are a member of God's royal family and make decisions to protect the mission of God's royal family as compared to protecting your self interest?

The third reason Paul was sure he had finished was because God told him he was getting close to the end of his time on earth. He knew he had not hesitated to do all that he could in the open doors he had. So as far as he was concerned, he is done. God is the one who will continue His own dream. Paul's part is over. He said in Acts 20:25-27, **"Now I know that none of you among whom I have gone about preaching the kingdom will ever see me again. Therefore, I declare to you today that I am innocent of the blood of all men. For I have not hesitated to proclaim to you the whole will of God".** NIV.

Did you know God will protect His own goals? All we can do is to work towards the goal with all our heart in whatever open door we have. Then when God shows us our time is coming to an end, we need to feel the release in knowing we have finished. How will Paul's example guide you today in what you are feeling about your goals and what you have accomplished to date?

The longer I wait to obey God's calling, the longer I keep myself in a state of loneliness. When God has spoken, the longer I hesitate, the more I am operating where my heart is disconnected from its source of true life. I walk around living an artificial life because I have disconnected myself from God's timing and purpose. It is only when I step out in obedience that my heart will beat as one with God's. God and I being on the same page is a place of wholeness. When God is with me, I find He is all that I need. We can conquer the world together!

"When Jesus said the Son of Man did not have a place to rest His head, this was an invitation into greater freedom."

There are times when I wish God would give me a five year business plan but I am learning that God does not need my vote. He will not give me His plans for me to review. I will discover God's plan by clinging to Jesus as my source of life and direction.

In Matthew chapter 8, verses 18-20, someone said to Jesus, **"Teacher, I will follow you wherever you go." To this declaration, Jesus replied, "Foxes have holes and birds of the air have nests, but the Son of Man has no place to lay his head."** NIV.

Jesus' answer taught me to trust His person as my plan. First I must hear His call in Matthew 28:19-20, **"Therefore go and make disciples of all nations, baptizing them in the name of the Father and of the Son and of the Holy Spirit, and teaching them to obey everything I have commanded you. And surely I am with you always, to the very end of the age."** NIV. Next I must ask if His call is more specific than the general call to help advance His message on earth. Once I settle on the specificity of His call for my life, I then follow His person through any open doors and opportunities that will put me further along in the end goal He has given me.

We are not responsible for doors that don't open but from the doors that have opened, which one helps you reach the most for Christ? Have you chosen the door that gives you the most opportunity to advance God's purpose on earth? If not, why not?

From all the doors that were open to me for ministry, I walked through the one to inspire women from all ethnicities and denominations and economic levels to connect their lives with God's purpose. The reason I chose this door was because it was my best opportunity to reach the most for God's kingdom. It was not a door I had designed nor was it one I would have chosen for myself. It was simply the door that was in front of me and it became my choice as to whether I would walk through it.

Before walking through the door, I asked these questions, "God, where does this door lead? What is our destination? When will I know we have finished?" He said He wanted a perpetual infrastructure that will inspire His daughters and provide the funds and opportunity for their training for missions and ministry. He said He wanted a trust fund to perpetually send the message to the world that He affirms the potential of His daughters for His mission and will invest in their training. He said He has chosen the empowering of His daughters as His way to complete His spiritual army. Not only will He do this through His daughters but He will use both young and old. He will call out the older generation and give them His dreams.

Acts 2:17-18 reads: **'In the last days, God says, I will pour out my Spirit on all people. Your sons and daughters will prophesy, your young men will see visions, your old men will dream dreams. Even on my servants, both men and women, I will pour out my Spirit in those days, and they will prophesy.** NIV.

I know God chose to begin His vision for the financial provision of His daughters across ethnicities and denominations in Houston, Texas. I know I will have finished when Houston, Texas has a basic level of funding for women for biblical training. I know that God wants this vision to travel to cities throughout the world. I don't know if I will live to witness the vision implemented in every city but I know there will come a day when the vision will be completed.

Although I know what the end goal is, what I don't know is how God will implement His vision. So I go to Him and ask for the plan. I have found that He gives us each day our daily bread. My security is in a person. When Jesus said the Son of Man did not have a place to rest His head, this was an invitation into greater freedom. I have found how little I actually needed in terms of my environment in order to succeed. If God gives us a building to operate from, then praise Him. If He gives me a tent, then praise Him. I have found that the treasure is in us. It has totally floored me that God has done so much with so little.

When the Inspire Women's office is full today with women streaming down the halls, I marvel at God's victory to fill what used to be empty space. When the women scholarship recipients came to orientation to open their scholarship award letters, I felt God's heart rejoicing. At one time we were a concept. Today, we are becoming a household name.

God continues to astound me. His fingerprints are all over Inspire Women. He moves out of His heart of mercy for His daughters and His global personnel plan to recruit and to send His spiritual warriors with His message to the ends of the earth.

I still don't know how I ended up here as the Founder and President of Inspire Women. Did I ever want to start my own 501 (c) 3 nonprofit ministry? Never in a million years! But God did not ask me what I wanted. What has surprised me is how over time, I discovered that doing what God wanted fulfilled the desire of my heart. What brings me to my knees is to realize that at a time when I felt my life was unraveling God had a plan for my life. How strange that when I found myself in Houston, Texas thinking my entire world had become unglued, God was saying, "We are right on time because the Founder of Inspire Women has landed in Houston, Texas!" It is simply a fact that although God does not need us He has chosen at this time to work through earthen vessels.

God was sure of His plan but I discovered it moment by moment by walking through the next open door that aligned with His vision. One day, no daughter will be left behind. Those who do not have the opportunity to be trained for missions and ministry will have the chance to be equipped. Oh how sad to think that we would be sending our military into battle without ammunition! In the same way, God wants His daughters to be fully equipped before He sends them to intervene in the battles of life.

When God told me to flow with Him, I discovered how insecure that made me feel because I didn't know Him. I knew Him in head knowledge, but I had to get out of the boat before I could experience walking on water with the person of Jesus. God, in His mercy, carried me one day at a time and allowed me to witness His faithfulness. Where I failed, He covered me with His grace. He reconnected the dots. He repaired damages.

If you think you know God, let me ask you how you know Him. Do you know Him in the way you can quote His Word and quickly notice when others quote Him incorrectly? How have you shown that you know Him in ways beyond just quoting His teaching?

God has shown Himself in my life to be the ultimate navigation system. When I first experienced the navigation system in my car, I could not believe how smart this car was to keep track of me. No matter what turn I was forced to make because of a road construction I did not expect, the system re-plotted my direction. No matter what wrong turn I made, the system immediately recognized the wrong turn and spoke into my life to get me back on track. It never lost focus. It always knew what the end goal was and it relentlessly instructed me to make the turns to get me back to where I was going. When I finally arrive, the system announces, "You have arrived at your destination." When I first experienced my car's navigation system, God showed me how I could count on Him to guide me in my life as the ultimate fool proof navigation system. He will re-plot, He will relentlessly instruct, He will not give up until I get the point. And then one day when I step into heaven, He will say, "You have finished. You have arrived at your destination."

One day, I was sobbing in my room when I felt I had totally missed God's voice. God reminded me of how He had returned for Peter. Oh how I relate to the feeling of not knowing how to get myself back on track. John 21:3-5 tells the story: **"I'm going out to fish," Simon Peter told them, and they said, "We'll go with you." So they went out and got into the boat, but that night they caught nothing. Early in the morning, Jesus stood on the shore, but the disciples did not realize that it was Jesus. He called out to them, "Friends, haven't you any fish?"** NIV.

God always returns to rescue a heart that longs to follow Him. From the depths of my soul came this song. The lyrics went like this:

He has come for me,
just as He promised,
He has come for me.
When I heard my name,
my heart began to sing again.
So I ran to His embrace
and as I looked into His face
I saw my Savior,
and He was claiming me.
He came for me.

I praise God for all the times He returned to help me to re-connect the dots. In the same way God decided the timing of when He began to take the gospel to the Gentiles, I believe God has chosen this time and place to affirm His daughters. The miraculous unprecedented success of Inspire Women confirms in my spirit God's timetable to inspire the full potential of His daughters to complete His spiritual army.

There are 6.7 billion people in the world and the population is growing daily. Nearly 2 billion are Christians, which leaves 4.7 billion who have not heard the message of Jesus. It will take every believer to be engaged in battle for every knee to bow and every tongue to confess that Jesus is the Lord. Can we afford to leave behind any undeveloped potential? Inspire Women was birthed from God's heart to shout to the world that no daughter will be left behind in His spiritual army.

God did not ask my opinion as to His timing and methodology. He has chosen to work through His daughters in whom He trusts with His mission. Are you one of God's daughters? Then I pray you will become part of God's victory story and fulfill the dreams He puts in your heart to complete His vision to save the world.

Transforming Loneliness to Fulfill God's Purpose

As I said in the introduction, you will learn that a life of faith is not some mystical feeling but a concrete application of God's Word in the following ways:

- No matter what family background you came from and how things were done in your earthly family, all believers belong to God's royal family and are therefore expected to act according to the customs of the royal family.

- Whenever I experienced an emotion because of a challenge or a decision I needed to make, God taught me to do the following:

  - I ask myself, "What am I feeling? Is it loneliness, rejection, or fear? What exactly is the emotion I am dealing with?"

  - I ask myself, "Is the level of the emotion I am feeling in proportion to what just happened? If not, what wound did it open from my past to cause me to over react?"

  - I ask myself, "Is there a teaching in God's Word that parallels the situation I just encountered? Are there verses that speak to the situation that will give me guidance on how to respond?"

    If I cannot find specific verses, then I look for biblical examples of someone who dealt with a parallel situation. Since I am to act as a member of God's royal family, I ask myself, "What is the custom of God's royal family and how would God expect me to act?" A tangible way to learn the customs of the royal family is to study the lives of God's faith heroes and how they responded in a parallel situation. I was then able to imitate how the faith heroes responded. There are times I learned from the mistake of a biblical character as described in my concluding thoughts which shares a situation that almost made me abandon the dream.

    A life of faith then is a concrete way to respond based on what God has revealed in His Word. A person who lives by faith is one who intentionally models behavior after the right choices of the faith heroes in the Bible and trusts that making such a choice is the best choice, no matter what the outcome. The result is a life that moves with conviction and confidence by making choices that are anchored in truths from God's Word and learning from the responses of those who are part of our spiritual heritage.

In applying the above steps, below is what I learned from God's Word to overcome loneliness. I pray you will believe God's instruction from His Word and model these truths to your life.

When something is missing from your life

- **Turn to God as your true North and your only sure compass. No mortal human can be our permanent pillar. Only an eternal unchanging God can complete us and walk with us for the rest of our lives.**

- **God clarified Adam's mission first before shaping Eve to be Adam's perfect counterpart. Therefore, before we know what relationship we need in our lives, we must first know our mission and then trust Him to give us whoever is missing on the team or in our life to fulfill His purpose and mission.**

- **Our security should come from knowing that if we lose someone in our life, that God will shape and send another person if they are needed to fulfill His mission.**

- **Be confident in knowing that no matter what happens, your Heavenly Father doesn't slumber, He loves us with all of His heart and everything will be all right.**

When God releases you from a leader

- **Trust God's goodness and know that His personnel reassignment is for your good and the expansion of His kingdom.**

- **Trust God to have** finished what He meant for you to learn under a leader and step into God's new vision for your life.

- **Don't live in your past relationships and embrace the new relationships God gives you to forward His purpose.**

- **Realize that God is not trying to take something from us but He is trying to give us so much more.**

When you lose a co-laborer in ministry

- Focus on the mission you shared together. Realize that person has just simply gone ahead of you and is waiting for you on God's mountaintop. The best way to honor their memory is to finish well.
- Be reminded that God did not weave your lives together to fulfill each other's dreams. You were not made to fulfill each other's dreams but to fulfill God's dreams.
- When everything changes, the one constant we can count on is the unchanging heart and mission of God.

When you release your child to God

- In Hannah's story learn to commit your child to God all the days of his life.
- Trust that when you are obligated to leave your child in a situation where he is surrounded by ungodly influence, there is power in a mother's prayer to protect her child. Samuel grew in wisdom in spite of the evil in Eli's sons. God is perfectly able to protect those who belong to Him.
- God sees all things and He will bring justice to all situations. Trust God to avenge those who are evil.
- When God's dreams become the reason for our lives, it will help us to hold on loosely to our earthly relationships.

When you accept God's decision to move on

- Know that God expects your loyalty to first be for Him and not in your dreams for another individual. Do not violate God's first and greatest commandment which is to love the Lord Your God with all your heart.
- The second commandment is to love your neighbor so don't justify loving your neighbor above following God first.
- Whether God is moving on for a season or for that person's lifetime, you will remove the loneliness in your heart by being on the same page with God.

- When you put God's plans first you can trust that, if it fits God's plans, He will bring back the person you let go of in due time if they continue to mature in their faith.

When God is silent in the storms of life

- Find comfort in the experience of the disciples who panicked even when Jesus was in the boat with them. Understand, therefore, that it is normal to feel lonely in the midst of challenges even when you are in God's will. Remember it takes an intentional choice not to panic.
- The next time we turn the corner to find that something has blown up in our lives, instead of being in a panic have the faith to trust in God's protection. He has already secured our future for eternity and is worthy of our utmost faith and confidence.
- God's grace is sufficient and His power is made perfect in our weakness.
- Embrace your challenges as one in God's family who is experiencing what other family members are trusted with. When you see that your life is no different than the lives of the disciples in Jesus' day, you won't feel so alone anymore. You will feel a connection with the faith heroes of the past.

When God delays

- God draws us into His purpose for our lives. This drawing process includes experiences that we must go through first that develops greater faith and readies us for our calling. Ask yourself if you are the one causing the delay because of your lack of faith or your lack of preparation.
- Find comfort in knowing that God is silent because once He speaks you are held accountable. So He waits. His delay is an act of grace because He is more involved with you than you realized.
- God sometimes delays for our protection, so trust God in knowing when to hide you and when to bring you back out into the public's eyes.
- Before God can trust us with His ministry, we must first learn that life is not a question of me doing great things for God but a question of God doing great things through me.

- When God finally speaks, what holds me back is whether I am willing to pay the cost to follow Him.
- Our willingness to pay the cost of our calling comes from answering the question Jesus asked Peter, "Do you love me?"
- Even in our love for Him, God is the one who empowers us to pay the cost of following Him. Jesus grew Peter from "phileo" love to "agapao" love.
- When we find ourselves sitting on a shelf, use this time to learn that though God invites us to join Him, His plans are not dependent on us. Then when God opens the door again, celebrate any opportunity to join God in what He is doing. God humbles us before He can trust us with success.
- When Jesus was on Calvary, he experienced God's silence. Jesus stayed the course in the midst of the silence. Know that God desires to conform us to the image of His Son. So when you experience delays in God's silence, just continue doing what you last heard Him say.

When you feel no one is serving with you

- John the Baptist was a voice in the wilderness. He started serving in his unique calling. Is it time to embrace your uniqueness and just start serving?
- Elijah felt overwhelmed by God's calling. He missed the fact that God had already set apart a spiritual army of seven thousand. You were not created to save the day. God is the one who will save the day. Let God be the commanding officer in your life.
- Paul was focused and diligent his whole time of ministry. He had great challenges but was never stressed. All we are responsible for is to serve in our open doors with what we have. God is the one who guarantees results.
- Any stage God gives us the privilege to build is for Him. There are times when we can let our own success overwhelm us to the point that we feel we have to top ourselves. When you experience success, learn to lay your gift on the altar. Follow John the Baptist's example in decreasing so God can increase.

When you've totally let God down

- Give yourself freedom to grieve your mistakes. Peter took time to weep.
- Don't make excuses for your mistakes. Instead go humbly before God and trust Him to repair damages and restore you to His purpose. The loneliest place to be is when you are separated from your Creator. So confess quickly and seek restoration.
- Use your smaller story to direct the focus on God's greater story. He can transform any failure into His victory song.

When God expects you to follow His voice

- God's eyes are on the world. Don't be surprised when He calls you out where you are settled and familiar to go to uncharted territory with His message.
- Jesus' statement that He had no place to rest His head is an invitation to freedom. God wants us to know His treasure is in us. You will be surprised at how much God can do when you no longer have encumbrances that artificially limit you.
- There is no biblical example for retirement. When you are financially secure and settled, this is the time God wants you to serve His purpose, not your own personal agenda.
- Always know the end goal. Though you may not know the "how's" you must know the "what". Then keeping the end goal in mind, follow God one day at a time through any open door or opportunity that will get you closer to the end goal.
- When God speaks, you become the protector of the dream. He has chosen to work through earthen vessels at this time. Ask God for the details and then implement. You and God can conquer the world together!

Additional Testimonies on Loneliness

In the appendix, you will find additional testimonies from friends of Inspire Women. If you wish to personalize this curriculum as your way to build authentic friendships and community, please add to or replace the testimonies in the appendix with those from those God has woven into your community. Below is a letter you may use to invite your friends to be part of this personalized curriculum

Dear _____,

When God entrusts you with a dream for yourself, your family, your church, your workplace, your ministry or community, your emotions can either empower you or they can cause you to crater on the inside. When the protector of the dream craters, you can kiss goodbye any dream that was meant to make a difference. I am writing you because I am embarking on an exciting journey to share God's truths to transform the emotions in our hearts into a positive energy for His purpose. Unlike other curriculums, I am so excited to be working with a "personalized" leadership curriculum and therefore need your help to make this adventure to be a success. The personalized curriculum I will be teaching has the following format:

- *The curriculum is divided into 3 modules, each focused on an emotion. The three emotions we will cover are loneliness, rejection, and fear. I will begin the discussion of each emotion with transparently sharing my personal journal entries from times in my life when I experienced the emotion being discussed.*

- *Following my personal journal entries will be a Bible study with God's truths to transform our emotions into passionate divine purpose.*

- *Included in our study are additional testimonies from friends such as you. If you did not keep a journal you can draw from, I invite you to relive those times in your mind when you experienced either loneliness, rejection, or fear and write a personal testimony describing your situation and what you felt as if you were experiencing it today. Then also add any truths God taught you in the midst of your emotion.*

I am inviting you to be a special part of this personalized curriculum to affirm your presence in our community and to help you to see that you have a message of hope to share with the community God has placed you in. I pray too that in this personalized curriculum, you will celebrate your divine appointment to be part of a personalized keepsake that will build the bond between us and create a lasting teaching instrument that will bless the members of our community for generations to come.

Please let me know if you will join me in creating this personalized teaching material for our _____ (church, workplace, ministry, family, etc.). If you choose to participate, specify which emotion you wish to write about and what God taught you about it through His Word. Please keep your testimony under 3 typewritten 8.5 x 11 pages.

Grateful for your special friendship,

Transforming Rejection to Fulfill God's Purpose

In the Bible, God reveals Himself as the one who was rejected, yet returned over and over again to restore the relationship with those who rejected Him. In the Old Testament, we hear God saying in Leviticus 26:43-45, **"They will pay for their sins because they rejected my laws and abhorred my decrees. Yet in spite of this, when they are in the land of their enemies, <u>I will not reject them or abhor them</u> so as to destroy them completely, breaking my covenant with them. I am the LORD their God. But for their sake I will remember the covenant with their ancestors whom I brought out of Egypt in the sight of the nations to be their God. I am the LORD.'"** NIV. If you have been rejected by someone for missing the mark, realize that the Israelites missed the mark in God's books. However, unlike rejection by the world, God's heart continues to give us a second chance.

> **"We serve a God who offered us Himself as the perfect choice but was voted off the team."**

1 Samuel 8:6-8 tells us: **But when they said, "Give us a king to lead us," this displeased Samuel; so he prayed to the LORD. And the LORD told him: "Listen to all that the people are saying to you; it is not you they have rejected, <u>but they have rejected me as their king</u>. As they have done from the day I brought them up out of Egypt until this day, forsaking me and serving other gods, so they are doing to you.** NIV.

If you have felt like you were the perfect match for a company, ministry or personal relationship but no one else seemed to think so, realize that we serve a God who offered us Himself as the perfect choice but was voted off the team by an ignorant crowd.

In the New Testament, Jesus said in Luke 9:22, **"The Son of Man must suffer many things and <u>be rejected by the elders, chief priests and teachers of the law</u>, and he must be killed and on the third day be raised to life."** NIV. (underline added for emphasis).

If you feel like you have sacrificially laid down your life for someone only to have them reject you and hurt you, then know that you serve a God who experienced similar rejection, to the point of being nailed on a cross.

Against God's repeated example of total stubborn love that returns to affirm and to claim us for Himself in spite of his own experience with rejection is the devil's counter strategy to distort our self image. He uses fallen humanity to accomplish His purpose. Through misunderstandings, unjust criticism, and emotional abuse, we become human missiles that put each other out of commission by sending messages of rejection that cause the recipient to want to crawl into a hole and never emerge again.

God wants to know today "Whose family do you belong to?" If you belong to God's royal family, then start viewing the family tapes you now belong to. You belong to a family heritage with faith heroes who did not allow rejection to change their appointed destinies. Jesus came to be a blessing and no matter how people responded, He would fulfill His calling to be a blessing. When you rise above rejection, you are acting as a member of God's royal family. You are saying, "This is how someone in my family responds to rejection!"

I wonder today if God has whispered in your ears something He desires you to establish but you have allowed past scripts of rejection to distort your self image. Did you know that God's calling is without repentance? God knows your resume because He wrote it. He allowed every incident in your life to shape you into the perfect vessel for what He desires to accomplish through you in His appointed time. Even in the rejection He has allowed in your life, He can use your heartache and transform it into passionate purpose for Him.

As guardians of dreams for a family, business, church, ministry, community or nation, we must allow God to give us His vision for our lives. It is from Him that we must get our clear script for what we are to accomplish in our season. God does not take lightly the roles and places in life He assigns us. He moves us with a purpose in mind. When we misuse our time or allow someone else to release us from God's assignments, we miss our divine appointments.

In Module Two of "Transforming Emotions in a Leader's Heart", I will share with you how God taught me to stay focused on His mission in spite of rejection. We will look at God's truth to rise above rejection in the following situations:

- **Rejected by your family**

- **Rejected by a culture or community**

- **Rejected as being imbalanced**

- **Rejected by those with greater business sense**

- **Rejected by those who question your calling**

- **Rejected by your peers or team mates**

- **Rejected by the leader you esteemed highly**

- **Rejected by those you are leading**

- **Rejected by those who withdraw their money**

- **Rejected by those who criticize you**

Rejected by Your Family

Situation: Do you have parents who favored your siblings or never affirmed your potential? Do you find those in your own family do not validate your calling?

The purpose of the personal journal entries shown below is to capture the rejection I experienced from family. Some entries were taken from an actual journal, others were written more recently as I reflected on what I was feeling at the time. The dates of the entries are approximate and were included to give the reader some sense of chronological history. After reading the personal journal entries capturing the emotion of rejection, please go to the section in the Bible Study that contains God's truths which addressed this emotion. In teaching this material, feel free to use my personal journal entries as illustration or personalize your lesson with writing your own personal journal entries or testimony to capture the emotion of rejection you felt in your own life. If you did not keep a journal, then try to relive the situation in your mind and write an entry today to capture what you felt at the time.

Feb 2, 1974

Dear God,
Today would have been my Mom's birthday but she is not with us anymore. I feel like someone just threw a grenade into my world. She promised me that she would always walk with me. No matter what the challenges, we said we could conquer the world together. How could she have had an exit plan without telling me about it? I knew she was depressed but she told me about a friend who committed suicide and she said her friend left such a mess. She said that no matter how bad things got, she would never do something like that. What happened God? Did the pain get too much for her?

I want to tell myself that it had nothing to do with me. Yet something inside me tells me that if she really cared about me she would not have left me. We dreamed so many dreams together. I am scheduled to leave for America in June. I promised her I would find a way to bring her with me. Did she not believe me? What will I do now God? The dream of reaching America began in her heart. What am I supposed to do when I get to America? Am I on my own? How will this story end?

May 5, 1976

Dear God,
After my Mom died, I didn't know where I fit in anymore. Other people have aunts and uncles and extended family. My Mom came from China and my father was born in Indonesia. So when they started their family in Hong Kong, we had no extended family. All we had was each other. When the family unit is small, the impact is great when you lose a family member. It's a frightening thought to realize that if this is all we have, then what happens if everyone

dies and only one is left alive. Who are we when we no longer have family?

Other than my sister and brother, my Dad was all the family I had to cling to. Then when he said he was getting married, it was as if he was leaving too. He said I would always be special to him but I know things will never be the same. I hate it when people tell me I am grown now. It's like grown people shouldn't feel a need for a family or that we're just supposed to be grateful for whatever we had and go and have our own family. I don't understand why it's wrong to want roots or to need roots. Is there something wrong with me? I know the healthy thing to do is for me to move on and make my own life. But God, it's hard to soar when you feel there is no ground under your feet. Please help me be stronger God. I don't want to be a drain on those around me. I need to get stronger.

The corresponding truths God taught me from His Word to address my situation
Feel free to continue reading all my personal journals in Module Two expressing feelings of rejection before reading the Bible Study. Or you may continue with the corresponding Bible study which contains God's truths in addressing the situation described in the above journal entries with additional truths God taught me to address situations that were not included in my journal entries. If you choose to personalize this curriculum as your way to bond with the group you are leading, feel free not only to use your own testimony and personal journal entries but in the Bible study part, include what God taught you from His Word in your situations of rejection.

Rejected by Your Family

Situation: Do you have parents who favored your siblings or never affirmed your potential? Do you find those in your own family do not validate your calling?

Reminder: Let's learn the truths from God's Word that speak to our situations. Remember that as a member of God's royal family, we are to act according to the customs of the royal family. This means reinforcing our royal identity by living according to God's specific instructions in the Bible. When we cannot find specific instructions that speak to our situation, we are to search our spiritual heritage and model our lives after God's faith heroes who responded correctly to situations that parallel our own. We can also learn from their mistakes to avoid making the same mistakes in our own lives.

The wounds inflicted upon us during childhood cut deep. When those wounds are the result of family members and loved ones who abused their influence during our formative years, it is as if someone burned negative tracks in our memory bank that distort our view of ourselves for the rest of our lives. Some numb the pain from those memory tracks through drugs. Some escape into a fantasy world of their own making. Some cry silently on the inside while acting like a carefree spirit on the outside. Some check out of life and no longer care to make a difference. With these coping mechanisms we may experience some relief but we start to feel empty because we are disconnected from our divine mission. We were never meant to sit on the bench! We were meant to get up and make a difference.

As the Founder of a women's ministry, I hear from many women. In their stories, I have witnessed the crippling effects of rejection. Before we can step into God's purpose, God has to transform our poor self image into a true self image and erase the negative tapes from childhood. Can you imagine the God of the Universe trusting us with a dream that is close to His heart? What a completely different message from the one many women grew up with that said that they could not possibly amount to anything.

How many women come from backgrounds where they were never affirmed? How many were never encouraged to dream? How many were self conscious of their talent or their desire to exercise their gift for fear of being accused of being ambitious? How many have cried out silently to God knowing there is something in them waiting to be born but also knowing that the fetus is dying inside them?

From heaven's throne, God heard the cries from His daughters' hearts and when the time had fully come, God spoke the word "Enough!" Something supernatural happens when God has had enough. It's as if you can hear the cavalry of military horses coming your way! You hear the hoofs and you see the dust swirling in the air. When the dust settles, you see the King of Kings standing tall on His holy mountain to claim His daughters for a royal kingdom.

The heart of Inspire Women is to inspire women from all ethnic backgrounds, denominations and economic levels to step into God's purpose. As proof of the seriousness with which we believe in the potential of God's daughters, Inspire Women funds scholarships to train those called to missions and ministry. The astounding facts of the way God established Inspire Women provided evidence of God's power to transform any background. He picked a Founder with deep wounds of rejection by a mother who took her own life and a culture that esteemed the male children higher than the girls. There are incidents in our lives where we can try to logically talk through them but when the wounds are emotional and deep, certain incidents continue to trigger our pain. Yet, God intentionally chose one with a wounded background to show His daughters that He can shape anyone for His passionate purpose.

I grew up in an environment of scarcity. Although my parents tried to give me all that I needed, the fact that there was so little to spare made me feel that any need I had was an intrusion. My mother even told me that I was an unexpected pregnancy and an unwelcome one at that because of what my needs meant to the family finances. Her words scarred the first chapters of my life. I felt like a bad beginning that the world had to put up with.

"How incredible that the one man rejected was the one God had chosen!"

God taught me from His Word that the only image I needed to concern myself with is God's image of me. Genesis 1:27 tells me **"So God created man in his own image, in the image of God he created him; male and female he created them**." NIV. Since God made

me to reflect His image, I should get my self image from God and not from anyone else. In fact, anyone else who tries to give me an image that falls short of my royal heritage is offending God and usurping His authority. All human opinion falls by the wayside when God has spoken. God showed me this truth in the story of Samuel who was sent to anoint one of Jesse's sons as King.

In 1 Samuel chapter 16, God shows us through His choice of David how God makes up His own mind and totally ignores the opinion of the family. When Samuel told Jesse that he was there to anoint the future king of Israel, Jesse revealed his heart and his personal evaluation of each of his sons by bringing before Samuel each of his sons, except for his son David. Was this because in Jesse's eyes, David was the dreamer? How could God possibly pick the one who spends his day alone on a hill tending the sheep and writing poetry?

Despite fallen humanity rejecting those around them based on outward appearances, God tells Samuel in 1 Samuel 16:7, **"...The LORD does not look at the things man looks at. Man looks at the outward appearance, but the LORD looks at the heart."** NIV. With this instruction, Samuel seeks God's confirmation as he evaluates each of Jesse's sons.

As Samuel met each of Jesse's sons, he repeats the same message in 1 Samuel 16:8-10 in three different ways: **"The LORD has not chosen this one either"** and **"Nor has the LORD chosen this one."** We can almost feel Samuel's mounting frustration through the words, **"Jesse had seven of his sons pass before Samuel, but Samuel said to him, "The LORD has not chosen these."** NIV

Have you ever been in a place where you have gone down a list and exhausted the whole list only to know deep in your heart that something is missing? This was how Samuel felt. He had no way of knowing that Jesse was withholding someone from him. But he had a spiritual hunch that he had missed a prospective candidate. So he says to Jesse in 1 Samuel 16:19, **"Are these all the sons you have?"** To this direct question, Jesse replied, **"There is still the youngest. but he is tending the sheep."**

How incredible that the one rejected by man was the one God had chosen! Samuel tells Jesse to send for his youngest son. As soon as David walked in to the room, 1 Samuel 16:12-13 tells us: **Then the LORD said, "Rise and anoint him; he is the one." So Samuel took the horn of oil and anointed him in the presence of his brothers, and from that day on the Spirit of the LORD came upon David in power…**NIV

Did you hear the words, **"he is the one"**? Oh the incredible peace in knowing that God has the final word. It matters little what your parents thought of you or what your siblings thought of you. It only matters what God thinks of you. David was away from the family but God saw his heart. In the poetry that he wrote, David honored God and cherished being in His presence. He wanted what God wanted. In Jeremiah 3:15, God said, **"Then I will give you shepherds after my own heart, who will lead you with knowledge and understanding."** NIV.

In 1 Samuel 13:14, Samuel said to Saul, **"But now your kingdom will not endure; the LORD has sought out a man after his own heart and appointed him leader of his people, because you have not kept the LORD's command."** NIV. The Apostle Paul described David as the one God appointed and said of him in Acts 13:22, **"After removing Saul, he made David their king. He testified concerning him: 'I have found David son of Jesse a man after my own heart; he will do everything I want him to do.'** NIV

Did you know that when God has an assignment that is close to His heart, He will pick the one He can trust? Are you the one God has chosen? If so, then shut your ears to the opinions around you. No matter how difficult the assignment, remind yourself, "I am the one. I am the one God picked and God never makes a mistake.

"The more impact you were designed to have, the more attack you can expect to come your way."

Against God's appointment always comes the challenge from the devil who is God's enemy. In fact, the more impact you were designed to have, the more attack you can expect to come your way. Perhaps you have suffered from domestic abuse from the hands of those you trusted as your authority figure. Realize that incidents from your past have left deep scars in your spirit. Those incidents that caused you pain in the past will also be your current vulnerabilities. Therefore, when you find yourself responding emotionally to an incident, ask yourself if your reaction is proportional to what just happened. Be alert to the fact that you might have walked into a trap set up by the devil to bring back the pain of your past to disable you from making good decisions in the present.

When you have distrust issues with authority figures from your past, what better way to knock you off course than to plant doubt in your mind for authority figures who are currently in your life? You will not trust godly leaders who try to intervene in your life to help you. You will live with an attitude of thinking you have to protect your own future in order to survive. Your whole psyche will be geared towards being safe. At the end of your life, you may be safe but you will have missed your divine purpose and those God sent your way to grow you in maturity. Samuel was a godly leader who spoke truth into David's life. Paul spoke truth into Timothy's life. If you find that you can't trust your current leader, then find a leader you can trust. Then submit to their instruction and trust their guidance.

"When someone godly invites you to do something, take it seriously."

At the crossroads of my life, I had to decide if I would allow the messages of rejection from my background determine my self image and what God could call me to do or if I would allow God to have the final word. It was after studying this passage in God's Word and learning that "If someone godly invites you to do something, take it seriously", that I made a decision that changed the course of my life.

God did not want me to live with the self image I developed from my childhood and He put a godly leader in my life to transform the image developed from memories of rejection into His purpose for me. He brought me to Houston and put me in Beth Moore's Sunday School class to learn under a godly teacher. One day I received a phone call from Beth asking me to teach her class. At the time she had nearly 300 in her class. I could not imagine why she called me. I had never expressed a desire to teach. I did not believe I had the gift to teach. I was happy every Sunday to simply sit under her teaching. Why in the world did she call me? But I had studied in God's Word that when

someone filled with God's Spirit invites you to something, you should take it seriously. God was using Beth to change my image of myself. By faith in God's Word as the direction for my life, I submitted to the fact that God leads us through godly leaders. So I taught the class. I was sure it would be the only time I would teach, thinking that God was simply testing me. My own self image was disconnected from God's view of me. I was surprised when I was invited to teach my first women's retreat. Beth was in the audience. She came up to me afterwards and said, "I don't know how to tell you this but I believe God has called you to be a speaker."

I trusted Beth's word for my life and decided that if God called me to teach His Word, then I ought to get some preparation. So I enrolled at Dallas Theological Seminary. I wonder today if you are living off the rejection scripts of your past that have distorted your view of yourself. God has a plan for your life. Is it time to hear Him say to you, "You are the one"?

No matter what background you come from, when God transplants you to a healthy environment, He wants you to flourish and not live in your past. As an illustration, when my son Robbie was five, we went to a landscape place and the owner pulled up this very shriveled looking plant from the ground and handed it to him and told him to plant it. The plant was barely a foot tall and its leaves were all brown and withered looking. Robbie took the plant home and stuck it in the ground in a place where it would get tons of sunlight and rain. Well guess what?

Below is what the plant looks like now. No matter where we began, when God transplants us to fertile ground, we have what we need to reach our full potential. When the devil brings us back to the bad memories of past years, what we must do is to remind ourselves, "We don't live there anymore!"

"You don't have to go looking for God's will. God knows where you live."

The other truth God showed me from His Word was this: You don't have to go looking for God's will. God knows where you live. Samuel was sent by God to invite David to step into a divine appointment. David was out in the pastures taking care of the sheep, praising God and writing poems. Could it be that what God looks for is a heart that is being purified? When we focus on getting the vessel ready, God then comes with the assignment.

Is there something you need to change in your life to surrender yourself as a holy vessel for God's divine appointments? On a scale of 1 to 10 with 10 being the highest, how would you rate yourself on holiness in the following areas? How holy is your thought life?

How holy is your business life?

How holy is your love life?

How holy are your responses when you've been wronged?

God is in search of a holy vessel with a heart that is willing to serve Him. 2 Timothy 2:20-21 reads: **In a large house there are articles not only of gold and silver, but also of wood and clay; some are for noble purposes and some for ignoble. If a man cleanses himself from the latter, he will be an instrument for noble purposes, made holy, useful to the Master and prepared to do any good work.** NIV.

Are you an instrument for noble purposes? If so, then God knows where you live. He is perfectly able to intersect your path to point you to where He wants to take you. The question is, when God knocks on your door, will you recognize that heaven has invaded earth?

What self image do you have based on rejection from your family that is limiting you from answering God's call on your life? How will things change when you are able to receive God's appointment that you are the one He has chosen?

When my son was a senior in high school, he decided he did not want to go to the prom and then changed his mind at the last minute. By this time all the girls had been asked except for a few. The girl he wanted to go with did not know who he was. So he decided to make her an introductory video on himself. The DVD began with a scene from New York City with these Broadway neon lights flashing around the title of the Broadway play. In this case, the name of the play was "Robbie invites someone to the prom." Then he taped himself saying, "Lauren, I know you don't know me so I thought I would make a video of myself so you would know who I was." He included on his video the testimony of girls in his grade testifying to his character.

When his father saw the tape he said to me, **"Did you tell Robbie what I said to you when I proposed to you?"** I said "No." He said, "Did you realize that he used the exact words I used? Robbie said, 'Lauren, I have considered all the factors and I think it might be a good idea if you and I went to the prom together.'" My husband said, "When I proposed to you, I said, "I have considered all the facts and I think it would be a good idea if we got married." I said, "How did Robbie know to use those words?" My husband said, "Because he thinks like me."

God wants us to know that no matter what family dynamics we have experienced, He is our heavenly Father who created us in His image. Like Father, like son, like Father, like daughter. He wants us to operate out of the image He gave us, not one distorted by rejection. The only voice He wants us to listen for is His voice. And in His voice, He wants us to hear His affirmation, that we are His beloved in whom He is well pleased.

Rejected by a Culture or Community

Situation: Have you ever felt like you were on the outside looking in because you were excluded from events or gatherings by friends or family or co-workers? Do you long to be accepted by your community despite their lack of affirmation?

The purpose of the personal journal entries shown below is to capture the rejection I felt from a culture or community. Some entries were taken from an actual journal, others were written more recently as I reflected on what I was feeling at the time. The dates of the entries are approximate and were included to give the reader some sense of chronological history. After reading the personal journal entries capturing the emotion of rejection, please go to the section in the Bible Study that contains God's truths which addressed this emotion. In teaching this material, feel free to use my personal journal entries as illustration or personalize your lesson with writing your own personal journal entries or testimony to capture the emotion of rejection you felt in your own life. If you did not keep a journal, then try to relive the situation in your mind and write an entry today to capture what you felt at the time.

Sept 15, 1973

Dear God,
I don't like talking to the kids at school who make me feel bad on the inside. Can anyone actually make me feel bad God or is it my fault for letting them? Everyone's talking about where they are going for college. Some kids don't ever have to worry about money. I don't know why some kids have all the breaks and others have to make their own breaks. God, don't you think that's unfair? My Mom says not to worry about what's fair or not. Just be the best and then you'll have all the opportunities. I've written to over a hundred colleges in the United States. I don't get many responses. The answers I get always say something about not having funds for scholarships. There must be someone out there who will believe in me. But where are they God?

Today one of the rich kids in school looked at me like I was a hopeless dreamer. Is it wrong to believe that we are all supposed to become all we can be? Why do certain people have more privileges? There is something very wrong with the system. It's like a bunch of people are trying to feel important by putting others down. How could you possibly be pleased? I don't know how to change the thinking of a whole community. God, what do you think? Is it possible to change the thinking of a whole community? Maybe the beginning of change must begin with me.

October 20, 1973

Dear God,
My Mom is always depressed these days. It's like all the sadness from her past is drowning her. I don't quite understand what happened. Things were different when she was raised in Mainland China.

Her father was always unemployed and because she was the oldest, she got a job when she was 15. She was working as a maid in a hotel when a businessman came into the room. He locked the door and raped her. She said she was so ashamed and she bled while walking quietly back to her home. She never dared tell anyone. She said in China at that time, she would be thrown out of the family if she weren't a virgin anymore. She knew her chances for marriage were over. Then she met a westerner who was twenty years older. He treated her like a porcelain China doll and she married him when she was sixteen. Their son had a hard time because his hair was blonde. He used to put black shoe polish on his hair to hide the fact that he was half Caucasian. God, is she depressed because all the rejection of the past kills you slowly on the inside? She cries a lot these days. She has that stare in her eyes as if she is playing all the scenes of yesteryears. I don't know what to do to help her.

All her life she was upbeat and bubbly and I think she just repressed all her pain. God, why can't you just take away the bad memories? I know she had some happy times but it seems like every time she starts to be happy, something happens to open the wounds from the past.

I'm not sure what happened recently. She was doing some sewing for someone and she said they treated her badly. It reminded her of the times in her childhood years when her family was financially desperate. Her father could not hold down a job. She was the oldest and was sent by her Mom to beg for food from their rich friends. She hated how those she went to for help made her feel bad for asking. She said you know who your friends are when you have to beg for a bowl of rice. Why did she allow the cutting words of others to enter her heart? It seems to me that those who let the world hurt them are the ones with a kind and gentle spirit. If she were meaner herself she would not care what someone said. She could be mean back. But she just backs off and sits quietly in a corner and hurts quietly. And then it's as though the hurt turns inward and I see her self destructing. What do I do God? Can the world's rejection drive us to the place where we self destruct?

God, my Mom heard from U.S. Immigration that her petition to the United States had been denied. Something died inside her when she received that letter. It was like it was the worse rejection ever. Will this rejection kill her? I don't hear her singing anymore.

Jan 5, 1975

Dear God,
I don't know what I'm supposed to do. It's a fact that I wasn't raised in this country. It's a fact that my skin color is different. This guy I was dating, it was supposed to be just for fun. But now it's turned into something that makes me feel like I have to apologize for who I am. What did his parents mean by cutting off his tuition if he continued to see me? They have never even met me. They judged me by my background. I can't change the facts. I guess it's also a fact that people are more comfortable with those who look like them and think like them.
I wish someone would give me a chance to show them my heart. I guess no one cares about my heart. They judge what they see from the outside and they cast their vote.

Do you care God? Sometimes it must tire you out to try to change how people think. I told him to date someone else because the complications aren't worth it. I don't want to spend my whole life trying to get people to accept me when they have already made up their minds about me.

Nov 18, 1975

Dear God,
Why do the kids with money make me feel bad? I didn't want to stay on campus during Thanksgiving. I wanted to visit my sister at her college. I saw a sign at the student center for those who needed rides. So I called this girl up. She seemed really nice. She was supposed to take me to the city closest to her hometown and then I could get on a bus for the rest of the way. We arrived late and I missed the bus. She told me I had to stay at a hotel. We went from hotel to hotel and I kept telling her the rate was too high. How do I break the news to her that any rate would be too high because I didn't have the funds for a hotel room?

She got tired of driving around and brought me to her house. It was a huge mansion like the ones you see on television on that soap opera Dallas. Her Mom wasn't pleased at all when I walked in with her. She looked at me like I was some stray puppy or something. At least people feed puppies. So I must have looked worse than a stray pup. She showed me the guest room and then I never heard from her again. I think she wanted me to just disappear. I felt very awkward in the guest room. I wish I had the money to just take a taxi and go away.

God, did you ever feel bad about yourself when you were turned away by unkind people? I feel bad about myself. Why do I let people cause me to feel bad about myself? God, when I get through with college, things will change. Who knows? Maybe I'll live in a mansion like this one day. But wherever we're going God, please don't let me forget how this feels. I don't ever want to make anyone feel as badly as this family made me feel.

November 15, 1981

Dear God,
I don't like being in a country where I can't speak the language fluently. My husband tells me it actually wouldn't matter even if I were fluent. Some cultures won't accept anyone who isn't from their culture anyway. Forget the idea of being cosmopolitan and learning from each other.

I went to the bakery today. I hate the system here. You stand in line and when it's your turn you're supposed to call out your order. I tried saying my order in the country's language. I know that the girl at the counter knew exactly what I meant. But she kept asking me to repeat myself. Some kind soul behind me then shouted out my order to help close the transaction. It was so humiliating. I think I'll go without bread during my stay in this country. Who needs bread from the bakery if it means being ridiculed in public? It just occurred to me that your Son called Himself the bread of life and He allowed Himself to be ridiculed to save the world. If we're going to be ridiculed, then maybe it needs to be for something eternally significant!

God, what are you teaching me in this country? You don't seem to care that the people around me look at me like I don't belong here. You must have a bigger plan but what is it?

July 22, 1998

Dear God,
I don't know what happened. It's like someone said something and a grenade blew up inside me. I don't even know why I signed up for this class. I heard it advertised on the radio. Who is this man that is teaching? Does my pastor agree with what he is saying?

He organized the class in groups and then he made the statement that in accordance with the teaching in the Bible, the women were not allowed to lead the group discussion. This is a classroom. If we can't learn in a classroom, where can we learn? How can we develop women to serve at their highest potential if we don't teach them how to lead a group? How will the women learn to work with those in their women's ministry?

God, I don't think this class is good for me emotionally. The professor reminded me of the stories my mother told me about the many families in China who viewed a daughter as inferior. It's like a son was what every father desired but a girl was a waste of time. What percentage of the world are women? Did we allow our culture to write off the potential of a major percentage of the world's population?

After the resurrection, your son appeared to Mary Magdalene first. She was entrusted with the greatest news on planet earth. What other news would surpass announcing the fact that Jesus rose from the dead and the incredible implication of what His resurrection meant to humankind? I remember reading once that those who teach should never teach a student they don't believe in because their opinions will show through and will limit the student. Well, it certainly is true in this case. It's like this teacher made one statement to wipe out the women and we allowed him to redefine and limit your calling in our lives.

God, what should I do? You gave me the gift of leadership but I can't use my gift if those around me won't let me. I think I should just work in the doors that open and stop feeling like a victim. No one can make me a victim. I am the one who makes myself a victim. I can always go where you have enlarged my space. So, where are we going God? Did Jesus slip through the crowds when He was rejected by a particular audience? Did He simply go where He could share your message? Are you making a way for me to slip through the crowd so your Word can reach as many as possible? Life is too short to live under rejection. We need to go where we are free to serve.

Sept 11, 1999

Dear God,
How long O Lord, how long? When I hear someone limiting me by their own biases, how long do I listen before I start to believe them? I find myself apologizing for having creative ideas. I feel like I have to act dumber or be regarded as a threat. If it weren't for my husband who so totally encourages me to ignore the comments of those who are short sighted, I think I would just crawl into a hole and never come out.

God, what do women do when they don't have an affirming husband or pastor? What about the single Moms out there who don't have someone speaking encouragement into their lives? What about the women who are verbally abused and told that they could never amount to anything? It hurts when someone says the women are not worth investing in. Is that why you have me raising funds to provide scholarships for women in biblical training? Is it because there are so many who do not believe in training your daughters. A pastor's wife came to me in tears because the church did not have the funds to train her. She felt overwhelmed because as the church grew, she realized she wasn't equipped and wanted to be trained to help her husband as much as she could. I made an appeal to an individual and the person said to me, "Why does she need to be trained? She just needs to be the pastor's wife." That hurt my heart God. I didn't have the heart to tell her. I know it hurt your heart too.

Feb 5, 2002

Dear God,
One of my professors told me I could do more for the Kingdom if I just went home and had a baby. I called the seminary and they said this professor did not represent the views of the seminary. I am learning that those with influence have the power to kill the dreams you trust to your daughters. I think this means we need to get our green light from you. We can't expect others to protect the dream. We must hear you for ourselves and then we must let your voice lead us forward.

A male classmate saw one of my Bible studies that had been published and he tossed it aside. His attitude was that he could never learn from a woman. But then another male classmate picked up the article, read it and said to the others, "I really learned something." So I guess God it means it might not be a question of dealing with a culture, a community or an institution. It might be a question of dealing with people as individuals. Some live by their biases. The secret is to slip pass them until we soar pass them. No human can thwart God's plans.

The corresponding truths God taught me from His Word to address my situation
Feel free to continue reading all my personal journals in Module Two expressing feelings of rejection before reading the Bible Study. Or you may continue with the corresponding Bible study which contains God's truths in addressing the situation described in the above journal entries with additional truths God taught me to address situations that were not included in my journal entries. If you choose to personalize this curriculum as your way to bond with the group you are leading, feel free not only to use your own testimony and personal journal entries but in the Bible study part, include what God taught you from His Word in your situations of rejection.

Rejected by Culture or Community

Situation: Have you ever felt like you were on the outside looking in because you were excluded from events or gatherings by friends or family or co-workers? Do you long to be accepted by your community despite their lack of affirmation?

Reminder: Let's learn the truths from God's Word that speak to our situations. Remember that as a member of God's royal family, we are to act according to the customs of the royal family. This means reinforcing our royal identity by living according to God's specific instructions in the Bible. When we cannot find specific instructions that speak to our situation, we are to search our spiritual heritage and model our lives after God's faith heroes who responded correctly to situations that parallel our own. We can also learn from their mistakes to avoid making the same mistakes in our own lives.

I did not grow up in an environment where those around me believed in my potential and wanted to sow into my life. I grew up in an environment with people from various ethnic backgrounds, each group vying for position and wanting to be treated as an equal citizen. Within each ethnic group there were even differences of opinions as to who was superior depending on whether you came from the North, the South, the East or the West. It was as though people wanted a way to classify each other and to find some reason why they should be ranked higher.

How do you grow up with a strong self esteem when you come from a country where you were classified as a second class citizen? Because Hong Kong was a British colony, those born in England were the true citizens of the Queen but those born in the colony were given an inferior passport with restricted travel privileges. This concept of inferior citizenship followed me through different arenas of my life. I can always tell when I am in the presence of someone who has formed opinions about me because of my economic background, my ethnicity or my gender. If I were to pick someone to lead the charge at Inspire Women, I would definitely not have picked me. In fact, I told the Lord that I come with way too much emotional baggage. I have seen how those who were brought up in an affirming environment are able to just let rejection roll off their backs. I have a friend who is able to look me straight in the eye and say, "What do I care what they say?" and totally means it and never loses a beat no matter how many people are against her. The Lord should have picked her to lead the charge. Was it God's sense of humor that He picked me with a fragile heart to lead the charge in an area with a high potential for rejection?

God had to do much repair work before He could trust me with a mission to affirm the potential of women to change the world. First, I had to have a correct concept of how God felt about His daughters. I did not grow up in a culture that was affirming of the potential of women. I was not raised believing I could make much of a difference in the world. The deep tracks of poor self image in my memory bank had to be transformed with the sword of God's mighty Word. Are you at a crossroads of life and need God's truth to show you who He is and how He sees you?

"The criterion God uses to assess how well we can represent His image is our dependence on the holiness and power of His Son. All other criteria are human made and misguided."

Genesis 1:27 reads, **"So God created man in his own image, in the image of God he created him; male and female he created them."** NIV. In this verse, God tells us that all humankind was created to represent God on this earth. Although we may have different roles, what we must rise above is the artificial limitation we impose on each other. When I live in a culture that unashamedly states that it is a better stewardship of one's funds to invest in the potential of men than in women or in one ethnicity than another, I know that God's heart is broken.

To say that one gender or one race has greater potential to represent God's image on earth is not substantiated in Scripture. When we create artificial ceilings for each other, we block God's image from being fully expressed in the world.

Genesis 5:1-2 reads, **"When God created man, he made him in the likeness of God. He created them male and female and blessed them. And when they were created, he called them "man."** NIV. In these verses, God defines the word "**man**" to include both male and female. He tells us that He "**blessed them**," God's Word did not say "He blessed him." God even repeats Himself and says that "**when they were created**", He gave the "**they**" the name "**man**." How eye opening to read in God's Word that from the very first pages of

creation, God valued both male and female and saw that they, as a united force, would represent God as "**man**" on planet earth.

The Apostle Paul tells us in Galatians 3:28, **"There is neither Jew nor Greek, slave nor free, male nor female, for you are all one in Christ Jesus."** NIV. Did you see the words that we are "**all one in Christ Jesus**"?

It is Christ who has made us acceptable to God. He is the one who pleases God. When we accept the blood of Jesus for the forgiveness of our sins, Christ places a covering over us with His sacrifice. When God looks at us, He no longer sees our imperfections but He sees Christ. In our human logic, we find ourselves arguing for the equality or superiority of gender or race. In God's eyes we are fighting the wrong battle. The ultimate question we must answer is how each of us compares to God's holiness because this is the only criterion that will matter for our eternal destination.

It matters little how we compare to each other in characteristics such as gender or race. When it comes to anything of eternal significance, God evaluates us on the basis of holiness. In this regard, Romans 3:22-25 tells us, **"There is no difference, for all have sinned and fall short of the glory of God, and are justified freely by his grace through the redemption that came by Christ Jesus.** NIV.

Based on our holiness, we have all failed, whether male or female, Jew or Greek, slave or free. We are all in the same boat of not quite making it according to God's standards. We are all saved by faith and offered the same gift of the blood of Jesus Christ as the full payment for the penalty of our sins. So when someone has the attitude that they are superior and reject you based on gender, race or what they perceive as your inferior role in life, rest in the fact that God sees all as equal under the covering of the blood of His Son. We are all equal at the foot of the cross of Jesus.

Find strength in knowing that it is by the power of the blood of Jesus that we will represent God's image on this earth. The criterion God uses to assess how well we can represent His image is our dependence on the holiness and power of His Son. All other criteria are human made and misguided.

If you were reaching for a cookie jar on the top shelf I could say to you that you won't be able to reach the jar because you're dressed in red. Perhaps I could even cause you to believe that your being in red will affect your ability to reach the cookie jar. But the reality is, the fact that you are in red has absolutely no connection with your ability to reach it. The premise is a misguided criterion. Your ability to reach the cookie jar is by having the right ladder to reach the height you need to reach. Christ Jesus is our ladder to God. We belong to Him and it is through Him that we will be part of a united community that represents God's purpose on earth.

How does knowing that God trusts both genders of all ethnic backgrounds to represent Him on earth affect your expectations for what God might call you to do? How have you limited God by your own self image?

"When your heart attitude is one of service and not rights or titles, you will find yourself praising God wherever you find yourself, wherever there is a need, wherever God sends you to save the perishing."

Before God could trust me with His mission, I had to settle in my heart that God would trust His daughters with His work. There were some churches that invited me to speak in their pulpit, there were others who felt I should only be allowed to address a Sunday School. There were some who felt I could only speak to women and there were some who felt I could address both men and women. The permutations were many. There were so many opinions I felt one could spend years fighting over what was the right answer. I knew God did not want me wasting my time arguing with other believers.

As I inquired of the Lord as to where He wanted His daughters to serve, He gave me the following illustration: When a house is burning, no one asks who should run in to save the children. Whoever has the courage and is able and willing to risk their lives will be applauded as a hero. What God taught me was to ask the question, "Who will be first to die for Christ?" Answer this question first and then all other roles will fall into place. When your heart attitude is one of service and not rights or titles, you will find yourself praising God wherever you find yourself, wherever there is a need, wherever God sends you to save the perishing.

Time is too urgent to be wasted in arguments among those who are saved while billions will perish without the gospel. Luke 19:37-40 tells the story: **When he came near the place where the road goes down the Mount of Olives, the whole crowd of disciples began joyfully to praise God in loud voices for all the miracles they had seen: "Blessed is the king who comes in the name of the Lord!" "Peace in heaven and glory in the highest!" Some of the Pharisees in the crowd said to Jesus, "Teacher, rebuke your disciples!" "I tell you," he replied, "if they keep quiet, the stones will cry out."** NIV.

Like the Pharisees in Jesus' day, there will always be those who reject you and demand your silence. God knows when time on planet earth will be over. He knows when the last day will be over for those who have not heard the gospel. He knows when He will unleash the potential of all believers to shout His message to the world before the curtain falls on planet earth and the opportunity to accept the gift of Jesus is over.

Acts 2:17-18 tells us: **"'In the last days, God says, I will pour out my Spirit on all people. Your sons and daughters will prophesy, your young men will see visions, your old men will dream dreams. Even on my servants, both men and women, I will pour out my Spirit in those days, and they will prophesy.** NIV.

Although Peter spoke the above words during Pentecost when the believers received the gift of the Holy Spirit, the women lived in a culture where biblical training was not available to them. So their potential was limited by what their culture allowed in their education. However, today, tradition has changed and our culture has lifted its limitations on educational opportunities based on gender or race. Communities are more open to hear from **"sons and daughters"**, **"young and old"**, and welcome "servants" who are filled with God's Spirit and ready to pour out His hope to the world.

Are we living in a time and age where God is moving to empower His daughters for maximum missions and ministry? A wise and godly pastor once said to me, "The ministry of Inspire Women can only snowball." Another said, "Your venue in Houston cannot contain this ministry". A third said, "This ministry will go global." As God builds Inspire Women, our confidence in His growth plans comes from knowing that we have stepped into the pages of His history. Our supernatural growth in a few short years can only be attributed to the fact that God touched this ministry to invest in His daughters to change the world because it pleased Him to do so.

Have you been allowing rejection of those who do not affirm your potential to stunt your service? How would life change if you recognized that the harvest is full and simply serve wherever doors are open?

There have been times when the words of those around me discouraged me to the point that I no longer wanted to serve. I find that when people are threatened, they have a tendency to accuse you of the very thing they are guilty of. So if they are the ones who want power, they accuse you of being ambitious. What they are really doing is protecting their turf. When you have a gift that is having an impact, expect those who are insecure to find fault with you.

"God's counsel to me was to stay out of sight when emotions run high."

Luke 4:28-30 tells us, **"All the people in the synagogue were furious when they heard this. They got up, drove him out of the town, and took him to the brow of the hill on which the town was built, in order to throw him down the cliff. But he walked right through the crowd and went on his way."** NIV.

I wonder if you have ever expressed the truth only to find the community members are furious because of the words that came out of your mouth. What encouraged me was to see how Jesus **"walked right through the crowd."** This tells me that God protected His message bearer. More than that, I read that Jesus **"went on his way."** Could it be that there are crowds we will never win and the best use of our time is to keep going in our mission elsewhere?

Have you been fighting against a community who refuses to accept you? Instead of wasting your time in trying to force a relationship, how will God's mission advance if you simply went on your way and served elsewhere?

When Jesus told the crowd in John 8:58, **"I tell you the truth…before Abraham was born, I am!"** this resulted in the following response: **"At this, they picked up stones to stone him, but Jesus hid himself, slipping away from the temple grounds."** NIV.

Did you notice the words **"Jesus hid himself"**? God's counsel to me was to stay out of sight when emotions run high. When people are so offended by you because what you are saying rearranges their world and what they believe, know that there are times when the best thing to do is to say nothing and keep a low profile. Notice too that Jesus responded by **"slipping away."**

What a relief to know that there are some battles God does not want us to fight. I wonder today if God is releasing you from a battle. State ways you can slip away from a community where the emotions are high and from those in the community who are threatened by you?

"When we are more worried about protecting our own turf than we are pleasing God, we are threatened by God's movement in anyone else and instead of embracing them, we move mountains to crush them."

When Jesus was placed before the crowds and they could choose one person to free, they did not pick Jesus. If you have ever felt the total unfairness in having an unworthy candidate picked over you, learn from your spiritual heritage and know that you are not alone in your experience. Matthew 27:20-23 tells the story: **But the chief priests and the elders persuaded the crowd to ask for Barabbas and to have Jesus executed. "Which of the two do you want me to release to you?" asked the governor. "Barabbas," they answered. "What shall I do, then, with Jesus who is called Christ?" Pilate asked. They all answered, "Crucify him!" "Why? What crime has he committed?" asked Pilate. But they shouted all the louder, "Crucify him!"** NIV

Did you notice the words "**But the chief priests and the elders persuaded the crowd to ask for Barabbas and to have Jesus executed.**"? Oh the incredible freedom we get from God's Word. Barabbas was a criminal as compared to Christ who spent His entire life blessing others. How could it be that the crowds would have picked to release Barabbas over Christ? In this story we learn that when someone who is not qualified gets picked, there is often a hidden agenda going on. Those in leadership at the time were protecting their own interest. Their concern was not the people. They did not care about releasing a criminal who might hurt the people. All they cared about was to protect their benefits and territory.

No matter how much Jesus blessed those around Him by healing the sick, the blind, the lame and even raising the dead, He still faced a community who rejected Him because someone was protecting their own benefits and turf. The ones who experienced the blessings were grateful. It was the ones whose positions were threatened by Jesus' work to bless the people who wanted to get rid of Him.

As a member of God's royal family, learn from your spiritual heritage. Observe what happened in Jesus' life that parallels your situation. When you are experiencing rejection, ask the question, "Who is doing the rejection and why? What are you doing that threatens them? Is it because they are enjoying a certain status in society? Do your activities take away from their importance?"

Those who opposed Jesus the most were the religious leaders at the time. How could it be that the ones who are supposedly closest to God would be the ones who did not recognize God's movement in their midst? When we are more worried about protecting our own turf than we are pleasing God, we are threatened by God's movement in anyone else and instead of embracing them, we move mountains to crush them.

"I will conform to the image of Christ by loving those who reject me but follow God's lead to enter a season where I will take the blessing intended for one group and redirect it to another."

Jesus responded to the doors that closed to him to reach the Jews by taking the blessing to the Gentiles. However, He kept a heart of love and forgiveness towards those He originally came to bless. From reading God's Word, we know God's plans will be to recycle back one day to give those who first rejected Him the opportunity to accept Him.

As a member of God's royal family, I found my comfort in following our family's royal customs. So my walk of faith is to act like a royal family member. I will conform to the image of Christ by loving those who reject me but follow God's lead to enter a season where I will take the blessing intended for one group and redirect it to another. All the while I will maintain a heart of forgiveness and desire for relationship. I will keep my heart open to discern God's timing to once again try to extend a hand of friendship to those who have rejected me.

Do you need guidance from God's Word for your life? When you hear His voice, will you do what He says? Oh what comfort we have from God's Word. In His Word, I find my marching orders to confirm the direction of my life!

Is God leading you to serve elsewhere? Has He enlarged your space where you can use all the gifts He has deposited in you to bless those around you?

I received word one day of a 27 year old medical student who was four months from completing her program. During a semester when she was overloaded with working overtime and studies, she took a final exam in one of her subjects and missed the mandatory score by a few points. As a result, she was told she could no longer be in the medical program. All her life, her dream was to serve children through medicine. She was so close to her goal she could almost touch it. She begged everyone she knew to pray for her and proceeded to make an appeal to the medical school's appeals board. The whole time, her aunt who was working with me on this manuscript kept instructing her about God's sovereignty. She wanted her niece to know that even when we pray, prayer is not our way to get what we want but to trust God with His plans for our lives.

Her niece received word that the Appeals board was upholding their decision to reject her from continuing in the program. Have you ever received a verdict that changed the rest of your life? Whether justified or not, the vote of a community can change our world. Or can it? How would the daughter of a King respond?

As believers, we are part of God's royal family. Our family consists of a line of faith heroes who role model how God expects us to live our lives. In our faith heroes we discover our royal family's code for behavior. What the devil tries to do is to confuse us with an illusion as to what is reality. He wants us to believe that our circumstances control our reality. This is not God's reality. What the devil tries to

kill, God restores in ways that astound the world. God's story is one of displaying His resurrection power over what the devil tries to bury.

In the midst of the worse rejection in the world, when God's one and only Son was rejected by a community to the point of being nailed on a cross, God brought about the greatest victory on planet earth. What will you allow to be the truth that controls your life and your responses? In Jesus' example, we witness how He shared His message wherever He had an open door. He was not responsible for the choices of those who voted against Him and shut their doors to Him. He kept going in His mission through whatever door was open. He kept going down to the last minute on the cross when He was blessing his mother Mary and the disciple John who were the only two left with Him. In His final moments on earth, He ministered to their needs and was the blessing God sent Him to be.

Oh the freedom to know that God has the final verdict on our lives. No one can throw us out of God's plans for us. We don't ever need the approval of a community to fulfill God's purpose. When God has allowed a rejection that has catastrophically affected our lives, remember the examples in our spiritual heritage. Jesus deserved to be King but instead He was nailed to a cross. From the depths of our greatest rejection, royalty rises above the darkness to save the world. This is the royal way. This can be your way if you live as a royal member of God's royal family.

Rejected as Being Imbalanced

Situation: Have others made you feel guilty for giving God priority in your life? Do others hold you to a different standard when it comes to God's work versus your secular job? Does it seem like those things with eternal consequences are not valued as much today?

The purpose of the personal journal entries shown below is to capture the rejection I felt from those who accused me as being imbalanced. Some entries were taken from an actual journal, others were written more recently as I reflected on what I was feeling at the time. The dates of the entries are approximate and were included to give the reader some sense of chronological history. After reading the personal journal entries capturing the emotion of rejection, please go to the section in the Bible Study that contains God's truths which addressed this emotion. In teaching this material, feel free to use my personal journal entries as illustration or personalize your lesson with writing your own personal journal entries or testimony to capture the emotion of rejection you felt in your own life. If you did not keep a journal, then try to relive the situation in your mind and write an entry today to capture what you felt at the time.

June 5, 1974

Dear God,
All my friends in high school used to go to the beach while I went to the library. They did not have the same sense of urgency. But somehow in my family, when the door opens, we know we have one chance to go through it and if we are not ready, we won't have what it takes to go through that door. The only hope our family had for the future was in my academics. The plan was for me to win a full scholarship to an American University. Then I would be able to get a good job and turn the financial situation around for the rest of the family. The beach could wait. There will be many more days in the future to run on the beach but there are only so many days to get ready for the moment the door opens to leave the country.

I hear people say to my Mom that her daughter spends too much time studying.

I'm sure they think I'm unbalanced. My Mom just smiles but she and I know that whenever you have a dream for the family, someone must pay the cost. It's not that I'm abnormal or that I would not rather spend the day at the beach. It's not that I don't rest either. But my rest is planned and I only take the rest in order to keep going. There is just no time to waste. By the time I'm ready to apply for a scholarship, all my transcripts must be strong enough to set me apart from everyone else who is applying. I know people don't understand because they live in the here and now. But my Mom tells me it's just an illusion when you build your life in places where you are not free. We must begin to build your life in a place where you are free and then we can reach our potential.

So here I am God. I finally reached the beginning of the dream my mother dreamed for our family. But she didn't make it God. The dream began in her but she is not here to see it come true. She helped me to be urgent and I stayed focused till the dream became a reality. She told me to ignore the criticism of those who called me imbalanced. Maybe it's possible to have balance when the dream is smaller. Those who are less urgent probably don't see those who are desperate and waiting for help. And even as fast as I went, and as urgent as I was, I was still not fast enough. Why didn't my Mom give me a chance to get stronger so I could deliver her from the challenges in her life? I was already on the right track. It was just a matter of time.

What do I do now God? Do we need urgency anymore? Who was the dream for? My Dad is depending on me now. He is all alone. He needs me to finish quickly so I can send for him. Do you know what God? I think when there is no one waiting for a dream to come true, there is no urgency. But when you know someone cannot make it without your help, you tell them to hang on, and you see their faces as you run as fast as you can.

Jan 16, 1982

Dear God,
I wonder if people in all companies work this hard. No one in this consulting firm leaves before 10 every evening. We all go out to dinner and then we come back to work. Everyone acts like this is normal. It must be normal for people who have worked at this pace all their lives. But why do they work at this pace? Do they have families depending on them? How much does the family need? How much will be enough? When you know why you're working it gives meaning to your

sacrifice. It must be sad though when some people go at this pace out of habit and they don't remember anymore why they are working. I'm not afraid of hard work. I'm not afraid of long hours. I can keep going without even thinking about how many hours I have kept going. But I think if I'm going to sacrifice, then I want to be sure I know for whom and for what I am laying down my life. It must be for more than a vacation home, another car or for more stuff. I think I need sacrifice to be connected to saving people.

Feb 6, 1991

Dear God,
It's the strangest thing. I don't think I'm any different today than when I was in corporate America. Yet, it seems like the general public has a different idea as to how hard someone should work in ministry. So it's applauded if you spend hours building a financial empire, or writing a paper to get your doctorate, or building a new company to secure the future of your family. But it's not o.k. to pour your life out to build a ministry that impacts the eternal future of souls that will perish without God. Now is that not the total deceit of the devil? He convinces us we are off balance for working hard for God but it's perfectly o.k. to work at an insane pace when it comes to working in the secular world. What's so sad is that even believers buy into the lie. Some are irritated if those who serve in ministry are too urgent. They throw themselves into their secular work and they want to do God stuff in a moderate way. I'm not sure what's going on God. Does it grieve you to see that we see no problem with being extreme when it comes to our secular job but we justify being balanced when it comes to you? Is

152

there anyone out there who will defy the norm and offer you extravagant worship

through their personal diligence in ministry?

The corresponding truths God taught me from His Word to address my situation
Feel free to continue reading all my personal journals in Module Two expressing feelings of rejection before reading the Bible Study. Or you may continue with the corresponding Bible study which contains God's truths in addressing the situation described in the above journal entries with additional truths God taught me to address situations that were not included in my journal entries. If you choose to personalize this curriculum as your way to bond with the group you are leading, feel free not only to use your own testimony and personal journal entries but in the Bible study part, include what God taught you from His Word in your situations of rejection.

Rejected as Being Imbalanced

Situation: Have others made you feel guilty for giving God priority in your life? Do others hold you to a different standard when it comes to God's work versus your secular job? Does it seem like those things with eternal consequences are not valued as much today?

Reminder: Let's learn the truths from God's Word that speak to our situations. Remember that as a member of God's royal family, we are to act according to the customs of the royal family. This means reinforcing our royal identity by living according to God's specific instructions in the Bible. When we cannot find specific instructions that speak to our situation, we are to search our spiritual heritage and model our lives after God's faith heroes who responded correctly to situations that parallel our own. We can also learn from their mistakes to avoid making the same mistakes in our own lives.

Do you find people criticizing you for being extreme? Do you hear them instructing you to be balanced? When I read about the life of the Apostle Paul, I don't see anything that is balanced about it. He led an extreme life.

Paul said in 2 Corinthians 11:23-29: **I have worked much harder, been in prison more frequently, been flogged more severely, and been exposed to death again and again. Five times I received from the Jews the forty lashes minus one. Three times I was beaten with rods, once I was stoned, three times I was shipwrecked, I spent a night and a day in the open sea. I have been constantly on the move. I have been in danger from rivers, in danger from bandits, in danger from my own countrymen, in danger from Gentiles; in danger in the city, in danger in the country, in danger at sea; and in danger from false brothers. I have labored and toiled and have often gone without sleep; I have known hunger and thirst and have often gone without food; I have been cold and naked. Besides everything else, I face daily the pressure of my concern for all the churches.** NIV

> **"Each of us must settle in our own hearts what God has entrusted us to finish."**

Could it be that God does not empower everyone to serve at Paul's pace but He chooses some for this level of momentum? The reason is not to cause everyone else to feel guilty. The reason is because there are some called to lead a movement, there are some called to lead a church, there are some called to lead a company, there are some called to lead a family and there are some called to lead a few individuals. There are also some called to lead all of the above.

Don't be surprised when you find people rejecting you for your momentum. They will accuse you of tiring them out. Instead of encouraging you, they will avoid you. Rest assured that there were those who avoided Paul as well. Not everyone is comfortable being in the midst of those who are radical for God or who are called to run at a different pace.

Each of us must settle in our own hearts what God has entrusted us to finish. What you must think about is how you will feel about your life the day your time on earth is over. I remember reading the biography of a missionary who said, "Oh that I would have more than one life to lose for Christ." When I am no longer on this earth, praise God that some will remember me as being radical for God. I would rather be remembered as being radical than being lukewarm. God instructs me in Revelation 3:16, **"So, because you are lukewarm-neither hot nor cold-I am about to spit you out of my mouth."** NIV

If left to my untransformed mind, I would spend my days shopping and sitting by the pool. I could go to lunch with my friends, putter around in my garden, and enjoy the days of my life. Instead, what do I find myself doing? I find myself building a ministry that will impact the spiritual lives of women for generations. I find myself developing a ministry that will find God's gems in our city and invest in their biblical training. I find myself beat up and poured out because I am seized by God's heart and what He wants to accomplish through His daughters. Jesus said in John 5:16-18, **"My Father is always at his work to this very day, and I, too, am working."** NIV. What I learned from Jesus is simply to stay on the same page with God. This doesn't mean we don't rest but we rest the way Jesus rests. He pulled away for prayer time, and one on one God time. He allowed God to be His replenishment.

"I hear people criticize those who are passionate for God, cautioning them to be more moderate."

Has someone rejected you for being extreme in your service to God? Have you been labeled as radical? I hear people criticize those who are passionate for God, cautioning them to be more moderate. The thing that catches my attention is why this counsel for moderation only applies to God's projects. I don't hear people advising moderation when it comes to the amount of time professionals and executives spend in building a business or trying to get the next promotion. In any new startup business when the owner wears many hats and is short on resources, it's considered normal to burn the midnight oil. When we send our troops into enemy territory, we do not criticize them for having meals at irregular hours or going without sleep. We see it as normal and applaud them for doing whatever it takes to win the battle. But when it comes to starting ministries and expanding God's kingdom into enemy territory, we seem to have a double standard. My heart breaks for the leaders who are criticized for doing what is necessary to advance God's mission. Has the thinking in our society become so influenced by our culture that we see God's work as some pass time we fit into our lives with moderation as compared to being the only activity that will count for eternity?

Describe a home project or a project in corporate America that consumed you. How much time did you devote to solving the problem?

Now name something you built that has eternal significance. How much time, energy, and resources were you willing to commit?

I once told a friend the dream God put in my heart for ministry. What I overlooked was the fact that this friend was not sold out to God in her life. The response I received was, "I don't think you should be so extreme. I think you should have balance in your life." If I had listened to her, Inspire Women would never have been born.

When God trusts you with a dream, be careful who you share it with. Remember that King David shared his dream to build the temple with Nathan, the prophet. This man of God told David to do whatever God had put in his heart. He said in 2 Samuel 7:3, **"Whatever you have in mind, go ahead and do it, for the LORD is with you."** NIV.

I praise God for the godly people He surrounded me with. In 2003 when I had to make the decision as to whether I would leave an established institution to build Inspire Women, I called Pastor David Self and Pastor William Taylor. They listened to the challenge that was ahead of me and then both of them said, "Anita, know that your church is with you."

No one can do your calling for you but oh how it feels like a cup of water in Jesus' name when someone wants God's will for your life and will pray for you to succeed. Inspire Women was established by God to listen with ears of faith to the dreams God has entrusted to His daughters and to train them for missions and ministry. If you are a leader God has entrusted with His dreams, know that we are with you in our prayers and friendship. We believe in your dreams because we believe in our God, the Dream Weaver of dreams of eternal significance.

Rejected by Those with Greater Business Sense

Situation: Have others judged you for being radical for the Lord? Do they question your logic when it comes to spending your money or time on the Lord's work? Do you use business logic to change God's marching orders in your life?

The purpose of the personal journal entries shown below is to capture the rejection I felt from those with greater business sense. Some entries were taken from an actual journal, others were written more recently as I reflected on what I was feeling at the time. The dates of the entries are approximate and were included to give the reader some sense of chronological history. After reading the personal journal entries capturing the emotion of rejection, please go to the section in the Bible Study that contains God's truths which addressed this emotion. In teaching this material, feel free to use my personal journal entries as illustration or personalize your lesson with writing your own personal journal entries or testimony to capture the emotion of rejection you felt in your own life. If you did not keep a journal, then try to relive the situation in your mind and write an entry today to capture what you felt at the time.

Oct 22, 1986

Dear God,
Are you telling me to leave corporate America? This is really bad timing. I am working at a time when companies are looking for MBA graduates, women and minorities. I have everything corporate America is looking for. Why would I leave? It defies all business sense. This is my time to make it big in corporate America. I can work in ministry any time. Are you telling me that you have a perfect timing too? Is it going to be a battle of which timing will drive me? Is it the timing of being in the right place at the right time in the business world or the timing of being in the right place and at the right time in God's battle to save the world?

March 1, 1989

Dear God,
I know my Dad does not understand. He spent a lot of money to send me to college. He sees me as having a thriving career. Why would I walk away from all of that when I am still young and able to work and save my money for my old age? I know he thinks I shouldn't work so many hours for the church. He always felt I was extreme and told me to be more moderate. It's so hard to explain that you called me out of corporate America. I wish I could show everyone the plan but you won't give me a five year plan. Maybe you don't give us a plan because you are not asking for our opinion. You won't show us a plan ahead of time for us to review. When you call, we don't get to compute the rate of return for time spent or resources sacrificed. Are you simply asking for obedience?

Feb 22, 2004,

Dear God,
I don't really understand how you do math.
If we give to encourage our sisters in
ministry instead of taking care of our own
needs, then what will happen to us? But
you keep leading us to walk by faith and to
go the extra mile to encourage our sisters
to serve at their full potential. Someone
offered us a percentage today for helping
them with a fundraiser and you said not to
take the money. You said to serve them as
our gift to them. You said that if we have a
strength that others need to advance the
kingdom, then we are to offer it freely. If
they choose to bless us, then let it be an
offer from their hearts. You show me
every day that ministry is not business. It
is an expression of your servant hood and
a heart that pours itself out to bless others.

The corresponding truths God taught me from His Word to address my situation
Feel free to continue reading all my personal journals in Module Two expressing feelings of rejection before reading the Bible Study. Or you may continue with the corresponding Bible study which contains God's truths in addressing the situation described in the above journal entries with additional truths God taught me to address situations that were not included in my journal entries. If you choose to personalize this curriculum as your way to bond with the group you are leading, feel free not only to use your own testimony and personal journal entries but in the Bible study part, include what God taught you from His Word in your situations of rejection.

Rejected by Those with Greater Business Sense

Situation: Have others judged you for being radical for the Lord? Do they question your logic when it comes to spending your money or time on the Lord's work? Do you use business logic to change God's marching orders in your life?

Reminder: Let's learn the truths from God's Word that speak to our situations. Remember that as a member of God's royal family, we are to act according to the customs of the royal family. This means reinforcing our royal identity by living according to God's specific instructions in the Bible. When we cannot find specific instructions that speak to our situation, we are to search our spiritual heritage and model our lives after God's faith heroes who responded correctly to situations that parallel our own. We can also learn from their mistakes to avoid making the same mistakes in our own lives.

As one who has an M.B.A. and climbed the ladder in corporate America, I am very familiar with the concept of "value added" and "return on investment." What God transformed in my heart was in understanding that although God wants us to be good stewards of our resources, ministry is not a business. This means, sometimes the greater faith is to understand that in spite of the cost, the activity is something God desires. There are times when God desires our extravagant worship.

Matthew 26:6-13 tells us: **While Jesus was in Bethany in the home of a man known as Simon the Leper, a woman came to him with an alabaster jar of very expensive perfume, which she poured on his head as he was reclining at the table. When the disciples saw this, they were indignant. "Why this waste?" they asked. "This perfume could have been sold at a high price and the money given to the poor." Aware of this, Jesus said to them, "Why are you bothering this woman? She has done a beautiful thing to me. The poor you will always have with you, but you will not always have me. When she poured this perfume on my body, she did it to prepare me for burial. I tell you the truth, wherever this gospel is preached throughout the world, what she has done will also be told, in memory of her.** NIV.

In this story, I learned that even among those who serve God there will be those who instinctively analyze God's ministries like some kind of stock market portfolio. The disciples were **"indignant"** when they said, **"Why this waste? This perfume could have been sold at a high price and the money given to the poor."** You will find among God's greatest leaders the attitude that you are wasting your time to minister to a few if you have opportunity to minister to thousands. This kind of attitude is not substantiated in God's Word. If Jesus' time had been managed by an agent, would they have sent him to speak to one woman at a well? God does not make decisions based on a return on investment of time spent measured against the number of people saved.

For example, Peter and John were sent to preach in many Samaritan villages. Acts 8:25 tells us: **"When they had testified and proclaimed the word of the Lord, Peter and John returned to Jerusalem, preaching the gospel in many Samaritan villages."** NIV. At the same time, we see God sending Philip to share the gospel with one eunuch. When God commissioned the disciples to share the gospel with the world, surely there is a more efficient way than transporting Philip to meet one Eunuch?

Acts 8:26-40 tells the story: **"Now an angel of the Lord said to Philip, "Go south to the road-the desert road-that goes down from Jerusalem to Gaza." So he started out, and on his way he met an Ethiopian eunuch, an important official in charge of all the treasury of Candace, queen of the Ethiopians. This man had gone to Jerusalem to worship, and on his way home was sitting in his chariot reading the book of Isaiah the prophet. The Spirit told Philip, "Go to that chariot and stay near it." Then Philip ran up to the chariot and heard the man reading Isaiah the prophet. "Do you understand what you are reading?" Philip asked. "How can I," he said, "unless someone explains it to me?" So he invited Philip to come up and sit with him...Then both Philip and the eunuch went down into the water and Philip baptized him. When they came up out of the water, the Spirit of the Lord suddenly took Philip away, and the eunuch did not see him again, but went on his way rejoicing. Philip, however, appeared at Azotus and traveled about, preaching the gospel in all the towns until he reached Caesarea.** NIV.

In God's marching orders, He sent Philip to reach one eunuch. God's Word tells us that **"both Philip and the eunuch went down into the water and Philip baptized him."** When they came up out of the water, we are told **"the Spirit of the Lord suddenly took Philip away."** This time, we find God's Spirit leading Philip in such a way that we find him **"preaching the gospel in all the towns."**

Observe how God reserves the right to send us to minister to one person some times and in some instances to crowds. God has the timetable for the world and He decides whom He will reach and how many He will reach at one time.

Jesus fed the five thousand but He also ministered to Nicodemus who sought Jesus out in a one on one meeting in the middle of the night. John 3:1-2 tells the story: **Now there was a man of the Pharisees named Nicodemus, a member of the Jewish ruling council. He came to Jesus at night and said, "Rabbi, we know you are a teacher who has come from God. For no one could perform the miraculous signs you are doing if God were not with him."** NIV. Jesus took the time to answer Nicodemus' question. He did not say, "I am an important person. I don't have time for one-on-one conversations."

Interestingly, God's Word showed me that those around the leader are usually the ones trying to manage the leader's time in an efficient way. Matthew 19:13-15 tells the story: **Then little children were brought to Jesus for him to place his hands on them and pray for them. But the disciples rebuked those who brought them. Jesus said, "Let the little children come to me, and do not hinder them, for the kingdom of heaven belongs to such as these."** NIV. In this situation, the disciples **"rebuked those who brought them"**. The implication in the rebuke was, "How could you expect Jesus to take time for such an activity? It's not worth His time!"

160

"I learned there are times God makes decisions that violate all business sense."

As you try to respond to individual needs, be ready for rejection from those who have their opinion on how you should spend your time. When I am weary, my human logic tells me to eliminate appointments with small groups or individuals. The problem is, there is no biblical evidence to justify that Jesus ever served this way. I remember responding to an appeal by a church to substitute teach for a class. I sensed that God wanted me to serve this class. It took me many hours to prepare the lesson. When I arrived at the class, I found there were three people in the class. I remember feeling bad as I left the class, knowing that those who were more business minded would question my wisdom to take on an assignment that impacted so few in an audience.

God reminded me of Philip and the eunuch. God reminded me of Jesus with the woman at the well. God reminded me of Jesus' grand finale on earth and how only two of His disciples were present at Calvary, and one was His mother. I learned there are times God makes decisions that violate all business sense. God will not allow us to use a formula to schedule our days. This way, we are forced to seek Him every day and to give Him the full reign to prioritize our activities.

Have you tried to reduce the scheduling of your time to a formula? Jill Briscoe taught me that it is an artificial formula to say "God first, family second, work and ministry third." She said the biblical model is to ask God, "What is first today?" There are days when we will be called to focus on one area of our lives more than others. When we go to God everyday, He gives us our priorities.

Have you allowed an artificial human made system to control your life?

How do you decide what you do every day?

How would life change if you simply allowed God to order your day and celebrate the fact that you have been obedient?

In the scholarship program at Inspire Women, I find myself helping supporters to evaluate scholarship candidates with God's mercy rather than business logic. I heard a leader once who steered a supporter away from helping a woman in ministry by using the argument that it was better stewardship of resources to invest in the training of a Pastor who was reaching hundreds in a congregation. As I listened to this argument, I looked at this woman who came out of an abusive background and realized it was a miracle that she was even walking around. She lived in a home where she was sexually molested by her brothers in a gang rape. She was on the verge of suicide when God intervened to set her apart for His work. God has healed her heart and she is excited about building a bridge from her past suffering to ministering to at risk teens. She was excited about Inspire Women's scholarships to train her in ministry. At the guidance of an influential Christian leader she was rejected from a supporter's funding because she was judged as not having as much "value added" to dollars spent as compared to someone with a larger platform.

In contrast, God commanded Inspire Women to listen with ears of mercy to the dreams He entrusts to His daughters. We do not place our personal biases on the different dreams God births. We do not say it is worth more to invest in those with a calling to a particular ministry versus another. Whether someone's ministry is with the lost, the homeless, the ill, the old, the young, the deaf, the home bound, the mentally retarded, the survivors of abuse, war or rape or to minister to a few or to thousands of other needs, all ministry born from God's heart is urgent. What we evaluate in our scholarship applicants is whether they have sincere passion and evidence of commitment. Our role is to equip our sisters to help them worship God

extravagantly through their service as they serve with excellence at their God-given potential.

When someone says to me, "I have always wanted to teach" we say, "Then be the best teacher you can be for God!" If someone says, "God has given me a gift in music," we say, "Then design worship the best way you can to tell the world about Jesus!" There are some God will train to shape ministries in Africa and China and in third world villages around the world. There are some He will send into abuse centers, pregnancy crisis centers, homeless shelters, prisons, and various ministries in the community. There are some He will lead to be authors or poets or playwrights or worship leaders. There are those God will set apart to encourage a leader who is on a difficult mission. There are some He will assign to face to face ministry with disabled veterans in a veterans' retirement home or patients in an Aids hospital.

"The more extravagant the sacrifice, the greater the worship"

The next time someone criticizes you for where you pour out your resources and time, find your healing in the fact that you serve a God who is extravagant. When He leads you to give in a way that violates business sense, then rest in knowing that the more extravagant the sacrifice, the greater the worship! Also know that God displayed His mercy when He sent Philip to meet with a eunuch, when He led Jesus to talk to one woman at a well and when He called me to serve with equal excellence whether I teach a group of three or a crowd of thousands.

I often hear from writers whose work was rejected by a publisher. They tell me they are frustrated because no one has chosen to publish their work. They evaluate their success based on the opinion of a publisher and how many thousands get to read their materials. So I ask them, "What if God asked you to write this book just for Him? What if God chooses to reserve this writing just for Him? Would you say that it was a waste of your time?" The point being, can you work unto the Lord and allow Him to do with your offering as He will? Can you offer Him your work as your extravagant worship even when He chooses to keep your work for Himself and not share it on a public platform?" Rejection from others takes on a totally different perspective when we offer God our lives and no longer give others the power to determine our success.

The more I studied God's Word, the better I understood His economics. David wrote God many poems when he was tending the sheep. How insulting it would be for God to hear us say, "If God keeps our work just for Himself, then it isn't worth our time"!

Has God put an assignment on your schedule that impacts an individual or a small group? In spite of the rejection by those who question how you have spent your time, how will you respond knowing there are times God violates all business sense in how He leads us to serve Him?

When God called me out of corporate America, it was at a time when I had everything corporate America was looking for. I had an MBA, a track record of performance and I was a minority at a time when companies were looking for minorities and women to promote. When God opened the door for me to return to corporate America after my children were in full time school, I did not understand why He opened the door. Then I realized that God did not want my service when I had no other option. He wanted to know, "When offered everything you could dream of from corporate America, would you leave it all because you consider me your greatest treasure?"

Today when I look back at my choices, I praise God for my time in corporate America because it has given me the skills I needed to run an organization that reaches thousands. But I also know that it is in laying down my business logic that I learned that when you get to the edge of a challenge that no human logic can solve, it is then that God teaches you how to part the Red Sea.

Rejected by Those Who Question Your Calling

Situation: Have you ever been in a place where you are certain of God's calling on your life but some family members and friends don't understand? Do you get distracted from the assignment God entrusted to you just trying to dodge all of the torpedoes that try to stop you?

The purpose of the personal journal entries shown below is to capture the rejection I felt from those who questioned my calling. Some entries were taken from an actual journal, others were written more recently as I reflected on what I was feeling at the time. The dates of the entries are approximate and were included to give the reader some sense of chronological history. After reading the personal journal entries capturing the emotion of rejection, please go to the section in the Bible Study that contains God's truths which addressed this emotion. In teaching this material, feel free to use my personal journal entries as illustration or personalize your lesson with writing your own personal journal entries or testimony to capture the emotion of rejection you felt in your own life. If you did not keep a journal, then try to relive the situation in your mind and write an entry today to capture what you felt at the time.

Jan 16, 1976

Dear God,
What happens when you think you are called to be with someone the rest of your life and they don't want you to be in their lives? If someone won't let me in, then is it my fault that I can't fulfill my calling? Why would you tell me to do something and then not tell the other person? Is it your way to test my obedience?

Feb 16, 1999

Dear God,
Did I get my calling wrong? I don't understand how you can give me the vision for what you want to do but those I am serving do not see where you are going. They are concerned with other priorities. Does this mean the vision is premature? Does this mean I am to forget what you

spoke to me and just serve in what you spoke to those in authority over me? Why would you create all this confusion by telling me the vision prematurely?

Maybe the confusion arises because we are in a time of transition. Maybe when you are growing a leader under a leader, there comes a time when we must cut the umbilical cord. I experience a similar challenge when I was raising my sons. At some point, they are their own people and I need to get out of the way so they can lead in what you have called them to do. Although they may have been part of what our family was doing in service, they were not created to serve me, but to serve you.

So God, does this mean I am in transition? If I find that those in authority over me do not see the value of the vision you have given me, it doesn't mean they are wrong.

It just means that you are multiplying leaders to expand your kingdom on earth.

The challenge then is to respect each other's calling and not accuse each other. I hear people whispering behind my back. They say I'm not a servant. Well, I think they mean I'm not their servant and they are right because I exist to be your servant. They don't realize that we don't call ourselves. I actually have very little to do with my calling. It's all about you, God. I'm really quite insignificant in the scheme of things except you needed someone in human form to work through so the world can better understand your heart and what you are building.

May 1, 2002

Dear God,
I don't know why you called me to raise an endowment for your daughters for biblical training. I don't have the experience or any idea how to do this. It's such a grand calling and I know no one believes me. Surely God would not have called one such as me. But how do I explain your calling to others when I don't understand why you picked me? I just know you heard the cries of your daughters and you are responding in mercy.

It's so funny how people will say to me that God did not call them to something because they believe they are called only when they personally want to do it. You did not ask my opinion. You simply showed me your heart and how it makes you cry when your daughters are not treated as equal heirs of your kingdom and trusted with the training so they can share in your mission to save the world. I just know that what compels me is simply my wanting to

be where you are working. So if you go up the mountain I want to go. If you go down to the valley I want to go. Is it wrong God to just want to be in your presence?

I hear you say you want a trust fund for your daughters so the women of this city will always have a basic level of support to be trained for your service. I hear you say that you want this established now. Why now? Could it be because you are urgent and now is the time to develop the potential of your spiritual army? I just know God that a remnant believes me. I just wish the rest would stop stabbing me behind my back. I know they think I am a fool.

Aug 12, 2006

Dear God,
I was telling a friend of mine what you led me to do in appealing for the ministry. She thought it was absolutely hilarious that I would go and ask a stranger to donate something that big. I didn't think it was strange because in my culture it would be an insult not to recognize someone's place of influence. It's like sitting next to Bill Gates and asking him for a cup of coffee when he can buy you the whole coffee chain. I don't know Bill Gates personally but I know that if you opened the door for me to sit next to him, I would ask him to ensure an education fund to train those who share your hope with others. I know he is focused on medical research. However, I have also seen in my mother's loss of hope, that without hope, people perish. We need physical, emotional, and spiritual health.

God, did you think it was pretty funny when my friend said, "God asked you to do it because He would never ask a Southern Belle to do something like that. That's because we would never do it!" We laughed about that. But the more I reflect on her words, the more I see how profound they were. Could it be that you already know what background and culture we come from before you choose us for the assignment? Could it be that the way we do things as our best way to honor you is exactly what you intended?

Maybe we need to stop judging how people do things but ask the bigger question about their motives and what they are trying to build. If we focus on the end result, then maybe we can find common ground instead of finding reasons to be divided. Maybe what's really important is to know that each of us will stand before you one day and all that matters is that we served with a pure heart in the best way we knew how, based on our backgrounds.

God, you tell the story of how one of your generals marched around the walls of Jericho seven times as your strategy to defeat the enemy. Now, how silly did that look? I can just imagine the comments. I'm sure someone said, "God could not possibly have asked you to do that!" God, maybe there are times you invite us to look silly to see how obedient we are and if we will trust you no matter how ridiculous the calling appears. Maybe at the end of the day, all that matters is our obedience.

The corresponding truths God taught me from His Word to address my situation
Feel free to continue reading all my personal journals in Module Two expressing feelings of rejection before reading the Bible Study. Or you may continue with the corresponding Bible study which contains God's truths in addressing the situation described in the above journal entries with additional truths God taught me to address situations that were not included in my journal entries. If you choose to personalize this curriculum as your way to bond with the group you are leading, feel free not only to use your own testimony and personal journal entries but in the Bible study part, include what God taught you from His Word in your situations of rejection.

Rejected by Those who Question Your Calling

Situation: Have you ever been in a place where you are certain of God's calling on your life but some family members and friends don't understand? Do you get distracted from the assignment God entrusted to you just trying to dodge all of the torpedoes that try to stop you?

Reminder: Let's learn the truths from God's Word that speak to our situations. Remember that as a member of God's royal family, we are to act according to the customs of the royal family. This means reinforcing our royal identity by living according to God's specific instructions in the Bible. When we cannot find specific instructions that speak to our situation, we are to search our spiritual heritage and model our lives after God's faith heroes who responded correctly to situations that parallel our own. We can also learn from their mistakes to avoid making the same mistakes in our own lives.

Have you ever felt called to serve in a way that no one else felt led to do? For example, in ministry, I have seen examples of this through those who felt called to serve the specific needs of a leader as compared to the needs of a ministry in general. Perhaps because the proximity is to the leader, such a calling creates suspicion especially among those who are protective and close to the leader. Since leaders often draw a following, the suspicion is, "Of course you would feel called to something that gets you more time with the leader. Everyone under the sun wants more time so what makes you different?" The suspicion is based on assessing such a calling as being more self serving and meeting the person's emotional need instead of meeting a need in the ministry.

"Don't be surprised when those around the leader will form opinions of you based on imperfect knowledge."

Luke 7:36-38 tells of an incident when a woman focused her attention on Jesus. It reads, "**Now one of the Pharisees invited Jesus to have dinner with him, so he went to the Pharisee's house and reclined at the table. When a woman who had lived a sinful life in that town learned that Jesus was eating at the Pharisee's house, she brought an alabaster jar of perfume, and as she stood behind him at his feet weeping, she began to wet his feet with her tears. Then she wiped them with her hair, kissed them and poured perfume on them.**" NIV.

Apparently, Simon must have had an issue with how the woman served Jesus because Jesus said to him in Luke 7:44-47, "**Do you see this woman? I came into your house. You did not give me any water for my feet, but she wet my feet with her tears and wiped them with her hair. You did not give me a kiss, but this woman, from the time I entered, has not stopped kissing my feet. You did not put oil on my head, but she has poured perfume on my feet. Therefore, I tell you, her many sins have been forgiven-for she loved much. But he who has been forgiven little loves little.**" NIV.

Why did the woman feel compelled to do something special and specific for Jesus? Jesus said in Luke 7:47, **"...he who has been forgiven little loves little."** I learned from this story that if a leader's message brought healing to a situation that plagued an individual for many years, you can expect that person to feel an extraordinary gratitude for how the leader's ministry set them free. If you are a leader who is experiencing the gratitude of someone who was blessed by your message, be sure to divert the attention from yourself to God Himself. If any healing occurred, it was by God's mercy and power. If you are the recipient of healing and feel called to serve a leader with extravagant devotion, be sure your ultimate loyalty is to God and to His ministry, which extends beyond one individual leader.

If God chooses to move His leader to a different assignment, how will that affect your service? How can you flow with God's timing and serve under a different leader God appoints? If you are not willing to transfer your service under a different leader, what is holding you back?

In this story, the woman focused her attention on God and was overwhelmed with gratitude for the forgiveness she received for her sins. One would imagine that God of all people is worthy of undivided attention. Yet, even with focusing one's attention on God, it drew raised eyebrows because the disciples did not discern the need to express such gratitude. Jesus' disciples were ministering with Him and were more focused on the needs in the crowd than in paying attention to what would bless their leader. You will find that those surrounding an earthly leader will be running with so many details that they may inadvertently overlook their leader. If God has called you to bless a leader, be aware that those around the leader may not discern the need for your service and may question your calling. The disciples' comments stemmed from their suspicion over why the woman's service was necessary. The idea was, "We don't see the need in this area so why do you?" Don't be surprised when those around the leader will form opinions of you based on imperfect knowledge. Find your assurance in knowing that God sees all things, examines your heart, and blesses a service that is pure and offered out of a heart of gratitude with no personal agenda.

"Is there a need that no one else is aware of that God revealed to you?"

Whatever was going on in Simon's mind about the woman was inaccurate, so Jesus corrected his thinking. Instead of finding fault in the woman, Jesus listed for Simon what he did not do. He said, **"You did not give me any water for my feet"**, followed by the words **"but she…"** He said, **"You did not give me a kiss"** followed by the words **"but she…"**. He said, **"You did not put oil on my head"** followed by the words **"but she…"** The next time someone rejects you for your service, ask yourself, "But are they doing what you are doing? Are they willing to pour out what you are pouring out?" If not, then ignore their comments and trust God to show them as Jesus revealed the truth to Peter.

If you have been assigned a **"but she…"** role, then instead of allowing the rejection to cripple you, say to yourself, "but for me, there would be no one taking care of this need." Write the words "But for me…" on a sheet of paper and tape it to the mirror in your bathroom. Then every morning, let God remind you that but for you, the need would fall through the cracks.

There are some people called to a cause and there are some called to a person. In this particular incident, the woman was set apart to be ultra sensitive to God's timing for a person. Is there a need that no one is aware of that God has revealed to you? Then let God's approval of your service be all that you need to keep going.

Are you the "but she…" woman in the life of one of God's leader or in the life of a specific ministry? What need were you called to meet? How have you responded to the need?

When my son turned 21, I found myself reflecting on key events in his life. I recalled an incident that could have permanently affected his image of himself. Robbie was always sure of his gift to make presentations. One semester, when he was in elementary school, he had gone to the extra work of getting some bonus points by making a costume to go with the character he was portraying. When I picked him up from school, he was visibly upset. "What happened?" I asked. He said, "The teacher hated my presentation. She took points off for the costume I made. That was supposed to be for bonus points. I have never heard of a teacher who took away points for the extra work you did to get bonus points!"

That night, while he was asleep, I went into his room and I placed my head on his chest while he was sleeping and poured out my prayers on his behalf. I begged God to protect him and not to allow a teacher's insensitivity to hurt him. I was so intense in my prayers that I began to heave and to weep. He woke up from his sleep and was panicked over my emotions. He said, "Mom, what's wrong? Did someone die?" I said, "No, son. I was just so devastated over what this teacher did to you. I don't want you to believe her opinion. I don't want her to rob from you the gift God placed in you." He said, "Mom, don't worry. I don't care what this teacher says. She doesn't have that kind of power over me."

Robbie was only 11 when he formed his conclusion but his words stayed with me. "She doesn't have that kind of power over me." I wonder today if you have given someone power to redefine your life that has no authority to do so. God is the only one who deposited His gift in us and is pleased with what He has created. Is it time for you to celebrate God's calling and return to God His right to control your life?

Rejected by Your Peers or Team Mates

Situation: Have you ever found yourself in a situation where you have been rejected by your peers and are not sure how to turn things around? Are you longing for your peers to accept you in their inner circle?

The purpose of the personal journal entries shown below is to capture the rejection I felt from peers and team mates. Some entries were taken from an actual journal, others were written more recently as I reflected on what I was feeling at the time. The dates of the entries are approximate and were included to give the reader some sense of chronological history. After reading the personal journal entries capturing the emotion of rejection, please go to the section in the Bible Study that contains God's truths which addressed this emotion. In teaching this material, feel free to use my personal journal entries as illustration or personalize your lesson with writing your own personal journal entries or testimony to capture the emotion of rejection you felt in your own life. If you did not keep a journal, then try to relive the situation in your mind and write an entry today to capture what you felt at the time.

Nov 5, 1994

Dear God,
I'm not really sure how to blend in with a group. When you give a leader a vision, are they pioneers? If they are pioneers, then who are their equals? When you entrust a leader with a vision, is it always lonely at the top? How do you get an existing group to be part of the vision or will every existing group always feel threatened?

I'm not sure what to do with the ideas you give me. I am working with a group and I see them struggling with a problem. I hear your answer but I'm afraid to open my mouth. On the one hand, I hear them saying they need answers. On the other hand, I don't think they want the answer to come out of my mouth. I think it takes time for a group to accept a new person. I think it's important to be accepted first before

offering any answers. What do you think God?

Jan 17, 2006

Dear God,
I think for some people it won't really matter what the evidence is, they will never receive me as an equal. It could be my age, it could be my ethnicity, or it could be my gender. Who knows? I asked my husband what he thought and he said some people form opinions based on what they are used to seeing. If they never grew up seeing a woman in leadership, or an Asian in leadership, or someone of a certain age in leadership, then they are uncomfortable with the person and will never let that person into their circles. They may go through the outward appearance of accepting someone but they don't really let them in.

God, do you think you could do something so extraordinary that your work in me will be evident? I feel like this is not my problem to solve. If you want me to be effective, then I have to trust you to make it so blatantly obvious that your hand is on my life that others will follow. It's your agenda God. I know you are perfectly able to establish the credibility of your leaders. I'll go where you lead God but I can only walk through the door if it is open.

The corresponding truths God taught me from His Word to address my situation
Feel free to continue reading all my personal journals in Module Two expressing feelings of rejection before reading the Bible Study. Or you may continue with the corresponding Bible study which contains God's truths in addressing the situation described in the above journal entries with additional truths God taught me to address situations that were not included in my journal entries. If you choose to personalize this curriculum as your way to bond with the group you are leading, feel free not only to use your own testimony and personal journal entries but in the Bible study part, include what God taught you from His Word in your situations of rejection.

Rejected by Your Peers or Team Mates

Situation: Have you ever found yourself in a situation where you have been rejected by your peers and are not sure how to turn things around? Are you longing for your peers to accept you in their inner circle?

Reminder: Let's learn the truths from God's Word that speak to our situations. Remember that as a member of God's royal family, we are to act according to the customs of the royal family. This means reinforcing our royal identity by living according to God's specific instructions in the Bible. When we cannot find specific instructions that speak to our situation, we are to search our spiritual heritage and model our lives after God's faith heroes who responded correctly to situations that parallel our own. We can also learn from their mistakes to avoid making the same mistakes in our own lives.

When God gives you answers to address a challenge, it seems He should inform those around you to welcome your ideas. Often, this does not happen. Be ready for an existing leadership team to be suspicious of any newcomer.

Even though an existing group may have been asking God for answers and help, it takes time for them to recognize God's answer through a new leader He has raised up.

If God is doing a new thing, chances are, the leader with the new vision will create a stir. God seldom comes through any territory without creating a stir. His priorities require us to re-adjust ours. You can be sure that whenever you expect someone to re-adjust their priorities, whether it is their time, energy, or money, you can expect resistance.

"If God is the one who sent you into a group, then trust God to prove to the group that He appointed you for His mission"

When God raised up the Apostle Paul to lead the charge in His vision to take the gospel to the Gentiles, Paul was not immediately accepted. Acts 9:26-31 tells us: **When he came to Jerusalem, he tried to join the disciples, but they were all afraid of him, not believing that he really was a disciple. But Barnabas took him and brought him to the apostles...So Saul stayed with them and moved about freely in Jerusalem, speaking boldly in the name of the Lord. He talked and debated with the Grecian Jews, but they tried to kill him. When the brothers learned of this, they took him down to Caesarea and sent him off to Tarsus. Then the church throughout Judea, Galilee and Samaria enjoyed a time of peace. It was strengthened; and encouraged by the Holy Spirit, it grew in numbers, living in the fear of the Lord.** NIV.

Have you ever tried to fit in with an existing group only to have them look at you with suspicion? God gave Paul a vision for ministry and he **"tried to join the disciples"** but **"they were afraid of him."** Depending on your background, expect there might be a clash between where you came from and the new group of people you are to work with. If they reject you, it may be because of incomplete knowledge about you and about God's vision. If God is the one who sent you into a new group, then trust God to prove to the group that He appointed you for His mission.

In Paul's case we see God raising up Barnabas to introduce Paul to the group to the point that everyone is now convinced that Paul is safe to include on the team. **"So Saul stayed with them and moved about freely in Jerusalem."**

How have you been having trouble in assimilating with an existing group?

What do you think are the concerns?

Who could serve as your Barnabas to introduce you and what God has been doing through you?

"No one can ship you out anywhere unless God allowed it"

After Paul was accepted by the disciples in Jerusalem, he then went around freely and "**debated with the Grecian Jews**." The result was, "**they tried to kill him**." Now watch what happens next.

The brothers who learned of this issue decide to pack Paul up and "**sent him off to Tarsus.**" If someone has shipped you off, don't be too quick to respond to the outcome as rejection. They may be sending you off because it is safer for you to be outside the target range for a season. They may be sending you off because they question the timing even though they accept your calling. Perhaps all the issues around you is creating a distraction and hurting the programs that were working before you showed up on the scene.

If your presence has caused problems and diverted a team from focusing on what was working before you arrived, could it be that you will serve the team better by getting off the team? Where could you go as your Tarsus till God brings you back in His perfect timing?

While Paul was in Tarsus, imagine him hearing through the grapevine that "**the church throughout Judea, Galilee and Samaria enjoyed a time of peace. It was strengthened; and encouraged by the Holy Spirit, it grew in numbers, living in the fear of the Lord.**" NIV.

In our human flesh, we may want to feel like everything crumbled when we left. We want to know that our presence made a difference and that people will miss us when we are gone. But in God's plan, He may choose to bless the team or ministry that shipped us out. What Paul did was to serve wherever He was sent. Then in God's perfect timing, as God's vision to reach the Gentiles matured, we are told in Acts 11:25-26, "**Then Barnabas went to Tarsus to look for Saul, and when he found him, he brought him to Antioch. So for a whole year Barnabas and Saul met with the church and taught great numbers of people. The disciples were called Christians first at Antioch.**" NIV

Oh the incredible encouragement God gives us in His Word. If you are in a place where the community you are in does not value your contribution, instead of taking it personally, receive it as God's open door for you to serve elsewhere. Know that if you were meant to continue with this community, then God will bring you back at a time when they now see you as their greatest asset. Instead of licking your wounds and feeling rejected, know that no one can thwart God's plans. No one can ship you anywhere unless God allowed it. Even in your exile when you may feel isolated and forgotten, God is working His grand purpose.

Have you recently left an institution and find yourself sitting in a Tarsus? What can you be doing in Tarsus to position you to return stronger than before?

"If you find a team rejecting you because of the way you are relating to the leader, then ask yourself if you are the one creating the problem."

The disciple John was someone who felt a special bonding with Jesus. He described himself in John 13:23 as "**the disciple whom Jesus loved, was reclining next to him**." NIV. Did you notice that it is in the book of John that John refers to himself as "**the disciple whom Jesus loved**"? No other book of the Bible refers to John in this manner. I wonder if John showed his heart and his longing to be special to Jesus by the way he described himself.

In the dynamics with his peers Peter, James and John, John was usually quiet and low keyed in manners. However interspersed with this low keyed demeanor were outbursts that demonstrated his belief in his exclusive relationship with Jesus. Luke 9:49-50 recounts an incident where John was singled out and identified as viewing himself as set apart from the rest when he said, "**Master…we saw a man driving out demons in your name and we tried to stop him, because he is not one of us.**" "**Do not stop him,**" Jesus said, "**for whoever is not against you is for you.**" NIV

Did you notice John's words, "**he is not one of us**"? Anytime there is someone in the group who has the attitude that they have some special "**one of us**" with the leader, this tendency may develop from "the team" being the "us" to the individual being the "us" with the leader. In Mark 10:35-36, both John and his brother were referred to as wanting some place of honor next to Jesus. The story reads: **Then James and John, the sons of Zebedee, came to him. "Teacher," they said, "we want you to do for us whatever we ask." "What do you want me to do for you?" he asked. They replied, "Let one of us sit at your right and the other at your left in your glory."** Mark 10:41 tells us that "**When the ten heard about this, they became indignant with James and John.**"

If you find a team rejecting you because of the way you are relating to the leader, then ask yourself if you are the one creating the problem. Realize that when anyone on the team tries to possess the leader in any way, it will create resentment from the rest of the team who will be saying, "What makes you so special to deserve a place of honor next to the leader?" As the leader, Jesus called them together and said, "**You know that those who are regarded as rulers of the Gentiles lord it over them, and their high officials exercise** authority over them. Not so with you. Instead, whoever wants to become great among you must be your servant, and whoever wants to be first must be slave of all. For even the Son of Man did not come to be served, but to serve, and to give his life as a ransom for many." NIV

If you are experiencing rejection because of some exclusive relationship you are trying to secure for yourself, then ask God for forgiveness. Thank God for the rejection of those around you because their rejection may be God's way to steer you back on the right track. Jesus did not condone any attempt for exclusivity. Instead, He wanted those who followed Him to understand that He came to serve. Therefore, those who love Him best must be ones who serve others best. God showed me in the situation with James and John that He does not encourage exclusive relationships as some kind of status symbol. Instead, the Son of Man came to serve and if there is any kind of exclusive relationship we desire, then let it be that of wanting to drink from a cup that requires more sacrifice. The closer a follower desires to draw near to the leader, the more the sacrifice God will require.

If you have experienced rejection from the team, could it be because you have inadvertently or intentionally sent out messages through either your body language or your verbal communication that you have some special relationship with the leader? In John's case, God tested his allegiance when Jesus ascended into heaven and was no longer physically present. God wanted to see how John would respond when he was on an island and separated from the crowd. Would John still be committed? If you want to be the disciple who a leader loves, then be aware of the level of sacrifice God will require from you.

If you profess to be devoted to a leader, then show your genuine devotion by being devoted to the mission that is dear to the leader's heart. What will you do to continue the mission if the leader is no longer physically with you?

About a year ago, my family brought home a new puppy. I was naive to think that our older dog would welcome this new addition. Instead the older dog growled at the puppy and showed him in no uncertain terms that he was King. I found myself saying, "Stop it!" a lot. I found myself breaking up fights. It was like the older dog was saying, "Who do you think you are? I was here first. Therefore, I am more special." It was as though the younger pup was saying, "I am new and different, so I am more special." Interestingly, when a stranger walked into the yard both dogs united in barking at the stranger. They joined forces as they served together to defend the property.

In addressing the disciples who were indignant over James and John wanting to feel more special to Jesus, our Lord said to His team in Matthew 20:26-28, "...**whoever wants to become great among you must be your servant, and whoever wants to be first must be your slave- just as the Son of Man did not come to be served, but to serve, and to give his life as a ransom for many**." NIV. As with my pups who joined forces in serving by protecting the property, Jesus recognized that the focus on service is what will eliminate the disunity among team mates.

When there is disunity on the team and jealousies over privileges and places of honor next to the leader, God's Word tells me the reason is because there is not enough service. When God raises the bar to service, we have no time to critique each other. All Jesus' disciples ended up dying for the cause. When we serve to the point of laying down our lives for the cause, what will unite us is our shed blood. Through our sacrifice, we see each other's heart for pure service. There is no vying for position when one is being martyred; there is only prayer for the saints. God's royal way to overcome rejection among peers is to raise the bar to service. It is in the way we bleed for the cause that we will unite through our common sacrifice.

Rejected by the Leader You Esteemed Highly

Situation: Have you been rejected by a leader that you once seemed to have a great rapport with? Are words getting back to you through the grapevine that someone you think highly of is talking negatively about you to others?

The purpose of the personal journal entries shown below is to capture the rejection I felt from a leader I esteemed highly. Some entries were taken from an actual journal, others were written more recently as I reflected on what I was feeling at the time. The dates of the entries are approximate and were included to give the reader some sense of chronological history. After reading the personal journal entries capturing the emotion of rejection, please go to the section in the Bible Study that contains God's truths which addressed this emotion. In teaching this material, feel free to use my personal journal entries as illustration or personalize your lesson with writing your own personal journal entries or testimony to capture the emotion of rejection you felt in your own life. If you did not keep a journal, then try to relive the situation in your mind and write an entry today to capture what you felt at the time.

August 1, 1977

Dear God,
I know I am only in undergraduate school and I probably shouldn't be worried about marriage. This is the time to discover my interests and to find out what I am about before connecting my life with another person. But I really thought he was the one. I thought he could have been the spiritual leader in my family.

I'm not sure what changed but something did. It's as if one day I was the perfect person and the next day I fell short of his ideal woman. He said he wanted something different. What was it about me that failed the test? Do I hang around hoping he will change his mind? How degrading this feels to hang around hoping someone might love you.

God, I heard through my friends that he is with someone else. So someone else was able to pass the test that I failed. What does she look like? What does she have that I don't? God, please take this feeling away. I don't like walking around feeling like I didn't make the cut.

March 6, 1987

Dear God,
I offered to help a leader but was told by the leadership that I was too gifted and that I was a threat. How could this be happening? Has ministry turned into some kind of monopoly? Is it all about exclusive contracts and making sure you get the largest share of the market? I am disillusioned God. What is really going on?

Jan 7, 1999

Dear God,
There are times when I feel my value to anyone is only when I serve their purpose. As long as I can help them with what they are doing then they treat me like I hung the moon. But heaven forbid that you should ever lead me to do something outside of their area. Then all of a sudden, I am a bother and they don't want anything to do with me. I feel used God. How foolish of me to think that my leader actually cared about what you were doing in my life.

April 16, 2005

Dear God,
I think some people are just mean. They know how much their words of affirmation would mean so they deliberately withhold their blessing. It's like the more they know how much you need them, the more they delight in rejecting you. There must be something going on in their past. Is this their way to get back at someone who walked out on them? I don't really know what's going on. I just know what happens behind closed doors. To the public they act kind because they know someone is watching. And then when no one is watching, they abuse you verbally and emotionally. They draw you close and then they push you away. It's like some kind of power play. They must need to control the relationship. Is it because they are afraid? What are they afraid of? Here I am begging for a crumb of affirmation from someone I esteemed highly. I probably had them on a pedestal. How could it be that I came to serve but they are afraid of my gift and see me as a threat. How strange! Is it something to do with me or is it really something to do with them?

The corresponding truths God taught me from His Word to address my situation
Feel free to continue reading all my personal journals in Module Two expressing feelings of rejection before reading the Bible Study. Or you may continue with the corresponding Bible study which contains God's truths in addressing the situation described in the above journal entries with additional truths God taught me to address situations that were not included in my journal entries. If you choose to personalize this curriculum as your way to bond with the group you are leading, feel free not only to use your own testimony and personal journal entries but in the Bible study part, include what God taught you from His Word in your situations of rejection.

Rejected by the Leader You Esteemed Highly

Situation: Have you been rejected by a leader that you once seemed to have a great rapport with? Are words getting back to you through the grapevine that someone you think highly of is talking negatively about you to others?

Reminder: Let's learn the truths from God's Word that speak to our situations. Remember that as a member of God's royal family, we are to act according to the customs of the royal family. This means reinforcing our royal identity by living according to God's specific instructions in the Bible. When we cannot find specific instructions that speak to our situation, we are to search our spiritual heritage and model our lives after God's faith heroes who responded correctly to situations that parallel our own. We can also learn from their mistakes to avoid making the same mistakes in our own lives.

Whether you are a biological child or a spiritual child, the wounds from the one who was meant to shepherd you has a way of totally crumbling the ground on which you are standing. Have you ever trusted a spiritual leader only to discover that they were using you for their purpose and never had the development of your potential as their priority? What do you do with this kind of rejection?

In the relationship between Saul and David, 1 Samuel 16:14-18 tells us: **Now the Spirit of the LORD had departed from Saul, and an evil spirit from the LORD tormented him...So Saul said to his attendants, "Find someone who plays well and bring him to me." One of the servants answered, "I have seen a son of Jesse of Bethlehem who knows how to play the harp. He is a brave man and a warrior. He speaks well and is a fine-looking man. And the LORD is with him." NIV.**

We discover from these lines that what initiated the relationship between Saul and David was a need that Saul had. In trying to meet this need to minimize a situation that was tormenting him, Saul started a recruiting campaign. Have you ever been recruited to meet a need of the leader of an organization?

David had the right set of skills so he was chosen for the vacancy in Saul's court. 1 Samuel 16:21-22 tells us, **"David came to Saul and entered his service. Saul liked him very much, and David became one of his armor-bearers..."** NIV.

Perhaps you have been serving under someone who needed your skills. Perhaps this person is older than you and someone you truly respected and wanted to serve with all your heart. Perhaps you even saw yourself as this person's armor-bearer the same way David became **"one of Saul's"** and you were excited to use any skill you had to protect your leader. All seems wonderful in the court but then the tide turns.

"The more successful the ministry grew, the more I knew I was the target of someone's jealousy."

As God blesses you with success, there are some leaders who will be excited to see your development and to encourage you and to step out of the way to allow you to soar. Then there are others who become insecure and jealous. They may even be threatened because they never had your interest in mind. Your only value to them was what you brought to them. There are some leaders who are happy to pour into your life as long as you served their agenda.

Oh the incredible comfort from God's Word to show us examples through one such as David who was rejected by his leader. 1 Samuel 18:5 tells us the problem began with David's success as described in these words: **Whatever Saul sent him to do, David did it so successfully that Saul gave him a high rank in the army. This pleased all the people and Saul's officers as well.** NIV.

Not only did David have success but his success was public and resulted in the crowds bragging about him. Then God's Word tells us in 1 Samuel 18:9, **"And from that time on Saul kept a jealous eye on David."** NIV

I remember my friend Jill Briscoe telling me about her radio program "Telling the Truth" on which she teaches with her husband Stuart and her son, Pete. She said, "Listeners order Pete's teaching more than Stuart's or mine." As she said this I saw how she beamed with joy. She was thrilled to see how God was using Pete in ministry.

In contrast, we find Saul growing in jealousy towards David to the point that he began expressing it in outward harm to David's person. 1 Samuel 18:10-11 tells us: **The next day an evil spirit from God came forcefully upon Saul. He was prophesying in his house, while David was playing the harp, as he usually did. Saul had a spear in his hand and he hurled it, saying to himself, "I'll pin David to the wall." But David eluded him twice.** NIV

I was in a situation once when I was totally disillusioned by a leader I served under. I heard through the grapevine that this leader was trying to turn supporters against me. I was broken hearted that the person I so respected would be the one to use their standing in the community to destroy a young disciple. I could not bear the rejection and everything in me wanted to just throw in the towel and go home. But a godly mature leader in the city held my feet to the fire and told me I did not have the freedom to give up. He said, "The future of thousands of women will be affected. God has trusted you with this ministry and you must keep going."

God in His grace protected me in spite of the darts that were thrown my way. As I recognized the parallels between my situation and the story of God's faith heroes in the Bible, I found guidance and encouragement for my life. In David's case, 1 Samuel 18:12-16 told me, **"Saul was afraid of David, because the LORD was with David but had left Saul. So he sent David away from him and gave him command over a thousand men, and David led the troops in their campaigns. In everything he did he had great success, because the LORD was with him. When Saul saw how successful he was, he was afraid of him. 16 But all Israel and Judah loved David, because he led them in their campaigns.** NIV.

In these verses I learned that my success would be my greatest protection.

Saul was afraid to touch David because he was so publicly successful. At the same time, my success would make me an even greater target in the same way Saul continuously looked for a way to destroy David.

I remember a time when a sister in Christ was in a divorce court and she was up against her husband who was an attorney while she was fighting to protect her children. She was a homemaker who had no experience in a court of law and here she was, up against those who were trying to intimidate her. She was lost as to how to defend herself against those who were trying to discredit her character. In a way, I felt what she must have felt. Here I was, with little experience in ministry politics and I was up against those who were very shrewd in convincing the public of a spiritual image that was cleverly orchestrated. But dare I tell anyone? Who would believe me?

"Our vulnerability becomes our weakness because we have given someone the power to destroy us from the inside out."

At the same time, I still felt a need to protect the leader under whom I had served. Perhaps it was because David was Saul's armor bearer that he continued to protect Saul.

In 1 Samuel 24:3-7, we read how David had the chance to rid himself of Saul but he didn't take advantage of the opportunity. The story unfolded as follows:

He came to the sheep pens along the way; a cave was there, and Saul went in to relieve himself. David and his men were far back in the cave. The men said, "This is the day the LORD spoke of when he said to you, 'I will give your enemy into your hands for you to deal with as you wish.'" Then David crept up unnoticed and cut off a corner of Saul's robe. Afterward, David was conscience-stricken for having cut off a corner of his robe. He said to his men, "The LORD forbid that I should do such a thing to my master, the LORD's anointed, or lift my hand against him; for he is the anointed of the LORD." With these words David rebuked his men and did not allow them to attack Saul. And Saul left the cave and went his way." NIV

No matter how much someone has tried to harm you, have you found yourself wanting peace and reconciliation? Do you find yourself appealing for friendship? In 1 Samuel 24:11, David said to Saul, **"See, my father, look at this piece of your robe in my hand! I cut off the corner of your robe but did not kill you."** NIV. Did you notice David called Saul **"my father"**?

There are some leaders who we feel so close to that they become like a parent to us. Whether as a mother or a father, we have allowed them into our heart. Our vulnerability becomes our weakness because we have given someone the power to destroy us from the inside out.

Who have you allowed into your heart? Have they proven to be safe or how have they hurt you?

Sadly, some leaders who know they have an impact on a disciple fully use this situation to manipulate their own interest. Instead of using their influence to help a disciple reach their God-given potential, they are filled with envy and jealousy and justify their action as protecting the kingdom. Sadly, what they are protecting is their own kingdom.

In David's story, time and time again, he tried to reason with Saul. In response to David's appeals, Saul said in 1 Samuel 26:25, **"May you be blessed, my son David; you will do great things and surely triumph."** NIV.

No matter how much David wanted to believe Saul's kind words of affirmation, he had to assess whether he could trust Saul's statements. In my own life, I would leave meetings thinking there was peace, only knowing in the core of my being that I was just kidding myself. When jealousy is the root of someone's behavior, they will stop at nothing. From the beginning pages of the book of Genesis, God showed me

how Cain's jealously resulted in his killing of his brother Abel. In a similar way, once jealousy takes root in a leader's heart, those who threaten them become the target of their vengeance.

1 Samuel 27: 1 taught me through David's assessment of his situation with Saul. It reads: **"But David thought to himself, "One of these days I will be destroyed by the hand of Saul. The best thing I can do is to escape to the land of the Philistines. Then Saul will give up searching for me anywhere in Israel, and I will slip out of his hand."** NIV.

Learning from David, I knew the best strategy for me was to hide in a cave. This means I had to accept the rejection and move on. This means writing the words "The End" and stop regretting how things could have been. This means no longer trying to have peace and simply staying out of the way of the person who is writhing with jealousy.

Is there someone in your life who is jealous of you? How have they hurt you by the way they expressed their jealousy?

"No matter what had transpired, I still held a deep love for the one who I once esteemed highly."

Through David's story, God showed me how the story ended. 1 Samuel 31:2-6 tells me: **The Philistines pressed hard after Saul and his sons, and they killed his sons Jonathan, Abinadab and Malki-Shua. The fighting grew fierce around Saul, and when the archers overtook him, they wounded him critically. Saul said to his armor-bearer, "Draw your sword and run me through, or these uncircumcised fellows will come and run me through and abuse me." But his armor-bearer was terrified and would not do it; so Saul took his own sword and fell on it. When the armor-bearer saw that Saul was dead, he too fell on his sword and died with him. So Saul and his three sons and his armor-bearer and all his men died together that same day.** NIV

When I read how the story ended for Saul I was broken hearted. I asked myself how I would feel if the leader I so loved were to lose a place of honor. I found myself grieving. I knew then that no matter what had transpired, I still held a deep love for the one who I once esteemed highly. I wonder if this is the situation for many biological or spiritual children. No matter how you have been abused, there is something in a child's heart that longs for reconciliation with the parent. In David's case, we are told in 2 Samuel 1:11-12, **"Then David and all the men with him took hold of their clothes and tore them. They mourned and wept and fasted till evening for Saul and his son Jonathan, and for the army of the LORD and the house of Israel, because they had fallen by the sword."** NIV.

We know the depth of our love when we find ourselves wanting forgiveness more than we want justice. No matter how someone has hurt us, we desire restoration. We find ourselves ready to forgive before they even ask for it.

But the sad truth is, some will never ask for forgiveness. Instead of seeking peace, they look for reasons to stay divided. I wonder today if it's time for you to let go of a relationship and let God work out the end of the story.

Have you been keeping a low profile to avoid the wrath of a leader you served? How does knowing how God protected his calling in David's life help you to feel less alone in your rejection?

I remember a time when I served a leader who was a mover and shaker in the community. Over time, I observed he was still dealing with wounds from a past rejection. As a result, he would project on me attributes I did not possess. If he asked me to do a project and I was unable to do it, he would take things personally. Every time someone said "No", he was unable to see what was going on in their lives. He saw everything through the lens of his own personal rejection. Everything was about him. Every time I saw him coming towards me, the lyrics of a particular country western song would play in my head. The lyrics of that song went something like this, "You've picked a fine time to leave me Lucille. Four hungry children and crops in the field…" I found myself wanting to scream out, "I am not Lucille!"

Sadly, there are leaders who live with phantoms from the past. No matter how much you try to interrupt their negative patterns with new evidence, they will convince themselves that they are always right. They will gather evidence against you to reinforce and to justify their own behavior. I wonder today if you need healing from God's Word over rejection from a leader you esteemed highly.

As a member of God's royal family, I am to model the behavior of faith heroes who finished well. From the example of David, God taught me to keep my distance, to forgive immediately and regularly, and to always have a heart that is open to restoration and friendship. Are you part of God's royal family? Then may you follow His royal way!

Rejected by Those You are Leading

Situation: Has your team ever changed your marching orders because they have their own agenda or solutions to the issues? Do your team members blame you for the decision when challenges are encountered in the mission?

The purpose of the personal journal entries shown below is to capture the rejection I felt from those God called me to lead. Some entries were taken from an actual journal, others were written more recently as I reflected on what I was feeling at the time. The dates of the entries are approximate and were included to give the reader some sense of chronological history. After reading the personal journal entries capturing the emotion of rejection, please go to the section in the Bible Study that contains God's truths which addressed this emotion. In teaching this material, feel free to use my personal journal entries as illustration or personalize your lesson with writing your own personal journal entries or testimony to capture the emotion of rejection you felt in your own life. If you did not keep a journal, then try to relive the situation in your mind and write an entry today to capture what you felt at the time.

May 15, 2001

Dear God,
We are in the middle of a high risk project. In a first time event, we are trying to rally three thousand women.

I will do as you instruct God but you know as well as I do that we live in a culture that has a short attention span. If we don't show success, we will have major mutiny among the troops. It's just a fact God. So I just need to ask you to give us a miracle if you want the people to keep following.

If you want me to look totally silly God, that's your prerogative. I'm o.k. with looking silly because I know you want this conference for the women of the city. But I don't think this dream is about me. I think it's about what you want to build for the women. So I just wanted to say God, that I am trusting you to give favor to your leader so the people will keep following.

I know there are those who have already declared defeat. They are waving the white flag when we haven't even begun. God, why is it that we have to make up for the faith that others lack? It's like we have to believe for them. Do we also add to our task list and the number of hours we have to work to make up for what they fail to do? Is this what leadership is all about? Is it about believing you and walking with you even when others have stopped?

August 15, 2004

Dear God,
I know you say you don't want anyone on the team who acts like hired help. You are offended when someone negotiates their wages. You want servants who serve as sons and daughters. I let them go God, I know that's what you wanted. Still, inside, I am broken hearted that they did not trust

you as their leader and provider. Did they think you would not protect those who honor you? God, how do you feel about the person who left? Are you broken hearted too?

Sept 7, 2006

Dear God,
Anytime you require more faith, I see how those who feel stretched will start taking shots at the leader. I get blamed a lot God for what you are asking for. I wish there was some way you could shout from heaven so people will know it's your idea and not mine. I wonder how Moses felt when the people he was leading rebelled against him. All he was doing was leading people to your blessing. Yet when what you require is faith and when people don't want to take a risk, they will resent the request. If you were standing here, would they take a swing at you? When they take a swing at me, are they really hitting you?

What do you want me to do God? It breaks my heart to think that those you intended to receive the blessing will lose what you had originally designed for them. God, will you give them a second chance?

The corresponding truths God taught me from His Word to address my situation
Feel free to continue reading all my personal journals in Module Two expressing feelings of rejection before reading the Bible Study. Or you may continue with the corresponding Bible study which contains God's truths in addressing the situation described in the above journal entries with additional truths God taught me to address situations that were not included in my journal entries. If you choose to personalize this curriculum as your way to bond with the group you are leading, feel free not only to use your own testimony and personal journal entries but in the Bible study part, include what God taught you from His Word in your situations of rejection.

Rejected by Those You are Leading

Situation: Has your team ever changed your marching orders because they have their own agenda or solutions to the issues? Do your team members blame you for the decision when challenges are encountered in the mission?

Reminder: Let's learn the truths from God's Word that speak to our situations. Remember that as a member of God's royal family, we are to act according to the customs of the royal family. This means reinforcing our royal identity by living according to God's specific instructions in the Bible. When we cannot find specific instructions that speak to our situation, we are to search our spiritual heritage and model our lives after God's faith heroes who responded correctly to situations that parallel our own. We can also learn from their mistakes to avoid making the same mistakes in our own lives.

There are times when I feel like I am on a major performance treadmill. I would love to think that those I lead would remain faithful and consistent no matter how turbulent the challenges. But I know we live in a microwave culture. I know that if those who follow do not see results quickly, many will wander off to other causes. It's like God is on some kind of deadline. People will commit to following God for six months, for a year, perhaps even three years. But drag out the timeline and you will be amazed how many will wander off to follow a different dream.

When Moses accepted God's call to lead the children of Israel out of Egypt, I wonder if he expected the people to question his leadership every time they faced a challenge. If you have been entrusted with dreams you are bringing to reality for a family, business, church, ministry, community or nation, manage your expectations. No matter how the people may be praising you one day, rest assured they have a tolerance level for challenges. As soon as the challenges mount past their point of tolerance, be prepared that they will be ready to throw you out. It matters little how much you have endured or sacrificed. It matters little how long you have served. Yesterday's miracles are yesterday's headliner stories. People will make decisions based on what you have done for them today to protect their own comfort level.

"Anytime the situation calls for a greater level of faith, you can be sure that most people will question the mission."

When the children of Israel arrived at the Promise Land, Moses sent in scouts to survey the land. They returned with the following report in Numbers 13:27-29, **"We went into the land to which you sent us, and it does flow with milk and honey! Here is its fruit. But the people who live there are powerful and the cities are fortified and very large. We even saw descendants of Anak there. The Amalekites live in the Negev; the Hittites, Jebusites and Amorites live in the hill country; and the Canaanites live near the sea and along the Jordan." NIV.**

I wonder if those you are leading have ever received a report showing them that it will take more than they expected to win the victory. Perhaps the battle will require longer hours. Perhaps it will require more resources. Perhaps there will be losses and risks along the way in order to win the battle. Anytime the situation calls for a greater level of faith, you can be sure that most people will question the mission.

When the grumbling begins, praise God for raising up one such as Caleb who said in Numbers 13:30, **"We should go up and take possession of the land, for we can certainly do it."** Praise God for an Aaron who will fall on his face with you before God to plead His mercy. Numbers 14:5-9 tells us: **Then Moses and Aaron fell facedown in front of the whole Israelite assembly gathered there. Joshua son of Nun and Caleb son of Jephunneh, who were among those who had explored the land, tore their clothes and said to the entire Israelite assembly, "The land we passed through and explored is** exceedingly good. If the LORD is pleased with us, he will lead us into that land, a land flowing with milk and honey, and will give it to us. Only do not rebel against the LORD. And do not be afraid of the people of the land, because we will swallow them up. Their protection is gone, but the LORD is with us. Do not be afraid of them."** NIV.

"If God gave you the specifics for a mission, know that God's leader is entrusted with the mission until it is accomplished."

You will need your Calebs, Aarons and Joshuas during the times when the people do not have the faith to keep going. But woe is the day when you find your own leadership siding with the people and rising up against you. Even in such a situation, know that God expects His leader to keep going forward with the vision. Even in times when no one believes, the leader must have the faith to believe for the entire community.

How are those you are leading rebelling against you? Who are your Aaron, Caleb, and Nun? How have your Aaron, Caleb, and Nun shown their support?

Unfortunately in Moses case, even with the backing of a few of his leaders, Numbers 14:1-4 tells us, **"That night all the people of the community raised their voices and wept aloud. All the Israelites grumbled against Moses and Aaron, and the whole assembly said to them, "If only we had died in Egypt! Or in this desert! Why is the LORD bringing us to this land only to let us fall by the sword? Our wives and children will be taken as plunder. Wouldn't it be better for us to go back to Egypt?" And they said to each other, "We should choose a leader and go back to Egypt."** NIV

The sad truth is, when the people rise up against God's leader, not only do the people pay the price but the leader pays the cost as well. In judgment of the people, God says in Numbers 14:26-35, **"How long will this wicked community grumble against me? I have heard the complaints of these grumbling Israelites. So tell them, 'As surely as I live, declares the LORD, I will do to you the very things I heard you say: In this desert your bodies will fall...For forty years — one year for each of the forty days you explored the land — you will suffer for your sins and know what it is like to have me against you.' I, the LORD, have spoken, and I will surely do these things to this whole wicked community, which has banded together against me. They will meet their end in this desert; here they will die."** NIV.

In the ministry of Inspire Women, God taught me that even when the mission is delayed by those who lack faith I don't get to say to God, "Well, I led them to the edge of the Promise land. If they don't have the faith to enter, that shouldn't impact my life."

I tried to argue with God that He should release me and that I have finished the assignment. But God showed me in His Word that when the people will not follow God's leader, it will delay the timing to reach God's intended end. I learned that I do not have the freedom to give God a deadline. I don't get to say, "God, you have one year to finish this assignment or else I'm leaving."

God called Moses to lead the children of Israel to the Promise Land, Moses is not finished until God's people enter the Promise Land. God does not change the mission He stated at the beginning. If God gave you the specifics for a mission, know that God's leader is entrusted with the mission until it is accomplished.

If you have been rejected by those you are leading, how will you respond knowing that God still wants His mission finished?

"Don't water down God's requirements as a way to get people to follow."

Have you ever tried to put artificial deadlines or terms of employment on your calling? In the New Testament, God shows me the story of how a teacher of the law went to Jesus in Matthew 8:19 and said, **"Teacher, I will follow you wherever you go."** NIV. To this declaration, Jesus replied in Matthew 8:20, **"Foxes have holes and birds of the air have nests, but the Son of Man has no place to lay his head."**

From this interchange, God taught me that Jesus had to tell the teacher that God will not give you the terms of service. There is no contractual agreement for location, wages, or work hours. What God wants are sons and daughters who will serve an eternal agenda! God is not looking for hired help who wants to negotiate the terms. This truth helped me greatly to understand the kind of personnel God appoints for a God-sized mission.

As a leader, be careful that you don't water down God's requirements as a way to get people to follow. At Inspire Women, we don't try to paint an easy picture of ministry. We are not trying to get women to sign up like a recreation club. There are times when God will lead me to deliberately change the terms just to see how someone will react. Are they able to flow with God or do they see their ministry as a contract? By their reaction, they reveal their motives. Ministry is not a career, but the sad truth is, it is looking more and more like corporate America.

Has someone left the team because they negotiated different terms for themselves elsewhere? How does knowing that Jesus would not guarantee terms help you with handling your response to those who have left?

"If you are a leader wrestling with the fact that some have left, ask yourself if they really understood the mission."

Before Jesus ascended into heaven, He commissioned His followers to share the gospel with the world. In fulfilling this mandate, we read in Acts 13:2-3: **While they were worshiping the Lord and fasting, the Holy Spirit said, "Set apart for me Barnabas and Saul for the work to which I have called them." So after they had fasted and prayed, they placed their hands on them and sent them off.** NIV. Observe that Barnabas and Saul were "**set apart**" for the work God called them to. Both were equally called and set apart. We also discover that John Mark was on the team. However he did not stay to complete the mission. Acts 13:13-14 reads: **From Paphos, Paul and his companions sailed to Perga in Pamphylia, where John left them to return to Jerusalem.** NIV

Why did John Mark leave the team? The International Standard Bible Encyclopedia said: "Not because of homesickness, or anxiety for his mother's safety, or home duties, or the desire to rejoin Peter, or fear of the perils incident to the journey, but rather because he objected to the offer of salvation to the Gentiles on condition of faith alone." Did you know that when your heart is not aligned with the mission, it's hard to stay committed to the leader?

If you are a leader wrestling with the fact that some have left, ask yourself if they really understood the mission. As with Mark, there could be a fundamental difference in what they believed God wants in ministry compared to the ministry God called you to do. Mark did not recognize God's timing and His method to reach the Gentiles by faith alone. When those who were so excited to be part of Inspire Women wander off, God's Word tells me that they may not have understood God's timing and method to mobilize His daughters as His way to complete His spiritual army.

In the midst of those who might leave, we see how God sets apart those who will remain faithful. Paul and Barnabas and Mark were a team. Imagine losing a third of your personnel or assets! God, in His grace, kept Barnabas and Paul walking together. For the trials that were ahead, Paul needed a Barnabas by his side.

Acts 13:49-50 tells us **"the Jews incited the God-fearing women of high standing and the leading men of the city. They stirred up persecution against Paul and Barnabas, and expelled them from their region."** NIV.

As the journey unfolded, Acts 14:19-20 tells us: **Then some Jews came from Antioch and Iconium and won the crowd over. They stoned Paul and dragged him outside the city, thinking he was dead. But after the disciples had gathered around him, he got up and went back into the city. The next day he and Barnabas left for Derbe.** NIV.

Did you notice the words "**he and Barnabas left for Derbe**"? In the midst of his personal suffering, can you imagine what it meant to Paul to have a Barnabas to walk beside him on his way to Derbe? Can you imagine getting up after the world has left you for dead without having a Barnabas to continue the journey with?

In your life, if those you are leading choose to leave, will you trust that God is perfectly able to set apart a Barnabas to walk with you till the finish? Who do you think is your Barnabas? How will you know when you have finished?

In the story "Lord of the Rings" by J.R.R. Tolkien, the story of Frodo who is a young hobbit entrusted with carrying a ring to Rivendell. In the face of fear, despair and betrayal, Frodo finds the only person he could trust was Sam. After many miles of travel when Frodo was exhausted, he faced the daunting challenge of going up a mountain from which he was to toss the ring into the valley thereby destroying its power to enslave the inhabitants of Middle-earth. As fatigue overwhelmed him, he turned to Sam and appealed to him to take the ring to the top of the mountain. Sam refused saying that he was not the one entrusted with the ring. Then in a grand gesture of friendship, Sam carried Frodo. He would not carry the ring but he would carry Frodo to the top of the mountain so he could then toss the ring into the valley.

In a similar way that Sam was to Frodo, Barnabas was to Paul. Paul was the one God entrusted with sharing the gospel with the Gentiles. Though Paul and Barnabas were together, it was Paul who was identified as the leader. Those Paul was called to lead rejected him, but Barnabas stayed by Paul's side as an encouragement to help him to continue in their missionary work. The story ended in Acts 14:27 when the two of them "**sailed back to Antioch, where they had been committed to the grace of God for the work they had now completed.**" NIV Did you see the word "**completed**"? In the midst of those who may reject you, trust God to send a Barnabas to walk beside you till you complete the work God has set you apart to do.

Rejected by Those with Money

Situation: Have you ever counted on someone for your financial provision based on their pledge and later they decided to redirect their funds to something else? Do you feel the rejection of those with financial ability?

The purpose of the personal journal entries shown below is to capture the rejection from those who withdrew support. Some entries were taken from an actual journal, others were written more recently as I reflected on what I was feeling at the time. The dates of the entries are approximate and were included to give the reader some sense of chronological history. After reading the personal journal entries capturing the emotion of rejection, please go to the section in the Bible Study that contains God's truths which addressed this emotion. In teaching this material, feel free to use my personal journal entries as illustration or personalize your lesson with writing your own personal journal entries or testimony to capture the emotion of rejection you felt in your own life. If you did not keep a journal, then try to relive the situation in your mind and write an entry today to capture what you felt at the time.

July 15, 1988

Dear God,
In corporate America, when people make a financial commitment they usually keep it because they are bound by contract. I am learning so much about how things work in church. Someone offered to pay for a church mailing and then it was though they got a different message from you and switch directions. I am seeing that those who say they are led by you are really led by themselves. How could it be that you have all this start and stop commotion?

I don't understand why people don't just admit that they are breaking a commitment. They want to hide behind some spiritual front. They say you led them elsewhere. Why would you lead them elsewhere when nothing has changed in the mission? In fact, things are going stronger than ever before. So what sense would it make for

you to launch a rocket and then instruct someone not to give the rocket any fuel? But I'm new to all this in the ministry world, so I had better keep my mouth shut. I'm just watching God. Teach me how I should respond. Do I let people believe they are spiritual when they have clearly hurt your mission?

Sept 22, 2003

Dear God,
I'm not sure what happened. You were there when the promise was made. When someone walks away from a commitment, are they breaking the promise to me, to our ministry or are they really breaking the promise to you? I have never seen this kind of duplicity before God and I feel like I've had my head in my seminary books for so long that I am totally disconnected from the real world. Out here in real life, I see those who quote your word. I see their

names in programs as role models of generosity; I also see a big show going on. How did giving turn out to be such a show? Am I supposed to say something God? Or do I just let people say unkind things to me because you will talk to them?

Aug 4, 2006

Dear God,
Why are we playing this game? Do you need money to advance your work? Since you own all the cattle on the hill, you can just say the word and the finances will be provided. I see those who raise funds tiptoeing around the supporters who are volatile. Someone called today to threaten the ministry. They said they had influence and will tell all their friends if we don't do what they say. They wanted us to know that if it were their word versus our word, their friends would support them. How did it come to this God? Will you let your leaders be blackmailed? I think you would choose for us to do without the funds if we have to compromise your honor to accept the funds. I told her "No". I know she was not pleased and assured me she would let others know of her displeasure. God, why are my insides trembling? Why am I afraid to be rejected by those who use their influence to lord themselves over others?

The corresponding truths God taught me from His Word to address my situation
Feel free to continue reading all my personal journals in Module Two expressing feelings of rejection before reading the Bible Study. Or you may continue with the corresponding Bible study which contains God's truths in addressing the situation described in the above journal entries with additional truths God taught me to address situations that were not included in my journal entries. If you choose to personalize this curriculum as your way to bond with the group you are leading, feel free not only to use your own testimony and personal journal entries but in the Bible study part, include what God taught you from His Word in your situations of rejection.

196

Rejected by Those with Money

Situation: Have you ever counted on someone for your financial provision based on their pledge and later they decided to redirect their funds to something else? Do you feel the rejection of those with financial ability?

Reminder: Let's learn the truths from God's Word that speak to our situations. Remember that as a member of God's royal family, we are to act according to the customs of the royal family. This means reinforcing our royal identity by living according to God's specific instructions in the Bible. When we cannot find specific instructions that speak to our situation, we are to search our spiritual heritage and model our lives after God's faith heroes who responded correctly to situations that parallel our own. We can also learn from their mistakes to avoid making the same mistakes in our own lives.

When God first trusted me with appealing for funds to train women for ministry, I had never attended a fundraiser. I had no idea how to organize a fundraiser. I was also totally ignorant of how some donors expected to be treated. I had spent seven years in seminary with my head in God's Word. My reality was God's Word and I felt like a fish out of water while swimming through waters in the physical world.

"God will not tolerate those who lie to Him and portray themselves as being more sacrificial or giving than they are."

God's Word has always been my counselor and safe place. So when I experienced the rejection or unkind criticism from those God entrusted with wealth, I asked God to show me in His Word what the problem was.

God brought me to the story of Ananias and Sapphira in Acts 5:1-6. The story goes like this: **Now a man named Ananias, together with his wife Sapphira, also sold a piece of property.**

With his wife's full knowledge he kept back part of the money for himself, but brought the rest and put it at the apostles' feet. Then Peter said, "Ananias, how is it that Satan has so filled your heart that you have lied to the Holy Spirit and have kept for yourself some of the money you received for the land? Didn't it belong to you before it was sold? And after it was sold, wasn't the money at your disposal? What made you think of doing such a thing? You have not lied to men but to God." When Ananias heard this, he fell down and died. And great fear seized all who heard what had happened. Then the young men came forward, wrapped up his body, and carried him out and buried him. NIV

What God taught me through this story was not to take things personally if anyone portrays themselves publicly as giving to the ministry when the facts do not line up with what they have truly given. He showed me that there exists a community that gives to have their names displayed. They think of themselves as doing God a favor. They know nothing about the concept of sacrificial giving. Their gift is small relative to what they have been trusted with but they want everyone to think that they have given much. They want their name on a program and desire the credit though they know full well that they have not done their part. It helped me to see in God's word that He will deal with those who give insincerely.

The story of Ananias and Sapphira showed me that God is not blind. He will reveal all secrets. He does not play games. God will not tolerate those who lie to Him and portray themselves as being more sacrificial or giving than they are.

I learned that the godly leaders entrusted with wealth are kind hearted. They do not lord themselves over others. They are grieved when they are unable to help. I also learned that my ability to get up every time I am rejected is the result of purifying my own heart. God showed me in His Word that the Apostle Paul encouraged the church to give and to keep their pledges. He said in 2 Corinthians 8:8-12, **"I am not commanding you, but I want to test the sincerity of your love by comparing it with the earnestness of others. For you know the grace of our Lord Jesus Christ, that though he was rich, yet for your sakes he became poor, so that you through his poverty might become rich. And here is my advice about what is best for you in this matter: Last year you were the first not only to give but also to have the desire to do so. Now finish the work, so that your eager willingness to do it may be matched by your completion of it, according to your means.** NIV.

"Have I given all that I am able? If not, let me focus on myself."

When I look at the life of the Apostle Paul I discover that one reason he is so able to appeal to others to give radically is because he personally has given radically. We cannot lead others where we have not been ourselves. Paul said in Acts 20:33-35, **"I have not coveted anyone's silver or gold or clothing. You yourselves know that these hands of mine have supplied my own needs and the needs of my companions. In everything I did, I showed you that by this kind of hard work we must help the weak, remembering the words the Lord Jesus himself said: 'It is more blessed to give than to receive.'"** NIV.

In the example of the Apostle Paul, God taught me how to get up every time I am rejected when I make an appeal for funds. Instead of taking rejection personally and being offended by the person who did not respond to my appeal, I need to examine my own heart in the way that I give. Have I given all that I am able? If not, let me focus on myself.

Paul encouraged believers to give cheerfully. His ability to lead others to give was a result of his own generosity. In 2 Thessalonians 3:7-10, he tells us, **"For you yourselves know how you ought to follow our example. We were not idle when we were with you, nor did we eat anyone's food without paying for it. On the contrary, we worked night and day, laboring and toiling so that we would not be a burden to any of you. We did this, not because we do not have the right to such help, but in order to make ourselves a model for you to follow."** NIV.

In Paul's words, I see the attitude of his heart. He did not go around demanding rights or payment for his services. He gave freely of himself so that no one would question his motive. He did not get a commission nor did he negotiate a raise. His service was pure. As a result, he could with clear conscience challenge others to give radically for God's purpose.

If God has called you to be the leader to inspire others to give, what have you done sacrificially? Does your team or those watching your life see you as sacrificial? Or do they resent what you are requiring of them as compared to what you require of yourself?

The more I serve in ministry, the more I find God requiring of me. What I also see is how iron sharpens iron. The staff who serve at Inspire Women inspire me. When I see how they walk away from the security of a corporate career to trust God for their provision I know they are not serving God for a paycheck. When I found out that one of them closed her bank account because there were no funds in it or cancelled a medical insurance policy to trust God with her health, it moves me to give more. When a volunteer gives Inspire Women her house, I am moved to tears by that level of commitment to biblical training for God's daughters. When I see each of the staff purchase a table at our annual luncheon fundraiser when the lowest table cost is $1200, I know someone is fasting and doing without in order to pay for this table. In learning from the Apostle Paul and how he inspired others to give, I know that one reason God continues to bless the efforts of the staff in their appeals to the city to fund the training of women for ministry is because they give cheerfully.

The next time you experience rejection from those who resist giving, ask yourself how cheerful is your giving. Do you feel like you have given God all your time and that actually God owes you something? Do you feel like you could have this big paycheck from corporate America so God should pat you on the back for serving in ministry at such a reduced rate? If you have this kind of attitude, thank God for the rejection you have experienced. Could it be because God is blocking your efforts to try to get your attention? What is God requiring from you before you can ask the same sacrifice from others?

"God's servants are to serve out of a cheerful heart that gives freely of our time and resources."

When David was rallying the people to give to building the temple, he said in 1 Chronicles 22:14, "**I have taken great pains to provide for the temple of the LORD a hundred thousand talents of gold, a million talents of silver, quantities of bronze and iron too great to be weighed, and wood and stone**." NIV. David began by being an example in giving. Not only did he give of his resources but he gave in the way he appealed to all his connections.

1 Chronicles 22:17-19 reads, "**Then David ordered all the leaders of Israel to help his son Solomon**." If you have asked others to bring their friends on board to support the cause and have encountered resistance, then ask yourself, "Have you rallied all your friends and connections?" We cannot lead others down a road we ourselves have not traveled.

God's servants are to serve out of a cheerful heart that gives freely of our time and resources. It is with this heart attitude that we can then make our appeals for God's kingdom. This heart attitude is also for our protection. If you are rejected, you know you had nothing personal at stake. You were not asking for yourself but for the Kingdom. You were simply inviting someone into the same cheerfulness you have as God invited you to give.

Have you ever been offended by those who turned down your appeal? If so, why? Did you have anything personal at stake in your appeal?

"It is through the conviction of our message that we will not apologize for the request every time we hit resistance."

I love the story of how Jesus instructed his disciples to ask for something specific. The story goes like this in Mark 11:1-6: **As they approached Jerusalem and came to Bethphage and Bethany at the Mount of Olives, Jesus sent two of his disciples, saying to them, "Go to the village ahead of you, and just as you enter it, you will find a colt tied there, which no one has ever ridden. Untie it and bring it here. If anyone asks you, 'Why are you doing this?' tell him, 'The Lord needs it and will send it back here shortly.'" They went and found a colt outside in the street, tied at a doorway. As they untied it, some people standing there asked, "What are you doing, untying that colt?" They answered as Jesus had told them to, and the people let them go.** NIV.

What God taught me through this story was how I must always test the motive of my heart. Am I asking because of my own reputation? Am I asking because I have something to gain from the request? Or am I asking because **"The Lord needs it"**. What's so amazing in God's economy is how we can never out-give God. Even in this story of Jesus needing the colt, Jesus instructed the disciples to say that they will **"Send it back here shortly."** Could it be that when God asks for something, we never really lose any assets? Instead God will use what we give but we always get back what we give in one way or another.

Interestingly, in this story, there were those who questioned the disciples and said, **"What are you doing, untying the colt?"** What God taught me through this story is to be sure of what I am asking for. Therefore, any question that surfaces is not a rejection of me or the project. Instead, it is our opportunity to answer, **"just as Jesus told them to"**. It is through the conviction of our message that we will not apologize for the request every time we hit resistance.

If you are raising funds, what is your cause? How sure are you that the Lord needs it? How will you respond when someone questions what you are doing?

"When you ask for something to build God's kingdom, you are protecting your supporters from having God blow away their wealth."

When God puts a name on your heart to ask and that person rejects you, trust God's leading. Just because someone said no is not an indication that you misheard God. Realize that you are in the middle of a spiritual warfare. The devil will try to distract those who hold the resources because he does not want God to bless them for their generosity. When you are persistent, be sure you are acting out of a motive to protect the blessing for those God has invited to underwrite His projects. So you are asking for their blessing and not your own.

God showed me this truth in Haggai 1:9-11, where God tells the people, **"You expected much, but see, it turned out to be little. What you brought home, I blew away. Why?" declares the LORD Almighty. "Because of my house, which remains a ruin, while each of you is busy with his own house. Therefore, because of you the heavens have withheld their dew and the earth its crops. I called for a drought on the fields and the mountains, on the grain, the new wine, the oil and whatever the ground produces, on men and cattle, and on the labor of your hands."** NIV

I learned from this dialogue that the people **"expected much"** because their logic dictated to them the return on their investment. But God deliberately blew away the wealth that was projected based on their human made plans because their focus was on being **"busy with his own house."** Next time you make an appeal, know that when you ask for something to build God's kingdom, you are protecting your supporters from having God blow away their wealth.

How will you make your appeal knowing that when you ask someone to support God's cause, it is your best way to love them and to help them to protect their wealth?

God proves to me time and time again that He does not need our assets. However, He allows us to be part of something significant. He tests our hearts through how we handle our treasure. I wonder today if you heard God's spirit prompt you to release your assets. Did you pass the test?

One of Inspire Women's supporters called me one day and said God told her to share her story with me. She said she had been to an event where I had invited the audience to fund a scholarship for women for biblical training. She said the Holy Spirit prompted her to give but she was trying to stall. So she said to herself that she would wait till she got home to check on her finances first. But then something compelled her to write the check. She said she wrote the check and turned it in to one of the staff. On her way home, she ran into something on the road and her car began to flip. She said it turned over several times and she saw her life flashed in front of her. The next thought that entered her mind was, "I am so glad I wrote that check." Although God spared her life, she wanted me to know how much she appreciated me for asking for her support. She said, "If you had not asked I would not have given. What would have happened had I died that day when my car flipped over? I did not want my last act to be that of not writing the check when God asked for my help."

God shows me time and time again that when He places on my heart to make an appeal for support, it is God's way to bless those He is inviting to sow financially into His work. Those who lord it over others because of their financial ability and make God's servant feel bad about asking are misinformed. God does not need their money. On the other hand, they are the ones who need to give for their own protection. They will not be able to take their funds with them when their time on earth is over. Jim Elliot who died as a missionary among the Auca Indians once said, "He is no fool who gives what he cannot keep to gain what he cannot lose."

Rejected by Those Who Criticize You

Situation: Have you ever felt like someone has been critical of you to the point of rejection? Do you find yourself having a hard time rising above their negative opinions?

The purpose of the personal journal entries shown below is to capture the rejection I felt from those who criticized me. Some entries were taken from an actual journal, others were written more recently as I reflected on what I was feeling at the time. The dates of the entries are approximate and were included to give the reader some sense of chronological history. After reading the personal journal entries capturing the emotion of rejection, please go to the section in the Bible Study that contains God's truths which addressed this emotion. In teaching this material, feel free to use my personal journal entries as illustration or personalize your lesson with writing your own personal journal entries or testimony to capture the emotion of rejection you felt in your own life. If you did not keep a journal, then try to relive the situation in your mind and write an entry today to capture what you felt at the time.

May 15, 1974

Dear God,
My father does not want people to know how my mother died. So we are to tell everyone that she died of a heart attack. He says people will ask fewer questions. It's so amazing how people form opinions all the time with incomplete knowledge. It wasn't my Dad's fault when my Mom lost hope. She allowed hopelessness to consume her heart till it finally suffocated the life out of her. God, can we feel so hopeless to the point that our heart just dies? I don't know how to make it through the next days. The teachers at school nominated me to be the President of the study body. I'm declining the nomination. I don't want any kind of limelight. I feel like I have this big secret to hide. What am I ashamed of God? Is there something I'm supposed to be ashamed of? Is it the criticism of the others that I dread? I'll just transfer to a different school where no one knows me. That way, I can pretend better. If no one knows the details then no one can criticize.

Feb 22, 1992

Dear God,
I can't believe I forgot my own testimony. If you hadn't rescued me, I would have just stood on that stage and nothing would have come out of my mouth. What happened, God? I looked into her eyes and I allowed her look to distract me. You did not send me to an audience to win their approval. You sent me with your message and I totally blew it. I forgot my calling and I started trying to win some popularity contest. I wasn't sent there to get votes. I was sent because you have a purpose and the people in that audience only have so much time before their time is over. You sent me with an urgent message to refocus them to what you cared about. I totally blew it God because I allowed their lack of urgency to throw me off track.

How could I have allowed myself to be afraid of people I don't even know? I traded my fear of the Lord for my fear of man. I am so sorry God. Please forgive me!

June 15, 2002

Dear God,
Did you see the look in his eyes when he looked at me? I could tell in his eyes that he thought I was just a silly woman who had these grandiose ideas that God could possibly use me. I got scared God and when he asked me a direct question on how I planned on raising an endowment for women for biblical training I did not have a plan. How do I tell him that you speak daily and you give me your instructions at your pace? He would think I fell off a truck.

The way he talks, I feel like he knows all the Bible facts but he doesn't know your heart. So why would I let someone like that make me feel stupid? I'm so sorry God that he made me afraid. I was embarrassed to tell him that I was following your plan. Was there something in me that longed for his acceptance? Why would I even care to get the blessing of someone who showed no mercy for your daughters?

I am grateful for the leaders in seminary. They told me to keep going. They told me to keep believing. I wonder what people do when they don't have encouragement to balance the criticism. I think unless you intervened, I would have been so crushed. I know I say I'll just go home but you know and I know that I would never have any peace. I would always feel like I left something unfinished. So I guess, God, this means it doesn't matter how much people criticize, I will keep going. I would rather be criticized as being radical for you than criticized for not finishing. God, please help me to finish well.

The corresponding truths God taught me from His Word to address my situation
Feel free to continue reading all my personal journals in Module Two expressing feelings of rejection before reading the Bible Study. Or you may continue with the corresponding Bible study which contains God's truths in addressing the situation described in the above journal entries with additional truths God taught me to address situations that were not included in my journal entries. If you choose to personalize this curriculum as your way to bond with the group you are leading, feel free not only to use your own testimony and personal journal entries but in the Bible study part, include what God taught you from His Word in your situations of rejection.

Rejected by Those who Criticize You

Situation: Have you ever felt like someone has been critical of you to the point of rejection? Do you find yourself having a hard time rising above their negative opinions?

Reminder: Let's learn the truths from God's Word that speak to our situations. Remember that as a member of God's royal family, we are to act according to the customs of the royal family. This means reinforcing our royal identity by living according to God's specific instructions in the Bible. When we cannot find specific instructions that speak to our situation, we are to search our spiritual heritage and model our lives after God's faith heroes who responded correctly to situations that parallel our own. We can also learn from their mistakes to avoid making the same mistakes in our own lives.

Have you ever wondered why the number one fear in adults is the fear of public speaking? When I read this in a report, it brought back memories of the time when I was sharing my personal journey with an audience. In the past when I shared my story I was on a stage with bright floodlights which lit up the stage, but also blinded me. I was unable to see the expressions on the faces in the crowd. But in this particular speaking engagement, I was standing a few feet from the front row and could see the look in the eyes of the women who were listening to my talk. Half way through the talk, while giving a chronological account of my life I could not remember what happened next. For a moment, there was absolute silence. A friend of mine who was sitting in the audience said to me later, "Everyone else thought you were just feeling emotional but I knew you had completely lost your train of thought and started to pray like crazy that God would help you to remember."

"God did not send me into the crowd to get their acceptance. God sent me to redirect their focus to His plans for the world."

I remembered praying a panic prayer and saying to God, "If you don't rescue me we're just going to stand here and say nothing." I could literally feel the second God rescued me and I finished the talk as if nothing had happened. But I knew something happened on that stage and I needed to get to the bottom of it lest it happens again. That evening, in my hotel room, I inquired of the Lord. "Examine my heart, God", I cried, "and show me what happened tonight!"

God took me back to the exact moment when I froze. It was when I looked into the eyes of one of the women sitting in the front row and saw her critical spirit. Was it my hair, my clothes, my ethnic background, my way of speaking that she was criticizing? What trivia was she focused on? I had to face my own insecurities and how I wanted to be accepted. God showed me how He and I had conflicting goals.

God did not send me into the crowd to get their acceptance. God sent me to redirect their focus to His plans for the world. I had to make the decision whether I was living to win the crowd's approval of me as a person or whether my life will be about inspiring those around me to be on the same page with God.

I cannot lead others where I have not gone. So God used the speaking experience to test my heart and to invite me to make a decision. Will I be on God's page, focused on the message He wants to tell the people, or will I be more concerned over trying to fit in so others would not reject me?

"Is my life about getting others to love me or is it about getting them to love God?"

Once you settle in your heart that life is about God then He is the one on stage. We are simply His mouthpiece. Whether we are at home, in the workplace, in a ministry or in the community God sees us as representing His image. In all that we do, God expects us to represent His character and His purpose. He has a purpose for everything not just what happens in church. He has an opinion for your family, your business, your ministry and your community.

When we put ourselves in the correct pecking order of God first, me second, life falls into place. When we accept our calling to serve His purpose in whatever environment He places us in, we are simply earthen vessels who go in His name.

Jesus said in Luke 13:34-35, **"O Jerusalem, Jerusalem, you who kill the prophets and stone those sent to you, how often I have longed to gather your children together, as a hen gathers her chicks under her wings, but you were not willing! Look, your house is left to you desolate. I tell you, you will not see me again until you say, 'Blessed is he who comes in the name of the Lord.'"** NIV.

In Jesus' words I learned that the message He brought was meant to be a blessing but just because our motives are right is no guarantee that the audience will receive us. The fact is those who come to hear us often come with their own personal agendas. What we say may threaten their turf. When we represent God's message, we need to manage our expectations and realize that God often speaks words that will require someone to adjust their priorities. What we say therefore may threaten someone's resources, their career plans or their own aspirations for where they were heading in business or in a ministry. It's not our fault when God's message challenges someone's personal agenda. But the fact is they will take it out on the message bearer.

In Jesus' words I saw how Christ did not allow the critical spirit of those who did not like His message to stop Him from fulfilling God's call on His life. He focused on what His message was intended to do for the people. He did not allow their response to dampen His passion or His zeal because He stayed connected to God's original intentions. I wonder today if the message you are speaking was designed to bless. Then focus on the fact that you were designed to be a blessing and keep blessing no matter what people think.

Have you allowed someone else to convince you that you are a curse instead of a blessing? Has someone's insecurity made you afraid? How have you been apologizing for your calling instead of staying in the blessing of what God has called you to do or say?

"When you know your heart is connected with God's heart, message and timing, then no matter what criticism is directed against you, keep going!"

I am not saying we should treat criticism lightly because a critical spirit could lead to aggressive action to stop you in your tracks. Acts 7:54-60 tells us what happened to Stephen. It reads: **When they heard this, they were furious and gnashed their teeth at him. But Stephen, full of the Holy Spirit, looked up to heaven and saw the glory of God, and Jesus standing at the right hand of God. "Look," he said, "I see heaven open and the Son of Man standing at the right hand of God." At this they covered their ears and, yelling at the top of their voices; they all rushed at him, dragged him out of the city and began to stone him. Meanwhile, the witnesses laid their clothes at the feet of a young man named Saul. While they were stoning him, Stephen prayed, "Lord Jesus, receive my spirit." Then he fell on his** **knees and cried out, "Lord, do not hold this sin against them." When he had said this, he fell asleep.** NIV

In this account of what happened to Stephen, it teaches me that someone's critical spirit could cause them to take action against me. Yet, in spite of this, Stephen never questioned whether he was to speak out. Stephen did not demand God's protection. He trusted in God's decision to do with the situation as He willed. All he was focused on was the content of his message and his certainty that he was in God's timetable.

If we judge situations by the outcome, we might find ourselves saying, "Stephen, maybe you should have been more diplomatic. Maybe you should have won your audience over before you shared so many facts. You didn't have to lie but maybe you shouldn't have revealed all the truth." But Stephen was sure of his content and his timing because God's Word tells us that he was "**Stephen, full of the Spirit**". When you know your heart is connected with God's heart, message and timing, then no matter what criticism is directed against you, keep going! If the outcome turns out in such a way that you get thrown out or your mission is killed, trust that what happens next will fit into God's overall plan!

How incredible that Stephen was so in tune with God that before he was killed, he looked up into heaven and actually saw Jesus standing in his honor. Stephen was the first martyr. Jesus did not apologize for the message He gave Stephen to speak. He knew the people would reject Stephen. He stood in honor in anticipation of the first martyr to be murdered.

Observe that Stephen did not have any kind of personal crisis. He did not say. "God, how could you have allowed this to happen? Here I was doing the very thing you asked me to do. If you are in this, why am I about to be killed?" Up till the very end, Stephen kept his mission pure by keeping his heart connected with God's heart. God sent him with a message to bless the people, so Stephen stayed true to being a blessing up till his last breath. He appealed to the Lord not to hold the people's misguided actions against them.

Have you allowed yourself to be resentful of those who are critical of you? Have you found yourself striking out at them instead of forgiving them? Have you wished for God to judge them and for them to get what they deserve when they stand before God instead of appealing to God for their forgiveness? When we operate out of being the blessing God intended us to be, then no matter how anyone reacts, we find our compass by staying on course.

No matter how someone has tried to hurt you, how can you reel your emotions back to the place of being a blessing to those around you?

"The criticism of a few can entice an entire community against us."

Acts 14:19 tells us of yet another incident where the anger of an audience resulted in their striking out at the message bearer. God's Word reveals the following incident with the Apostle Paul. It reads: **Then some Jews came from Antioch and Iconium and won the crowd over. They stoned Paul and dragged him outside the city, thinking he was dead.** NIV

Did you notice the words that they **"won the crowd over"**? Be prepared that when anyone harbors a personal dislike, they will try to influence everyone else. So don't be surprised if you hear about closed door meetings and you sense people are talking behind your back. When something is brewing, know that it's a matter of time before the discontent boils over. In Paul's case, the anger resulted in his being dragged out of the city and stoned.

This incident taught me that there would be seasons in our journey where the criticism of a few can entice an entire community to be against us. But Paul's story also taught me that when God has a message, we don't get to choose to walk away and never come back. In Paul's case he continued to Derbe and stayed true to his mission.

But then we read in Acts 14:21-22 that **"They preached the good news in that city and won a large number of disciples. Then they returned to Lystra, Iconium and Antioch, strengthening the disciples and encouraging them to remain true to the faith. "** NIV.

Could it possibly be that Paul headed back into Antioch? Realize this is the same Antioch where the Jews came from, who enticed the crowd to stone Paul. In other words, he walked straight back into the very group who was critical of him. We do not get released from our calling just because someone is critical. In fact, you may find that God leads you to walk right back into a critical crowd until God's mission is accomplished. The outcome of Paul's decision was he ended up **"strengthening the disciples and encouraging them to remain true to the faith."**

What group or situation has driven you to take a different path? If God were to send you back into the very group who criticized you, would you go? If not, why not?

"God had to teach me to keep obeying even if I looked like a fool. At the crossroads of life, I learned from Mary's example how to discern God's favor."

There are times when God allows us to be in a place where we become the target of the public's criticism. Luke 1:26-38 tells us the story of how an angel told Mary she would be with child. The angel said, **"Do not be afraid, Mary, you have found favor with God. You will be with child and give birth to a son, and you are to give him the name Jesus. He will be great and will be called the Son of the Most High. The Lord God will give him the throne of his father David, and he will reign over the house of Jacob forever; his kingdom will never end."** NIV.

You can be sure that Mary was afraid. Why wouldn't she be? God was putting her in a situation where she would be the target of everyone's criticism? Do you sometimes feel like God has placed you in a situation where everyone finds something negative to say about you?

What would Mary say to the criticism? If she tried to defend herself, it would be even worse. How would people take the information that she was called to be the mother of the Messiah? Such a claim would sound arrogant. It would evoke further criticism, "Who do you think you are to think that God would appoint you to such a privileged place?"

In Mary's example, we see that she did not dwell on fear or on what people would say. Instead, she focused on the awesomeness of God's appointment and said in Luke 1:46-49, **"My soul glorifies the Lord and my spirit rejoices in God my Savior, for he has been mindful of the humble state of his servant. From now on all generations will call me blessed, for the Mighty One <u>has done great things for me</u>- holy is his name."** NIV. In spite of the expected criticism, she clung to the fact that God **"has done great things for me"**.

When Inspire Women separated as its own independent nonprofit organization, I walked away from a Vice President level at the largest multi-ethnic Bible College in the country to drive off with all my boxes piled up in my backseat. Have you ever handed in the keys to your office and driven off, not knowing where you are heading? I knew some felt I was being stupid. They did not hear the hound of heaven nipping at my heels and pushing me out the door.

I wish I could say that I left boldly but I didn't. I left with tears streaming down my face as I looked at the building I was leaving in my rear mirror. I wonder if you have ever felt silly while following God's voice. Do you wish you could follow quietly where no one can witness the change in your physical condition? I wish God didn't have to display the gestation periods in broad daylight. I wondered if this was how Noah felt when he was building the ark. Everyone watched the silly man build something when there was no rain. I wondered how many thought the very concept of focusing on developing the potential in women was a waste of time! Yes, I must have looked very silly. But then I concluded that God didn't care how silly I looked.

God had to teach me to keep obeying even if I looked like a fool. At the crossroads of life, I learned from Mary's example how to discern God's favor. She must have felt the public ridicule as she walked around unwed and pregnant. In a similar way, the world saw me as walking around with a ministry that was homeless.

It was not exactly a condition that made you want to broadcast it to everyone.

I wondered if Mary wished her pregnancy could be over with quickly so God would announce the Messiah and show the world that her condition was necessary for what He was birthing. I felt like I was carrying the ministry of Inspire Women in my womb but before God established it, I would experience the ridicule of those around me. No one understood how ridiculous I felt to drive away from an established institution to build something with no resources. No one but those close to me understood how much I personally longed for community and staying where I could put down roots.

How do we endure an embarrassing situation that is part of God's plan? The only way is when we know God's Word and therefore can discern His timing and favor in the midst of what appears to the public eye to be a bad situation. I knew this was God's timing for His daughters. I knew that God was showing favor to Houston, Texas to allow the saints of my city to birth the Inspire Women's ministry.

Describe a time when you knew you had found favor with God but your outward situation resulted in rejection by the community.

How does knowing this help you to overcome the rejection?

Did you know that God always has the last word? Inspire Women did not stay homeless for long. Someone who was invited to speak at our conference sent me a tape to show me her teaching style. On it she mentioned the name of someone I had been trying to reach. I was told that this person owned office buildings in the city. I called her to ask if she knew this person well and she said she was best friends with his wife. I found out that the wife in the conversation was Cathy Cameron. When she heard that I needed office space she said, "I know Anita Carman. She does not remember me but I met her when she spoke at the Texas Women's Retreat. I overfilled my table and was put at the speaker's table next to her." Cathy spiritually discerned that God had woven our lives back together and determined she was meant to help me. Within less than a month, Inspire Women moved into prime office space which was donated to the ministry.

Did you know that when you follow God's voice, even if He allows an embarrassing physical condition, it is only for a season? God never ends up looking silly. God tells us in 1 Samuel 2:30, "…**Those who honor me I will honor**". NIV.

Mary did not go down in history as an unwed mother. Even though God allowed the criticism for a season, He made sure the ones who really needed to see God's truth were given the truth. God made sure the angel also appeared to Joseph so Mary would have the support she needed. In a similar way, in spite of the criticism, God opened the eyes of those He hand picked to see His movement among His daughters. No human manipulation or criticism can keep God's plans from going forward. The next time you face criticism, learn to focus on where God is going. The greater plan will silence the noise around you and help you to stay focused in spite of the criticism.

What is the ultimate destination of where you are going? In spite of the criticism, can you celebrate that the end result will be worth enduring any criticism along the way?

When I was wrestling with feeling silly, I remember reading the story about how Walt Disney started Disney Land. The story tells of how he went from door to door trying to sell a Mickey Mouse doll during the time of the depression. He had a vision for the future and was not afraid to look silly to bring that vision to reality. What God entrusted to me was a vision that far exceeded being entertained in this lifetime. If those who have a vision for business are willing to take chances then how much more should I be willing to look silly for a cause that will have eternal consequences! I found myself saying, "You take chances in business all the time, and so what's so wrong about taking a chance for God?"

When I look back at how life unfolded, what I realize is the awesome grace of God. You see, when God has a plan, God will bring His vision to pass. I was never the one who was taking a chance on God because God always finishes what He begins. Instead, God was the one taking a chance on me. He was watching to see if I would stay on the saddle. Will I keep riding until I reach my destination?

A friend of mine said, "Try riding backwards." I asked her, "What do you mean?" She said, "If you ride backwards, you will see how many miles you have already covered. Then the future won't seem so daunting."

Transforming Rejection to Fulfill God's Purpose

As I said in the introduction of this curriculum, you will learn that a life of faith is not some mystical feeling but a concrete application of God's Word in the following ways:

- No matter what family background you came from and how things were done in your earthly family, all believers belong to God's royal family and are therefore expected to act according to the customs of the royal family.

- Whenever I experienced an emotion because of a challenge or a decision I needed to make, God taught me to do the following

    o   I ask myself, "What am I feeling? Is it loneliness, rejection, or fear? What exactly is the emotion I am dealing with?"

    o   I ask myself, "Is the level of my emotion I in proportion to what just happened? If not, what wound did it open from my past to cause me to over react?"

    o   I ask myself, "Is there a teaching in God's Word that parallels the situation I just encountered? Are there verses that speak to the situation that will give me guidance on how to respond?"

    If I cannot find specific verses, then I look for biblical examples of someone who dealt with a parallel situation. Since I am to act as a member of God's royal family, I ask myself, "What is the custom of God's royal family and how would God expect me to act. A tangible way to learn the customs of the royal family is to study the lives of God's faith heroes and how they responded in a parallel situation. I was then able to imitate how the faith heroes responded. There are times I learned from the mistake of a biblical character as described in my concluding thoughts which shares a situation that almost made me abandon the dream.

    A life of faith then is a concrete way to respond based on what God has revealed in His Word. A person who lives by faith is one who intentionally models behavior after the right choices of the faith heroes in the Bible and trusts that making such a choice is the best choice, no matter what the outcome. The result is a life that moves with conviction and confidence by making choices that are anchored in truths from God's Word and learning from the responses of those who are part of our spiritual heritage.

In applying the above steps, below is what I learned from God's Word to overcome rejection. I pray you will believe God's instruction from His Word and model these truths to your life.

When rejected by your family

- Remember you were made in God's image and no one else has the right to distort your self image.

- In God's appointments, He will look at your heart.

- God will choose "the one" for His mission and makes up His own mind. He is not influenced by the opinions of your parents or siblings. Therefore, listen only for God's calling for your life.

When rejected by a culture or community

- Remember God's word is the sword to cut through the lies that distort our self image.

- Don't let your culture, community or past emotional baggage put artificial limitations on you that God never intended.

- Live as a citizen of God's kingdom instead of allowing your culture or community to define your role in life.

- Learn from Jesus when to slip away when emotions are high instead of fighting every battle.

- Jesus was rejected by a religious community so expect your hardest darts may come from the church or those you consider Christian leaders.

- Keep a heart of forgiveness towards those who have rejected you.

- Take your blessing to others and serve in your open doors, trusting God's timing for you to recycle back one day to extend your hand of friendship to those who once rejected you.

When rejected as being imbalanced

- Settle in your heart what God has called you to finish. It is far better to be remembered for being radical rather than lukewarm.

- Recognize the world's

- double standard that cautions us to have balance and moderation in our lives concerning God's projects but accepts without question the same passion and zeal for your job or career.
- As a leader you may be criticized for doing what is necessary to advance God's mission but remember the only thing that matters is that you are moving at God's pace and per His instruction.

When rejected by those with greater business sense

- Remember there are times when God desires our extravagant worship.
- Although God wants us to be a good steward of our resources, ministry is not a business. God oversees all projects birthed by His spirit and He wants to direct your time and resources to cover the spiritual needs in the world.
- Some projects will be large, some will be small, some may involve crowds, and some may involve one individual. God has not called us to make decisions with a business model but with a ministry model.
- Follow God's heart and let Him reprioritize your schedule and the use of your resources.

When rejected by those who question your calling

- Recall that it even raised eyebrows in Jesus' day when the woman who poured out her perfume on Jesus was criticized for focusing her attention on Him. Jesus told the disciples that they overlooked the need "but she.."
- Know that there are some called to encourage the leader. Let the rejection be further confirmation that you are on track and let God's approval be all that you need to keep going.

When rejected by your peers or team mates

- Remember God raised a Barnabas to introduce Paul to the apostles. So even for Paul, it took time to be accepted by his peers.
- Paul's peers shipped him off to Tarsus when his presence created tensions. If you are sitting in a Tarsus, serve God in your open doors and trust Him to

bring you back to the team in His perfect timing. Where once you might be the misfit, in God's timing, you will be the perfect fit.

- Instead of feeling the team does not value you, focus on the current needs of the team and the challenges they face. Be sensitive to the needs of the team. God wants us to grow in relationship with Him and with each other.

When rejected by a leader you esteemed highly

- Stand firm in the mission that God has entrusted to you and be determined to keep going.
- Don't let your vulnerability become a weakness by giving someone else the power to destroy you.
- Praise God for your season with a leader, then have the courage to walk with God the rest of the way.

When rejected by those you are leading

- Know that God expects the leader to keep going forward with the vision. There will be times the leader must have faith for the community.
- Even when God's timing is delayed because the people reject the leader, the leader is not released from the mission unless God specifically says so or until the mission is completed.

When rejected by those who withdraw their money

- Don't take rejection personally since you are representing God. Help supporters see that God is the one who is asking them to step into their divine appointment. If they reject you, they are actually rejecting God's invitation.
- You cannot lead others where you have not been so set the example of radical giving with a pure heart. If you sow sparingly, you will reap sparingly.
- Encourage those who give to be a cheerful giver. We can never out give God.

When rejected by those who criticize you

- Settle in your heart if it's more important to you for your audience to love you or if you have been sent to lead them to love God.

- Stay true to your calling to be a blessing and continue to bless no matter how people accuse you or criticize you.

- Find your confidence in the content of your message and in God's timing to deliver it.

- Don't be surprised if God will not release you from a group that is critical. God is not afraid of criticism and He will fulfill His mission in spite of it.

- If God has put you in a place where you become the target of public criticism, focus on where God is heading. Ask yourself, "What blessing did God mean for me to be to this audience?" Let the celebration of what God intended to do through you silence the noise of the criticism along the way.

Additional Testimonies on Rejection

In the appendix, you will find additional testimonies or journal entries from the friends of Inspire Women. If you wish to personalize this curriculum as your way to build authentic friendships and community, please add to or replace the testimonies in the appendix with those from those God has woven into your community. Below is a letter you may use to invite your friends to be part of this personalized curriculum

Letter of Invitation to invite a friend to share personal experience

Dear _____,

When God entrusts you with a dream for yourself, your family, your church, your workplace, your ministry or community, your emotions can either empower you or they can cause you to crater on the inside. When the protector of the dream craters, you can kiss goodbye any dream that was meant to make a difference. I am writing you because I am embarking on an exciting journey to share God's truths to transform the emotions in our hearts into a positive energy for His purpose. Unlike other curriculums, I am so excited to be working with a "personalized" leadership curriculum and therefore need your help to make this adventure to be a success. The personalized curriculum I will be teaching has the following format:

- *The curriculum is divided into 3 modules, each focused on an emotion. The three emotions we will cover are loneliness, rejection, and fear. I will begin the discussion of each emotion with transparently sharing my personal journal entries from times in my life when I experienced the emotion being discussed.*

- *Following my personal journal entries will be a Bible study with God's truths to transform our emotions into passionate divine purpose.*

- *Included in our study are additional testimonies from friends such as yourself. If you did not keep a journal you can draw from, I invite you to relive those times in your mind when you experienced either loneliness, rejection, or fear and write a personal testimony describing your situation and what you felt as if you were experiencing it today. Then also add any truths God taught you in the midst of your emotion.*

I am inviting you to be a special part of this personalized curriculum to affirm your presence in our community and to help you to see that you have a message of hope to share with the community God has placed you in. I pray too that in this personalized curriculum, you will celebrate your divine appointment to be part of a personalized keepsake that will build the bond between us and create a lasting teaching instrument that will bless the members of our community for generations to come.

Please let me know if you will join me in creating this personalized teaching material for our _____ (church, workplace, ministry, family, etc.). If you choose to participate, specify which emotion you wish to write about and what God taught you about it through His Word. Please keep your testimony under 3 typewritten 8.5 x 11 pages.

Grateful for your special friendship,

Transforming Fear to Fulfill God's Purpose

When Jesus was carrying the cross on the way to Calvary, the gospel of Mark, chapter 15 verse 21 tells us, **"A certain man from Cyrene, Simon, the father of Alexander and Rufus, was passing by on his way in from the country, and they forced him to carry the cross."** NIV. The sad truth is, Simon's experience is more the norm than the unusual. We will find that while we are "**passing by**" and while we are on our way, the same way as Simon was "**on his way in from the country,**" God intersects our lives with a divine agenda. When the invitation first shows up on our radar screen, we are caught unaware because our mind is focused on other things. Simon finds himself walking into a situation, and a Roman guard grabs him and pulls him onto the scene. Have you ever asked yourself, "How did I end up in this situation? How did I get involved? Why am I involved?" More than that, do you find yourself dreading your situation and saying like Simon probably said, "How do I get this over with so I can get back to what I was doing?"

Imagine the scene Simon was pulled into. There is a major mob following the activity around Jesus. There are big Roman guards who are not exactly your neighborhood friendly welcome wagon. They had whips in their hands. They had swords. They had a commanding presence and demanded your utmost allegiance. To have one of them look your way would probably make you wither on the inside. To have them command you to be next to the very person they are executing is not exactly a job for which you would volunteer. You

do not want to touch the cross or be close to the one being executed, but now here you are with the cross on your shoulders and your skin rubbing against the prisoner who is on death row. While carrying the cross next to Jesus, what do you think Simon was feeling? Do you feel his heart beating faster? Do you see the beads of sweat on his forehead? Do you see the glazed look in his eyes that comes when a situation catches us off guard and scares us? Do you feel his dread of what he might be required to do next? Heaven forbid that the sweat from this prisoner should rub against his skin or that drops of his blood would get on him or his clothes!

Fast forward to the future. What do we know about Simon, this certain man from Cyrene? Observe how Mark described him as "**the father of Alexander and Rufus.**" Who are Alexander and Rufus? Church history tells us that they were prominent leaders in the early church. Could it be that their father's encounter with God and his realization that he carried the cross with the Messiah transformed not only Simon's life, but also the lives of his children? Did you know that it is God's grace to involve us in spite of our fear?

God's Word tells us that in Simon's case, "**they forced him to carry the cross.**" The "**they**" in this story were the Roman guards who represented a secular force. I wonder today if God has used a secular system to force you in a certain direction. Perhaps your company has mandatory retirement, perhaps you were laid off, perhaps your need for employment or the need to take care of a family situation has forced some changes. Perhaps you see yourself as helpless in your circumstances when God simply used circumstances and secular and monetary forces to put you exactly where He designed you to be. While you might interpret your situation as forcing you to be where you are, God is thinking, "You are right on time!"

In our minds, we might find ourselves saying, "Oh God, don't send me!" "Oh God, please don't look my way!" In God's grace, He allows circumstances to force our footsteps not because He is trying to take something away from us but because He desires to give us more. Simon was "**on his way in from the country**" when God intersected his life. Were you on vacation and thinking about getting home to water the plants? You weren't exactly thinking about being part of some major movement in your city. If you feel pressure, instead of getting mad, try changing your paradigm to think about the following. Our human mind is too short sighted to see the blessing God has put in front of us. So praise God for pressure because sometimes it takes pressure for us to be on the same page with God.

Next time you find yourself shrinking from an opportunity, ask yourself, "Am I like a Simon of Cyrene?" Are you missing your divine appointment by allowing your dread of the situation cloud your vision? Are you concerned with what the assignment will require from you personally? Perhaps it's time to stop and to ask, "Where was I on my way from? Where was I on my way to? Was what I was doing as critical as what God has redirected my time, my energies, or my resources to do? What is God's timing and plan for this world? Am I disconnected from God's spiritual movement? Is my life cluttered with my own stuff instead of breaking free to connect with an agenda that impacts beyond my world and family? It is so incredible how God works. His plans always give us more than we could ever imagine for ourselves. Alexander and Rufus were impacted eternally because their father was forced to be part of God's agenda! Have you asked yourself, "Where is God going with this? How will this story end? What blessing am I forfeiting by my reluctance to become involved in God's plans for me?"

Pastor Leonard Barksdale, an attorney who God called out of corporate America to serve as a Pastor in a fifth ward church once said to me, "Remember, Anita, that Simon only got to help carry the cross, but Jesus was the one who went all the way to Calvary." What comforting words at a time when God's call on my life feels daunting. From his counsel, I was reminded that God is the one who has paid the price for His own dreams. He's not putting the weight of the whole world on my shoulders. He carries the world. What He does is to invite me to be part of the journey. I was not called to be Savior. I might be called to be a Simon of Cyrene, on my way to do something else, when God in His mercy allows me to be part of a plan with eternal significance.

As guardians of dreams for yourself, your family, business, church, ministry, community, nation, or the world, have you allowed your fears to cause you to abandon what God intended to do through you? Fear is not from God. In God's perfect love, there is no fear.

In this third module of our study on "Transforming Emotions in a Leader's Heart", I will share with you how God taught me to stay focused on His mission in spite of fear. We will look at God's truth to rise above fear in situations:

- **When your physical welfare is at risk**

- **When you fear unemployment and poverty**

- **When the odds are against you**

- **When you fear failure**

- **When you face suffering**

- **When someone is angry or jealous**

- **When choices you can't control affect you**

- **When you lose your children, assets, or health**

- **When you fear divorce or widowhood**

- **When someone breaks a promise**

We may not always be able to control how we feel, but we can choose what we do. The Apostle Paul said in 1 Corinthians 2:3-4, "**I came to you in weakness and fear, and with much trembling.**" NIV. Yet his fear did not make him shrink back from God's calling. Paul's summary of his choices was stated in Acts 20:25-28, "**Now I know that none of you among whom I have gone about preaching the kingdom will ever see me again. Therefore, I declare to you today that I am innocent of the blood of all men. For I have not hesitated to proclaim to you the whole will of God.**" NIV.

Did you see the words "**I have not hesitated**"? Oh, the victory to arrive at the end of our lives and be able to make the statement that we have a clear conscience because we did not hesitate to do the things God intended to do through us! As a member of God's royal family, I praise Him for the role models of faith heroes who have gone before me and finished well. God's Word and the examples of their lives serve as my compass. I don't get to pass this way again. In the time that I have, I can't control how I feel, but I choose to allow God to harness my emotions and transform them into a passionate purpose to fulfill His dreams.

When Your Physical Welfare is at Risk

Situation: Are you in an environment that is threatening to your physical body? Are you experiencing fear because of physical, emotional or sexual abuse?

The purpose of the personal journal entries shown below is to share with you incidents in my lifetime when I experienced the emotion of fear when my physical welfare was at risk. Some entries were taken from an actual journal, others were written more recently as I reflected on what I was feeling at the time. The dates of the entries are approximate and were included to give the reader some sense of chronological history. In teaching this material, feel free to use my personal journal entries as illustration or personalize your lesson with writing your own personal journal entries or testimony to capture the emotion of fear you felt in your own life. If you did not keep a journal, then try to relive the situation in your mind and write an entry today to capture what you felt at the time.

December 9, 1967

Dear God,
I hate the sound of an angry mob. People get so crazy when they are all angry and in the same place at the same time. It's like their anger feeds each other's anger and before long, no one really knows what they are fighting about. It's like they reinforce each other's insanity. The policemen look weary these days. It must be hard to always be on the alert for some bomb to explode. The teachers try to keep us focused but I can tell that they are distracted as well. It's hard to sit through a history lesson on something that happened a hundred years ago when history is happening right outside our own window. What is going on in the city? I don't know what all the commotion is about. I wonder if most people just want to get on with life but things happen around them and they get pulled into the drama. What if a bomb explodes at the school gate? What if I died tomorrow, God?

What if I get a limb blown off? Do other kids my age worry about things like this?

May 5, 1969

Dear God,
Sometimes I don't know where to hide. There is a war zone in my own home. I don't know what my Mom and Dad are fighting about. The screaming gets so loud the pictures are going to fall off the walls. I'm not sure who threw it but someone threw a glass bottle against the wall and it burst into a thousand pieces. There is glass everywhere. I thought a bomb had exploded in our own household. My sister and I are holding each other in the bedroom and crying. I told her I could pretend to faint. Maybe then the fighting will stop. God, I don't know what to do? I just want peace. I hid in the chapel today. It felt peaceful in there. I just sat there for hours looking at the cross in front of the chapel. The cross dominates the room. I don't know why but the cross gave me

peace. It's strange how a cross that symbolized your death could give me peace. How could a death that took place 2000 years ago give me peace today? What was it about your death that makes me feel that as long as I stay close to you, things will be fine? Is there something about your death that is the secret to the peace I am looking for? Or maybe the answer is in your resurrection. What kind of power did it take to raise Jesus from the dead? Is that power available to me today?

January 15, 1970

Dear God,
Why did you let someone break into our home? I can't believe they locked our watch dog up in the back room. What's the point of having a watch dog if he can't protect us? Now the dog is traumatized so I'm scared and the dog is scared. I'm not sure that makes much sense at all. Someone knocked on the door and my heart jumps and the dog hides. Who needs a dog that is scared of robbers?

It feels so strange to think that someone was watching the house and broke in when the family was gone. What would have happened if we had walked in on the robbers? There are so many things in life that's a question of timing. Do you control time, God? When you protect us, is it for a reason? And when you don't protect us, is that for a reason as well?

Nov 7, 1975

Dear God,
I guess it was pretty stupid of me to put up a notice at the student center to find someone to teach me how to drive. I was

surprised that the man who answered the ad was not a student. I should never have gotten in the car with him. He seemed like such a kind gentleman. He said he wanted to help. We drove around for a while and then he said he wanted to go by his house to pick up something. When we got to his house he asked me to go in. It must have been you who warned me to say no. So I stayed in the car. Then on the way back to campus, I was driving his car. When my hands were on the wheel, he put his hands on my right leg. He said he was trying to guide my leg into pushing on the brake at the right time. But I knew something wasn't right. I didn't know what to do God because my hands were on the wheel. So I drove the car into the ditch. Well, that got his attention and he was more worried about getting the car out of the ditch and took his attention off me. I got out of the car and walked back to campus. I feel like I escaped but things could have turned out differently. When I got back to my dorm room, I locked the door. I wish I could lock out the whole world. Tomorrow I'll go to class and act like nothing happened. Life goes on God, doesn't it? I guess we just keep going.

July 1, 1979

Dear God,
I had to get a car so I could drive to my first job. Here you and I are in Washington D.C. and I'm in a new city again. I can't believe I actually got my driver's license when I've been behind the wheel three times. I can't believe there was a thunderstorm on my first day of work. I don't know what happened God but my car began to hydroplane. I stomped on the brakes which was probably a stupid thing to do. The car spun around and I

almost hit a concrete wall. I can't believe there was no one else on the road or else I would have caused a major wreck. Did you hear my heart pounding God? I could have died on the road today. You must have spared me for a reason.

Aug 22, 1980

Dear God,
I can't believe when I rented this house I did not realize the house next to mine was a bar. I guess there must not be any zoning in this part of town. The house was partially hidden behind trees so I didn't notice the sign. This house is not the safest place to be because the bar next door is loud and filled with people every night who drink to get drunk. I heard loud singing close to the house this evening and then a beer bottle flew into the window. My heart stopped. It reminded me of the riots in Hong Kong. At least then I had my family around me. But this time, I was all alone by myself in the house. I wasn't sure what to do next. Should I go downstairs and see if someone broke in? What would I have done if I heard footsteps in the house? God, I locked the door to my bedroom and stayed very still? I hid under the blankets but that felt stupid because what safety is a blanket! God, are you watching over me? There must be somewhere I can go that is safe.

The corresponding truths God taught me from His Word to address my situation
Feel free to continue reading all my personal journals in Module Three expressing feelings of fear before reading the Bible Study. Or you may continue with the corresponding Bible study which contains God's truths in addressing the situation described in the above journal entries with additional truths God taught me to address situations that were not included in my journal entries. If you choose to personalize this curriculum as your way to bond with the group you are leading, feel free not only to use your own testimony and personal journal entries but in the Bible study part, include what God taught you from His Word in situations where you faced fear.

When Your Physical Welfare is At Risk

Situation: Are you in an environment that is threatening to your physical body? Are you experiencing fear because of physical, emotional or sexual abuse?

Reminder: Let's learn the truths from God's Word that speak to our situations. Remember that as a member of God's royal family, we are to act according to the customs of the royal family. This means reinforcing our royal identity by living according to God's specific instructions in the Bible. When we cannot find specific instructions that speak to our situation, we are to search our spiritual heritage and model our lives after God's faith heroes who responded correctly to situations that parallel our own. We can also learn from their mistakes to avoid making the same mistakes in our lives.

I remember I was eleven when there was political unrest in my city. A curfew was declared at 7 p.m., and everyone had to be off the streets. I was late leaving school, and as I was rushing home, I could see there were fewer and fewer people around me. My heart started beating faster, and I rushed as fast as I could to get home. That evening I found myself hiding under my covers while hearing the explosion of tear gas in the distance and the sounds of angry mobs running down the streets. I prayed that they would not come near our building or throw anything through the windows.

When we were past the political unrest, I still had to face the growing crime in my neighborhood. My mother informed me that the daughter of one of our friends was raped in an elevator. The thought of being trapped in an elevator with an assailant made my heart stop. My mother gave me strict instructions on what to watch out for. I was to walk quickly and run two flights of stairs to our apartment on the second floor in case anyone was waiting for me after school. The thought of someone stalking me or waiting to attack me filled my heart with fear. I thought my mother was just imagining things till I

came home one day to find that someone had broken into the house. When I saw all my clothes on the floor, it made my stomach turn. It was such an eerie feeling to think that a stranger had invaded the sanctuary of our home. I wanted the police to search every room, every closet, and every corner of the house just in case someone was still hiding behind some closed door. The very thought of an assailant jumping out at me made me tremble. I desperately wanted to find a place on earth where I would feel safe.

Our family's lack of finances forced us to stay in conditions that were unsafe. I hated where I lived. I felt like a prisoner of my circumstances. I could not stand the feeling of being trapped in my environment. But there was nowhere else to go.

Although my mother did not know the Bible, she had a simple faith in God. She kept reminding me that God looks at the heart, and if we will keep our heart pure, He will protect us. I counted the days and could not wait for the day when God would take me out of a neighborhood that was growing more unsafe by the day.

"Anytime I allow a person or a situation to frighten me, I am focusing too much on the enemy and need to redirect my focus to God."

Years later, I learned from David who said in Psalm 27:2-3, **"When evil men advance against me to devour my flesh, when my enemies and my foes attack me, they will stumble and fall. Though an army besiege me, my heart will not fear; though war break out against me, even then will I be confident."** NIV. As I read these words, I asked myself, "How did David get himself to a place where He could be sure of God's protection? As I read on, I discovered his secret. David said, in verse 4, **"One thing I ask of the LORD, this is what I seek: that I may dwell in the house of the LORD all the days of my life, to gaze upon the beauty of the LORD and to seek him in his temple."** NIV.

From David's example, I learned that anytime I allow a person or a situation to frighten me, I am focusing too much on the enemy and need to redirect my focus to God. Though someone may have invaded my personal sanctuary, I need to allow myself to be transported in my mind to God's sanctuary. I need to visualize God sitting on His throne in heaven. I need to visualize Jesus sitting next to the Father. I need to see the angels singing and praising God around the throne and the son of God saying as He did in Matthew 28:18, **"All authority in heaven and on earth has been given to me."** NIV. Instead of focusing on the evil around me, I need to focus on God's power to overcome evil.

"The best way for me to experience God's protection is for me to be about God's business."

The more I read God's Word, the more He taught me how to transform the emotions that cripple me into a passionate purpose for His plans on earth. The authority Jesus referred to in Matthew 28:18 was in the context of the activity of sharing God's message on earth. The context read, **"Therefore go and make disciples of all nations, baptizing them in the name of the Father and of the Son and of the Holy Spirit, and teaching them to obey everything I have commanded you. And surely I am with you always, to the very end of the age."** NIV. Perhaps what Jesus is teaching us is that we will feel God's promise of "**I am with you always**" when we are doing what He commanded us to do. The best way for me to experience God's presence and protection is for me to be about God's business.

What does going and making disciples mean? Jesus is sending us to the ends of the earth with His full authority. Instead of hiding in fear, it is time for us to make disciples of all nations by sharing the message that God has come to earth through His Son. He is offering us the gift of forgiveness and eternal life. Moreover, when we accept His gift and become a part of His royal family, He gives us His power to represent Him and proclaim His name on earth.

We are not victims, we were designed to be conquerors. We are warriors of the King of Kings and God is sending us into our communities to transform the world with God's power. When we enter any environment, we are to represent our Father's heart. We are to look at things with our Father's eyes. When we leave a neighborhood, a workplace, or a community, something should have changed as evidence that God's daughter visited this place.

"How could it be that the personal attacks on Paul did not make him afraid of life?"

If you are in a situation where you are being threatened physically, know that God has authority over your situation, and He does not want you to live in such circumstances. Therefore, exercise authority in your heavenly Father's name, and take action to transport yourself to safer grounds instead of just allowing others to hurt you. If you are unable to get out safely, then pray and ask God for an escape plan. The courage to leave comes from knowing that all authority in heaven and earth has been given to Jesus, and He has commissioned us to represent Him in the world. So we are to step into our appointment with confidence. We are to say, "No more" to situations that God would never bless. We are to say, "Something must change" to situations that grieve God's heart. I wonder today if God has allowed you to experience threats to your physical welfare because He wants to strengthen your faith before He sends you in His name to change a similar situation in a family, neighborhood, or community.

What physical threat to your person do you need to confront in the name and power of Jesus?

How will you act differently knowing that all authority has been granted to Jesus, and He is sending you in His name to share His gospel and to subdue this earth in His power?

When we represent God's heart of justice and mercy, we become an active member of God's army. The Apostle Paul did not skip a beat in spite of the attacks on his personal body. He was not surprised by the assault on his personal being. He kept going in spite of the physical injury. Paul tells us in 2 Corinthians 11:25-26, **"Three times I was beaten with rods, once I was stoned, three times I was shipwrecked, I spent a night and a day in the open sea, I have been constantly on the move. I have been in danger from rivers, in danger from bandits, in danger from my own countrymen, in danger from Gentiles; in danger in the city, in danger in the country, in danger at sea; and in danger from false brothers."** NIV.

How could it be that the personal attacks on Paul did not make him afraid of life? I learned from Paul that even if we have been hurt physically, we don't have to allow the attack to traumatize us. If our mindset is that of making our personal safety our goal, then any breech to the fortress we have built around us will create major panic. But if our mindset models Paul's attitude, and we see ourselves as being about God's business, then we will interpret any attack on our personal being as part of the battle we are in to advance God's purpose on earth. Like Paul, we will wear the scars of battle as a mark of a hero for Christ.

Have you experienced a violation of your physical being or an invasion of your personal space? How can you allow God to transform what you have experienced as His victory story to overcome the enemy?

The devil has declared war on planet earth. We will experience casualties of war because we are under attack. If we don't accept we are at war, it will not change the fact that we are at war. However, it will cause us to be unprepared for the war. God wants us to heed Peter's warning in 1 Peter 5:8, that **"Your enemy the devil prowls around like a roaring lion looking for someone to devour."** Jesus tells us in John 10:10, **"The thief comes only to steal and kill and destroy; I have come that they may have life, and have it to the full."** NIV. It is when we cling to Jesus and the life and power He offers that we will overcome the fear of the life the devil tries to destroy.

Has someone stolen your innocence? Has someone or something tried to destroy you? Know that God has sent you a Deliverer. No matter what someone has taken from you, know that God has the power to renew you with His life. Take a moment now to feel God's light shining through you and illuminating the dark places of your life. Set aside time to do this every day.

One of Inspire Women's scholarship recipients was continuously sexually molested by her step father during her teenage years. She became so sick of the abuse that she ran away from home at the age of fifteen. She was homeless and lived under a bridge. Imagine her as a scared teenager running from home and sitting in the dark under a bridge only to find herself raped by a stranger who took advantage of her vulnerability. Years later, she felt so desperate she did not know what to do. No matter how things improved on the outside, she felt she was running on the inside. Then she went to church one day and heard the message of Jesus and His power to save us. She prayed to accept Him as Savior. She said she felt this bright light go through her and it melted away all the ugliness she felt was in her. It was like Jesus washed her white as snow. She emerged from the experience with a renewed spirit and an excitement to serve God. She heard His call to be trained to work with children who have been abused.

What physical danger are you facing in your life today? Is it time to trust God's authority in you to represent Him and transform your situation with God's power? Is it time to allow God's power to heal you from wounds from the past?

My mother was born in China. At the age of 15, she was the victim of rape. When someone has violated you in a brutal way, I can imagine how she would have a fear to ever trust again or to leave familiar territory. I think it's easier to be adventurous or to take risks when you have never been hurt. But when you have experienced violence, it's as if your whole body is put on the alert and you view the world with suspicion.

In spite of the trauma in her background, she found herself in a place where her family needed her to leave the country to find work in order to send help home. She had to decide if she would leave all that was familiar to her to go to a land where she had no connections and no idea how she would make it. She knew that someone had to go in order to protect the rest of the family. Her courage to leave changed the future for her entire family and opened the door to opportunities we would never have enjoyed had she not taken a chance and left home.

My mother's desire for safety was outweighed by her greater drive to fulfill her mission to protect the family. When you have a choice between fear and courage, what will drive your life? Your sense of greater mission or purpose in life will give you the courage to take the chance on risking one life for the saving of many lives.

When You Fear Unemployment and Poverty

Situation: Do you fear not having enough funds to pay the rent and to take care of your needs? Do you fear unemployment and the loss of a title, a role, and a purpose for waking up every morning?

The purpose of the personal journal entries shown below is to capture the emotion of fear from not having enough resources or being disconnected from a community through unemployment. Some entries were taken from an actual journal, others were written more recently as I reflected on what I was feeling at the time. The dates of the entries are approximate and were included to give the reader some sense of chronological history. In teaching this material, feel free to use my personal journal entries as illustration or personalize your lesson with writing your own personal journal entries or testimony to capture the emotion of loneliness you felt in your own life. If you did not keep a journal, then try to relive the situation in your mind and write an entry today to capture what you felt at the time.

Feb 7, 1970

Dear God,
My Mom wants to leave this city but she said she can't take me with her. She said she could not feed me. I told her I didn't care. She made me promise that I would study hard so I could find a job and feed myself. She told me never to depend on anyone for a roof over my head. I wish I could make things better God. Maybe one day I'll be rich. Maybe one day I can buy my Mom a grand mansion and she won't ever have to worry about money to buy food. Maybe one day she'll have the dress she's always wanted. Maybe one day she can visit her family in China before someone dies. She was really broken hearted when she did not have the money to visit her Dad when he was ill. Then when he died, she cried for days. It feels so bad to want to do things and not have the money. One day, maybe she won't have to feel desperate anymore.

April 6, 1973

Dear God,
There is no money for college. I have written over a hundred letters. The Dean of the University of Pennsylvania wrote me back and told me not to give up. He said there were no scholarships but that I should keep trying. It's so hard to wait for a letter and to open it only to find bad news. There must be someone who will believe in me. My Dad said he could not possibly afford the tuition. I think if I can get a full tuition scholarship he might be able to help with food. Even then, it will be very hard for him. What should I do God? Should I just forget about going to America? What is this dream going to cost us? Do all dreams cost this much?

My mother said my brother left the country with enough money for six months. He studied all day and worked in the restaurants in the evenings. He rented a cot to sleep on for $25 a month. He lived on crackers and water. She said he is really smart and he will make it one day. People love inviting him to their homes because he fixes everything for them. He's always trying to help others. Mom said God will take care of him because he has a giving heart.

Feb 5, 1997

Dear God,
I know you have set me apart for your work but is it wrong to want to be part of an organization so I can have a sense of community? I don't have a title or fill a role in an organization. I guess I'm unemployed. I don't have to call in anywhere or report anywhere. I could disappear from planet earth and no one would notice. Maybe that's why people go to work. It's more than a paycheck. It's a way to feel connected.

God, it's so strange to feel disconnected from the world. I wonder if you made us to be part of a community. I know there are some people who can be on vacation all the time. There are some people who have the luxury to go from one hobby to another. But what is it in me that makes me feel like the moments are ticking away and there is something I am supposed to be finishing. I wonder if being unemployed simply means being free to listen to your own voice everyday since there is no company dictating my schedule. Is my title "child of the King", fully owned by my heavenly Father, commissioned to finish His work? Is this the lesson you wanted to teach me by disconnecting me from a company?

The corresponding truths God taught me from His Word to address my situation
Feel free to continue reading all my personal journals in Module Three expressing feelings of fear before reading the Bible Study. Or you may continue with the corresponding Bible study which contains God's truths in addressing the situation described in the above journal entries with additional truths God taught me to address situations that were not included in my journal entries. If you choose to personalize this curriculum as your way to bond with the group you are leading, feel free not only to use your own testimony and personal journal entries but in the Bible study part, include what God taught you from His Word in situations where you faced fear.

When You Fear Unemployment and Poverty

Situation: Do you fear not having enough funds to pay the rent and to take care of your needs? Do you fear unemployment and the loss of a title, a role, and a purpose for waking up every morning?

Reminder: Let's learn the truths from God's Word that speak to our situations. Remember that as a member of God's royal family, we are to act according to the customs of the royal family. This means reinforcing our royal identity by living according to God's specific instructions in the Bible. When we cannot find specific instructions that speak to our situation, we are to search our spiritual heritage and model our lives after God's faith heroes who responded correctly to situations that parallel our own. We can also learn from their mistakes to avoid making the same mistakes in our own lives.

I grew up in a home where we had four in the family with four bedrooms, two of which we rented out for extra income. I grew up where I hated the fights over finances and was determined that when I grew up I would never be poor. I hated not having options. I hated needing to depend on someone else for my provision. God, in His mercy, gave me a way to secure my financial future. And then when I thought I was ensured of a lucrative career, God invited me to leave corporate America. How do we keep our fear of poverty from influencing our choice to follow God?

"Would I allow my mother's fears to dictate my future, or would I trust God to lead me?"

I could hear the tapes from my childhood blaring in my ears when I walked away from corporate America. Even though I had a husband, my mother continually warned me to never trust a man for my provision and to always be able to take care of myself. The thought of having to trust another human being for my finances made me feel like I was betraying my mother. She would have been so disappointed in me for walking away from a lucrative career. Would I allow my mother's fears to dictate my future, or would I trust God to lead me?

What fears do you carry with you? Are these your fears based on your personal experience or did you inherit your fears from your parents?

The most amazing thing happened when I walked away from corporate America. I have found that no matter what I give, I can never out give God. As I reflect on my life, I realize God taught me to live by some principles which protected me financially. These principles are so second nature to me that I do them without thinking. Do you need God's wisdom to manage your finances?

Solomon was the wisest man on planet earth. He wrote the book of Proverbs which contains much wisdom for our lives in many areas, including the area of financial stewardship. Proverbs 6:9-11 reads, **"How long will you lie there, you sluggard? When will you get up from your sleep? A little sleep, a little slumber, a little folding of the hands to rest — and poverty will come on you like a bandit and scarcity like an armed man."** NIV

From an early age, God taught me to use my time well. When I was on the bus traveling between school and home, I would be reading and learning. If I was sitting in the waiting room of a doctor's office, I would be reading and learning. When I was waiting in car pool line for my children, I would be reading and learning. I find myself always trying to read and learn from others. I devour information. I'm not sure when the change took place, but I used to waste hours of the day watching television. I now find myself resting by spending time with God and talking to Him, or other times I am writing, or reading, or studying. What I did not realize at the time was that I was in continuing education. What I did not realize was how I was engaged continuously in "on the job training" so I would never stagnate and I would always be growing and learning. When you do this, the most incredible thing happens. You find yourself sought after. You'll find yourself with a reputation where people want what you have to offer because you are regarded as being an expert in your field. I remember someone telling me once that the goal in life is to be so good at what you love to do that someone will pay you to do it.

"I wonder if you have a teachable spirit or do you get defensive so that those with wisdom shy away from sharing any wisdom with you?"

Proverbs 13:18 reads, **"He who ignores discipline comes to poverty and shame, but whoever heeds correction is honored."** NIV. Did you notice the words **"whoever heeds correction"**? I wonder if you have a teachable spirit or do you get defensive so that those with wisdom shy away from sharing any wisdom with you?

God taught me through Proverbs 13:18 that He puts people around me so I can learn from their experiences. My mother used to tell me that very few people care enough about you to correct you. So if someone takes the time to correct you, receive it with humility and learn from it. No matter what someone says or whether I agree with a person's constructive criticism, I find myself saying, "Surely there is something in what they have shared that can help me improve in some way." It is a sad day when we are beyond reproof. I wonder today if you are stunting your own growth because you are more concerned with impressing someone than in learning from their counsel?

Proverbs 14:23 reads, **"All hard work brings a profit, but mere talk leads only to poverty."** NIV. I have met many dreamers in my life. They talk about dreams, they talk about having the faith to trust God. And then nothing happens. It's as if they have mastered the talk but they don't walk the walk. Their faith consists of letting God do the work while they wait. I have found that God does not hand me life on a silver platter. He has chosen to work through me, but He expects me to get up and go. God's Word continues to prove itself true in my life. It says that "**All**" hard work brings a profit. Notice that "hard work" is an essential part of the equation.

When people ask me about Inspire Women, I want them to give credit to God and tell them God is the one who built Inspire Women. What I sometimes fail to be clear about is that God has chosen to work through earthen vessels. So Inspire Women did not get built by sitting around and waiting on God. It was built where every second of my time was spent praying, asking God what the next step was, and then immediately obeying and doing what He said. It resulted from

getting up every time I was knocked down. It was birthed out of begging God to help me to subdue the circumstances that stood in the way of God's vision being fulfilled.

I have found some who talk about the future without understanding that any future will come if all we want is some random future. But when we have been entrusted with a vision, then we must make choices and work daily to bring about the fulfillment of God's vision.

When Noah built the ark, God gave him the plans but while building, he had in mind the end product. As a leader entrusted with God's dreams, we must be clear on what the dream is. Then instead of talking about it, we must get up and get moving.

What dream have you been talking about? How long have you talked about it? What can you do as your next step to get moving on it?

Proverbs 28:19 reads, **"He who works his land will have abundant food, but the one who chases fantasies will have his fill of poverty."** NIV. When I was a child, I used to sit around day dreaming. I lived in a fantasy world. Then the older I got, the more I realized that I was running out of time daydreaming and there was much real work to be done.

In this verse God also taught me to understand which **"land"** is mine to work. God did not entrust me with all land, just the area He has given me. When I work someone else's land, I am living with the fantasy of being over something I have not been given. God will not bless my efforts because I am standing on someone else's property.

For example, I remember several situations where I attempted to make myself available to individuals who were hurting emotionally, thinking that I could be of help. What I have learned is that I do not have the physical energy to minister to thousands and to serve in a counseling capacity to those who need attention because of personal problems. God's calling for my life is to inspire women to God's purpose and provide more specific training to those called to missions and ministry. Though I may inspire thousands via the internet or speaking at conferences, my one on one time is spent with those in leadership and a few close friends. This is the **"land"** God has given me to farm.

When I step beyond my land and get involved in one on one counseling with unfamiliar individuals who are going through major trauma, I find I have exceeded my boundaries. Someone who is called to walk with those in crisis needs to be handling the need. What I had to learn was to put those who need special attention with others who are called to work with individuals in crisis.

When I allow myself to be pulled into the details of other people's deep emotional needs, it's like I've attached myself to someone whose arms are flailing and who might hit me in the face in the process. It's like jumping in to save a drowning person when I have no training in handling the responses of someone who is desperate. Some situations need to be handled by those who have special training and can give focused attention to the person who is hurting. When I get involved in the wrong **"land"**, instead of helping anyone, I end up allowing someone who is drowning to bring me under with them. In spite of the toll on my time and my emotions, I end up being accused of being insensitive and uncaring. The criticism defeats me at a time when I feel like I've jumped through hurdles to be available. What follows is a deep discouragement while trying to minister to the thousands God has brought to the ministry. My failure with a few makes me want to quit as a leader because I feel like I have no business trying to lead anyone!

What "land" has God given you to farm? Are you focused on farming your "land", or are you chasing fantasies?

"God calls me to work where the doors have opened. I can only make the best of opportunities that I have."

What "**land**" are you working? There are some people who totally overlook what is in front of them because their eyes are on another field. God calls me to make my moments count for Him because I will be held accountable for my moments. I don't have the time to fret over doors that haven't opened yet in my life. God calls me to work where the doors have opened. I can only make the best of opportunities on the "**land**" that I have. So I begin where I am, and I continue where I am until God expands my territory. And what I do with the land I am farming today must somehow tie in to the overall mission for my life or else I am just filling my time with activity. The hours tick away and every minute brings me closer to the end of my time on earth. The question is, when the last minute ticks, what will I have left behind that is of eternal significance?

I have found there are times when God is preparing to expand my territory, and I find myself working the current land while putting down stakes in another. Instead of being overwhelmed, it helps me to understand my seasons. All farmers must understand the season when they are farming land. If God is leading me to have a different crop next year, I know I need a certain amount of crop from my current plantings while beginning to sow different seeds for the future. There will be days when I feel there is too much on my platter. The truth is, I am in a time of transition and when the new crop begins to grow, I can gradually transition to the crop that bears most fruit for God.

Are you in a time of transition? How does it comfort you knowing that the normal life for one who is in transition involves feeling overloaded for a season?

Proverbs 11:24 reads, "**One man gives freely, yet gains even more; another withholds unduly, but comes to poverty.**" NIV. Oh, the incredible wisdom of God's Word! I have known those who have a scarcity mentality. They think small because they live in their scarcity mentality. So when someone needs help, their tendency is to say, "When I have enough for myself, then I will help you." What God taught me was to give out of whatever I have. So even if I don't have much, I give what I can to encourage others, and I have a hand that is always open. I wonder today if you have an open hand or if your hand and your heart are always poised in a closed position? What is so amazing to me is that people respond to those who have a spirit of generosity even if they don't have much to give. Moreover, people find reasons to pour resources into the lives of those who are generous. God shows me time and time again that the more I give, the more is given unto me. Do you live with a scarcity mentality? Then you will find that there will never be enough.

When I reflect on my life and the times God has asked me to give freely, the gift has always involved grace. In any organization, when a mistake is made, someone has to pay for it. When you are the leader, the buck usually stops on your desk. There are times when the easier thing to do is to remove the person who has made the mistake. Sometimes the royal thing to do is to absorb the mistake and to give the person a second chance. I have found that just because I show grace there is no guarantee that the one receiving the grace will show gratitude. Often they express gratitude in the beginning, but there is something about the pride in fallen humanity that takes them from a place of gratitude to a place of accusation. I have discovered that those who begin by saying "Thank you" sometimes end with saying it was my fault to give them a project with unrealistic goals. I am not sure why it always comes back around to be my fault, but it is human nature to blame others rather than take responsibility ourselves. When you give freely with no strings attached, you will protect your heart and continue to be happy with your gift.

"Backup plans are actually biblical."

Perhaps because I grew up in an environment of political unrest, I was never sure of what was going to happen. One day, my mother would tell me it was politically unsafe to be a foreigner so be sure never to tell anyone my father was born in a different country. Another day she would tell me it was better to be a foreigner so be sure to tell everyone my father was not born in China. I woke up each day realizing that there was a different formula for success that depended on factors that had changed in the environment. So when you are unsure of the stability of your environment, always have your script ready to go with plan A, plan B, plan C or however many plans you need to address the situation.

This mindset has translated into how I respond to changes in ministry and in the work I do. For me to be a good steward of any project, I ask God for the best plan. And then I ask Him for a backup plan in case someone does not keep his promise. I operate knowing that we live in a fallen world, so we should expect people to act fallen. This means that those who make promises tend to break their promises. When people upon whom I am relying break promises to me, I need to know how I will respond.

God confirmed to me in His Word that having backup plans is actually biblical. Ecclesiastes 11:6 reads, **"Sow your seed in the morning, and at evening let not your hands be idle, for you do not know which will succeed, whether this or that, or whether both will do equally well."** NIV. There have been so many times when I was weary and would rather go to bed after a long day's work. But God instructs me, **"at evening let not your hands be idle"**, so I continually seek God's wisdom and plan what to do if someone I count on leaves, or if income we counted on is diverted elsewhere, and rehearsing the various "what if's" scenarios. I don't live in fear of the "what-if's", I simply live in preparation for the "what-if's". The preparation might mean scaling down to bare bone minimums or cutting expenses immediately. It might mean storing any overflow in the storehouse in preparation for times of famine. God continues to help me to manage my expectations so I am not caught off guard, nor do I find myself in a panic if the worse happens.

Is there someone or something critical to a project or a mission you are on? What succession plan can you design in order to protect God's purpose if that vital person or thing is not there?

There are times when no matter how well we manage our lives, unexpected situations in the economy may catch us by surprise. Did anyone anticipate the fall of Enron? Could anyone have anticipated the 9/11 terrorist attack and its rippling effects on companies that were affected? If you find yourself unemployed, what could God possibly be doing during this time in your life?

"God had a plan for my life, and when I forgot who He was and what He wanted to accomplish on earth, I forgot who I was."

We live in a culture where our jobs and our titles often define us. Sometimes I wonder if God deliberately allows circumstances to rock our world so we can stop relying on human made foundations. Do you fear severing ties with an organization or a ministry because of your need to fit into the society with a title and a role that others recognize? Do you fear being lost in a crowd and not knowing what you're supposed to be doing with your time when you wake up every morning?

I remember a time when I was not working anywhere and entered the ranks of the unemployed. I thought perhaps I should get some training as a way of preparing myself for a time when I might re-enter the work place. So I signed up for a class. During the break, I noticed that everyone was busy calling their office on their cell phones. I had no one to call. I wandered around by myself during the break trying to look busy and needed. But the fact was, no one missed me because I was disconnected from any purpose that would make a difference. It is a painful experience to know that your existence or lack of it will not make any difference. What I totally missed was the fact that God missed me. God had a plan for my life, and when I forgot who He was and what He wanted to accomplish on earth, I forgot who I was.

What I failed to realize at the time was that my identity was established by God Himself when I accepted the gift of His Son. How could I walk around like a hobo when I have executed a transaction that secures my future for eternity? I had forgotten about this divine transaction with a God who keeps His promises. I wonder today if you have executed the same transaction. If so, did you know that from all the contracts you have signed or all the decisions you have made in your entire lifetime, this transaction with the Almighty is the most important one in your portfolio of transactions? If you were to ever file this transaction, it should be in a file that glitters. In fact, let it be in a custom made musical folder that sings every time you open it up. It should sing the song "Amazing grace!" Indeed that's how this transaction came to exist. It was birthed from God's amazing grace to offer us ridiculous terms where we get all the benefits, and He paid all the cost!

God reminded me of this divine transaction to show me I was misguided to fixate on an earthly title, or role, or any kind of identity that is defined by a company, a ministry, or another human being. God defined my identity through this divine transaction. In God's rule book, He has laws and standards He does not break. In His assessment, no matter how perfect I think I am, any mistake misses His perfect and holy mark and bans me from heaven. In my own strength, I did not qualify for heavenly citizenship because it takes being perfectly holy to make it past heaven's gates. A just God could not let sin go unpunished but a loving God chose to pay the penalty of my sins by sending His Son to die on the cross for me. In this divine transaction God ordained, He granted me heavenly citizenship when I received the gift of His Son as the full payment for my sins. When was the last time someone handed you more than a billion dollars for non-performance? Along with the acceptance of God's gift came the inclusion of my name in God's spiritual family tree. This is an identity that will not only carry me through life but through eternity! It is an identity that no court of law or human decision can rob from me!

When my son Thomas was fifteen, I remember being angry with him for something and took away his privileges, I said, "No more TV, no more games!' His brother jumped in on the act and said, "No more food!" He stormed to his room in a rage. Then within a few minutes, I saw him skipping down the stairs, as happy as can be. He was singing the words, "I believe…I believe…" I said to him, "You believe what?" He sang, "I believe Jesus loves me. Jesus died on the cross for me!" Then he looked me straight in the eye and said, "And you can't take that from me!" He was right. No one can take from us what God has granted. When we receive the blood of Jesus for the forgiveness of our sins, we are a citizen of a heavenly kingdom. We are employed forever as a royal ambassador for God's purpose.

Have you ever received the gift of God's son as your qualification for heavenly citizenship? If not, will you pray this prayer now?

God, I confess that no matter how hard I try, I cannot meet your perfect and holy standards. Please forgive me for missing the mark. I accept the gift of your son who paid the full penalty of all my sins. As I pray this prayer, I trust you as the God who is unchanging. You promised that for those who accept your Son, you will forgive us all our sins and grant us eternal life with you in heaven. So I trust my acceptance of your offer as a binding unbreakable contract between you and me to forgive me of my sins. I accept the gift of your Son and receive your forgiveness and the assurance that you have written my name in your spiritual family tree and count me as an eternal citizen of heaven. Amen.

If you have prayed this prayer, please sign your name here:

Signature: _____ **Date:** _____

God reinforced my heavenly citizenship through a specific encounter with someone who recognized me as a heavenly citizen even when I forgot my identity. I was in a store, and a lady came up to me in tears. She said she recognized me from a Christian event I had attended. She told me her husband was dying of cancer, and she was crying tears of joy when she saw me because she was sure God sent me to encourage her. She asked me to pray for her. So right there in front of the cashier's line, I prayed for her.

When I left the store, I heard God say, "You felt lost without a title. Didn't you know that a title will limit you?" God took me through a time of unemployment so I could learn that He was all the title I needed. I don't need a company or anyone else to give me a title. I am the daughter of the King of Kings. I am a free agent to go on a divine mission. God reserves the right to send me where He wishes. My identity is in God's family tree and in representing the values of my royal family wherever I go.

"When I cut the umbilical cord to human made structure, I am free to flow with God to the ends of the earth."

When the Apostle Paul was in chains, one could say that he had his wings clipped. Yet in this limited state, he said in Ephesians 6:19-20, **"Pray also for me, that whenever I open my mouth, words may be given me so that I will fearlessly make known the mystery of the gospel, for which I am an ambassador in chains. Pray that I may declare it fearlessly, as I should."** NIV

What chains do you feel around you? What have you assessed as being your limitations? How would life change if you viewed yourself like Paul did, as God's "ambassador in chains"?

I praise God for a time in my life when He stripped me of all titles. It was during this time that He gave me my identity in His purpose. His purpose is not confined in one organization or ministry. His purpose is not limited by geographic location. When I cut the umbilical cord to human made structure, I am free to flow with God to the ends of the earth.

I was observing some preschoolers during a summer camp. They all marched around a set of chairs when the music began and when the music stopped, they scrambled to find a seat. The game began with one seat fewer than the children in the group. Whoever did not get a seat was invited to leave the game. Then the music played again and more chairs were taken away. The game ended with one chair in place, and whoever grabbed the chair first was the one who won. As I watched the children, I wondered if we adults are the ones who brain wash our children into scrambling for a particular chair and pushing everyone else out of the way. We have programmed our minds to live in a scarcity model. We also zero in on a particular chair we must grab and discount all others.

God did not create the world as a musical chairs game. Matthew 6:31-34 tells us, **"So do not worry, saying, 'What shall we eat?' or 'What shall we drink?' or 'What shall we wear?' For the pagans run after all these things, and your heavenly Father knows that you need them. But seek first his kingdom and his righteousness, and all these things will be given to you as well."** NIV.

Observe the words "**all these things will be given unto you**". Do we really believe that God owns the universe and will give us all the things we need? Do we believe He can move us from one company to another and into new opportunities that He owns throughout the world? We are the ones who limit God by setting artificial boundaries. As in a musical chairs game, we dictate to Him which chair we want. Meanwhile God is saying, "My spirit flows where it wills. I will not be limited by your human made rules and boundaries." Are you ready to be in God's royal family? Is it time for you to learn how to flow with His spirit?

When the Odds are Against You

Situation: Are you in a situation where the odds are against you to succeed? Do you question God's calling and accuse Him of being unreasonable?

The purpose of the personal journal entries shown below is to capture the emotion of fear in situations when the odds for victory are against you. Some entries were taken from an actual journal, others were written more recently as I reflected on what I was feeling at the time. The dates of the entries are approximate and were included to give the reader some sense of chronological history. In teaching this material, feel free to use my personal journal entries as illustration or personalize your lesson with writing your own personal journal entries or testimony to capture the emotion of loneliness you felt in your own life. If you did not keep a journal, then try to relive the situation in your mind and write an entry today to capture what you felt at the time.

May 6, 1971

Dear God,
There are so many in my class applying for full scholarships in America. There are not enough scholarships for all of us. Who will get to go? It seems like there are so many trying to find a way out? Every time someone says they got accepted, I can feel the tension in the air. I don't know if I should be happy for them or sad that there is one less scholarship for someone else. Are you in control God? It seems to me that if you really want me somewhere you can make a way. That's what the teachers at the mission school say. They say God can make a way.

September 2, 1973

Dear God,
I don't know how I got in. I was given a full scholarship to Mississippi University for Women. I never imagined I would be in Mississippi. I think some Christians made this scholarship available. I'm not

sure why. I'm just grateful I got it. I'm scheduled to leave in June of 1974. I guess God it doesn't really matter how much the odds are against me. I just need one open door. I feel like you opened this door. Thank you, God, for giving me a way to the free land of America.

Jan 8, 1977

Dear God,
What are the odds in getting a scholarship for graduate school? Yet today I received a letter from New York saying that I got accepted into the MBA program. You opened the door again. I'm not sure I understand why everyone focuses on the statistics. You keep showing me that you defy statistics. It's like you're taking me somewhere and no one can stop you. I think you want me to have this degree. I know my Mom would be proud because she always wanted me to be financially independent. They tell me I'll have a great starting salary. I can't imagine having money one day.

Oct 3, 2001

Dear God,
I don't know what will happen but I feel like I am on this moving escalator and the event will be here whether I'm ready or not. There are some things in life that will happen because they are scheduled to happen. This is one of them. How could I have controlled something like 9/11? Something major has taken place and it has rippling effects on thousands. Our conference is in November but I know the event of 9/11 will have some impact on the conference. This isn't the time to be marketing a conference. Or maybe it's the perfect time. But people are distracted and it takes time before they start to look for answers. Maybe the conference will be right on time. Maybe they will be ready to question their purpose in life.

But what if things don't settle down fast enough? What if after all this time and resource commitment, the attendance drops dramatically? What will it mean for Inspire Women if this assignment crashes? God, I don't have time to be afraid. Fear is not from you. The fact is, you knew about 9/11 before it happened. You also knew what the dominoes effect would be. You are not surprised. So if you are not in a panic, why should I be in a panic? Do you know something God? This life is about your dream not mine. So why am I afraid that you will let your own dream crash? And should you choose to do so, isn't it your dream to do with as you will? I am learning that there is great freedom when I just let you manage your own dream. I need to separate myself from the results. My calling is to obey, your role is to bring the results you want.

April 3, 2003

Dear God,
This is not a good year to start a nonprofit organization. Donations are down. Everyone is warning me against going independent. The crazy thing is, I have never had the desire to start my own organization. God, I like being part of a community. I hate feeling like an immigrant. Why would I do something so contrary to what I personally and emotionally need? And to do this when the odds are against me is totally insane. Yet, why do I hear your voice pounding on my heart? What is it that you want for your daughters? There are so many other women who have connections and influence who would be so effective at doing the very thing you want to do. I don't understand God why you don't entrust this vision to one of them. I feel like you picked the one who is weakest and least likely to succeed. Is that because you know I would never imagine there was anything in me that can establish what you long for? Is this how you will get credit for the entire ministry? All I have is you God. Maybe that's what you want everyone to see. Maybe you want people to see that all we need is you and you will provide us with the resources to build your dream. Just promise you'll go with me God. If you don't go with me, I'm going home. Remember this is your dream God. So I'm trusting you to show me the way.

When the Odds Are Against You

Situation: Are you in a situation where the odds are against you to succeed? Do you question God's calling and accuse Him of being unreasonable?

Reminder: Let's learn the truths from God's Word that speak to our situations. Remember that as a member of God's royal family, we are to act according to the customs of the royal family. This means reinforcing our royal identity by living according to God's specific instructions in the Bible. When we cannot find specific instructions that speak to our situation, we are to search our spiritual heritage and model our lives after God's faith heroes who responded correctly to situations that parallel our own. We can also learn from their mistakes to avoid making the same mistakes in our own lives.

When Moses led the children of Israel to the edge of the Promise Land, he sent scouts into the land to survey the territory. They came back to report to Moses and the whole assembly and said in Numbers 13:27-28, **"We went into the land to which you sent us, and it does flow with milk and honey! Here is its fruit. But the people who live there are powerful and the cities are fortified and very large. We even saw descendants of Anak there. The Amalekites live in the Negev; the Hittites, Jebusites and Amorites live in the hill country; and the Canaanites live near the sea and along the Jordan."** They were staring into the face of a situation where the odds were against them.

"Do you focus your time analyzing the odds or do you focus your time being clear as to what you heard God say?"

God does not hide the facts. He shows us clearly how the odds are stacked against us. He does not want warriors who enter a battle not realizing the challenge ahead. However, in spite of the facts, when God says "Go!", He means "Go!" Numbers 13:30 tells us:

Then Caleb silenced the people before Moses and said, "We should go up and take possession of the land, for we can certainly do it." NIV.

Are you staring at odds that are against you? Do you focus your time analyzing the odds or do you focus your time being clear as to what you heard God say?

When my mother prayed that God would open the door for her children to reach the free land of America, she did not focus on the odds against her; she focused on God's character to protect those who cried out to Him. How did she, an uneducated woman, trust God to educate her children at an American University? Although she never went past a third grade education, she started to drill her children in academics trusting God to one day open the door. All her children left on full scholarships to American universities. Today my brother is the Senior Vice President of Fidelity Investments, my sister runs a museum store, and I was a management consultant in companies such as Exxon and Booz, Allen, and Hamilton till God called me out of corporate America into full time ministry. Do you allow statistics to manage your life or do you believe in the God who defies odds?

Caleb was focused on what He heard God say. He knew God wanted the children of Israel to claim the Promise Land. He knew they were at the edge of the blessing. He knew God would not have taken all that trouble to bring them this far only to have them shrink back. He was clear that the next thing to do was to go forward. The people, however, were afraid of the odds. So instead of remembering God's dream, they started to worry about what it would take to go forward.

"When the odds are against you, those who are faithless will always complain."

Numbers 13:31-33 tells us: **But the men who had gone up with him said, "We can't attack those people; they are stronger than we are." And they spread among the Israelites a bad report about the land they had explored. They said, "The land we explored devours those living in it. All the people we saw there are of great size. We saw the Nephilim there (the descendants of Anak come from the Nephilim). We seemed like grasshoppers in our own eyes, and we looked the same to them." NIV**

Have you been dwelling on the facts to the point that the facts have a voice louder than God's voice? What was God's mission for your life? Do you even remember what the original calling was? Have you allowed the facts to cause you to abandon the mission?

God's Word shows us how history repeats itself. When the odds are against you, those who are faithless will always

complain. Numbers 14:1-4 tells us: **That night all the people of the community raised their voices and wept aloud. All the Israelites grumbled against Moses and Aaron, and the whole assembly said to them, "If only we had died in Egypt! Or in this desert! Why is the LORD bringing us to this land only to let us fall by the sword? Our wives and children will be taken as plunder. Wouldn't it be better for us to go back to Egypt?" And they said to each other, "We should choose a leader and go back to Egypt."**

"…once the cost is higher than expected, don't be surprised when followers will accuse the leader."

God shows through His Word the patterns that repeat in history. If the journey does not require sacrifice or risk, everyone is happy to go on the journey. But once the cost is higher than expected, don't be surprised when followers will accuse the leader. The situation somehow ends up being the leader's fault. If you know this to be the pattern, then you will know that you are right on tome. You will soften your own pain when you manage your expectations.

God shows us through the story of Moses that when God tries to stretch the faith of the people, the pattern of those who are faithless is to accuse the leader. It is human nature for our fear to drive us to blame someone else for our predicament. The problem is, the leader is not the one stretching us. If we are to blame anyone, we should blame God. The leader is simply under God's authority and is in the same boat of having their faith stretched and needing to trust God. There are times when I see those on my team struggling with God's call for their lives. I see them getting mad at me as if I was the one who set the goals.

Before I can help those on my team to trust God, I must first have settled my own fears. If I don't have the faith to go forward, how can I encourage others to take a leap of faith? In this story, praise God that Moses and his inner circle weren't having a crisis of faith. Numbers 14:5-9 tells us: **Then Moses and Aaron fell facedown in front of the whole Israelite assembly gathered there. Joshua son of Nun and Caleb son of Jephunneh, who were among those who had explored the land, tore their clothes and said to the entire Israelite assembly, "The land we passed through and explored is exceedingly good. If the LORD is pleased with us, he will lead us into that land, a land flowing with milk and honey, and will give it to us. Only do not rebel against the LORD. And do not be afraid of the people of the land, because we will swallow them up. Their protection is gone, but the LORD is with us. Do not be afraid of them."** In so many words they were telling the people that the victory is not based on facts or analysis. The victory is simply based on one criterion "**If the LORD is pleased with us.**"

"God intentionally allowed the odds because He wants a people who will live by faith."

What causes the LORD to be pleased with us? It is not our performance but our surrender and our faith. God wants to know, "Who are you afraid of? What are you afraid of? Are you more afraid of a person or your circumstances than you are afraid of God's displeasure for not obeying and trusting Him?" Moses and the leaders instructed the people that **"their protection is gone, but the LORD is with us. Do not be afraid of them."** The flip side of the statement is this, "If you disobey God, then your protection is gone. If you take yourself out of the center of God's will, then you are on your own to protect yourself. So here is the choice, "Do you want God to protect you or do you want to protect yourself?"

When God launched the first Inspire Women's conference, it was scheduled right after 9/11. On top of that, it came after a global women's conference that took place in our city. The last thing the city needed was another conference and an unknown one at that. The uniqueness of Inspire Women is in our follow up programs to offer women targeted leadership training, fund scholarships to accredited seminaries and specialized programs, and to best train them for their calling. But after a major crisis, how many care about training and preparation for God's mission when their worry and focus is on their families and immediate needs? If the devil wanted to create panic, he certainly succeeded. Nevertheless, we could choose to trust God's leading and ignore our circumstances.

When the odds are against you, know that God is not surprised. God intentionally allowed the odds because He wants a people who will live by faith. God will never eliminate the need for faith in your life. Once you understand God's patterns, you will know what to do.

When Moses first left Egypt, he set out to lead the children of Israel to the Promise Land. What did you set out to do when you began your journey with God? What has changed?

"When I fast forward the tape and imagine myself on my deathbed, I don't want to look back and wonder what could have happened had I chosen to have more courage."

At the crossroads of life, cling to what you first heard God say. Then make the decision that best aligns with what you first heard Him say. When given an option, pick the one that will allow you to demonstrate more faith. The most important thing is for God to be pleased with your choice. In His pleasure, you will find your protection.

When I reflect on the growth of Inspire Women, I cringe to think that I could have turned back. If I had turned back, I would have lost the blessing of seeing a ministry established to inspire thousands of women to step into God's purpose. I would not have seen how God established a ministry to provide scholarships for women for biblical training. I would not have seen the establishment of the Inspire Women's Leadership Institute where leaders from ministries all across the city can grow together in leadership, fellowship, and spiritual maturity.

When I fast forward the tape and imagine myself on my deathbed, I don't want to look back and wonder what could have happened had I chosen to have more courage. What's wrong with taking a few chances, living on the edge, and being willing to jump in, even when the odds are against you? Is it time for you to do something that is bigger than your fear? Is your fear the only thing standing between you and God's blessing?

The incredible thing I have discovered about God is that He has already planted steps of faith in our past. Before we climb a mountain, He has already taught us to climb a hill. When a friend said, "God is inviting you to fly without a parachute," she also added,

"But that's o.k. because you have done this before." Her words really made me think.

When have I trusted God before when I wasn't sure of the plan? Then God brought me back to the time years ago when I had to go back to my country to be interviewed by the U.S. immigration to get my residency papers to stay in this country. I knew there was a chance they would say no and then I would not be able to get exit papers to return to this country. I also knew that my only grounds of immigration were to prove that I was related to my brother who is an American citizen. But my brother was born in China during the war and my mother did not have a birth certificate on him. Immigration said we could take a blood test from my mother but then my mother died. So I was going into this interview knowing that my only chance for immigration was my relationship with a brother that I could not prove was my brother.

When I walked into the interview I had been in school in Mississippi and I am the kind of person who absorbs her environment so I was talking like someone from Mississippi. Ten minutes into the interview, the immigration officer started laughing.

Then he said, "I have been out of my country for ten years and I never imagined I would hear a Mississippi accent out of the mouth of a Chinese woman. You want to live in our country?"

I said quietly, "Yes."

He said, "Fine." He stamped the papers and told me the interview was over.

When I left U.S. immigration, I felt God's Spirit in me celebrating. God showed me years ago that when there is something I needed for His purpose to continue, He would open the door. I did not know then that God had Inspire Women on my platter. I did not know I was going to be the Founder of a ministry God would birth in Houston, Texas. For me to be the Founder of a ministry that is birthed in Houston, Texas, I had to be in this country. So God opened the door for me to be in this country. Having climbed that hill with God, He already trained me in the little things before He put a mountain in front of me. I have seen God carry me past situations when the odds were against me. Before God calls you to climb a mountain, He has already taught you to climb a hill.

Are the odds against you? Then remember you serve a God who specializes in impossible odds. More than that, He specializes in designing a custom tailored program that trains His vessels to fulfill His dreams, no matter what the odds.

When You Fear Failure

Situation: Are you in a situation that is demanding more than your capabilities? Are you afraid to fail because of what it will mean to your livelihood and your future? Do you feel the stress even thinking that you might not make it?

The purpose of the personal journal entries shown below is to capture the emotion of the fear of failure. Some entries were taken from an actual journal, others were written more recently as I reflected on what I was feeling at the time. The dates of the entries are approximate and were included to give the reader some sense of chronological history. In teaching this material, feel free to use my personal journal entries as illustration or personalize your lesson with writing your own personal journal entries or testimony to capture the emotion of loneliness you felt in your own life. If you did not keep a journal, then try to relive the situation in your mind and write an entry today to capture what you felt at the time.

Aug 6, 1979

Dear God,
I heard the Partner of the company throw someone out of her office today. People are very intense here. They throw a project at you with no instructions and expect you to figure it out. I can't believe I am supposed to oversee the financial data for all government offices in Washington D.C. People are handing me their data in the hallways. Meanwhile my office is piled high with information and I have no idea what I'm doing.

God, I don't know anyone in this city. What do I do if I can't do this job? How much is my rent? How much money do I have in the bank? How long could I last before I run out of money? I don't think it's an option anymore to move back home. I can't think God. I'm trembling on the inside. I didn't expect work to be like this. Is it me or is it the job? Maybe I'm not cut out to do management consulting.

Nov 11, 1979

Dear God,
I can't believe the clients for my next project will be admirals of the U.S. navy! What do I know about the U.S. navy? The partner said the company pays us top dollar to figure things out. They don't expect us to know anything but they expect us to learn while we do. I think everyone else is in the same boat. Is this how work is supposed to be? I thought school was hard and I couldn't wait to work. Now I wish I could return to school. At least in school, I knew my dorm was paid for and I didn't have to worry about whether I could afford the rent.

July 16, 1980

Dear God,
I must be getting better with handling the unknown. What do I know about the oil business? Nothing! But I don't feel the same level of fear anymore. Exxon is a big

company and I know they hire top people but somehow, I feel like you'll guide me through my projects. I had my first presentation today. I walked into the room and it was filled with men in dark suits. I had a peach suit on. Maybe that's not exactly the Exxon colors. Oh well....I think the men thought I brightened up the room. They seemed to like the project. They told me I did well. I think I'm learning how to make it in corporate America.

Aug 19, 1982

Dear God,
Booz Allen and Hamilton is one of the top management consulting companies in the world. The partner said the company pays us top dollar and he expects us to deliver. He said the company has no mercy. If we don't deliver we'll be gone. It looks like everyone works till 10 p.m. or later every evening. I'm used to working hard so that won't bother me. God, I'm making a lot of money in corporate America. Is this the American dream? The partner said if we do well, we'll fly up the corporate ladder. They don't care about our age, they reward performance.

July 1, 1985

Dear God,
I flew up the corporate ladder. It seems like every time I do well, the goals increase. Some days I feel like I'm competing with myself. Everyone is in such a hurry to do more. When we finally finish all that we're doing, what progress will we have made? Is it about getting a bigger house, a bigger car, or maybe an additional house or car? And then what

happens? Where does all this success lead? It seems like the more you achieve, the more afraid you are of losing what you have achieved. It's like we've built a prison for ourselves.

April 1, 2001

Dear God,
I never expected that the goals in ministry would be harder than the goals in corporate America. At least in corporate America, we did preliminary studies to see if a project was viable before we took it on. But here in ministry, it's like the leader decides what needs to be done and then we jump in. The analysis tells me we will crash but we go anyway. This is major stress city. How could we launch without adequate personnel or funds? It's like launching a rocket knowing you'll run out of fuel with no plan as to how to get more fuel. Is this how things work in ministry? I've never worked full time in ministry before so all this is new. What do I do God? Do you want me to throw out all my spreadsheets? What does trusting you mean? I know you don't mean for me to park my business hat because you gave me an M.B.A. So did you give me that business background so I can sit here and stress? Maybe I should just go in any open door that will get me closer to the goal and stop looking at the score board? Is that what living by faith means?

Oct 1, 2001

Dear God,
I used to be afraid of failure but I'm not afraid anymore. I'm tired of living a safe life. If you want this conference and you want it done with limited budget and

resource, who am I to tell you it can't be done? Maybe you design the kind of worship you want. Maybe it pleases you to know that I am willing to do this with so little resources. Maybe you're not impressed with human skills. Though you use those skills, what you want is a trust relationship with you. Well, God, I think you got what you wanted because I wake up talking to you, I talk to you all day, and you are the last person I talk to before I go to bed. I think the reason you gave me a God-sized project is so that I will desperately cling to you. You are all I have God. The only reason I'm not afraid to fail is because you are walking with me. Please don't ever leave me God or I'll crash.

June 11, 2002

Dear God,
There is absolutely no way I can handle two finals for seminary while producing a citywide conference and luncheon. No human being could possibly handle this. And on top of all that, you're asking me to keep a 4.0 GPA. Why, God? I think you're trying to push me to the place of unraveling. If I unravel God then everything will start to crash.

The strangest thing is how you have used this time to completely own my mind. There is no time for one extra thought that is not related to your mission. If I get distracted I will fail. I need you to guard my mind. You are the gatekeeper. I don't think about anything but what you have

put on my platter. I don't get to choose who I spend time with, what I do, or what I feel. You own it all God. I know this is the only way to make it. If I just watch for your signals and follow your marching orders completely, I will succeed. I have no opinions of my own God. Forget whatever I learned in corporate America. It takes more than skills to part a Red Sea. Let me listen to your voice God. Let me listen so closely that I can almost hear you breathe. God, I can actually hear you. It's like you're standing right behind me and I can almost feel your breath on my neck. I know this is your dream God. I just don't know why you picked me to fulfill it.

July 2, 2003

Dear God,
I can't believe we separated from an established organization to start our own non profit ministry. God, do you know I have no idea how to do this? Who in their right mind does something like this? Yet I am so sure this is what you want. God, my confidence is in knowing that you are sure. I know you have the plan. If left to me, I would crash. But when you lead, I'll just follow. I can hear you God. I don't know when I started hearing you so clearly. Is it because you get louder when I follow longer? Is it because you want to be sure of our obedience first before you speak? Is it because unless we step into a God sized mission there's no reason for you to speak louder?

254

When You Fear Failure

Situation: Are you in a situation that is demanding more than your capabilities? Are you afraid to fail because of what it will mean to your livelihood and your future? Do you feel the stress even thinking that you might not make it?

Reminder: Let's learn the truths from God's Word that speak to our situations. Remember that as a member of God's royal family, we are to act according to the customs of the royal family. This means reinforcing our royal identity by living according to God's specific instructions in the Bible. When we cannot find specific instructions that speak to our situation, we are to search our spiritual heritage and model our lives after God's faith heroes who responded correctly to situations that parallel our own. We can also learn from their mistakes to avoid making the same mistakes in our own lives.

I remember when I was in corporate America, the partners of the company used fear as an incentive to get the young consultants to work. I remember attending an orientation with the top graduates of Harvard, Stanford, Cornell and M.I.T. I was surrounded by highly competitive people who were used to succeeding. I was totally stressed out with the pressure to perform and then the pressure to outperform myself. I could not understand why being successful was so important. I just knew it was and the idea of failing tore me up on the inside.

"The only way I can be perfect is if I simply receive God's perfection."

When God took over my life, something dramatic took place. I didn't get smarter but I worked smarter. God said in Romans 3:22-25, **"There is no difference, for all have sinned and fall short of the glory of God, and are justified freely by his grace through the redemption that came by Christ Jesus."** NIV. This verse brought me from the arrogance of thinking that I could do something perfect to realizing that only God is perfect. In fact, if I could accept my imperfection, I could relax.

Psalm 103:15-16 helped me to take myself less seriously. It reads, **"As for man, his days are like grass, he flourishes like a flower of the field; the wind blows over it and it is gone, and its place remembers it no more."** NIV.

When I ask myself, "What will this matter a hundred years from now?" I find myself letting go of details that used to send me into a tailspin. A friend of mine once told me, "Anita, you need to lighten up or you won't make it." So I started researching jokes and sending them to him. I think he now has a joke library with all that I have sent him over the years. I think I passed the test when in the middle of a major crisis, he received a joke from me. He replied, "I'm glad to see that you are still laughing."

One of the greatest truth in God's Word that helped to set me free is in Romans 8:3-4 which reads, **"For what the law was powerless to do in that it was weakened by the sinful nature, God did by sending his own Son in the likeness of sinful man to be a sin**

offering. And so he condemned sin in sinful man, in order that the righteous requirements of the law might be fully met in us, who do not live according to the sinful nature but according to the Spirit." NIV.

What these verses taught me was that God's son was the only one who was able to fulfill the perfect requirements of God's law. What I finally understood was that God is the only One who has succeeded in everything. In the areas of eternal life, He lived a perfectly holy life and then went to the cross to pay the penalty for my imperfection. He then offered me the gift of forgiveness for all my imperfections. More than that, He gave me the opportunity to fully meet God's standards "**according to the Spirit**."

How do I live the full requirements of God according to the Spirit? I do so by admitting that I in my human flesh cannot attain perfection. The only way I can be perfect is if I simply receive God's perfection. Then by faith, I allow God to live His perfect life through me. It took me a while to see the concept but it took me even longer to do it.

How do I do my job by the power of Christ's perfection? No matter what my job requires, I no longer try to be impressive. I begin by saying I have missed the standard. I then accept the gift of Christ's perfection and know that He has all the answers. So now, all I have to do is to ask God to show me His answers. I then get out of the way by not arguing with Him or acting like I know better. Instead, I offer my life as a living sacrifice and I say to God, "All my energy belongs to you. All my creativity belongs to you. All my diligence belongs to you. Use them as you will and direct me to solve this problem." Are you so focused on watching your goals that you have overwhelmed yourself? Perhaps it's time to focus on the perfection of Christ and then trust Him to show you day by day how to reach the goal.

Are you afraid of failure? If so, why? How can you alleviate your pressure by depending on Christ's perfection?

"The key to releasing stress is to give God my life as an act of worship and to let Him control the results."

My husband used to say to me, "Just keep shooting the ball. Don't watch the score board. Don't keep revisiting decisions. Just keep going in the same direction till the game is over." The key to releasing stress is to give God my life as an act of worship and to let Him control the results. If I have given God my best, then I need to rest in knowing that He is pleased with me. At the end of the day, He is the only boss I work for. I exist to fulfill His purpose. Colossians 3:23-24 teaches us, **"Whatever you do, work at it with all your heart, as working for the Lord, not for men, since you know that you will receive an inheritance from the Lord as a reward. It is the Lord Christ you are serving."** NIV.

Another way I render my life as a living sacrifice is to start by examining my motives. Why do I want to succeed? Is it to make myself look good? If so, why? The fact is, when I am gone this place will remember me no more. The only thing that matters is that I have left God's fingerprints behind me. His is the only story that's worth telling and worth remembering. So as I pour myself into my work I find myself feeling the sentiment as expressed by the Olympic medalist winner in the movie "Chariots of Fire." He said, "God made me fast and when I run I feel His pleasure. And to win, that is for His honor." So I ask God for the opportunity to win so His name will be honored.

When you operate out of your need to perform, you are meeting your own need to prove yourself. God has already given us His verdict. How can you live in the freedom of God's verdict that we have all failed? Begin from a place of humility and ask how you can offer your life as your form of worship to God.

I remember telling my son Thomas to work harder. He said to me, "Why?" I said, "Learn from your brother. He works hard" He said, "But I'm happier." I wasn't sure what to say to that. I said, "Thomas, do you think your purpose in life is to be happy?" He said, "I don't want to be stressed like my brother."

When his brother was in eighth grade, he represented his school in San Antonio in a Math contest. I was speaking at a women's retreat that weekend and could not be with him. I called him that evening and he said, "Mom, I'm scared." I asked, "Why are you scared? You're really good at Math and you love competition. It really gets your adrenalin going when you get to compete in the count down rounds where they give you a question and you have to press the buzzer and be first to answer the question." He said, "It was fun last year because there were no expectations. But this year, everyone looks to me to win. So I'm afraid. I don't want to disappoint anyone." I thought to myself, "But last year, he won not only because he practiced and is gifted in Math but there was a prayer warrior who was on her knees all morning." The thought hit me, "Do we really believe God is behind our success or is He just a tag along?" Is it really that we depend on ourselves and add a little dose of God as a lucky charm? Now, if God was the wind beneath his wings last year, then what's the difference this year? The stakes may be higher but his source of strength hasn't changed. Did we begin with God and then shift to depending on our own strength? I told my son what the Lord told me about leaning on His strength. My son said he felt better. The next day, he won the Math contest.

Today, I see both my sons work in their own styles but neither are ever stressed. They tell me, "Life is short, Mom. Let's be happy!"

When You Face Suffering

Situation: Are you in a situation where you anticipate suffering? Do you dread what is about to happen?

The purpose of the personal journal entries shown below is to capture the emotion of fear in anticipation of suffering. Some entries were taken from an actual journal, others were written more recently as I reflected on what I was feeling at the time. The dates of the entries are approximate and were included to give the reader some sense of chronological history. In teaching this material, feel free to use my personal journal entries as illustration or personalize your lesson with writing your own personal journal entries or testimony to capture the emotion of loneliness you felt in your own life. If you did not keep a journal, then try to relive the situation in your mind and write an entry today to capture what you felt at the time.

December 11, 1974

Dear God,
He said I was too emotionally needy and he didn't want me in his life anymore. He wrote me a letter to say the relationship was over. So I guess that means the engagement is over. I thought he said he would always be there for me. What happened, God? Was the distance between Hong Kong and the United States too much for him?

I have never split up with anyone before. What is this pain I feel in my heart? It's like my heart is actually hurting but there is nothing physically wrong with me. I feel like I can't breathe. I feel like someone cut me on the inside with a razor. I don't know what to do. I think I should just sleep so I can't feel the pain. I find myself crying all the time. What is wrong with me? I don't even know how long this pain will last because I've never split up with anyone before. Is it like a headache that will just go away in time? There is no medicine I can take. I wake up feeling emotional pain
and I go to bed feeling emotional pain. What is wrong with me?

May 1, 1980

Dear God,
What is wrong with me? I keep getting my heart broken. What is it that I am looking for? I'm trying to be what I am not. I've totally lost who I am by trying to get someone to love me. And then I find they leave me anyway. So why did I lose myself in the process? So now I've lost everything. I lost me and I lost him. What sense is that?

I hate this feeling I have. I wake up not wanting to be alive. I think it must be easier to be in physical pain because at least people can relate to physical pain. I can't handle one more heartbreak!

July 22, 2002

Dear God,
How could I be so sick and have finals to take? I have to listen to 4 audio tapes to listen to and they are six hours long. My head is pounding I can't keep my head up long enough to listen to a tape or to read my text book. I can't blow this test God, these are the last finals at seminary. I had to put my head down and sleep and wake up in fifteen minute intervals to study. I feel like I'm hobbling to the finish line and I don't know if I'll make it. I am so pitiful God. I feel like I'm dying but I know this suffering is nothing compared to what you went through. Stop my hands from trembling God, I have to write a paper. Help me to finish well. I want this final test to honor you!

Oct 1, 2005

Dear God,
I can't get rid of this migraine. I have so much to do but my head is throbbing and it feels like it's about to fall off. I can't stay down God so please help me to get up. You didn't get off the cross even when your head was throbbing. It's like you made up your mind to finish and you were prepared to do whatever it took. I want to finish too God.
My children are watching to see what I do. It will affect how they respond to life. I saw a film once that showed a father carrying his son to the finish line. I feel like you are carrying me. When we get to the finish line it's going to be just you and me. At the end of the day, it's always been just you and me. Even when others jump on the band wagon, it's still really just you and me. It's like we could just walk away together and I would have all that I needed.

What is it God that is so sufficient about you that you are all that I need? Even in this migraine, you show me that you are in control and you are not surprised. You used this migraine to remind me of when the crown of thorns went into Jesus' head. You are asking me to render my suffering as my form of worship.

Would I worship you through my suffering by showing the world that you are worthy? The greater the suffering, the greater the victory! I thought it was such bad timing to be struggling with physical pain at a time when there is so much work to do in the ministry. But I think you are telling me that the timing of this physical problem was perfectly timed to bring you the most honor. If I would serve you while in pain, how much more does that show the world what you mean to me! I am learning God that you don't waste anything. So when I ask you to remove suffering I am really asking if you will settle for less honor. I think I should just say, "Do what you will God. May whatever you decide be done to me according to thy will."

When You Face Suffering

Situation: Are you in a situation where you anticipate suffering? Do you dread what is about to happen?

Reminder: Let's learn the truths from God's Word that speak to our situations. Remember that as a member of God's royal family, we are to act according to the customs of the royal family. This means reinforcing our royal identity by living according to God's specific instructions in the Bible. When we cannot find specific instructions that speak to our situation, we are to search our spiritual heritage and model our lives after God's faith heroes who responded correctly to situations that parallel our own. We can also learn from their mistakes to avoid making the same mistakes in our own lives.

"Jesus recognized his suffering was His great opportunity to glorify God."

Over the years, I have often heard the teaching that the sole purpose of human kind is to glorify God. These words sounded spiritual but I had no idea what the word "glorify" meant. So how do I glorify God if I don't know what the word glorify means? Then I learned that the word "glorify" in the Greek has the idea of being "fat, heavy, important." So the concept of glorifying God has the idea of showing the world how important God is by the choices that I make. I think in our human minds, we want to think of glorifying God in terms of writing a best seller, drawing thousands in a crowd, having major success in our projects. What about the opportunity to show the world how important God is by our willingness to suffer or to sacrifice for Him? In fact, the more difficult the challenge we endure for Christ's sake, the louder the message we send to the world of how worthy our God is of our suffering.

In the Garden of Gethsemane, Jesus said in John 17:1-2, **"Father, the time has come. Glorify your Son, that your Son may glorify you."** NIV. Observe that Jesus recognized that His suffering was His great opportunity to glorify God. Is this how you view your suffering?

In Jesus' suffering, He was tempted as we are. Although He was God, He was in human form and suffered as a man. Hebrews 2:17-18 tells us that, **"...he had to be made like his brothers in every way...Because he himself suffered when he was tempted, he is able to help those who are being tempted."** NIV

What kind of God is that wonderful that would cause Jesus to go to the cross in obedience to Him? What are you telling the world about your God in the way you are handling your suffering?

"God wants to know if you will endure the cross as your way to show the world your God is worthy."

When God trusts you with dreams for yourself, your family, business, church, ministry, community, nation, or the world, know that suffering was part of God's plan through Jesus, and it will be part of God's plans for you. As God conforms us to the image of His Son, we cannot avoid suffering as part of our journey. It's not a question of whether you will ever suffer; it is more a question of how you will respond when suffering enters your life. It is not unspiritual to fear suffering but it is unbiblical to fear it to the point of trying to avoid it when God trusts you with a cross.

In Jesus' example, He anticipated that the time of His suffering was beginning. He said in Matthew 26:31, **"This very night you will all fall away on account of me, for it is written: 'I will strike the shepherd, and the sheep of the flock will be scattered.'"** NIV Have you ever anticipated a time when something or someone is about to strike you, and you know the blows will be hard and unmerciful?

In the midst of the imminent trials, Jesus also suffered the emotional loss of those who professed to be His friends. When Peter said in Matthew 26:33, **"Even if all fall away on account of you, I never will."** Jesus replied in Matthew 26:34, **"this very night, before the rooster crows, you will disown me three times."** NIV.

The abandonment began even before the trial began. Matthew 26:36-39 tells us that **"Jesus went with his disciples to a place called Gethsemane, and he said to them, "Sit here while I go over there and pray." He took Peter and the two sons of Zebedee along with him, and he began to be sorrowful and troubled. Then he said to them, "My soul is overwhelmed with sorrow to the point of death. Stay here and keep watch with me."** We are told that when Jesus returned, He found His closest friends fast asleep. Matthew:40-42 tells us, **"Then he returned to his disciples and found them sleeping."Could you men not keep watch with me for one hour?" he asked Peter.** NIV.

Did you see the words, **"Could you men not keep watch with me for one hour**?" Peter, who was so adamant in his profession of commitment to Jesus, was among those who fell asleep. He abandoned Jesus emotionally even before the trials began. Have you ever been in a place where those who were your closest confidantes were distracted and consumed with their own needs during a time of your deepest suffering?

Meanwhile, what was going on inside Jesus? Matthew 26:39 tells us, **"Going a little farther, he fell with his face to the ground and prayed, "My Father, if it is possible, may this cup be taken from me. Yet not as I will, but as you will."** NIV. Matthew 26:42 tell us, **"He went away a second time and prayed, "My Father, if it is not possible for this cup to be taken away unless I drink it, may your will be done."** NIV. Did you notice that Jesus went away a second time? How many times have you gone back to God with an issue that is weighing heavy on your mind?

Some of us have the opportunity to run the other way and often do. Others are not given an option. At the crossroads of life, God wants to know if you will endure the cross as your way to show the world your God is worthy.

Matthew 26:43-44 tells us, **"When he came back, he again found them sleeping, because their eyes were heavy. So he left them and went away once more and prayed the third time, saying the same thing."** NIV. Observe the words **"went away once more and prayed the third time."**

What does it mean when you have asked God the same question and He gives you the same answer? How have you discovered that God is sure of His calling for your life? How does it help you to be sure, knowing that God is sure?

"Jesus had one question to answer, 'Father, do you want this?' When He was sure the answer was 'Yes', that settled it for Jesus."

Was Jesus terrified of the cross? He was not oblivious to the facts. He knew what it would take to go to the cross. He knew what it meant to have the sins of the world put on His shoulders. Even though He was blameless, He was going to death row for all humankind. Worse still, He knew that for a moment in time, the entire wrath of God would be poured out on Him. Can you imagine God redirecting all His wrath towards you alone?

How did Jesus get past the fear? Jesus said in Matthew 26:29, "**Yet not as I will, but as you will.**" Don't miss the fact that it was the relationship between Jesus and His father that settled the question for Him as to whether He would go to the cross. Think of it this way. Aren't there people in your family or life that you would suffer for and sacrifice for more than others? And in the case that you choose to endure sacrifice on their behalf, is it not your relationship with them that causes you to decide what you will bear for them? In Jesus' case, He had one question to answer, "Father, do you want this?" When He was sure the answer was "Yes", that settled it for Jesus.

I remember growing up looking into my mother's face and seeing her longing to reach the Promise Land of America. I promised I would get her out of Hong Kong before the Communist takeover. One of the deepest disappointments in my life was the fact that I was unable to give her what her heart so longed for. But if you were to ask me, "Is there anything you would withhold to give your mother her dream?" The answer would be "No." I would have worked as many jobs as I needed to in order to save the money. I would have sacrificed not buying anything I personally wanted in order to give her the money. I would have depleted my savings in order to pay for the immigration attorney, the plane fare, or whatever was needed in order to get her out. Would I do this for anyone else? The answer is, "No." But I would do it for her because of the depth of our relationship. It would not even matter to me why it was so important to her to reach the Promise Land of America. All I would need to know is, "Mother, do you want this?" I know because of our relationship that she would never ask this of me unless it was absolutely critical.

Jesus knew how deep His relationship was with the Father. He knew how much the Father loved Him. The Father would never have asked Jesus to go to the cross had there been another way. But the only solution that would satisfy both the Father's utmost character of justice and the Father's utmost character of love was for Him to give up His one and only son to appease the law's penalty of death for sin and to satisfy the Father's love which then sent His Son to pay the penalty. If there is something you are unwilling to do for God realize it is because your relationship is not deep enough. Therefore you find yourself saying, "No way! There is no way I'm doing this for you!"

What is the depth of your relationship with the Father? Was there something God asked of you that you were unwilling to give earlier that you find yourself willing to give today because you have grown deeper in your relationship? If there is something God is asking of you today that you are unwilling to give, what can you do to deepen your relationship so you will be able to give it freely just because the Father asked?

We will find our peace when we trust our relationship with the Father to the point that we freely give as soon as we know it is something the Father desires. When God called me to establish Inspire Women, I did not understand why. The only question I asked was, "Father do you want this?" As soon as I heard in my spirit it was something He wanted, I had my marching orders. I knew that whatever it took, however long it took, I was to keep going in the direction of giving the Father what His heart longed for.

"God does not lead us to Calvary to leave us there."

It is one thing to say "Yes" with our mouths, it is another thing to do "Yes" with our lives. How did Jesus fulfill His commitment to the Father? It was His trust in the Father's heart. He knew God does not lead us to Calvary to leave us there. He leads us to Calvary to take us past Calvary to the resurrection. There is no value in suffering for suffering sake. God allows suffering because of what it accomplishes.

Hebrews 12:2-3 tells us, **"Let us fix our eyes on Jesus, the author and perfecter of our faith, who for the joy set before him endured the cross, scorning its shame, and sat down at the right hand of the throne of God. Consider him who endured such opposition from sinful men, so that you will not grow weary and lose heart.** NIV

In anticipation of suffering, Jesus focused on the victory after the suffering. It is the joy that is after the cross that will get us through. God will not waste suffering. When we allow God to use our suffering to forward His purpose, we can make sense of our suffering.

60% of Inspire Women's scholarship recipients come from backgrounds of abuse. When once they could not understand why God allowed them to suffer, they now embrace their past as God's way to shape them into the perfect vessel to minister to those with backgrounds similar to what they have overcome. A woman who was physically abused is being trained to work with women in an abuse center. A woman who was sent to jail for nine years because she was afraid to tell the name of a drug dealer for fear her children would be killed is being trained to minister to those in prison. A woman whose son died of Aids is ministering to families in Africa with children who have died of Aids. Story after story, Inspire Women listens to God's dreams in His daughters as He transforms our suffering for His greater purpose.

What cross has God trusted you to carry? How can God build a bridge from your suffering to help those around you?

Once Jesus was sure of God's will, He no longer wrestled with God's decision for Him to suffer. Matthew 26: 45-46 tells us: **Then he returned to the disciples and said to them, "Are you still sleeping and resting? Look, the hour is near, and the Son of Man is betrayed into the hands of sinners. Rise, let us go! Here comes my betrayer!"** NIV.

The moment had arrived and we watch Jesus walking right into God's divine appointment. He could have run the other way. No one could force Jesus to go to the cross. Even the nails could not keep Jesus on the cross. When Peter tried to block Jesus' arrest He said in Matthew 26:52-54, **"Put your sword back in its place...for all who draw the sword will die by the sword. Do you think I cannot call on my Father, and he will at once put at my disposal more than twelve legions of angels? But how then would the Scriptures be fulfilled that say it must happen in this way?"** NIV From Jesus' example, I learned that God takes care of our fear when we submit to His greater purpose.

Are you afraid of the suffering that is ahead of you? What details of the suffering scare you? How does it comfort you knowing that since God walked with Jesus through the hardest trial on planet earth that same God is present to walk with you?

1 Peter 5:8-9 instructs us, **"Be self-controlled and alert. Your enemy the devil prowls around like a roaring lion looking for someone to devour. Resist him, standing firm in the faith, because you know that your brothers throughout the world are undergoing the same kind of sufferings."** NIV.

Did you see the words **"your brothers throughout the world are undergoing the same kind of sufferings."**? Before you find yourself saying, "Well, Jesus is Jesus but I'm not Jesus", let God's Word show you that we are not alone in our sufferings. In fact, **"your brothers throughout the world are undergoing the same kinds of suffering."** Anyone called to represent God will have a cross to bear.

You may not always be able to see what someone else's cross is but you can be sure that everyone has one. If you come from a background of abuse, your cross may consist of walking back into situations of abuse to minister to the abused. Your cross may include having to work through your own memories from the past and continuously having to claim God's victory over wounds that are re-opened. God is the one who chooses the stage on which He will display His power. What the devil tries to do is to discourage us by causing us to compare our crosses and feel like what I have to carry is heavier than what you have to carry. The truth is, we are undergoing **"the same kinds of suffering"** though our sufferings may appear in different forms.

When my son was 20, I remember him telling me, "Mom, when you first came to this country, you were on the low end of Maslow's hierarchy of needs because you were concerned over your basic support. I am on the upper end of Maslow's hierarchy because I don't worry about bills but I worry about self actualization and

what my purpose is in life. I just wanted you to know that the pain is just as painful for those at the top of the hierarchy as for those at the bottom." What an incredibly insightful thing for a young man of twenty to say! I wonder today what kind of suffering you are going through. Although our crosses may be different, we are not alone in our sufferings.

"In spite of God's silence, will I step into my identity as a member of God's royal family tree and show the world how royalty responds to a cross?"

When Moses was treading unknown territory he said to God in Exodus 33:15-17, **"If your Presence does not go with us, do not send us up from here. How will anyone know that you are pleased with me and with your people unless you go with us? What else will distinguish me and your people from all the other people on the face of the earth?"** NIV.

In Moses' request, I find the cry of my heart. As I face unknown challenges and suffering, what I need the most is God's presence. Yet, for some reason, at times I find God choosing to be silent. Jesus' ultimate test of faith was when He was on Calvary and experienced the Father's silence. From Jesus' example, I know that part of my suffering will include God's silence during the hardest times of my life. Yet, knowing this ahead of time prepares me for the challenge. I know the silence will end the same way it ended for Jesus.

Jesus' death on the cross did not end with abandonment by the Father but resulted in His resurrection. God will not stay silent because God will rescue His own. When the time came for Jesus to completely let go of His body and die, He knew God would be there to receive Him and to agree with Him that the job was finished. Following Jesus' example, we must trust God's presence in the midst of our suffering, no matter how silent God is. We must trust God will break the silence and stay true to His character. Psalm 72:12-14 tells us, **"For he will deliver the needy who cry out, the afflicted who have no one to help. He will take pity on the weak and the needy and save the needy from death. He will rescue them from oppression and violence, for precious is their blood in his sight.** NIV

I know there will be seasons when I won't sense God's presence in the midst of my suffering. However, instead of being afraid, I will not treat my situation as being unusual but recognize it as a biblical pattern of God's activity to grow me to be more like Jesus. Like Jesus, I will trust that whatever suffering God allows to touch my life will be for the fulfillment of a greater plan. Therefore, I will choose ahead of time, even before the pillars of my life start to shake, that I will not be shaken. I will rejoice that God saw me worthy to share in the fellowship of His Son's suffering by trusting me with a situation where I am to trust Him like His Son did. In spite of God's silence, will I step into my identity as a member of God's royal family tree and show the world how royalty responds to a cross?

If you have trusted God with your salvation for eternity, can you also trust God with a suffering that is temporary on this earth? While trusting Him, will you praise Him for granting you the privilege to experience a microscopic version of what Christ endured on the cross? I pray for the faith to believe that even if God allows life to break me to pieces, He will put me back together in a way that will show the world His greatness! It is in deciding how to respond ahead of time that you will guard your heart and shape your emotions into a passion to fulfill God's purpose.

Describe a Calvary God custom tailored for you. As a member of God's royal family, how will you show the world how royalty responds to a cross?

God has a purpose for the suffering but **He does not like suffering for suffering sake**. When Jesus died on the cross to pay for the sins of the world, He cried out, "**It is finished**" and as soon as the suffering accomplished its purpose, it was over. In the same way, I have watched how God used my son's asthmas to accomplish His purpose as my son was growing up. He used it to grow character as my son learned to endure and to overcome his condition. But there came a point when God decided that the trial was over and my son's condition was under control.

There are sufferings we may endure for a long time and then there are sufferings God allows only for a season. I learned that what I need to do is to say to God, "Let this suffering accomplish your purpose." If I am going to suffer, then let it do in me what God wanted the suffering to do or else I will have suffered for no reason. If we are going to suffer anyway, let it at least be our form of worship unto a King who is worthy.

When Someone is Angry or Jealous

Situation: Are you afraid of someone who has an anger or a jealousy problem? Do you wish you had a place to hide?

The purpose of the personal journal entries shown below is to capture the emotion of fear due to an angry or jealous person in your life. Some were taken from an actual journal, others were written more recently as I reflected on what I was feeling at the time. The dates of the entries are approximate and were included to give the reader some sense of chronological history. In teaching this material, feel free to use my personal journal entries as illustration or personalize your lesson with writing your own personal journal entries or testimony to capture the emotion of loneliness you felt in your own life. If you did not keep a journal, then try to relive the situation in your mind and write an entry today to capture what you felt at the time.

Feb 15, 1980

Dear God,
Did you see how his anger flared up? If I had been closer I think he would have hit me. I'm not sure what I did wrong. Was it my fault that he's been lying to me and that you allowed me to discover the truth? How long did he think he could hide the fact of these other women in his life? He said he wants me out of his life. It was all right for me to be in his life as long as I didn't know the truth. But now that I know, it's like I remind him his life is one big lie. I am learning God that some people prefer to live a lie. It's like they have created a fantasy world that distracts them from their real pain. He doesn't want to talk about things that matter. He doesn't want to resolve the real issue. I just need to slip out of sight or else I fear he will turn on me. He will find reasons to be unhappy with me. He will continue to abuse me because I have gotten too close to the truth. What am I afraid of God? I have my exit papers. I need to just leave.

Dec 5, 1998

Dear God,
I am working with someone in ministry who has all kinds of baggage from his past. I don't think he ever got along with his mother. It's amazing to me that the hurt from our childhood has the power to affect our relationships today if we don't resolve our anger issues. I feel like I'm in some kind of love-hate relationship that has nothing to do with me but he is projecting on me all his repressed anger. I think his relationship with his mother resulted in major insecurities he has with women. I don't think it helped when his wife left him. How did I get pulled into his soap opera? I wish he would just go and get some counseling so we can all get on with kingdom work. Sometimes I feel like I am taking the blows for all the women in his life who walked out on him. Wish he could see the pattern. I wonder if women walk out because he takes out his anger on them. What should I do God?

December 21, 2004

Dear God,
Today I felt like the girl in a story I read about years ago. She went out into her neighborhood with a bowl of pops. The kids all ran over and grabbed a pop and then they rode off together on their bikes leaving her standing there all alone. I felt that way today except it was far worse. At least those kids who took the bike were just being insensitive but they weren't trying to be mean. But today I felt as if I was with someone who needed something from me but was resentful that I had what they needed. Our eyes reveal what is going on in our hearts and when I gave him what was needed, I think I saw anger come through his eyes. Or was it jealousy? Was it resentment that I had what was requested? So instead of being thanked, I was hated. I'm not sure God what else to do? Maybe I shouldn't try so hard? I should just accept that some people will always try to find fault with me because I am a threat to them. Maybe I should just avoid them and save myself from being hurt.

Feb 5, 2005

Dear God,
What should I do? Actually, it's our problem since I do what you tell me to do. So I think the question should be, "What should we do?" I can't wrestle someone to the ground to get them to use their influence for me. I can tell that they do not have kingdom perspective. They are only interested in building up their own turf. They have this arrogance that what they are building is superior. What happened to the idea of the united body of Christ? I can't believe I even got reprimanded for asking for help. The attitude was, "How dare you expect us to help? How arrogant of you to think we would spend time with someone like you?" Then when they hear we do well, I can see smoke coming out of their ears. It's the strangest thing God. Is this sibling rivalry? Is this like the Cain and Abel story? Abel should have run. Are you telling me to run God?

The corresponding truths God taught me from His Word to address my situation
Feel free to continue reading all my personal journals in Module Three expressing feelings of fear before reading the Bible Study. Or you may continue with the corresponding Bible study which contains God's truths in addressing the situation described in the above journal entries with additional truths God taught me to address situations that were not included in my journal entries. If you choose to personalize this curriculum as your way to bond with the group you are leading, feel free not only to use your own testimony and personal journal entries but in the Bible study part, include what God taught you from His Word in situations where you faced fear.

When Someone is Angry or Jealous

Situation: Are you afraid of someone who has an anger or a jealousy problem? Do you wish you had a place to hide?

Reminder: Let's learn the truths from God's Word that speak to our situations. Remember that as a member of God's royal family, we are to act according to the customs of the royal family. This means reinforcing our royal identity by living according to God's specific instructions in the Bible. When we cannot find specific instructions that speak to our situation, we are to search our spiritual heritage and model our lives after God's faith heroes who responded correctly to situations that parallel our own. We can also learn from their mistakes to avoid making the same mistakes in our own lives.

There are times when fear is warranted. In fact a healthy fear is God's way to protect us from evil. I have been around people who display one face to the public and one face behind closed doors. They are volatile personalities because there is a war raging inside them. They suffer from a deep insecurity and that insecurity causes them to lash out at anyone who threatens them. They need to be the one with the favor, they need to be top. They will eliminate anyone who steps into their space or their turf. Have you ever had someone lash out at you because you have invaded their territory?

"Have you ever been around someone who blames you for their failure?"

In the story of Cain and Abel, we see the first mention of anger. It was evoked because of jealousy. Genesis 4:4-8 tells us: **The LORD looked with favor on Abel and his offering, but on Cain and his offering he did not look with favor. So Cain was very angry, and his face was downcast. Then the LORD said to Cain, "Why are you angry? Why is your face downcast? If you do what is right, will you not be accepted?**

But if you do not do what is right, sin is crouching at your door; it desires to have you, but you must master it." Now Cain said to his brother Abel, "Let's go out to the field." And while they were in the field, Cain attacked his brother Abel and killed him. NIV

Cain was angry because God favored Abel. He had a similar opportunity to do what was right but chose not to. Then he was resentful of the consequences. Have you ever been around someone who blames you for their failure? Instead of recognizing their own mistakes, they seethe with resentment and choose to strike out at you.

God's Word warns us of situations where we ought to be fearful. We should have a healthy fear of those who are angry because their anger could lead to our physical harm. It would be foolish to ignore the fact that someone is jealous of you. God's Word shows us time and time again that it's only a question of time before those who are angry will strike at us.

"Have you ever had someone watch your every move because they were worried you might get ahead of them in accomplishments?"

In Module Two of this curriculum I referenced the story of Saul and David to illustrate a situation when someone was rejected by a leader they esteemed highly. I would like to look at this same story but from the angle of Saul's anger, which exploded from his jealousy.

Saul was a King who was threatened by a shepherd boy. Here was David who entered Saul's court to soothe him with music from a harp. Here was David who protected Saul by risking his life to face Goliath. Here was David who went out to fight battles under Saul's authority. The only problem was, Saul was only happy with David as long as David served Saul's purpose and when David's success was credited to Saul. But when Saul saw that the people were impressed with David, he became jealous. 1 Samuel 18:8 tells us Saul's thoughts: **"They have credited David with tens of thousands…but me with only thousands. What more can he get but the kingdom?"** NIV. In 1 Samuel 18:9, we are told, **"And from that time on Saul kept a jealous eye on David."** NIV.

God's Word specifically referred to Saul as having a "**jealous eye**" toward David. Have you ever had someone watch your every move because they were worried you might get ahead of them in accomplishments?

Name someone who is jealous of your gifts or your successes? How have they watched your every move and tried to counteract your successes?

Proverbs 29:22 tells us, **"An angry man stirs up dissension, and a hot-tempered one commits many sins."** NIV. Don't try to reason with someone who is angry because someone who is hot-tempered will commit many sins. They will stir up dissension because their way to handle the raging storm that is going on inside them is to wreak havoc around them as the waves of anger inside them spill over on those around them. God's Word tells us in Proverbs 15:1, **"A gentle answer turns away wrath, but a harsh word stirs up anger."** NIV. Don't try to confront an angry man because they are not operating out of logic but out of their own unresolved issues. Therefore, don't let them use you as their punching bag. Instead, start pedaling backwards and allow a gentle answer to turn away wrath.

God's Word tells us of times David used kind and gentle words to appease Saul. He showed grace and spared Saul's life and appealed to him to reconcile. It mattered little what grace David showed Saul. Saul's gratitude was short lived because his own jealousy always took over. In the incident where David showed Saul grace, 1 Samuel 24:17-19 reports Saul as saying to David, **"You are more righteous than I...You have treated me well, but I have treated you badly."** Then shortly afterwards we read in 1 Samuel 26:1-3, **"The Ziphites went to Saul at Gibeah and said, "Is not David hiding on the hill of Hakilah, which faces Jeshimon?" So Saul went down to the Desert of Ziph, with his three thousand chosen men of Israel, to search there for David."** NIV

We see David repeatedly extending a hand of friendship in an attempt to have reconciliation. In 1 Samuel 26:17, David says to Saul, **"Why is my lord pursuing his servant? What have I done, and what wrong am I guilty of?"** NIV. In realizing David's kindness to him, Saul said in 1 Samuel 26:21, **"I have sinned. Come back, David my son. Because you considered my life precious today, I will not try to harm you again. Surely I have acted like a fool and have erred greatly."** NIV Yet in spite of these words, David knew better.

Is there someone in your life who you long to maintain a relationship with? How have you tried to reach out to them in spite of their meanness towards you?

I had a situation when someone made a big financial mistake and asked my help to cover the cost. In an attempt to bring unity, I made the decision to cover them so they would not take the consequence of their error. They showed gratitude for a moment and thanked me profusely for my grace. Then almost immediately I heard through the grapevine that they were slandering me behind my back. I could not understand the behavior till God showed me the relationship between Saul and David and pointed out to me that you can never win the friendship of someone who is jealous of you. The best approach is to avoid them. This means I am to find reasons why I cannot make a meeting. I am to return their angry words with a gentle answer. I am to stop trying to reason with them. If I just stay out of the way, in time, their own ambition will destroy them.

Is it time for you to recognize that sometimes, fear is warranted? Is it time for you to hide in a cave and know that in time, an angry and jealous person will bring about their own destruction? If so, what steps do you need to take to protect yourself?

I remember watching a movie called "Homeward Bound" where three household pets were trying to find their way home from across the country. One was an old golden retriever, one an American boxer and one was a Persian cat. Where dogs and cats normally fought, this trio co-existed happily. At the end of the journey, the old dog fell into a hole in a construction site. The boxer coaxed him to climb out of the hole because they had traveled a long time together and the boxer wanted him to make it home. The golden retriever finally told the boxer to go on without him.

The scene flashed forward to the family's home where the kids heard the boxer's bark in the distance. There were many tears and hugs as kids and dog united. Then the family heard the meow of the cat and once again there was a major celebration. Then there was silence and one of the kids commented that the golden retriever was probably too old to make the journey. A few seconds later, the family heard that old familiar deep bark and the nothing but sheer mania filled the air.

As I watched this movie with tears streaming down my face, I thought the boxer probably was the one who pulled the old golden retriever out of the hole. Yet, in real life, I wondered how many who are older would accept the aid of someone younger. Would Saul ever have accepted David's help without experiencing conflicting emotions where, on the one hand, he enjoyed the benefit of David's help, and on the other hand, he resented David's youth and success?

I wish that all leaders who are growing physically weaker would respond like the old golden retriever to the young rambunctious leaders like the young American boxer. After all, at the end of the day, we are all heading homeward bound. And all that matters is that we carry each other along the way so that everyone will make it home safely.

When Choices You Can't Control Affect You

Situation: Are you in an environment where you feel like a victim because of choices that others are making that will affect your world? Do you feel it's unfair that someone else's choice will change the course of your life?

The purpose of the personal journal entries shown below is to capture the emotion of fear as you watch how your world is affected by the choices of others you cannot control. Some entries were taken from an actual journal, others were written more recently as I reflected on what I was feeling at the time. The dates of the entries are approximate and were included to give the reader some sense of chronological history. In teaching this material, feel free to use my personal journal entries as illustration or personalize your lesson with writing your own personal journal entries or testimony to capture the emotion of loneliness you felt in your own life. If you did not keep a journal, then try to relive the situation in your mind and write an entry today to capture what you felt at the time.

May 5, 1984

Dear God,
He ran a red light. I could not see the road on my left because a truck was next to me. The truck driver waved at me to drive on and so I did. Who would have imagined that this car would run the red light and crash right into the driver's side of my car? The paramedics said when they came to the scene, the entire car had collapsed around me. They did not expect me to be alive. I don't remember anything God. Is it your grace that I don't remember a thing? I just know that my hip is broken and I won't be walking for six months. I know that whatever project I had at work, it will be delegated. I know that someone made a choice that has changed my world. Yet, through it all, I have this feeling that no human can change my world or what you have planned for me. I wonder God if you allowed this accident to happen to get my attention. It showed me how little time I have on earth. It scared me to think that the day of the accident could have been my
last day on earth. What was I doing with my life? I was climbing the corporate ladder. But for what purpose? When I arrive, where will I be?

God if someone can make choices that totally destroy my life, then how in the world can anyone feel secure? It's like there are thousands of moving pieces around us and at any time, one of them could hit us. I'm going to be a total basket case if I live in fear of anything and everything that could go wrong. It's like waiting for the next terrorist attack or not knowing when you will step on a land mine.

God, I need freedom from fear. You are bigger than anything in this world. Surely you are not held hostage. You have a say so. I need to trust that if you allowed something to happen then there is a story you are telling about yourself. What did you want me to learn from this accident?

March 15, 2003

Dear God,
I don't know what to do. I trust in the leadership you have put in place. But what happens when that leadership leads in a way that is contrary to the vision you have given me? Do I get to go home then God? Or are you saying I am to keep going with whatever open door I have?

April 1, 2004

Dear God,
I don't think this medicine is working. I feel so helpless because I am at the mercy of the doctors. But what if they are wrong? I think I feel worse than before. This reminds me of the story I read about someone whose doctor gave her the wrong treatment and it affected her physically for the rest of her life. The amazing thing was, the changes in her life also created the environment where she drew closer to you. In fact, because she couldn't be up and about she spent her time writing about you and then her writings inspired thousands.

Could it be God that if we trust you, you are really the one in control of our lives?

I'm not quite sure how this works. It's like you give human kind free will and sometimes that free will can be used to hurt someone else. But even in the midst of those wrong choices, you already have a plan to turn lemons into lemonade.

Sometimes I think we should just fast forward the tape and know that when the words flash up on the screen and it reads "The End", the story will leave us with a big "Wow!" moment. There will be turns in the plot but no matter where it ends, you steer us towards home.

April 5, 2005

Dear God,
Someone is talking about me behind my back and I can't control what comes out of their mouth. They have a personal agenda but the people they are telling are so gullible they don't realize they are being misled. What do I do God? Do I just stand here and let life happen to me? At what point do I get to say I don't have to live like this? I don't think it's fair for me to suffer from the wrong choices others make. Don't you agree God? How come you're not saying anything?

The corresponding truths God taught me from His Word to address my situation
Feel free to continue reading all my personal journals in Module Three expressing feelings of fear before reading the Bible Study. Or you may continue with the corresponding Bible study which contains God's truths in addressing the situation described in the above journal entries with additional truths God taught me to address situations that were not included in my journal entries. If you choose to personalize this curriculum as your way to bond with the group you are leading, feel free not only to use your own testimony and personal journal entries but in the Bible study part, include what God taught you from His Word in situations where you faced fear.

When Choices You Can't Control Affect You

Situation: Are you in an environment where you feel like a victim because of choices that others are making that will affect your world? Do you feel it's unfair that someone else's choice will change the course of your life?

Reminder: Let's learn the truths from God's Word that speak to our situations. Remember that as a member of God's royal family, we are to act according to the customs of the royal family. This means reinforcing our royal identity by living according to God's specific instructions in the Bible. When we cannot find specific instructions that speak to our situation, we are to search our spiritual heritage and model our lives after God's faith heroes who responded correctly to situations that parallel our own. We can also learn from their mistakes to avoid making the same mistakes in our own lives.

When Enron collapsed, how many families were impacted? How many people spent years working and saving only to have their pensions and provision for their family disappear? Could they have controlled what happened to them? What do you do when you suffer the choices of those you have no control over? Do you fear being a victim of those you cannot control?

When a major donor who has committed to the staff's support, breaks a pledge when the ministry is experiencing major growth and the team is worn out from long hours and tireless effort, how do I break such news to the team? There were days when I allowed my fear of the bad news to throw me into depression. I wanted to just put my arms around those who had been so faithful and tell them we will all give up together. It is almost better to say we will all leave than to choose those who we will leave behind because of lack of funds to support them.

"Even in ministry, some of the very people we pour ourselves out to help can turn around and attack the ministry with their criticism and their demands."

What God taught me through His Word was to accept the fact that the choices of others will impact my world. As the leader, I do not have the option to leave just because someone has made a decision that completely changes my schedule and expectations as to what I will be doing with my time. In the story of Moses, he had the faith to enter the Promise Land. Joshua and Caleb, who served with him, were on the same page. But the Israelites that Moses was leading and who God wanted to bless were the ones who raised their hands against God's plans.

A very distraught business owner shared with me how she sacrificed to protect the jobs of her staff. Then she discovered that someone in her inner circle was stealing from her by using her signature stamp to withdraw funds from her account. Another business owner shared how the very employee she had mentored started a company to compete with her. Even in ministry, some of the very people we pour ourselves out to help can turn around and attack the ministry with their criticism and their demands. Things are no different today than during the time when Moses led. His mission was sabotaged by the very people he was trying to bless by leading them into God's promise land. After all the years Moses served the people faithfully, they rebelled against him and refused to enter the promise land.

God was not pleased with the people and judged them. He tells us in Numbers 14:21-23, **"...as surely as I live and as surely as the glory of the LORD fills the whole earth, not one of the men who saw my glory and the miraculous signs I performed in Egypt and in the desert but who disobeyed me and tested me ten times — not one of them will ever see the land I promised on oath to their forefathers. No one who has treated me with contempt will ever see it."** NIV.

Don't miss the fact that God allowed the wrong choices of others to impact the leader. God's judgment also affected others who were innocent. Whether you are leading a family, business, ministry, church, community, or nation, you will find that the wrong choices of those you are leading will not only impact you but will hurt those you are leading who are not at fault. The consequences of wrong choices others make may change your world, your schedule and impact many years of your life. What God showed me through this story was how Moses was forced to wander in the desert an additional 40 years. Joshua and Caleb who represented the ones who were faithful

also got to wander in the desert for 40 years with Moses. Has someone made a decision that has impacted not only your world but changed the future for your children, your ministry team or coworkers?

"When I no longer own my time, my energy or my resource, then all I need to do is be obedient to whatever open door I have in continuing with the original mission."

When I try to convince myself that God will spare me any consequences of someone's wrong choices, I know I am just kidding myself. God reserves the right to protect me, but He also has the liberty to allow the consequences of someone else's wrong choices to impact me. I will not mitigate my fear by sticking my head in the sand and convincing myself I won't be affected. The way to overcome my fear is to settle in my heart that even with the consequences, God will show me how to lead in the midst of a plan B.

Are you in the middle of plan B? Observe that Moses did not abandon the mission. Instead, he flowed with the changes and continued the mission the best way he knew how. In the same way, when life throws a curve ball your way, learn how our faith heroes responded and model after their right choices. In their right choices, we will discover the royal way to respond as one who is a member of God's royal family.

Moses did not abandon the mission. He stayed focused on what God entrusted to him to accomplish. Though the timeline had extended, the mission stayed the same.

What was your original mission? Is there any reason for you to believe that God has changed His original mission?

When the actions of the faithless impact the ministry, God taught me not to allow the changes to paralyze me with fear but to continue His mission in whatever open doors I have left. Could it be that the one constant thing in our lives that will give us stability is our choice to stay obedient to the original mission? So although we cannot control what others do, we can control what we do. We can choose to be obedient. Given that someone sabotaged plan A, is there a plan B to get us to the same goal? Know also that God is the one who designs plan B. He told Moses His judgment of those who were disobedient. He also told Moses about the extended deadline and the changes in the team of who gets to reach the Promise Land and who will lose their blessing. Have you asked God for a plan B?

The only time I get afraid is when I start to measure my expectations of how I want life to be as compared to what is required of me in the new plan. When I have given up my time, my energy and my resources then there is nothing anyone can take from me that I have not already surrendered. When I look at how long something will take, it overwhelms me when there is something else I wanted to do with my time. When I look at how much of my resources it will take, I'm resentful if there was something else I wanted to buy with the resources. But when I exist for God's purpose and He owns everything, then I am truly free. I can say, "God, whatever it takes but I can only give what I have. So if you want it, take it all." When I no longer own my time, my energy or my resource, then all I need to do is be obedient to whatever open door I have in continuing with the original mission. In my obedience I find my freedom and life continues with minimal drama.

Has something changed in your life that requires an adjustment to your time and schedule? What has changed?

What adjustments do you need to make in your time, your priorities, and your resources in order to continue the mission?

When my sons were little, they loved playing with a toy known as a transformer. It was made with different pieces that were assembled together but could be moved around to change the shape of the toy. The one they had looked like a robot but with a few moves of the different parts, it could look like a car. Then with another few creative moves, it could be transformed into a box. As I marveled at how the transformer could be reinvented, I wondered if God created some situations with built in transformation options. While we may think that someone's actions can throw our world out of control, could it be that God knows the limits and will not allow any situation to throw us off course to the point that we will not be able to fulfill His original intentions. Like the transformer my sons played with, they could affect its shape but only up to a point. In reality, they could only reinvent up to a number of ways and that they will have hit their limit. Ultimately the manufacturer of that transformer had already predetermined the level of change that is possible.

And so it is with God's plans. He is the ultimate manufacturer of all His dreams. He knows the breaking point and He has already pre-built the boundaries. Though you may feel there are decisions others make that can spin your world out of control, God ultimately controls His dreams. He will not allow His dream to deviate beyond its pre-designed margins of flexibility.

Losing Your Children, Assets, or Health

Situation: Do you fear the loss of your children, your assets or your health?

The purpose of the personal journal entries shown below is to capture the emotion of fear in the loss of children, assets or health. Some entries were taken from an actual journal, others were written more recently as I reflected on what I was feeling at the time. The dates of the entries are approximate and were included to give the reader some sense of chronological history. In teaching this material, feel free to use my personal journal entries as illustration or personalize your lesson with writing your own personal journal entries or testimony to capture the emotion of loneliness you felt in your own life. If you did not keep a journal, then try to relive the situation in your mind and write an entry today to capture what you felt at the time.

Aug 11, 1987

Dear God,
I should never have read that book about the kid who died during the night. Now I find myself afraid. I don't know what I would do if something happened to my son during the night. What if he has an asthma attack and can't breathe. What if I don't hear him? Would I blame myself the rest of my life?

I don't like pain God. I don't like being so close to someone that you're always afraid of losing them. Surely, God, there must be an answer. I know the answer is not to withdraw from everyone. So how do we love and still know that we will be all right if we lose those we love?

Oct 15, 2003

Dear God,
I think the whole world is worried about getting on a plane. We are all a little paranoid. We think everyone looks suspicious. It will take a while for
everyone to relax. When your mind is filled with images of disaster, you feel so vulnerable. You feel like a sitting duck. You feel like something is going to strike your life and destroy your world any minute. How could this possibly be the way you meant for us to live? Yet, you could have controlled events so disasters don't happen. But you don't feel a need to do that. So surely there must be another answer to experiencing peace in our lives "even if bad things happen to good people."*

I read a book that says that you are feeling helpless as well. The author says we find comfort in knowing that God is feeling as helpless as we feel because He gave humankind free will and so He can't do anything about how things are going. How could that give anyone comfort? Besides, the idea goes against everything you reveal in the Bible. Even Jesus said He did not stay on the cross because someone in their free will put Him there. He said He stayed on the cross because He chose to. So I must believe that you freely make up your own mind and you make your own choices. For some reason, you chose not to intervene. So the question I have to answer is whether I trust your decisions. Do I trust you to make decisions that affect my life?

Aug 9, 2007

Dear God,
My boys are leaving for college. I was just thinking about that shooting at Virginia Tech. How does a parent let go of their children and know that some calamity could be around the corner? There was some story in the paper that a car full of students turned over on the highway and all five kids were killed. These kids were top of their class. We can say God will protect but the facts shout at us. It's just a fact that there are times when you allow bad things to happen to us.

God, I wish there could be a formula. I wish I could know that if I do "A", then you will do "B". But you chose not to organize life on earth like a business contract. The only guarantee you give us is for what happens after our time on earth is over. But while on earth, you want a relationship, not a contract.

I think that in a relationship, it's not a question of what you do for me or what I do for you. It's more about you being King and me being here to serve your wishes. So what are your wishes? I know you don't report to me so that's probably why you don't run your ideas by me before doing them. But how do I get past being afraid of your unpredictability? It's like I never know what to expect. Will you choose to allow me to lose my children, my house and my health? How do you make these decisions? There must be something that drives you.

I wonder if what you want is for me to trust that you will always operate out of your character of goodness. So is this the bottom line, God? Am I to settle in my heart how good I truly believe you are? Will I let what you did for me on Calvary be the final verdict or will I continue to evaluate you based on what you allow to happen in my life? I don't think you like being put on a performance treadmill. I think you're pretty impressed by Calvary. I think you feel that Calvary is all we need to trust your heart.

It just occurred to me that when Job in the Bible trusted you, this was before Jesus came. Now how incredible is that? He was able to trust you even before Calvary. How much more should we be able to trust you?

The corresponding truths God taught me from His Word to address my situation
Feel free to continue reading all my personal journals in Module Three expressing feelings of fear before reading the Bible Study. Or you may continue with the corresponding Bible study which contains God's truths in addressing the situation described in the above journal entries with additional truths God taught me to address situations that were not included in my journal entries. If you choose to personalize this curriculum as your way to bond with the group you are leading, feel free not only to use your own testimony and personal journal entries but in the Bible study part, include what God taught you from His Word in situations where you faced fear.

284

Losing Your Children, Assets, or Health

Situation: Do you fear the loss of your children, your assets or your health?

Reminder: Let's learn the truths from God's Word that speak to our situations. Remember that as a member of God's royal family, we are to act according to the customs of the royal family. This means reinforcing our royal identity by living according to God's specific instructions in the Bible. When we cannot find specific instructions that speak to our situation, we are to search our spiritual heritage and model our lives after God's faith heroes who responded correctly to situations that parallel our own. We can also learn from their mistakes to avoid making the same mistakes in our own lives.

Job 1:2-3 tells us that Job "**had seven sons and three daughters**." NIV. Then he experienced one calamity after another in personal losses in his household. Job 1:18-19 tells us that a messenger came to Job and reported one of his losses. He said, "**Your sons and daughters were feasting and drinking wine at the oldest brother's house, when suddenly a mighty wind swept in from the desert and struck the four corners of the house. It collapsed on them and they are dead, and I am the only one who has escaped to tell you!**" NIV. Have you ever feared getting a phone call or a letter in the mail telling you that something terrible has happened to those you love?

In the past, I used to find myself negotiating with God.
I would say, "Oh God, please don't let this happen."

Like any parent who hears of the loss of his children, we can feel Job's grief and hear his wailing as Job 1:20a tells us, "**At this, Job got up and tore his robe and shaved his head.**" NIV. However, what was unusual was the second half of the verse which read, "**Then he fell to the ground in worship.**" NIV.

What does it mean to worship God in the midst of your losses? When was the last time you thanked God for losing something or someone you valued?

God allowed Job to lose his children, his home, his servants, his cattle, and his health. Have you ever lost your children? Have you lost your home to a foreclosure or a natural disaster? Have you lost your whole department because of a company reorganization? Have you ever lost your assets because of a recession, a stock market crash or an employee who cheats you? Have you lost your health? In spite of these losses, we hear Job saying in Job 13:15, "**Though he slay me, yet will I hope in him…**" NIV. What kind of thinking is this? Not only will Job continue to praise God but He will keep His hope in God. How could there be freedom in handing God the pen and letting Him write the rest of our stories? Yet in this total surrender we will find our peace.

In the past, I used to find myself negotiating with God. I would say, "Oh God, please don't let this happen." I had in my mind all the events I dreaded and then I lived in a nightmare of constant worry hoping all these dreadful things would never come to pass. Have you ever lived in the hypothetical world of "What if's". What if my mother died? What if I lost my son? What if I lost my husband? What if I lost my job? What if I lost my health? The hypothetical world can fill you with fear. Shakespeare once said, "A coward dies a thousand deaths but a brave man dies but once." He is so right. I think I have died a thousand times in my own imagination.

When Job said, "**Though he slay me, yet will I hope in him**", God is teaching us through His word that if we can handle the worse situation, then we can handle any situation. I can't imagine a worse situation than having God slay me. How in the world do you run when the God of the Universe raises His hand against you? Yet even if it comes to that, Job was saying that he would find his hope in God.

One thing that has helped me so much in life is to project myself into a worse case scenario and to say to myself, "And even if that happens, then what?" Instead of living in the fear of all the what-if's in my life, I then live in the world of "even if". Even if I loose my mother, yet will I hope in Him. Even if I lose my son, yet will I hope in Him. Even if I lose whatever it is that I am afraid to lose, yet will I hope in Him. And should I even lose my own life, then let me say as the Apostle Paul said in Philippians 1:23-24, "**I am torn between the two: I desire to depart and be with Christ, which is better by far; but it is more necessary for you that I remain in the body.**" NIV.

As a member of God's family tree, I find myself paying attention to the biblical patterns of how life unfolds for those who are serving God. I see the pattern of how those who walked in faith clung stubbornly to God because they trusted in His goodness. When you find yourself in a place where you feel you have no answers and you don't know what's up or what's down, then cling to what you know. I heard an old missionary say once, "When I don't remember anything else, I remember the children's hymn I learned long ago: Jesus loves me this I know, for the Bible tells me so."

What situation or loss do you fear the most? Can you fill in the sentence "And even if this happens, this I know…"

"I asked God to show me in the Bible how to get past the loss of a child."

God is an eternal God and lives from eternity past to eternity future. As a result, He does not view life from our earthly timeframe. Although God promises His protection, there are times when God allows our loved ones to enter eternity future as His way to protect them. I often hear parents who have lost children say to me, "This is not right. Children are supposed to bury their parents. Parents are not supposed to be burying their children." I was ministering to a woman once who moved from Chicago to Houston to get away from the gangs. She put her teenage son in a Christian school. He was doing very well in Houston and went to youth group at his church regularly. He was driving home after a youth meeting when someone broadsided into his car and killed him. The mother was devastated. She could not understand why God did not protect him. She asked me how she could fill the loneliness in her heart and get past the loss of her son.

In my desire to offer her words of comfort, I asked God to show me in the Bible how to get past the loss of a child.

God took me to John 3:16 which says, **"For God so loved the world that he gave his one and only Son…"** Did you observe that God let go of a son? How did He do it? The first part of the verse said, **"God so loved that he gave"**. God's emotion of love was greater than the sorrow of His loss. Therefore to learn from God, I must allow the emotion of love to be greater than my emotion of sorrow.

So I asked God, "How can my emotion of love be greater than my emotion of sorrow?" The Lord showed me that we can take our greatest loss and offer it to God as our greatest love offering. So we say, "Father, this child is my very life. I take my greatest treasure and I willingly give him up and lay him at your feet. Thank you for allowing me the privilege of letting go of my greatest treasure and to give you a gift that cost me something." When we do this, we have allowed the emotion of love to be greater than our emotion of sorrow. And then peace descends because we were created in the image of God and peace happens when we conform to our Father's image and make choices based on His example. Peace happens when our heart starts to beat in rhythm with that of the God who created us.

Write down what you feel is your greatest treasure. Now imagine going into God's throne room and laying your treasure at Jesus' feet. Describer the peace in worshipping God in this way.

My boys are now out of the nest. Some years ago, when they were still in elementary school, I thought it would be a good idea to take the family to the Schlitterbaum water park. So here we were, one happy family. I believe my boys were 8 and 6 at the time. They wanted to go down this huge slide that emptied into a big swimming pool. I told them to go ahead and I would wait for them by the pool. I waited and waited. No boys. I sent my husband up the flight of stairs that they went up, to see if they were at the top of the stairs. The stairs were four floors high. He came down and said, "These stairs lead to a slide that does not empty at this pool." "Where does it let out?" I asked. He said, "It lets out at the other side of the park, forty five minutes away."

A panic shot right through me. "Go after them!" I cried out to my husband. So I sat by the pool while he went looking for the boys. As I sat there, I started imagining the park closing down, I started imagining us looking for bodies, I started thinking about how well my younger one could not swim. This did not turn out to be that wonderful family day I had expected. I waited and I waited. Forty five minutes later, I see my husband walking towards me. No boys. He said he got to the end of the slide and they were nowhere to be seen. He decided to file a report with the park on our missing children. Meanwhile, I sat by the pool in case the boys showed up. While I sat there, I said to the Lord, "You can see them. You know where they are." I reminded the Lord of the one story I always taught my older son and that was the story of Cain and Abel. And I told him, "The moral of the story is, you are your brother's keeper." I said to the Lord, "Please help him remember that."

Another twenty minutes went by. Then out there in the distance, I see my two boys shuffling towards me dragging a big rubber tube behind them. I said to them calmly, "Come here, sit down, tell me all about it." My older son said, "Mom, when I saw we let out at the other end of the park, I figured you probably reported us to missing children." Then he said, "Halfway down the slide, the slide split. Thomas' tube started going down the left, mine was going towards the right. I paddled as fast as I could and I grabbed onto Thomas' tube so we would go down together on the same side. The whole time, all I could hear in my head was, "You are your brother's keeper! You are your brother's keeper! You are your brother's keeper!"

The first verse my son memorized in Sunday School was this, "**I have hidden your word in my heart that I might not sin against you.**" NIV. (Psalm 119:11). I know God does not guarantee me safety in this world but I praise Him for the times He protected my children by bringing His Word to their remembrance. And I praise Him for the times His Word carried me through my losses. In His Word I have found the counsel for all situations in my life.

When You Fear Divorce or Widowhood

Situation: Are you afraid to be on your own without the financial and physical protection of a husband?

The purpose of the personal journal entries shown below is to capture the emotion of fear in the loss of a spouse. Some entries were taken from an actual journal, others were written more recently as I reflected on what I was feeling at the time. The dates of the entries are approximate and were included to give the reader some sense of chronological history. In teaching this material, feel free to use my personal journal entries as illustration or personalize your lesson with writing your own personal journal entries or testimony to capture the emotion of loneliness you felt in your own life. If you did not keep a journal, then try to relive the situation in your mind and write an entry today to capture what you felt at the time.

June 21, 1992

Dear God,
What in the world happened today? I went with a friend to court. She is in a divorce and is fighting for custody of her children. I had no idea what I was walking into. She tells me later that her attorney quit and the judge told her she had to get another attorney. She was so emotional she could not get her act together to find another lawyer. On top of that, she was so devastated when her lawyer quit that she could not trust anyone. But the judge was not sympathetic. It was the wildest thing. Here she was without an attorney representing herself, while fighting a case against her husband who is an attorney and is represented by one of the best attorneys in town. I thought I was going to die when she told me to stay with her. What could I possibly do? I know nothing about the law.

During the intermission, her husband's attorney came into the conference room, slammed his hand on the table and said,

"Take the settlement. If you go into that court, we will cream you!" When she looked at me and asked if she had enough money for the kids, I could feel her panic. God, did you feel her panic too? Actually I felt my panic as well because how was I to advise her? I'm not an accountant. I don't know if she will have enough for the kids.

So God, we did the only think I knew how to do. I told her we are spending way too much time focusing on all that we don't know. We don't know the law, we don't know the financial implications, we are filled with all that we don't know. So how about refocusing to what we do know? We know that God is in control. We know God loves us. So God, we decided to pray and just ask you to show us what to do. I told her that whatever she sensed in her spirit after we prayed, that's what she is supposed to do. After we prayed, she said you whispered your Word in her ears and you told her that God appoints the judges of the land. So she decided to go with the judgment of the judge instead of taking the settlement from the enemy.

God, the judge gave her more than the settlement. I guess it could have ended up differently. I'm not even sure it matters what the settlement was. She said when she came off the stand she felt the bondage of fear had been broken. She said all these years she had been afraid but when she went on that stand, she broke through the fear barrier. She stood for what she believed to be right and that was all that mattered.

God, I see peace in her spirit. It was like you were in that courtroom and you came to be her husband. I know you will lead her now one day at a time into the rest of her life.

Jan 15, 2005

Dear God,
I can't imagine what it's like to lose someone you have been married to for forty years. It's like losing half of your heart. It's like losing the one who finishes your sentences and who knows you so well they can speak what you are thinking. I went to the funeral today and her husband's presence was sorely missing. How will she continue without him? He handled al l the details. More than that, she could trust him with all the details. Now she will need to know where the money is, how to invest it, and how to plan her finances for the future. Now she will need to figure out what to do when there is a plumbing problem or when the roof leaks. Meanwhile, it's not like life stops just to let you figure out all these details.

I feel the panic in her spirit. I see her walking into an empty house not knowing what to do with herself. I see her crying herself to sleep at night. I see her going to a social and feeling there is no one there she connects with and then being reminded that she used to have her husband to talk to at these socials and now she comes alone. Oh God, I know there is a plan in the heartache but sometimes, the pain feels so deep you can't even imagine a day when the pain will stop.

God, you are merciful to widows. I know you want to put your arms around the widows and show them you are the banner of love over them. Show me God how Inspire Women can help. Is this time for a widow to see herself as the daughter of the King, commissioned by you to share your message with the world? I know something miraculous happens when we let you fill the empty places in our heart. I've seen it time and time again. God, help us to receive your sufficiency. It's so hard to imagine you can fill our hearts when we can't see you. But I know you are real because I hear you. Help her to hear you God. I just know that you can open up a ministry for her beyond her wildest imagination. Oh that she will have the vision to see it!

We received a scholarship application from a woman who was a pastor's wife for 25 years. She is trusting in your plan for her life. If we can throw out all our preconceived ideas on how we can spend the rest of our lives maybe we can go to you with no strings attached. Just as we are, God, take us and shape us into a vessel you can send to make your dreams come true.

When You Fear Divorce or Widowhood

Situation: Are you afraid to be on your own without the financial and physical protection of a husband?

Reminder: Let's learn the truths from God's Word that speak to our situations. Remember that as a member of God's royal family, we are to act according to the customs of the royal family. This means reinforcing our royal identity by living according to God's specific instructions in the Bible. When we cannot find specific instructions that speak to our situation, we are to search our spiritual heritage and model our lives after God's faith heroes who responded correctly to situations that parallel our own. We can also learn from their mistakes to avoid making the same mistakes in our own lives.

A woman in my Sunday school class told me that she came home one day and found all her belongings packed in a suitcase and left outside her house. After twenty five years of marriage, her husband decided he did not love her and threw her out. Another woman shared how she went to use her credit card and found that it had been cancelled. She went to the bank and found her husband had withdrawn the money. She was in a divorce hearing and was up against a husband who was an attorney who fought to keep all the assets and to leave her with as little as possible. When once your husband might have been your best friend, you now find him acting as your worse enemy. Here is someone who knows all your vulnerabilities and he is using all of them against you. I wonder today if your heart is filled with fear over a divorce your spouse is demanding. Do you feel you have lost an umbrella of protection over you? Do you feel exposed and insecure?

The loss of a husband to death is different because it does not come with all the emotional baggage of betrayal. However, it still carries with it a deep loss of one who was our best friend, our confidante, our protector financially, emotionally, and physically. Who do you turn to as you face life as a single person?

In Isaiah 54:4-5, God says, **"Do not be afraid; you will not suffer shame. Do not fear disgrace; you will not be humiliated. You will forget the shame of your youth and remember no more the reproach of your widowhood. For your Maker is your husband — the LORD Almighty is his name — the Holy One of Israel is your Redeemer."** NIV.

In these verses God is not specifically addressing widowhood or divorce but is speaking of His restoration of a rebellious people. However, in these verses, we find God describing Himself as our Maker and our husband. During a time when we experience the fear of losing a husband, how comforting to know that our Maker is our husband!

I love the words that say "**The LORD Almighty is his name**". In the case of a widow, your name may feel like half a name since the two became one and now the two is only one. In the case of a divorcee, you may be suffering from the resentment of a spouse who not only wants to rip your ring off your finger but no longer wants you to use his name. At a time when you don't know what your name is anymore how comforting to know that our Maker, our husband has a name and He is called the LORD Almighty. Would you exchange the name you held with an earthly husband with that of being a wife who belongs to the LORD Almighty?

More than that, this husband is "**the Holy One of Israel**" and is "**your Redeemer**." So often in a divorce, the other side makes up lies in an attempt to win their case. There is little honesty in a spouse who does not want you to have any of the assets. Observe how the LORD Almighty is known as "**the Holy One**". He is honest and filled with integrity. You can trust His character. At a time when you don't know who you can trust, you can trust God.

Not only is your Maker, your husband, the Lord Almighty and the Holy One, He is also your Redeemer. If you have lost a spouse, do you find yourself with regrets over what you wish you had done while your spouse was alive? Were there words you wished you had said? Were there trips you wish you had gone on and now it's too late?

In the case of a divorce, no matter how right you may be, any time there is a conflict, there are always two sides to the story. No matter how little you are at fault, something in you dies when you feel like such a failure. We need a redeemer who will cover us with His grace. We need a redeemer who will heal our heart and restore us with His mercy. We need a redeemer who is our Maker and the creator of second chances and new dreams and beginnings.

Did you need to hear today that God is your husband? How has it comforted you knowing that your Maker is a husband who is holy and your redeemer?

A friend of mine who suffered from a terrible divorce has been single now for many years. She said that at first she was fearful of being alone. When things broke down in the house she didn't know what to do. She was in a panic over handling her finances. When she was ill, she did not have a person in the house who could drive her to the doctor. She was often reminded that she was all alone. Then she began to call on God as her husband. She said it was like God was in charge of personnel she didn't even know existed. When she needed someone to carry something into the house, a neighbor would show up unexpectedly. She said she would pray and somehow God sends reinforcements. He has met her needs for the past twenty years.

A widow came to the Inspire Women's conference and felt led to volunteer full time in our office. We have become her family. Then she felt led to give the ministry her house with rights to live in it during her lifetime. As a result, one of our other supporters who is a builder was moved to help her remodel her home at minimal cost. God wove relationships in her life she never knew was possible. Oh what blessings we forfeit when we fail to call on God. He is our Maker, our husband, the Holy One who is our redeemer.

When Someone Breaks a Promise

Situation: Are you in a place where you desperately need someone to keep their promise? Are you afraid those who committed to help you will abandon you?

The purpose of the personal journal entries shown below is to capture the emotion of fear when you needed someone to keep their promise to you. Some entries were taken from an actual journal, others were written more recently as I reflected on what I was feeling at the time. The dates of the entries are approximate and were included to give the reader some sense of chronological history. In teaching this material, feel free to use my personal journal entries as illustration or personalize your lesson with writing your own personal journal entries or testimony to capture the emotion of loneliness you felt in your own life. If you did not keep a journal, then try to relive the situation in your mind and write an entry today to capture what you felt at the time.

October 15, 1973

Dear God,
Many of my friends are leaving the country. They are the hope for their families. Mom says some kids make it to America and they remember their families. Others do well and they disappear to have their own lives. I wonder what it's like to depend on someone as your only hope. What if you poured everything into them and they leave, do really well, and then totally forget about you? Mom said that in China, the women depend on the men who leave to build a business and then they find a girlfriend and never return home. Don't they care about the kids? Some continue to send money, others don't care. I wonder how there could be a father who leaves his kids and not care if they are hungry? What do the women do? God, will you take care of the women? They must feel so desperate when they have no means to feed their kids. How could this be right, God? Do you see what is going on?

November 15, 2006

Dear God,
What happened to the one who promised to be there for me in this ministry? God, did you notice how some are called one day and then tell me they have been called out the next? They make you seem random. It's like you never finish what you start. They get offended easily when things don't go their way or when we don't go fast enough or when the journey will require more from them than they are willing to give.

All I know is, this is going to be a lonely journey because we live in a culture that wants things that are easy. Why does it seem like you don't really care who leaves? You are tired of being everyone's entertainment. I don't blame you. I guess we can be tired together.

So God, did you say you wanted a ministry to inspire thousands to fulfill your purpose? Did you say you wanted an endowment so your daughters would have a trust fund to be trained for missions and ministry? I guess all rich people set up trust funds for their children. I guess you're pretty rich. So you must want a trust fund for your children's education. I just wonder how many will give you what your heart longs for? How many will stay committed to their pledges? How many will give out of their own inheritance? How many will give their widow's mite just to be part of what you are doing for your daughters? And when Houston has a basic level of support, will the vision travel to other cities? When it's all said and done, God, how many will finish what you began?

God, are you telling me that you're the friend I can count on? No matter how many others break their promise, you are the friend who stayed on the cross to pay the full penalty of my sins. God, thank you for staying! Thank you for finishing! Thank your for showing me that as long as I have you, I am going to be all right. This story is going to end well after all.

Jan 15, 2007

Dear God,
When you parted the Red Sea for Moses, he turned the corner and there was no water. Is this the biblical pattern? Right after the miracle, do you allow life to unravel and watch to see how we will respond?

Never in a million years did I expect that the hardest challenges in Christian ministry would be from the actions of believers. There are times when I feel there is more integrity in corporate America. When I was in the workplace, there were contracts and people were expected to keep their word. In the Christian culture, it's like there are no consequences because people expect to be forgiven. There are some who abuse grace. What's sad to me God is that when a promise is made to a ministry, it's not made to me but to you. Do they think they can break their promise to God and not reap any consequence?

God, Moses wandered in the desert for forty years because of the faithlessness of the people. Are you telling me I will suffer delay because of promises others break? What I must guard against is the irritation Moses exhibited which disqualified him from entering the Promise Land. If we are to wander in the desert, God, then help me to just go with the flow. I have no priorities except to follow you. No matter how long your assignment will take, there is no place I would rather be than where you are working. Lead me one day at a time God and help me to finish well.

I'm sad that those who broke their promise erased their own name from being the one who could have been such a significant part of what you are doing. I don't judge them God because I am not responsible for their choices. I am only responsible for my own choices, so let me focus on that. Please don't let me break any promises. No matter how long it takes, strengthen me God. Help me to endure. Help me to love along the way. Help me to rejoice that the days are never too long when I am in your will.

March 6, 2007

Dear God,
I don't know how I can trust another person as long as I live. You never believed Peter even when he vouched to

stand by you forever. Perhaps my mistake was in believing someone when they told me they would walk with me forever. I wonder if they say they will walk with me because it meets an emotional need in them. Then when that need is met elsewhere, all of a sudden, they feel the calling has changed. So was it their own selfish need the whole time? I don't understand God. Jesus was able to keep eleven of the twelve and with Judas He knew from the beginning that Judas would not stay faithful. How many faithful disciples do we have through Inspire Women? Or do we live in a Nintendo culture where people can't stick with anything. They say they are called out but they make you look totally schizophrenic. It's like you start and never finish anything. God, is there someone out there who has the staying power to finish?

The corresponding truths God taught me from His Word to address my situation

Feel free to continue reading all my personal journals in Module Three expressing feelings of fear before reading the Bible Study. Or you may continue with the corresponding Bible study which contains God's truths in addressing the situation described in the above journal entries with additional truths God taught me to address situations that were not included in my journal entries. If you choose to personalize this curriculum as your way to bond with the group you are leading, feel free not only to use your own testimony and personal journal entries but in the Bible study part, include what God taught you from His Word in situations where you faced fear.

When Someone Breaks a Promise

Situation: Are you in a place where you desperately need someone to keep their promise? Are you afraid those who committed to help you will abandon you?

Reminder: Let's learn the truths from God's Word that speak to our situations. Remember that as a member of God's royal family, we are to act according to the customs of the royal family. This means reinforcing our royal identity by living according to God's specific instructions in the Bible. When we cannot find specific instructions that speak to our situation, we are to search our spiritual heritage and model our lives after God's faith heroes who responded correctly to situations that parallel our own. We can also learn from their mistakes to avoid making the same mistakes in our own lives.

I still remember the many stories my mother told me about her life in China. She often shared the heartaches of the women who depended on the men for their livelihood. She spoke of how many couples were separated when the men left the country in search of work and in order to send funds home to support the family. She said it was the fear of every woman with children that the man who promised to take care of her would direct his affections elsewhere. This waning in affection often shows up in the curtailing of contact. So for example, he would visit less and less. The letters or calls that used to come every week begin to spread out over a longer period of time. The period between visits becomes longer and longer. The final blow is when a letter arrives to announce that he has found someone else. Or the letter may never arrive. The person who promised to be there for you and the children has disappeared and you know that he has gone on with his life without you.

"I wonder today if there is someone who promised to stand by us we need to forgive? Even before they break their promise, can we already have forgiven them?"

As I searched God's Word for His comfort I asked the question, "Did someone ever make a promise to Jesus? How did Jesus handle a situation where someone broke a promise to Him? Did he ever fear that those who made commitments would break their word?"

During one of Jesus' most vulnerable times in His journey, the very disciple who professed he would never abandon Him was far from His side. In the same way we may find that the one who was closest to us has abandoned us during our times of greatest need. In such a situation, our human tendency is to be bitter or disillusioned. Some even give up the mission thinking that the disobedience of others releases us from our calling. I praise God for teaching me how to respond even before the abandonment occurs so I will not be shaken.

In the story of Peter, the book of Mark, chapter 14, verses 29 stated him declaring, **"Even if all fall away, I will not."** The amazing thing is, even when Peter made his statement, Jesus already knew that Peter would fail him. At that very instant, Jesus already forgave Peter. In the book of Luke chapter 22, verses 31-34, Jesus said, **"Simon, Simon, Satan has asked to sift you as wheat. But I have prayed for you, Simon that your faith may not fail. And when you have turned back, strengthen your brothers."** I wonder today if there is someone who promised to stand by us we need to forgive? Even before they break their promise, can we already have forgiven them?

"God's Word showed me that I needn't fret over the promises that are broken because God will be the one going after those who break their promises."

In my life, there were friends I trusted with all my heart and depended on greatly. I trusted their word because they presented themselves as a friend. During critical times in my life when I needed my friends to be true, I could not believe that those I trusted were the ones who abandoned me mid stream. I praise God for His Word because in it I found fellowship with those who experienced similar challenges to what I was going through. Knowing that Jesus kept going when Peter turned back showed me that no matter how close someone is to me, ultimately God is the one who will walk with me to the finish line.

God's Word showed me that I needn't fret over the promises that are broken because God will be the one going after those who break their promises. Luke 22:61-62 tells us: **The Lord turned and looked straight at Peter. Then**

Peter remembered the word the Lord had spoken to him: "Before the rooster crows today, you will disown me three times." And he went outside and wept bitterly. NIV.

In the words that showed me that Jesus **"looked straight at Peter"**, I knew that God has a way of confronting those who made promises to Him. No matter what Peter tried to tell the crowd, he could not run away from himself and what he had said. He could pretend all he wanted that he was not involved but God has a way of getting our attention. When faced with his broken commitment, Peter **"went outside and wept bitterly."**

I praise God for His Word that transforms my emotions. Instead of being disillusioned by those who abandoned me, God showed me that abandonment by those you trust is a biblical pattern. God's invitation to me is to learn from my role model in the Bible.

Like Jesus who forgave Peter, I must forgive immediately. Like Jesus who looked straight into Peter's eyes, I must trust that God has a way to remind those of the promises they made. Like Peter who wept bitterly and desired to be restored to Jesus, I must ask God to protect the blessings He originally intended for those who made a promise to protect God's mission. When I follow God's Word, I am no longer a victim of my circumstances. Instead, I choose to follow the example of God's faith heroes in order to be counted among God's faithful saints.

Even when Peter left Jesus, He was not alone. Jesus said in John 16:32, **"But a time is coming, and has come, when you will be scattered, each to his own home. You will leave me all alone. Yet I am not alone, for my Father is with me."** NIV. God walked with Jesus and stayed with His Son. Jesus in turn is walking with us and He stayed on the cross till He finished the work of our redemption. John 19:30 tells us, **"When he had received the drink, Jesus said, "It is finished." With that, he bowed his head and gave up his spirit. "** NIV.

"I am compelled to stay because of what is at stake."

In Jesus' example, I find the power to keep going until I have finished the work God trusted me to do. For all the examples of those who broke their promise and left, I have God's example of keeping His promise to stay until the work is done. Why did He stay? He stayed because of me. Jesus said to His Father in John 17:24, **"Father, I want those you have given me to be with me where I am, and to see my glory, the glory you have given me because you loved me before the creation of the world."** NIV.

In a similar way, I am compelled to stay because of what is at stake. Jesus knew that his staying and finishing would determine whether we get to spend eternity with Him. Our tenacity to work God's mission will come when we make the connection that our activities affect the lives of thousands for eternity. No other cause is worthy of your pouring out your life.

State how you can connect your life with God's mission. Once you are sure that your activities impact eternity, say how it affects your momentum knowing God will not break His promise to never leave you or abandon you as you serve His mission.

"What exactly am I afraid of?"

Jesus knew what was in Peter and in all fallen humanity. So He transferred His trust to God. When you are in a relationship with someone whose unpredictability creates major stress in you, ask yourself, "What exactly am I afraid of? Write your fear out in a sentence. Then ask yourself, "Should that happen, then what?" till you get to the bottom of what you are afraid of.

The answer could be "I won't have enough funds to keep going". So push yourself to understand your fear by repeating the question; "And if that happens, then what?" You might answer, "Well, then I won't be able to keep going." Then say again, "And then what?" You will find yourself wrestling for an answer and repeating yourself and saying, "Well, it's not good to not be able to keep going. Then I'll feel bad." But ask again, "And then what?" And the answer you might find yourself saying may be, "Then I guess it's not so bad. I guess I'll be fine. It's going to be all right." Sometimes the best way to face a fear is to confront it and to trust God to show you a way to break through it.

What promise are you afraid someone might break? And if what you are afraid of happens, can you answer the question, "And then what?"

"When I am filled with fear over the consequences of promises that others may break, I refocus to the promise of all promises that was kept."

I think sometimes the devil keeps us in a state of fear so we are not really sure what we are afraid of. In the first incident of fear mentioned in the Bible, we find Adam and Eve hiding. Genesis 3:8 tells us: **Then the man and his wife heard the sound of the LORD God as he was walking in the garden in the cool of the day, and they hid from the LORD God among the trees of the garden.** NIV. Genesis 3:9 tells us, **"But the LORD God called to the man, "Where are you?"** NIV.

If God were to ask you today, "Where are you?" could you answer that you are where God wants you to be? If not, what are you running from?

In spite of anything we may be guilty of, the incredible grace of God is that when He came searching for His children, He came with a plan of restoration. In Genesis 3:15, God tells Adam and Eve His restoration plan. He says, **"And I will put enmity between you and the woman, and between your offspring and hers; he will crush your head, and you will strike his heel."** NIV. In these words, God prophesied a time when there will come an offspring from the woman who will wage war against the devil. The devil will strike His heel but in his death, He will crush the serpent's head.

When I am filled with fear over the consequences of promises that others may break, I refocus to the promise of all promises that was kept. God kept His promise to send a seed from woman to crush the devil. When Jesus came into the world and died on the cross for us, He paid the full penalty of the sins of the world and crushed the devil's plan to rob God of His children. In the fulfillment of God's promise to offer fallen humanity a plan of restoration, I will find my confidence.

Since God has restored the greatest loss on planet earth, then surely He has the plan to restore me with the smaller losses in my life. It is with this confidence that I can say, "If someone promised to stay but chooses to leave, God has another plan", "If someone promises to provide for me but abandons me, God has another plan", "If someone made a commitment to finish but bails out mid stream, God has another plan". God who is the Master planner always has another plan. God came looking for Adam and Eve in the garden. When God came, He brought with Him a backup plan. But the greatest and most awesome truth of all is the fact that God came, ready to pay in full the cost of His backup plan.

Have you ever stressed yourself out over the cost of a backup plan? Did you know that when God brings restoration with a backup plan, He has already counted the cost? More than that, He has the power to provide for the cost.

What promise has someone broken to you? Instead of fearing the implications, will you pray the following prayer?

Father, My heart is afraid because I feel my life is being controlled by those who make promises they don't keep. I ask you today to help me to break free from the fear of broken promises by transferring my trust to you as the one who keeps all your promises. You have kept the greatest promise ever made on planet earth. You promised to send a Savior to pay for the sins of the world and you kept your promise. In the same way you provided a backup plan for restoration, I ask you for a backup plan for the promises I am counting on that will have major implications if broken. In the same way you provided the cost of the backup plan, I trust you to also bring a way to pay for the backup plan. Thank you God that I am not on earth to solve problems all by myself. I come from a royal family line of faith heroes with a track record of recovering from the worse losses. It is in the bloodline of my family to have the courage to dream again and the power to finish the dream. Thank you, God, for adopting me into your family tree and teaching me to live as the Daughter of the King. I pray this in Jesus' name. Amen.

I alleviate my fears when I no longer have to trust in the promises of fallen humanity. Instead I find my security in trusting in the promises of my heavenly Father. The prophet Habbakuk expressed his trust in God this way in Habbakuk 3:17-18, **"Though the fig tree does not bud and there are no grapes on the vines, though the olive crop fails and the fields produce no food, though there are no sheep in the pen and no cattle in the stalls, yet I will rejoice in the LORD, I will be joyful in God my Savior."**NIV. God restores the joy in our hearts no matter how our circumstances appear because we have the confidence that God will always come through for those who trust Him.

As God led me into ministry, what I realized was, there were some wounds in my life He deliberately did not take away. I found that certain events or situations would open up the wounds and I would ask God to just take away the memories and eradicate parts of my personal history, but He chose not to do that. For example, one of my biggest challenges in ministry is to trust those who make promises to me. Trust is something difficult for me perhaps because if you feel you have been betrayed by your own mother, it's hard to trust any one else on this earth. For so many years when I was growing up, she and I would dream of coming to this country together. No matter what the challenges, we promised we would always be there for each other and, together, we would make it. Then when I woke up at the age of 17 to find she had taken her own life, my whole world unraveled. I saw her exit as the greatest act of betrayal because she left without me and I had to continue the journey alone. In my intellect, I can argue that she was in a lot of despair herself and her suicide had nothing to do with me and I should not take it personally. But emotionally, her act made me afraid to ever depend on anyone in any journey I am on that is significant in my life.

I carried this emotional baggage with me as God entrusted me with His work. The problem is, in ministry, so much of the work requires teaming up and rallying the body of Christ. The reason is because God's heart is for the world so He is not interested in my taking some solo journey with God. He wants me to get to the mountaintop but my marching orders are to keep the team together and to bring a whole community with me. My emotional challenge arises when someone I depended on makes me a promise and then breaks it.

God healed my heart by telling me, "In your relationships, there may be some things you needed as a daughter, or as a wife, or as a mother but I am inviting you to operate as my ambassador. In that role, you set aside your needs as daughter, mother, wife and step into your calling as an ambassador of Jesus Christ. Your emotional need does not give you an excuse to compromise my calling in your life." I learned that God's power is there to overcome what is emotionally missing in my personal life. The devil's lie is that certain events or relationships will paralyze us. God's truth is that those He calls, He will empower.

Today, when I look back at the incidents when those I trusted broke their word to me, I realize God allowed them in my path to show me His power to overcome my past. If God did not remove the wounds or feelings of your emotional need, it was meant to remind you that whenever the need arises, His power will be there to overcome the wounds and to keep you going. God is not afraid of your past. You shouldn't be either.

Transforming Fear to Fulfill God's Purpose

As I said in the introduction of this curriculum, you will learn that a life of faith is not some mystical feeling but a concrete application of God's Word in the following ways:

- No matter what family background you come from or how things were done in your earthly family, all believers belong to God's royal family and are therefore expected to act according to the customs of the royal family.

- Whenever I experienced an emotion because of a challenge or a decision I needed to make, God taught me to do the following

  o I ask myself, "What am I feeling? Is it loneliness, rejection, or fear? What exactly is the emotion I am dealing with?"

  o I ask myself, "Is the level of my emotion in proportion to what just happened? If not, what wound did it open from my past to cause me to over react?"

  o I ask myself, "Is there a teaching in God's Word that parallels the situation I just encountered? Are there verses that speak to the situation that will give me guidance on how to respond?"

  o I look for biblical examples of someone who dealt with a parallel situation. Since I am to act as a member of God's royal family, I ask myself, "What is the custom of God's royal family and how would God expect me to act?" A tangible way to learn the customs of the royal family is to study the lives of God's faith heroes and how they responded in a parallel situation.

  o Any time I encountered an emotion, a challenging situation or a decision I had to make, God instructed me to find a situation in the Bible that paralleled my situation. I was then able to imitate how the faith heroes responded. There are times I learned from the mistake of a biblical character as described in my concluding thoughts which shares a situation that almost made me abandon the dream. A life of faith then is a concrete way to respond based on what God has revealed in His Word. A person who lives by faith is one who intentionally models behavior after the right choices of the faith heroes in the Bible and trusts that making such a choice is the best choice, no matter what the outcome. The result is a life that moves with conviction and confidence by making choices that are anchored in truths from God's Word and learning from the responses of those who are part of our spiritual heritage.

In applying the above steps, below is what I learned from God's Word to overcome fear. I pray you will believe God's instruction from His Word and model these truths in your life.

When your physical welfare is at risk

- Instead of focusing on the evil around you, focus on God's power to overcome the evil.

- The best way to experience God's protection is to be about God's business.

- Interpret any attack as part of the battle we are in to advance God's purpose on earth. Expect attacks and be prepared.

When you fear unemployment and poverty

- Practice God's wisdom in managing your time.

- Keep working toward your dreams and not just talk about them.

- If you are unsure of your circumstances, have a plan A, B, or as many back up plan(s) as you need to be prepared.

- Give generously out of what you have. Live life with an open hand and an open heart to give.

- If you are unemployed use the opportunity to express your identity as God's daughter who is free to represent her heavenly Father.

- Trust God in realizing that a title will limit you. Your greatest freedom will come from your title as the daughter of the King of Kings who will go wherever God is working. Flow freely with God and understand that God's priority is to share the story of His Son.

When the odds are against you

- Focus your time on hearing God's marching orders and trust His voice over your circumstances. The safest activity is to be obedient and the safest place is where God told you to go.
- Remember that God is perfectly able to protect His mission and purpose for your life.
- Make it your priority to please God. God is pleased when we obey. In His pleasure we are assured of victory.

When you fear failure

- Help to alleviate your stress by recognizing that God sees all of us as imperfect.
- The only perfection is through Christ so lean on His wisdom.
- Forgive yourself and take yourself less seriously.
- Beginning from a place of humility and imperfection, offer your life, energies, creativity and diligence to God as your form of sacrificial worship to Him.
- Let God take care of the results.

When you face suffering

- Jesus asked one question, "Do you want this?" When the Father said, "Yes" that settled the question for Jesus. He walked straight into Calvary and never wavered. Realize your willingness to suffer will depend on the depth of your relationship with the Father.
- Know that Jesus was terrified as well by the suffering that was in front of Him but He trusted God through His suffering.
- God's ultimate purpose is to conform us to His Son so learn to suffer the way Jesus did. He trusted God through it.
- In Jesus' greatest test before His death, He experienced God's silence. Don't be surprised if God leads us into a time when we don't hear Him. Follow Jesus' example and act like God is present the same way Jesus committed His spirit t the Father's hands.

- Jesus focused on the joy beyond the suffering. Learn from Jesus how royalty responds to a cross. If we endure our suffering like Jesus, we can celebrate our future reward.

When someone is angry or jealous

- Know that your fear is warranted as a way to protect you. Avoid an angry or jealous man.

- Turn away wrath with a gentle word.

- Intentionally create space between you and those who are jealous of you.

- Let the ambition of a jealous person destroy himself. The best strategy to take care of God's business is to stay alive.

When choices you can't control affect you

- Learn to assess how someone else's choices have affected your time, resources and schedule. Then adjust accordingly.

- Know that even if the choice of the faithless affect you, God expects you to stay with the mission until you have finished His plans

When you lose your children, assets, or health

- Remember you will only find your peace in total surrender.

- Settle in your heart that even in the worse situation, you can put your hope in God and He will see you through.

When you fear divorce or widowhood

- Remember God has promised to be your husband and redeemer.

- The Lord Almighty is known as the Holy One. He will heal your heart and restore you with His mercy.

- He is the creator of second chances, new beginnings, and new dreams. Call on and count on God to meet your needs.

When someone breaks a promise

- Remember that Jesus forgave Peter for abandoning Him. Forgive even before they ask for it.

- If someone breaks a promise trust God to know what happened and to confront the person.

- Put your trust in the God who keeps all His promises. Do not allow yourself to be desperate, transfer your expectations to a more reliable source.

Additional Testimonies on Fear

In the appendix, you will find additional journal entries or testimonies from the friends of Inspire Women. If you wish to personalize this curriculum as your way to build authentic friendships and community, please add to or replace the testimonies in the appendix with those from those God has woven into your community. Below is a letter you may use to invite your friends to be part of this personalized curriculum

Letter of Invitation to invite a friend to share personal experience

Dear _____,

When God entrusts you with a dream for yourself, your family, your church, your workplace, your ministry or community, your emotions can either empower you or they can cause you to crater on the inside. When the protector of the dream craters, you can kiss goodbye any dream that was meant to make a difference. I am writing you because I am embarking on an exciting journey to share God's truths to transform the emotions in our hearts into a positive energy for His purpose. Unlike other curriculums, I am so excited to be working with a "personalized" leadership curriculum and therefore need your help to make this adventure to be a success. The personalized curriculum I will be teaching has the following format:

- The curriculum is divided into 3 modules, each focused on an emotion. The three emotions we will cover are loneliness, rejection, and fear. I will begin the discussion of each emotion with transparently sharing my personal journal entries from times in my life when I experienced the emotion being discussed.

- Following my personal journal entries will be a Bible study with God's truths to transform our emotions into passionate divine purpose.

- Included in our study are additional testimonies from friends such as yourself. If you did not keep a journal you can draw from, I invite you to relive those times in your mind when you experienced either loneliness, rejection, or fear and write a personal testimony describing your situation and what you felt as if you were experiencing it today. Then also add any truths God taught you in the midst of your emotion.

I am inviting you to be a special part of this personalized curriculum to affirm your presence in our community and to help you to see that you have a message of hope to share with the community God has placed you in. I pray too that in this personalized curriculum, you will celebrate your divine appointment to be part of a personalized keepsake that will build the bond between us and create a lasting teaching instrument that will bless the members of our community for generations to come.

Please let me know if you will join me in creating this personalized teaching material for our _____ (church, workplace, ministry, family, etc.). If you choose to participate, specify which emotion you wish to write about and what God taught you about it through His Word. Please keep your testimony under 3 typewritten 8.5 x 11 pages.

Grateful for your special friendship,

I almost abandoned God's Dream

My husband came home early from work thinking he was going to take the afternoon off. I was in my study finishing the final pages to "Transforming Emotions in a Leader's Heart." He walked quietly into the room and just stood there. I looked up to see if he had something to tell me. He hesitated and then he said, "Yogi died." Yogi was our 15 year old French sheepdog whose vision grew worse over the years, whose legs collapsed from under him every other day but somehow he always bounced right back up, who we were sure would outlive us all!! He ran in the sun, he devoured his dog biscuits, he knew how to celebrate being alive. I heard Yogi this very morning when in his dementia he was just barking nonstop at the wind, still proud of his role as watch dog. So I said to my husband,

"What do you mean?" He said, "He's not moving. I think he's dead."

I went to check on Yogi and sure enough, there was no life in him. He must have slipped away during his morning nap. As I leaned over him and patted his head and body, he felt stiff as a board. That warm furry bundle of life was gone. As my husband made arrangements with the local S.P.C.A. to take care of the body, I started to reflect on the first days he came to our family. He was only 2 months old. How quickly the years have flown by and how precious our moments are. How much time will we really have before there will be no more life in us? And in the time that we have, are we soaring freely the way God intended or are we living in bondage to situations that break our heart and keep us prisoners in our own emotions?

My niece, Rachel, sent me a devotion she wrote titled, "I'm Free, are You?" It hit my mail box this very morning. I felt it contained a perfect message for my concluding thoughts to you. It read as follows:

*I used to work in a downtown area and, on occasion, walked past the county jailhouse. One day, as I walked past the entrance to the jail, a man came bursting through the doors dancing and shouting with his face towards the sky and his arms in the air. "I'm free!" he exclaimed, repeatedly, **"I'm free!"***

I often remember what I saw that day and marvel at the total abandon the man displayed as he embraced his freedom. And I wonder what it must be like to be released from prison - to one moment be standing in a small, dark cell and the next moment be breathing in fresh air and staring at a clear, blue sky. It must be a moment full of wonder and excitement…a moment that can cause a grown man to dance on a city sidewalk jubilantly shouting, "I'm free!!!"

I can almost hear the same fervor in Paul's voice as he writes his letter to the Romans. As he conveys the message of salvation by God's grace through faith in Jesus Christ, he is

urgently trying to convince the believers in Rome that they are no longer slaves to sin. **They are free!**

Listen to his words in Romans 6, verses 3-7. **"Or don't you know that all of us who were baptized into Christ Jesus were baptized into his death? We were therefore buried with him through baptism into death in order that, just as Christ was raised from the dead through the glory of the Father, we too may live a new life. If we have been united with him like this in his death, we will certainly also be united with him in his resurrection. For we know that our old self was crucified with him so that the body of sin might be done away with, that we should no longer be slaves to sin- because anyone who has died <u>has been freed from sin.</u>** *NIV.*

For reasons that even we can't explain, we don't always embrace our freedom. Can you imagine if, at the end of the day, the gentleman released from jail voluntarily walked back in to spend the night? Maybe he'd do it out of habit. Maybe he'd forget he was free. Maybe he'd decide that freedom was overrated. Sounds ridiculous, right? Who would give up freedom that was rightfully his?

Well, the sad truth is that we as Christians do just that, every day. We choose to remain slaves to sin and we buckle under the weight of our burdens until we can merely trudge through our days, finding no joy in them. That is not how free men live.

And so, if Paul were here today, he might start writing a letter to us, reminding us in a fervent voice that in Christ, we are free from the bondage of sin. And he'd beg us to embrace that freedom. And then he'd probably stop and say, "You know what? Just go read Romans. It's all right there."

How would you describe your life today? Is it a life of freedom? Or do still feel imprisoned by your old habits and ways? Has your new found freedom given you hope or do you feel bewildered by how to live your new life in Christ?

As we conclude this time in our journey together, my prayer for you is that you will walk into your future, free from being in bondage to sin and to emotions that keep you from fulfilling God's purpose for your life. Whether God has trusted you with a dream for yourself, your family, church, ministry, workplace, community, nation or the world, the dream is only as good as the vessel who is able to fulfill the dream. If the one appointed to fulfill the dream is derailed in some way, the dream will sit dormant or it will be totally abandoned. This curriculum was the attempt of a weak vessel to share how God transformed my emotions to empower me to complete His purpose. If you could only see the vessel God had to work with, you would marvel at how great God is. He is so able to create something out of nothing.

The overall principles I pray you will assimilate into the way you live for the rest of your life are as follows:

1. **As believers, we are members of the royal family**

2. **Our royal family has royal customs that are part of our heritage and identity**

3 **We reinforce our royal identity by continuously acting as a member of God's family**

4. **The customs of God's royal family are concretely stated in the Bible. We are to follow these instructions.**

5. **If a verse does not speak to our situation, we are to study the lives of the faith heroes in the Bible and learn from their parallel experiences how we are to respond.**

As a bow that represents the final touch to a thoughtful gift, let me share with you one last incident from my life where I used the above principles in response to a situation that crushed my heart to the point that I almost abandoned God's dream. The situation involved major disillusionment with a leader I had esteemed highly. I was broken hearted to watch how a friend who began so purely started to make decisions that were self serving.

"How do you get past the disappointment and keep going in spite of the hurt?"

Have you ever been in a place where the parent you trusted hurt you, where the boss you trusted cast the vote to disband your project or department, where a mentor God raised to sow into your life ends up being jealous of you and tries to destroy your progress, where a sibling or co-laborer who once dreamed with you for God has chosen a personal agenda? How do you get past the disappointment and keep going in spite of the hurt?

As soon as I felt the stabs in my heart, I ran to God for my counsel. As a member of the royal family, I desperately searched for something in God's Word to guide me. I was not satisfied with general guidance of forgiveness and the overall concept of trusting God. I needed something more concrete that I could sink my teeth into. So when I cannot find verses that specifically instruct me in my situation, I then ask God to show me a parallel situation in the Bible. Is there someone who experienced what I am going through? How did they respond?

In response to my confusion as to how someone who began so well could end so tragically, God led me to the story of Moses. The story is told in Numbers 20:2-12: **Now there was no water for the community, and the people gathered in opposition to Moses and Aaron. They quarreled with Moses and said, "If only we had died when our brothers fell dead before the LORD! Why did you bring the LORD's** community into this desert, that we and our livestock should die here? Why did you bring us up out of Egypt to this terrible place? It has no grain or figs, grapevines or pomegranates. And there is no water to drink!" Moses and Aaron went from the assembly to the entrance to the Tent of Meeting and fell facedown and the glory of the LORD appeared to them. The LORD said to Moses, "Take the staff, and you and your brother Aaron gather the assembly together. Speak to that rock before their eyes and it will pour out its water. You will bring water out of the rock for the community so they and their livestock can drink." So Moses took the staff from the LORD's presence, just as he commanded him. He and Aaron gathered the assembly together in front of the rock and Moses said to them, "Listen, you rebels, must we bring you water out of this rock?" Then Moses raised his arm and struck the rock twice with his staff. Water gushed out, and the community and their livestock drank. But the LORD said to Moses and Aaron, "Because you did not trust in me enough to honor me as holy in the sight of the Israelites, you will not bring this community into the land I give them." NIV.

"The sentiment was, 'hat else do you want from me after all my years of serving you?'"

What God led me to do in this story was to focus on what was going on in Moses' emotions. What was he repressing which finally erupted? Before he struck the rock he said, **"Listen, you rebels, must we bring you water out of this rock?"** He called the people **"rebels"**. In his words, **"Must we bring you water out of this rock?"** we hear Moses' resentment. The sentiment was,

"What else do you want from me after all my years of serving you?"

"Oh the danger of a leader who will end badly because of emotional burn out, feeling 'fed up' and ready to just get the project over with..."

Here was a leader who had served for years. Here was a leader who had put up with a faithless group and suffered the consequence of wandering in the desert for 40 years because of wrong choices others had made. Through it all, Moses was faithful. Could it be that after pouring out and pouring out, we can find ourselves irritated with the very people God trusts us to lead? Instead of serving them, we find ourselves criticizing them, angry at them, calling them names, talking about them to others instead of praying for them. Oh the danger of a leader who will end badly because of emotional burn out, feeling "fed up" and ready to just get the project over with so they can be done with the people!

In Moses' story, I saw how his frame of mind paralleled the leader in my life I had so admired. This leader had grown irritated because of all the years of service in the midst of those who have delayed the work because of their faithlessness. This leader no longer wanted to trust God for the strength to lead but had gone down the path of entitlement. The attitude was that of "After all I've done for you, what else do you want from me? I'll help because it might be the politically right thing to do or because circumstances force me to but my heart is not in it. And you can be sure that when no one is looking, I will not make one decision that will help you! It's payback time for you to bless me, not for me to bless you!"

My heart was broken to see what had happened to Moses. At the same time, God healed my heart with Moses' story because I saw the warning for my own life. I will spend many years building Inspire Women. I will have victories and setbacks. I will have delays caused by the faithless decisions of those around me that will cost me time, energy and require longer hours and more sacrifice from me and the staff. I will grieve to see how those who didn't trust God will lose the blessing God intended for them. But through this journey, what God wants to know is how I will respond at the end. Will I become irritated? Will I feel like someone owes me? Will I manipulate things because of what I think I deserve?

Oh heaven forbid that the leader who began as a "son" or "daughter" whose service was a representation of our royal family's fingerprints on earth, should end up negotiating like some hired help who comes with list of demands and a list of "you owe me".

In God's Word I have found concrete instruction to guide me in my life. As I said and continue to re-iterate, a life of faith is not some mystical experience. Being led by God or saying we feel peace about doing something should not be a feeling that has no basis. We are royalty and royalty has a royal code. We can let our emotions control us or we can submit our emotions to customs of God's royal family. Let God examine what we are feeling. Then let Him show us in His Word how we should respond to our situations in a concrete way that either follows a biblical instruction or models after the choices of our faith heroes. We learn from the right things our faith heroes did as well as from their mistakes.

In Moses' story, instead of my being disillusioned with a leader, I learned how vulnerable leaders are as they enter the ending season of their service. If someone like Moses could have fallen, then how much more could any leader fall into the same temptation? This story helped me to pray for those who were deceived at the end. It also helped me to focus on my own walk and to ask God to keep me from being deceived. Oh the absolute certainty of living according to the royal code and the confidence when we follow it, then no matter what the outcome, we are living a life God will bless.

I pray this study encouraged you in a special way. When I pray for you, I hear a victory song. I believe in you because I believe in the power of God's Word in you as you put His Word into action.

For extra copies of "Transforming Emotions in a Leader's Heart"

Or to invite Anita Carman to speak at your event

Please contact Inspire Women at 713-521-1400

or visit www.inspirewomen.org

APPENDIX

Additional Testimonies from

friends of Inspire Women on

Transforming

Loneliness

Rejection

Fear

According to God's Word

To Fulfill His Purpose

Option to personalize curriculum: Please invite the friends from your community to share their stories as a way to build authentic friendships and community.

The Loneliness of Childhood Abuse

I am a single executive and manage over a hundred people. In my personal life, I take care of a mother who has suffered with an illness for many years. There are days when I feel like the loneliest person on planet earth. No one else carried my burden nor had any compassion for it. I ended up not telling anyone my business. To the world I was a business professional. In my private world, I was a daughter who had to learn to be a mother to her own mother.

It seems that when life takes a turn for the worse, the devil delights in piling on more trauma in his attempt to destroy God's children. I was only twelve when my mother's illness caused her to be incapable to meet my father's needs. As a result, he turned his attention towards me. I felt trapped in a household with an ill mother and a father who was making sexual advances towards me. Who could I tell? I was scared and confused that the person who was my authority figure would take liberties with my body that made me ill. My innocence was destroyed by my own father.

In an attempt to escape, I decided to go visit a friend of the family who just had a baby. I thought perhaps I could be of help. During my stay with her, I found myself alone in the house one day. To my total shock, I was in the bathroom when her husband opened the door and walked in. I struggled for three hours as he pushed himself on me. Then, out of total physical exhaustion, he got what he wanted and raped me. I was in so much pain I did not know what to do with myself. I found a bottle of wine in the refrigerator and drank the whole thing. Every day for the next few days when I gained consciousness, I found this man on top of me. So I was repeatedly raped for several days.

How could I have escaped from home only to enter a worse situation? Here I was, a girl at the age of 12. I was sure I was not made for this earth and I wish I could just die and disappear. In God's grace, He gave me a godly friend who fed me God's Word as her way to help me heal the wounds. Then I met a young man who loved me gently. Although God had different plans for me, this young man gave me a glimpse for how God intended relationships to be between a man and a woman.

I don't know what I would have done had my friend not shared God's healing Word with me. In it I have found my restoration. King David said in Psalm 6:6-9, **"I am worn out from groaning; all night long I flood my bed with weeping and drench my couch with tears. My eyes grow weak with sorrow; they fail because of all my foes. Away from me, all you who do evil, for the LORD has heard my weeping. The LORD has heard my cry for mercy; the LORD accepts my prayer.** NIV

Kay

The Loneliness of Leaving Home

Below is an email exchange between me (Anita Carman) and my oldest son, Robbie. Robbie left home for college and went to school out of state. Unlike many of his friends who went to college close to home, he did not have the luxury of returning home during the weekends. After he left, I went up to visit him one weekend and when I returned home, I found an email in my inbox. Below was our dialogue with each other:

Subject: **Hey**
Date: **9/18/2005 10:58:35 AM Central Standard Time**

Hey family, I just got back to my room about 30 minutes ago and wrote an entry into my journal that I thought I would share with you. Hope the trip to Houston went smoothly.

Robbie

This weekend, my family came up to see me and from the moment that I saw them all waiting for me outside the dorm I felt something, something that I hadn't felt in over a month. It just felt so good to have them here with me but at the same time so weird that they would be leaving again in 2 days.

The look on my Dad's face when I first saw him made me realize, in one glance, how much he loved me and how glad he was to see me. And deep inside I was feeling the same thing, and it felt so good to see him. And even though I don't think I usually let any emotion show for some reason and don't think of myself as an emotional person, seeing him for some reason made me miss him so much more.

And then my mom was just like, typical mom, trying to look out for me. She was the same as she's always been and it made me think of my wonderful childhood and how awesome she made it and how big a part she was of it and made me miss her. And even though she's quirky sometimes I love her so much.

And then there is my brother Thomas who is nineteen months younger than me. I spent 2 nights with him and they were amazing. It's like when you're brothers you'll always have a connection and it doesn't matter what happens in between when you see each other because when you do, you'll pick up right where you left off. Just having him there to do the stuff that I do everyday made the experience so much better. And it made me, again, realize that I love him so much. And it's hard to think that I'm in college now and he'll be in college next year and there's a good chance that we won't be going to the same place and I can't imagine that, because ever since I can remember we always embarked on the new experiences, on one level or another, together. I remember going to science camp with him one summer and no matter how stupid or cool I thought it was, it was always so comforting to have him there beside me going into that new camp in the morning. And now he's gone and I'm here all alone and next year he'll probably be all alone.

And it's just tough for me because over the past 19 years I've always been so close to my family and I've had such a great time. And they were always the foundation, and I can't think of any time that we were ever really apart. I can't really remember the last time I cried about something but last night when I was laying in bed thinking about how we were breaking up I started crying. And I left the room so Thomas wouldn't hear me or be distracted and went into the TV lounge and just sat there crying. Something I've never done in my entire life. Then again this morning during breakfast I was on the brink of tears so many times knowing that they were going to leave soon and after I finally did see them pull away, I just went up onto a hill, found a spot underneath a tree, and cried again.

I just miss them so much. And I realized that it was, in a way, homesickness that I was dealing with because they are my home. Not Houston, not the street where we live, but where my family is. That's where I feel I belong and I wanted so bad to get into the backseat of that car and drive away with them, ready to tackle whatever comes next.

Up here at college, this isn't where I belong. This isn't my home. I'm merely here to study hard and get an education/degree. Then I'm out of here and going back to Houston where my family is, and where we'll all live together for the rest of our lives. And then it hit me, or the Holy Spirit revealed something to me—that our life on this earth is just like college. We don't belong here and we'll never feel quite at home here because this isn't where our home is. Our home is in heaven with God Almighty, with Jesus, and with all our other Christian family. That's where we should be longing for. We're living life right now for a specific purpose, to worship God and do what He sent us here to do. Just like in college we're here to get an education. But we should always keep the perspective that at the end of all this, we're going home. And it's going to be awesome because we'll finally arrive at our final destination. We will have finally arrived at the place that we were designed to be. I can have a good time at college, I can make some friends. But no matter how good it is here there will always be a huge part of me that will be unsatisfied unless I'm in the presence of my family. And that's ok. I shouldn't feel bad that life in college isn't as fulfilling as life at home because it's not supposed to be. It's a sojourn, a business trip. And as long as I know that, it's fine, and even good, to enjoy the perks of college life. But I can't try to turn this place into my home. Because it's not and wasn't meant to be. And life is the same way. Sure, life can be enjoyed, in fact Jesus said, "I've come so that you may have life and have it to the full." But we can't get too attached to this life because its very nature is that it's temporary. And just like college, it's going to pass before we know it. And when it does, if we lived it right, we will finally be able to go home.

Below was my email response to my son:

Subject: **Re: hey**
Date: **9/18/2005 9:29:48 PM Central Standard Time**

Well, gee, I couldn't stop crying in the car and I was wondering, "What happened? I was so strong when Robbie left Houston." I was so excited about God's plan for your life but seeing you at school so far from home made me realize that God's plan often requires a sacrifice. I really began to ask God, "Are you sure you want Robbie here or is it our human logic and reasoning that brought him here?" And then I was assured that God loves us more than anything and whatever He leads us to it is for our ultimate good. So when I don't understand

His plans, I must trust His heart. Would I trust Him with my son? Absolutely! It will be at this place far from home that you will hear God's voice. I believe God sometimes has to take us out of the familiar environment before we can hear Him clearly. So bravo on hearing the Holy Spirit today! You're so right about the university being a temporary place just like earth is a temporary place. Now the challenge is to use our experience as a segue to share the gospel. People relate to stories that touch them where they are. Jesus always used stories to share kingdom truth. What made me feel better is to know that because earth is temporary, what God cares about the most is that none should perish. If God wants my son at this university so he can lead those around him out of eternal condemnation to life in eternity, then would I let go of my son for a season the same way God let go of Jesus for a season? Someone once taught me that in our Christian walk, God will conform us to His image. I am finding this to be true more and more. It seems like He gives us opportunities to experience what He experienced. Maybe this is so we can have a greater appreciation of what He did for us.

Talk to you later and thanks for accommodating us this weekend. It was great to see you!

Love, Mom

The Loneliness of Losing a Child

It's been since June 22nd, 1989, when Kyle passed. He was born June 21st, 1981. Do you see God's hand in those dates? I always thought that was one of God's messages to us that Kyle's life was ordained to begin and end; it was up to us to learn the lessons from it.

Kyle's birth was bittersweet. We had looked so forward to welcoming our second son, exactly two years and two months after Clay was born. When we learned that he was born with life threatening congenital heart disease, my heart broke. I started crying and couldn't stop. I was told I had to go see someone and talk to them about what was happening. It was strongly encouraged by the pediatric cardiologists and my OB-GYN. Everyone could see I was fragile. So I made an appointment with the psychologist they recommended and went. He asked me why I was there and I said, "because I can't stop crying". This was when Kyle was born. I think my body was already beginning to prepare me for what was to come.

Kyle lived for 8 wonderful years. And, then his doctors felt he needed to have the reconstructive surgery in order to give him a chance at a full life. The surgery became a death sentence and 12 days after his surgery, he succumbed. After Kyle's death I went thru an intense period of grief and anger towards God. I was so unprepared to deal with the sorrow. My Jewish faith taught me "ashes to ashes, dust to dust"…when it's over, it's over. I had no reason to hope I would ever see my son again.

Then, thru a series of events over a period of years, God brought people to me to lead me to Him. At first I read books. Then, there were messages delivered through people. God was sending messengers to me to reel me back in. But, this time God sent His son to save me. And, not only did he teach me how to accept Kyle's death, but the greater message was to accept Him as my Savior. God lost His Son for a season in order to draw us to Him. Jesus said in John 12:32-33, **"when I am lifted up from the earth, I will draw all men to myself."** NIV. Jesus was lifted up on the cross when He died for our sins. He paid the full penalty of all our sins as His way to satisfy the Father's requirement for justice. He then fully embodied the Father's character of love by offering us the gift that reads "Paid in Full" as our covering to enter heaven. All we have to do is to say, "Yes, I receive it." Today, I see that in the same way God let go of His Son for a season to draw all the world to Him, God allowed me to lose my son for a season to draw me to search for answers that would lead me to Him. When I feel the loneliness of Kyle's physical absence, God reminds me that every grand destination has a cost. In fact, the grander the results the greater the cost. Kyle was put in my life for a reason. Now I know it was to change my eternal destination.

Bonnie Likover

Rejected in Childhood

Most of my childhood was plagued with fear, pain and anxiety. I was constantly on the run from the beatings and the verbal abuse of my parents. My mother was always mad and cursing me and my sisters with some old Chinese sayings that meant "dead girl". She cursed us for being born and complained incessantly about all she had to do because of us. She beat us with either the black belt or the bamboo stick. I thought if I hid them and she could not find them, then she could not beat us. My father worked long hours but he took his turn at night and on the weekends, usually after he had several drinks. My younger sister and I often hid in our "safe sanctuary", our bedroom closet among the piles and baskets of clothes writing "run away letters" on the wall in the dark.

When I was six, my younger sister was removed from the home because neighbors had witnessed my mother beating and starving her. A newspaper article said "the child was beaten about the face beyond recognition with evidence of starvation". Visions of her hiding like an animal under a red high chair still haunt me today. I just could not handle being connected with "that family who had too many children, whose mother beat and starved her child, the child who was taken away". The further I pushed it down the more it was covered and not real. I lived in constant fear of being exposed, and if the conversation came up, I quickly became busy and ran off. Yes, running away and covering up worked for me. Whenever conversations came up about our families, I would avoid talking about mine. I prayed and hoped no one would say, "What about your family, who are your parents, brothers, sisters...?" I did not have happy family stories to tell like everyone else, I wanted to be normal and to be accepted but, deep down inside, I knew I was different. I began to believe the lie that everyone had it better than me. If my family situation was not bad enough, the kids at school mocked and made fun of me because I was Chinese. I was afraid to even go to the water fountain for fear of hearing, "hey you Jap, why don't you go back to where you came from, hey you Chinaman, or just mocking my last name. The chains of fear kept me wishing I was someone else.

One time my father returned home late from work to the meager meal my mother prepared. He became angry and quickly prepared himself something different. He summoned me to the kitchen where he began to slap my face repeatedly and saying "no one would ever want me, and that I would never amount to anything, and that I was no good." I remember just standing there and letting him slap and hit me on the face as the tears and the anguish welled up inside of me because I thought this all must be true. I believed from this point, that I could not do anything to prevent my parents from beating me. But deep inside, I thought there was something I could do to make me worthy.

My career as a nurse brought me new heights. I climbed the ladder of success and enjoyed big titles, fancy offices, and being known among the important people. Things really looked great on the outside. My fear of unworthiness kept me on a performance treadmill. On the outside, people saw me as happy and successful. On the inside, my life was still a life imprisoned by fear, condemnation, shame, worthlessness, and rejection. When work or family was too much, I would overeat or sleep. Both were my comfort as alcohol was for my father. One year while my husband was on a six-month assignment out of the country, I was ready to change my job, sell our home, and get rid of everything.

I recognized my need for a Savior at the age of 18 but I didn't know how to let Jesus be my Lord. A co-worker friend said to me, "Do you have a personal relationship with Jesus?" I said, "No, how do you do that?" A relationship with God seemed foreign to me. All of my life, the cry of my heart was for someone to tell me that "I was accepted and special and that I was loved." God is faithful. In hindsight, I now realize God's sovereign plan looks nothing like the one I tried to build. By His divine appointments, He placed people in my life to enable me to find Him, His love, His acceptance through the Lord Jesus Christ. All of these relationships helped to break and cut the chains of my past. God gave me partners in ministries who worked alongside me, lightening my burden but trusting in God for the results. These friends taught me who I was and was not without Christ. God gave me mature women of faith who zealously taught the Word of God without compromise. God led me to INSPIRE WOMEN, a ministry that helped me to develop and further embrace my passions in the eternal kingdom. INSPIRE WOMEN allows me to partner in a vision that promises to support and train broken women just like me to and to allow God to write His victory story through ours.

Claiming God's victory with you,

Donna

Rejected in the Workplace

Although I was called to corporate American when I was 25, I did not have more than a "mustard seed" of God's wisdom so I was "clueless" about what I would encounter. The story of how the calling occurred is somewhat surreal when I reflect ---humorous actually but I knew it was God's hand. I entered through the door the Lord opened assuming once again I was in for "easy blessings."

Yes, I was so immature in my spiritual life that I expected to have it all which pretty much described my life up to that time. Born into a loving, godly family, baptized at 2 months, confirmed into church membership at 12 with my childhood being totally blessed---good education, opportunities to develop my gifts and talents, many friends, loving caring neighbors, church family and community at large. I had many successes and achievements on my "resume" by age 10. In fact, my wise father took the opportunity to humble me after I earned some grade school award which I did not fully appreciate or understand at the time but later in life drew upon as God molded and refined me. Dad said: "No matter how talented, smart or beautiful you are there is always someone who is more talented, smarter, or beautiful so forget about comparing yourself to others and "run your race" as God has designed you for perfectly and completely." You see my parents had the way of instructing us (that being my little brother Mike and me) by using the truths from God's word (like Hebrews 12:1, the basis for that particular discussion) and living the truths in deed and action.

So why after only a short period did I feel like an "alien" where God had sent me? The beginning of my "frustrating season" crept in. I clung to Jesus' words "you are from below; I am not of this world." (John 8:23) and pressed on seeking to impress the bosses who might open doors for me to climb the corporate ladder---I had big dreams and as the Lord began to bless me with one opportunity and success after another I became more prideful drifting away from God all the while becoming frustrated, confused and lost.

During my first year in the corporate world, I took my first business trip, redesigned and successfully implemented various financial, management systems and regulatory processes and reports. On the personal side, I discovered my husband had betrayed me and no amount of Christian counseling could restore a broken relationship. I was crushed----angry and FRUSTRATED! I poured myself into work and although I was going up the ladder, each rung brought more discontent and dissatisfaction. Things were not what they appeared; there were "mystery rules" which of course, I did not meet. Oh, the time and energy I wasted trying to achieve the elusive seal of approval---trying to be the "perfect" career woman. Unaware that approval is an evaluation and love is unconditional, as a perfectionist in the worldly way, equating the two! I kept trying to please and climb the ladder to the top.

When my company merged with another, I was asked to work on a small team to resolve "policy issues" so that necessitated my traveling to the East coast where both companies had corporate offices. At the kick-off meeting, I found myself as the senior representative for my company and the only woman in the group of 10, being grilled on my age, where I had been educated, my marital status rather than my credentials, experience and capability to accomplish the project at hand. I remember my disillusionment in being judged unfairly and to a standard of perfectionism that was totally foreign to me. One vice president of the other company even had the gall to say something like "how can a female in her early 30's who grew up and was educated in Kansas, handle this work?"

Yes, I was fooled by the appearance of things and wanted approval and acceptance by the important corporate leaders but that experience was instrumental in my awakening to how lost I was...how far from God and my upbringing I had wandered. Experiences like the one I recounted helped me release myself from the shackles of what others thought about me--- I stepped out to take a stand. What freedom to finally say: "I'm a unique person with special talents and qualities and I won't be held hostage to someone else's idea of what I should be or do." I learned I couldn't lead my life for external approval but rather I had to seek God's will and purpose for my life. Freedom is something you have to know from within. How true the paradox of "taking up the Cross and then my yoke is easy and my burden light" becomes. My frustration was lifted and I was free in Christ. I like the Chinese proverb that says "tension is who you think you should be, and relaxation is who you are." Wow, how thankful I am that God loves me unconditionally and sent me into the corporate world. The poet e.e. cummings (yes, he uses only the lower case for his name) writes: "To be nobody---but yourself---in a world which is doing its best, night and day, to make you everybody else---means to fight the hardest battle which any human being can fight; and never stop fighting." How true to be in the world but not of the world! Yet another paradox of Christianity: "I became my own only when I gave myself to Another!"

I came to learn that leadership and stewardship in the corporate world or anywhere else is about serving, encouraging and connecting in meaningful relationship for the collective good of all. I praise God for calling and equipping me for the 25 1/2 years I spent in the corporate world and for the blessing of "Loving in Jesus' name" wherever He sends me.

1 Peter 1:1 explains my question of why I sometimes feel like an alien where He has sent me. Peter said, **"To God's elect, strangers in the world...who have been chosen according to the foreknowledge of God the Father, through the sanctifying work of the Spirit, for obedience to Jesus Christ and sprinkling by his blood..."** NIV. We, believers, are only aliens on earth. We are citizens of heaven and are here on earth only temporarily---only as strangers, pilgrims, sojourners, aliens.......to hear **"Well done, my child"** is my aim.

Cathy Wining Thomas

ADDITIONAL TESTIMONIES ON REJECTION
Betrayal, the Heart Stabbing Rejection

I was taught from a very young age that your word was your bond, that truth and having a noble character were important. Honor, integrity and doing the right thing when no one is looking were all valued attributes. There was very little grey in my world. My father was an attorney who was part of the WWII generation that put a premium on all of the above mentioned values. My Mom was an honorable woman who loved my father unconditionally and enjoyed the same devotion in return. I was totally blessed with a loving family.

As a college student, I met and married my husband of 19 years. We grew apart and, although church -going, we had no true Biblical foundation. Eventually another woman brought an end of a weak marriage. I felt betrayed and a failure. Did he not vow to love me till death do us part? His choice violated all sense of integrity and what I valued in my life.

King David cried out in Psalm 69:1-4, **"Save me, O God, for the waters have come up to my neck. I sink in the miry depths, where there is no foothold. I have come into the deep waters; the floods engulf me. I am worn out calling for help; my throat is parched. My eyes fail, looking for my God. Those who hate me without reason outnumber the hairs of my head; many are my enemies without cause, those who seek to destroy me. I am forced to restore what I did not steal.** NIV

Perhaps if I had been more familiar with the Bible, I would not have felt so alone. Today I know that God in His grace gave us the story of David so we would see that if God could lift David out of the miry pit, He can deliver us as well. And indeed God lifted me out of my pit. God saved a wonderful single gentleman for me and, after dating for four years, we married. This godly man was used by God to bring me and my three sons to an understanding of how the virtues that we had been taught to value are worked out in God's plan for his children. However, in spite of the blessing of my marriage, I began to see a pattern in the kinds of crosses God allowed me to carry.

Out of necessity from my divorce, I jumped into the work force. Hard work has never been a problem for me, as it was part of what I had been taught. **I had learned to meet my responsibilities, deliver on my promises and hopefully show character.** I was blessed with job opportunities that were challenging and lucrative. In one of my jobs, I was in a rare position for a woman as a VP for a multi billion company. I didn't know the owners were planning to sell the company. Although my department was acknowledged as the most outstanding and effective in the company, I found myself targeted and publicly humiliated. I knew this was manipulated by the person who hired me who was supposedly on my side. The betrayal I felt from my first marriage was repeating in my corporate career.

I left the company after it was sold. While I was taking my time to determine my next step professionally, I accepted another high level position with an established institution and was entrusted with a major project. I found at every turn the leader and his good old boys were undermining my efforts. Their resistance blocked my progress and kept me from launching the major project I was hired to do. In spite of the challenges, my department reached revenue heights never seen before. But the mission I had dedicated my energy to never left the ground. I became ill and suffered from the frustration of betrayal. Why do those who promise me so much end up being the ones who clip my wings and keep me from soaring?

I was diagnosed with a disease with no known cure. By God's Grace, after eight years of trying everything including four years of antibiotic therapy, I am out of pain and am grateful to the Great Physician. Trust me, the doctors locally had no clue. This story is much too long to relay, but it was another betrayal of those who promised much but delivered little.

I've seen the pattern of betrayal show up in various areas of my life. As a community volunteer, I have always helped where I could with a number of non-profits. I was asked by one such nonprofit organization to help bring life back to an event. With a great deal of cajoling by the President, I agreed to chair an event to introduce a new concept to bring in the needed revenue. As soon as I took over the reins, the politics began. I was challenged at every turn. Still, being one who always kept her word, I endured to deliver what I promised. Once I agree to do something, my word is my bond. The event netted a wonderful sum to bless the city. In spite of the event's success, the opposition soon mounted to destroy all that had been built. Although the money was raised, the objectives met, and the guests were delighted by the event, the powers in charge decided to bury the concept. Once again, a journey that began in trust and mutual friendship ended up with my feeling used up and betrayed.

I have reconciled myself that problems are part of life. Rick Warren, author of A Purpose Driven Life writes; "Life is a series of problems: Either you are in one now, you're just coming out of one, or you're getting ready to go into another one. The reason for this is that God is more interested in your character than your comfort. The goal is to grow in character, in Christ likeness." Inspire Women taught me to find the patterns in my life and to connect the dots. The idea being, God does not entrust everyone with the same problems. What they have encouraged me to do is to celebrate that God reserves the right to choose who He wills for the crosses He wants them to bear. They have taught me that our stories pale by comparison to God's story and any story we have will take on eternal significance only if we let our story point to God's greater story. In applying this teaching, I praise God for allowing me to experience betrayals more so than the average person. If this is the cross God chooses for me to carry, then I carry it gladly. Since God's ultimate purpose is to conform me to the image of His Son, I ask God to teach me how His Son responded to betrayal. When Peter told Christ he would never abandon Him, Christ already knew that Peter would betray Him. Knowing this, Christ said to Peter that Luke 22:31-32, **"Simon, Simon, Satan has asked to sift you as wheat. But I have prayed for you, Simon, that your faith may not fail. And when you have turned back, strengthen your brothers."** NIV. In these words, I learned that Christ forgave Peter the moment He knew that Peter would betray Him. In the same way, when others betray me, God's invitation to me is to forgive. Christ continued to bless in spite of the hurt and He kept His heart and His arms open for Peter to be restored as a friend. In following God's example, I will also keep my heart open and not become jaded or cynical.

Betrayal is real but more importantly, so is God's example!! My desire is to rise above the darkness and be a giver of light in spite of the disappointments. So, onward and upwards, with God as my role model, I will stand as Christ would!

Cindy Crane Garbs

Rejected by My Husband

As I was packing for an out of town business trip last week, my husband in a fit of anger yelled, "You're crazy, you're crazy, you're crazy!" Lots of marriage counseling and hard work has finally taught me to respond peacefully and even with humor at angry outbursts. So, I completed the packing and flew to Canada. It seemed like everything should be OK. Forgive and forget, and go on with life.

While I forgave my husband, I began to spiral down emotionally until a few nights later, I was at an expensive restaurant with business colleagues having ordered a $40 dollar entrée. I could not stay at the restaurant. Emotionally, I was a wreck. So, I left early. I realized the next morning, that even though there is no valid reason to do so, I had internalized and subconsciously began to believe the words my husband had spoken.

I am a successful attorney with three healthy children and many wonderful friends. How could I allow one person who spoke out of anger hurt me so much? I realize that it is because I grew up with the message that something was wrong with me, or, "You are crazy." It is not that people told me this all the time, though at times they said it. Instead, growing up as a girl in a man's world sent plenty of messages that I did not think correctly. After all, I was more concerned with whether the family liked each other than with the family's financial success. This seemed extremely weird in my family that had bought into materialism "hook, line, and sinker" (as we used to say in East Texas).

I also realize that our society's view of life as revolving around material goods, and sex, and money can cause young girls to feel they do not think straight. This is especially true for extraordinarily intelligent or emotional girls. When we have feelings, we are scorned or laughed at because they do not contribute to the "important" things in life. Finally, I realized that things often do not make sense in life. Why was my sweet sister killed in an accident when she was fourteen? Why do the selfish children seem to be so popular?

After comprehending the root cause of my emotional distress, I did what Anita Carman has taught me, I went to the Bible and asked God to show me in His word what I should learn from this situation. I discovered that God is very serious about calling someone "crazy". In fact, Jesus compared it to murder.

In Mathew 5:21-22, Jesus says, "You have heard it was said to the people long ago, "Do not murder, and anyone who murders will be subject to judgment. But I tell you that anyone who is angry with his brother will be subject to judgment…. But anyone who says, 'You fool!' will be in danger of the fire of hell." NIV. Jesus knows the emotional damage caused by calling someone "fool" or "crazy".

Jesus also tells us what to do about our foolish ways. He says to pray for wisdom, and God will give it to us. However, as with anything else we ask God to give, we must ask in faith and believe in our hearts He will give it.

The Bible Study support group I attend is comprised of women who work, moms who stay home, and grandmothers. All are sane, caring Christian women who survived abuse as children. Almost all have expressed concerns about being crazy. Why are women so susceptible to this lie? It is possibly Satan's most effective weapon against women in our society. Maybe we need to be Jesus to each other and tell one another we are not crazy. The ones who called us this were angry or controlling, but that certainly does not make it true.

Obviously, we need to pray for wisdom. We also have to convince ourselves to believe that God will give us all the wisdom we need. It will not be "conventional" or worldly wisdom. As the wisest man who ever lived wrote in Proverbs 3:5-6, "**Trust in the Lord with all your heart and lean not on your own understanding; in all your ways acknowledge him, and he will make your paths straight**." NIV. Trusting in the Lord requires deleting our old tapes that play the internal message that we are fools. After praying for wisdom, thanking God for giving us wisdom will record a new tape for our brains, which cannot believe opposite information. Repeating to our selves and out loud, "Thank you God for giving me your wisdom, so I have the wisdom of God" will eventually replace the old tapes with God's truth.

In conclusion, when someone says, "You're crazy", take three steps:

1. Rebuke the lie and not allow it into your heart;
2. Pray for God to give His wisdom; and
3. Thank God repeatedly for giving you His wisdom.

Keep repeating God's truth until the Holy Spirit fills the hole caused by the emotional hurt and the peace of Christ returns. Then, enjoy the peace of Christ that passes all understanding. (Philippians 4:7).

Lisa

Are You Afraid of Being Alone?

When my divorce was finally over I felt like I had come out of a battle zone and was so relieved that I survived. As much as I felt that I would rather be alone than be miserably married, I still had to adjust to the fact that I was on my own. I was facing things like Valentines without a Valentine, thanksgiving dinner without the usual family, my birthday without the person who once was my counterpart. The aloneness was most vivid when I was ill and there was no one to drive me or when the car broke down and I felt stranded. It was during these times that I cried out to God to be my husband.

I remember right after Katrina, there was a major storm heading for Houston. Everyone was leaving town. I was terrified because I knew I could not drive myself. I felt so utterly alone and trapped while waiting for the hurricane to hit. I asked the Lord to help me. A friend who lived in Dallas offered to fly to Houston to drive me to her home in Dallas. Never in a million years would I have expected anyone to reach out to me that way. Once again, God showed me that even before we cry out to Him, He already has the answers.

I own a small building that I lease out to a company. One day, the company called to say a garbage truck had hit the fence while picking up the garbage and the fence could not close any more. I called the garbage company and they said they would take a look at the problem the next day but no one came. So I prayed: "Father, you know I don't have the money to replace this fence. I pray that the garbage company will fix it." The next morning I got a phone call telling me the fence was fixed. The garbage company had fixed it the night before. The Lord had answered my prayer while I slept.

While on my own, I had been praying for quite a while that the Lord would give me a world wide ministry one that would count for Him for all eternity. A number of months later I was bedridden because of my heart. I asked the Lord if I could do a ministry while in bed. A few days later Anita Carman, President and Founder of Inspire Women called me and asked me to be her Prayer Warrior. I said, "Yes!" because I knew this was God's answer to my prayers. Not only did the Lord answer my prayer while in bed but Inspire Women is beginning to go nation wide and will go world wide. God showed me that as long as He is in my life, we will be conquering the world together. It has been my utmost privilege to stay on my knees on behalf of Inspire Women. I have watched the ministry soar. Every time I hear of the doors God has opened, I say, "Thank you Father. I knew you would do it!"

Paul said in 1 Cor 7:34, "**An unmarried woman or virgin is concerned about the Lord's affairs: Her aim is to be devoted to the Lord in both body and spirit.**" NIV. God has been my husband and my life has been an adventure. I praise God for the women who have found an earthly counterpart to walk with them through life. But for those who are single, I want them to know that being single is not a liability or some inferior state you feel you are settling for as if life is better elsewhere. It is a different calling whether for a season or for a lifetime. And with all of God's callings, it is perfect because it was designed by a good God who loves us with all His heart.   Carol Logan Byrd

The Fear of Inadequacy

In my adult years I met Johnnie Lee Jr., while working at Dresser Industries Inc. We developed a warm friendship. I began to realize through Johnnie that I needed something more from God than I had. As we interacted I came to the conclusion that I knew of Christ but didn't really know Christ in a personal intimate way, as my personal Savior. Johnnie and I became engaged and during our engagement Johnnie became a Minister. Fearful yes! "Why?" I was thinking, "I can't be a Minister's wife because I don't know anything! I am just getting into Christianity."

My situation wasn't helped by others who had already picked the lady Johnnie should marry. I also had two sons to bring into the marriage and Johnnie didn't have any. I felt so unworthy, so inadequate. So now my fear was, I don't deserve him. He should marry someone else. After marrying Johnnie and watching him go out to minister, I was so afraid that I would have to say something to God's people. I watched other ministers and how their wives got up on stage and words would just flow out of their mouths. I would say, "Oh no, I can't do that, I am going to pass out if I have to speak! I can't speak like that; I am going to say the wrong thing." I would literally hide so Johnnie couldn't see me, hoping he wouldn't remember that I was there with him.

When Johnnie would have me stand, I would just stand and wave, praying it was a hole that I could go down into. I would sweat and my heart would pound. I made it through 10 years of being a Minister's wife by the Grace of God. After 10 years of being a Minister's wife, now I am going to become a Pastor's wife. I really wanted to say, "Oh no, I am barely making it as a Minister's wife, how am I going to be a Pastors wife?" Here came the fear again, which had never completely gone away.

Pastor's wife! I can't just wave and say two words. I asked Johnnie if he was sure that the Lord was calling him to this area of ministry. I began to realize that the Lord wanted, once again, to take me out of my comfort zone. I had fear of the unknown, fear of whether things would work out. I wondered if people will like me. Will I be able to be the perfect Pastor's wife? I said to the Lord, "Will I ever be able to get rid of this fear?"

God promised me in 2 Timothy 1: 7 **"For God did not give us a spirit of timidity, but a spirit of power, of love and of self-discipline." NIV.** Praise God for Johnnie constantly telling me, "Baby just say what the Lord gives you to say, don't worry about the people judging you, don't worry about saying it like Joyce Myers, you're Debra Lee, just be Debra". Praise God for one of Johnnie's friend who introduced him to College of Biblical Studies. Johnnie and I started going on a Pastor's scholarship, and our first class was Marriage and Family, the best class I had ever taken. I began to know and understand the real role of a godly wife and a mother. As time went on Johnnie began to take more classes, and Praise God he met Anita Carman, the best thing that could have ever happened to him. Anita began to get scholarships for Johnnie to go to seminary, he was flourishing in the Word of God. I was longing to go so I could flourish also but our lack of funds did not allow both of us to go.

At home one evening, Johnnie and I were talking about my taking classes knowing our funds would not allow it. He wanted me to be more comfortable with handling God's Word. One day, sitting at home on my day off work my phone rang and on the other end was Anita Carman. and she said; "Debra this is Anita and I have some ladies that want to sponsor you in school. They want you to keep up with Johnnie since he is being equipped you need to be equipped also". I just held the phone and began to weep tears of joy, saying the Lord is so faithful. He will give you the desires of your heart I knew that if I could be trained in the word of God then I wouldn't be so fearful. I explained to her how we both really wanted me to go but could not afford it. Through Inspire Women, off to school I went and now I am hooked on Bible College. I am taking class after class and learning God's Word.

Anita didn't know how fearful I was to get up in front of people to just give my name. She emailed me and asked me to share my testimony with some ladies. When I received the email FEAR immediately came over me. I began to sweat and shake. So I began to say to myself, "Oh no not me, I can't do that". I called Johnnie to tell him and he said, "Oh that's good, you can do it." I said, "No, I can't. I am scared to death!" but he began to minister to me. I calmed down and asked the Lord for his help and asked Him what I should do. The next day I emailed Anita and said I would do it. Yes, fearful and scared to death, I was going to have to get out of my comfort zone. The Lord told Jeremiah; "… **don't be afraid of their faces**". I began to put into practice the things I had been taught in the Word and realized that it's not about me, it's all about Jesus. It's about saying a word that will help someone. I made it through by the Grace of God and the prayers of the saints. Anita asked me again to share my testimony this time in front of thousands of women at the Inspire Luncheon. Anita still did not know how fearful I was of speaking in the front of people. So she continued to push me. I thank Anita for that. I still wanted to pass out or crawl into a hole but God is so faithful; He wanted me to get over the stumbling block in my life that was the spirit of fear.

Johnnie reminded me that I can do all things through Christ who strengthens me. He encouraged me to do what the Lord gives me to do. Be yourself. Don't act like anyone else. I am beginning to realize that we all are tools in God's hand. We are all different, and each tool has a different function so that we need each other. I can't be an Anita Carman, there is only one and God broke the mold when he made her. But there is also only one Debra A. Lee so I've learned to embrace my uniqueness, gifts, and talents and not compare to others. For me to not appreciate who I am and what I can do in ministry for the glory of God is to dishonor the Creator. Yes I do struggle a bit, but now my fear is a healthy reverential fear of the Lord. I don't want to shame God's name; I want to bring honor to it.

How to overcome Fear: 1) Ask the Lord to Remove it 2) Quote the Word of God 3) Be led by the Lord 4) Praise Him for His guidance 5) Praise Him for taking you through it.

Debra Lee, Pastor's wife, Victory in Jesus Evangelistic Center

The Fear of Man's Disapproval

Galatians 1:10 reads: "**Am I now trying to win the approval of men, or of God? Or am I trying to please men? If I were still trying to please men, I would not be a servant of Christ.**" NIV.

I was born Dec 4, 1943, Marilyn Price, to the parents of Paul and Jeanne Price. I was the second child. I had a sister Linda who was 3 years older and later I had a baby brother Joe who was 8 years younger. We were a fairly poor family as were most people in those days BUT I remember being a happy family. In fact the nickname my mother gave me was "Happy Chappy".

I came into my family very loved and very happy. God intended for me to mature in a safe environment but then something happened. When I went to school, I had trouble with schoolwork. I know now that I was dyslectic. I wrote left handed and did everything else right handed, except for fine motor skills-I can do them either hand. To this day I don't automatically know my right from my left. I have a "writing callous" on my left hand and I have to rub it to know my left from my right. I thought I was bad because I was always being corrected. My sister was the prettiest and she was very smart. My brother was the "cute baby". It felt like my mother just really did not care for me-but now I know that was not true.

When I was in the second grate I became close to my teacher, Jean Rodgers. In fact her husband traveled and sometimes she would walk home with me and spend the night. I had her approval but I didn't seem to have the approval of my parents.

When I was in the second grade, I was in the Brownies-Girl Scouts. When it came time to sell cookies, I walked for miles and miles. In those days it was safe. Since I was such a talker, it was easy for me to talk to people and sell cookies. Back then you didn't order them; you took them around and sold them on the spot. I walked so far and sold so many cookies that I earned a "free trip" to camp. This was the first success that I experienced. Camp was great!! Again the approval of men.

We moved when I was in the 4th grade and the only thing I was any good at was "ball", any kind of ball. And boy I was good!! And that felt great!! I became close to the PE teacher Peggy Cox, she thought I was great. Another time of approval of men.

When I started High School my longtime boyfriend broke up with me. I was devastated and embarrassed. I met a boy that was out of high school and we married the summer of the 11th grade. I didn't finish school. I felt like a real looser. I didn't love him but it seemed like a way out from under my mother's critical thumb. He was a nice guy and I was so immature that I thought it could work. We were married 2 years when I decided to go back home. I stayed home about 6 months under my mother's critical spirit and left again for the big city- Houston, TX.

July 1, 1963 I met the love of my life Billy Lewis. I knew it right away, though I don't think he felt the same way. We dated for 9 months and got married on March 6, 1964. We had a great time and marriage. Billy made me feel SMART & SPECIAL. No one had made me feel smart before.

Now Billy had been to college 1 semester and after we married he wanted to go back. He was going to start summer school. Well, I wasn't about to sit at home by myself. So I marched up to the registrar at South Texas Junior College and told her I hadn't graduated BUT I want to go to school. Do you know that lady, Mrs. Hutchinson, let me start on scholastic probation? She said if I could pass, I could stay. Well to my surprise I did pass!! And I stayed.

While we were going to college, we both worked part-time. I worked at an insurance agency. By that time, I had taken some classes to learn how to rate insurance policies. We finished our 2 years at the Junior College and now it was time to go to the University of Houston. Yes, I had the grades, average of B+. I couldn't believe it, nor could my mother BUT Billy could, he continued to tell me how smart I was!!

After six years we had our first child. I really wanted a child. I thought my child would love me completely. It seemed that even Billy's love was not enough. I was a stay at home mother for only 3 months. It just wasn't fulfilling like I had hoped. So, I went back to work part time.

In 1976, I had one child in Day Care, and another on the way. I thought it would be good to start a daycare center so the ARK CHILD CARE CENTER was started. The first one was so successful and we thought we should build another. By 1984 we had 5 locations.

We both continued to work hard and things seemed to be going our way. Again, I felt powerful and smart. Buy now I had 5 daycare centers, a home in Memorial, a ranch, 2 Cadillacs, a corvette, a truck, and a big diamond ring.

Well here is where to story gets GREAT. I met this lady at church, Dianne Nelson (yes we always attended church) and something just drew me to her. I know now it was JESUS. This lady talked about Jesus like he was a real person. For some reason, I had never encountered this before, even though I attended church. I thought to myself, I want to hire her and see how she acts at work. I knew I had a church face and a work face. I used vulgar language at work and I was a hard-nosed businesswoman. BUT I was successful and received the approval of men. I really had to talk hard to get her to come to work (and kept raising her starting salary). She finally agreed to come. Guess what? She was the same at work!!! Little by little she gently bathed me in scripture. I didn't know it though because despite the fact that I was in church every Sunday and bought the latest "cool" Bible, I NEVER opened it!!!

After 8 months of her influence and really counting the cost of a "real commitment to Christ, I knelt by my bed one night and prayed. "Dear Jesus, if I am a Christian, why don't I act like one"? Then "Dear Jesus, I don't know if I am a Christian, but I want to be, please come into my heart, change me and save me. Forgive me of my sins, I want to repent of my sins and turn toward you. I have been going my own way for a long time (I was 36), I want to follow your way, Jesus." This was April 6, 1980.

That night an unexplainable peace came over me. I returned to work interested in telling others about Jesus. My life did change. I was peaceful and happy. My life has not been perfect since than, I have had much heartache and I continue to sin, but now I immediately confess that sin and Jesus is "**faithful and just and will forgive us**" (1 John 1:9). I have a love for Jesus and people and I have a sense of purpose…the purpose we were all created for, to glorify God. When trials come, I can face them with the assurance that Jesus is there with me and He will direct my path. Romans 8:28 tells us, "**And we know that in all things God works for the good of those who love him, who have been called according to his purpose.**" NIV.

I no longer need or seek the "approval of man" I can finally rest in the arms of Jesus. I have had times of drought and times of plenty. In both I know and trust Jesus, that He is working all things to the good of those who love Him. And oh how I love Him!

I am so grateful God led me to pray this prayer
"Jesus I know that I am a sinner (Romans 3:23) for your Word says that all have sinned and fall short of the glory of God, I know that I want to go to heaven when I die but your Word tells me that the wages of sin is death but the gift of God is eternal life in Christ Jesus our Lord (Romans 6:23). So I want to receive the gift of your son so I can have eternal life in heaven. Thank you for telling me that you demonstrated your love for us in that while we were still sinners, Christ died for us (Romans 5:8). I thank you for helping me to believe your Word and for keeping your promise. You said that if we confess with our mouth that Jesus is Lord and believe in our heart that God raised him from the dead, then we will be saved (Romans 10:9). You said for it is by our heart (not our head) that we believe and are justified, and it is with your mouth that you confess and are saved. God, I believe with my heart and confess with my mouth that your son Jesus has the power to save me and I accept your gift. Thank you for giving me the gift of eternal life in heaven. I thank you in Jesus' name. Amen.

Marilyn Lewis

Are You Afraid of the Mess You've Made of Life?

God is there to redeem us even if the mess we're in is one we've made ourselves. In my struggles through life, deep in the valleys, I've learned about the way God restores hope and shows His grace through all kinds of tough times.

I learned early in my life that God is there to redeem me even if the mess I'm in is one I've made myself. I was a mess in the spring of 1969 when I was 18, a senior at Spring Branch High School, pregnant and unmarried. That is a tough predicament to be in today, but can you imagine what it was like to be in that spot 38 years ago? Especially when you're an only child of older parents and they are pillars in the Community and the Baptist Church! This was definitely a valley experience in my life!

There was pressure on me from people I would have never imagined would give me this "advice" – the pastor of my childhood church and my own father - to end the pregnancy, have an abortion and get on with my life so I would not embarrass them. I just knew I couldn't do that. I felt the hand of God leading me to decide to have the baby, despite how uncomfortable and awkward things were. I have never regretted it! NEVER!

At the time, I didn't know how things would turn out; I just knew that God was in charge. In Genesis 50:20, when Joseph is talking to his brothers after they are all reunited in Egypt, he says to his would-be murderers, **"You intended to harm me, but God intended it for good to accomplish what is now being done, the saving of many lives."** NIV.

You see, Joseph knew what I now know, that God "gives second chances" Sure, being unmarried, pregnant at 18 was tough, but God was with me the whole time and was able to redeem the situation. I wouldn't give anything for my son John, and for the joy of being his mother. John had worked his way up our family business and was marketing manager when we sold the company. Over the last several years he has had several jobs; he sold fleet cars and sold health insurance. He decided to postpone college once again. Ultimately God led him to work at his church; he's been a strong Christian most all his life. He's a wonderful husband and father of four, he's a leader in his church, and became an ordained minister this summer. He is a wonderful Christian man; I love him and am proud of him. I thank God that He allowed me the opportunity to be John's mother. Though I can not say I was totally unafraid by what my father and my church pastor had intended for evil (by encouraging me to have an abortion).... God intended for good...through my son -John-who has led many people to Christ. We can not see what Jesus has in store for us. We need to trust and obey.

I stand before you today...definitely more in the valley than on the mountaintop.... but still, unquestionably, in what Isaiah called the "Shadow of the Almighty". While there are things about the last few years that are still fuzzy to me, there are a few things that have become clearer and clearer through these difficult times. And that is that the hand of God, the presence of Jesus Christ and the comfort of the Holy Spirit are always as near to us as our next breath...as close as the very skin on our bodies. And that is made ever more crystal clear when we are in the challenging valleys of our lives. And EVERYONE HAS THEM...everyone!

Cheryl Thompson Draper

The Fear in Walking with a Mom with Cancer

Psalm 46:1-7 reads: **God is our refuge and strength, an ever-present help in trouble. Therefore we will not fear. The LORD Almighty is with us; the God of Jacob is our fortress.** NIV.

When the blow of cancer and the replacement of a hip strikes there is only one thing to do—go to Him. Even though there have been times when my mom and I have wanted to shout "that's enough!" we feel confident in our Lord. He gives us peace because we know that He is our refuge.

Mom has been dealing with cancer and hip surgery in a very quiet way. She is willing to do whatever the doctors say. She doesn't complain, she has a very sweet spirit, and that spirit seems to draw others to her.

1 Corinthians 12:7 reads: **Now to each one the manifestation of the Spirit is given for the common good.** NIV. The doctors, hospital staff, family and friends have all been God's gift to my mom. They have brought her healing, love, friendship, flowers, and notes.

It has been a long hospital stay. I pray everyday that she will sit up and begin to walk. I pray that God will heal her and make her strong and give her a few days of fun.
In Jeremiah it says that the Lord has plans for us. We are confident that He has plans and He knows what He is doing. He gave my mom and our family a glorious week in Colorado together to celebrate her 80th Birthday. He knows what lies ahead for her and He let each of us have a special time with her. We thank God so much for that.

Even though some days seem dark and long I know that God is with me because He promised never to leave me or forsake me. Through Christ I know that we will get through all of this because He gives us the strength to do so. There will be light again at the end of this dark tunnel because I know that God brings good out of the bad. Like Psalm 139:1-3 says, **"O LORD, you have searched me and you know me. You know when I sit and when I rise; you perceive my thoughts from afar. You discern my going out and my lying down; you are familiar with all my ways."** NIV.

Over and over again God tells us in His Word that He is here with us and is in charge. All He asks us to do is have faith in Him. Believing in Him pleases God. We have faith in our precious Lord. We believe in Him. We are looking ahead to see what He has in store for us.

Kim Watson

(Kim wrote the above on Aug 12, 2007. The next page contains Kim's additional thoughts on what the Lord taught her through her Mom's illness.)

Additional thoughts from Kim…

When I wrote about my Mom on August 12, I did not expect what was about to happen. I had different plans for our last days together.

It was Thursday night, August 17, and I was by myself with my Mom in the hospital. I talked to God a long time that night. I wish I could say I felt His presence but during my darkest hours, I could not hear Him. I kept saying to Him, "This isn't my plan." I was eager to bring my Mom home with me during her final days. I wanted us to have time together away from a hospital. I had visions of reading the Bible to her and just being able to have conversation. I wanted to be in the warm atmosphere of home as compared to the formal atmosphere of a hospital. My Mom told me several times that she loved me very much and not to leave her. I stuck close to her the whole time.

I had read a pamphlet on the signs of dying and they were all there, one after another. I did not recognize all of them at the time. First my Mom started pulling at her clothes, then she asked to talk to her loved ones, then she had a burst of energy and wanted us to leave the hospital and go somewhere together. When she breathed she would exhale with a puff of air. Then I started to hear a raspy sound in her breathing. All this was in the pamphlet. It really bothered me when I heard that raspy sound in her breathing. So I prayed and asked God to take that sound away. About five to ten minutes later, the nurse came into the room to give my Mom a breathing treatment. She suggested suctioning out the phlegm in her throat. She ran tubes down her throat and the rasping sound went away. I wasn't even thinking by then and did not see that God had answered my prayers for that horrible sound to go away.

I kept reading the Psalm and asking God to protect my Mom. My Mom was at the Houston Medical Center and my husband who was on a business trip in New York flew back to Houston to join me at the hospital. I was so relieved when he arrived. God knew I could not handle these final moments by myself and brought him to be by my side just in time. God kept my Mom alive till Chuck could be with me. I remember when he went out of the room I was so anxious for him to return. I did not want her to die when he was out of the room. My husband and I were in the same room when God took my Mom home. When the nurse came in to take her vital signs, I told the nurse she would not find any.

Although I know that there is no spiritual death and my Mom lives on in eternity, I must say that physical death is not pretty. When I think of that moment when my Mom's breathing stopped, I wish I could say there was a bright light in the room but I saw nothing. I had read that some people get glimpses of heaven. I did not. I wish I could say that God came into the room and I saw God ushering my Mom home. But I did not see God in the room. The final moments just came quietly and she was gone.

The nurses started taking the IV's out of her. At that time, I wasn't sure what to do with myself. The whole time I kept saying to God, "This wasn't my plan. My plan was for her to return home with me so we could have the next few months together." God's message to me was, "But Kim it was my plan. You wanted her home with you but my plan was to take her home with me." When I think about having this tug of war with God, I see me pulling one way and God pulling the other. I saw how when I finally understood what God wanted, I found myself letting go. God wanted my Mom in His home. How could my home possibly compare?

I started to fret over all the things I wish I had said to my Mom. Then a few days later, I found some cards I had written to her. God, in His grace, showed me, "Kim, you said all those things to your Mom. You wrote them on the cards you sent her." I thanked God for reminding me. At the memorial service, the minister told the story of how my Mom was always excited to go on a trip. When my husband Chuck called her to ask if she wanted to go she would always say, "I'm ready to go!" The minister said, "Jesus called her name and she said, 'I'm ready to go!'" She went on her best trip ever!

My son, Brian was working at a Young Life youth camp and two boys accepted Christ. Brian shared at the service that heaven rejoices when a sinner comes to salvation. He said that when those two boys prayed to accept Christ, it helped him to know that his grandmother was among the saints in heaven who were rejoicing. She was part of the heavenly celebration.

My Mom turned 80 on July 15 but the family came for a week long celebration starting July 4th as different family members flew into town. I remember her saying, "This will be my last fling." I did not agree with her but now I realize that she must have known. She thoroughly enjoyed her last fling on earth!

As I go through the days, I can still hear her voice when she said to me, "I love you so much. Please don't leave me." I'm glad I never left her. I was there till her very last breath. Though I could not see Him, I know I was in the room when Jesus came to bring my Mom home. If there is anyone I can trust my Mom to, it would be Jesus.

I thank God for my Mom and for the time we had together. And I thank God for keeping His promise to bring home those who belong to Him, when our time on earth is over.

Kim Watson

Are You Crippled with Fear over Your Children?

Fear visits us in so many circumstances of life, but it does not have to stay unless we let it. The Word of God can cast away all fear. The word says in 1 John 4:18 **"There is no fear in love. But perfect love drives out fear, because fear has to do with punishment. The one who fears is not made perfect in love."** NIV

I was a people pleaser. I wanted my family to be proud of me so I was very obedient. I walked in fear of not being liked as a teenager. I had no proof of it, as I was liked by a lot of people, but there was that nagging fear. That was before I knew the word of God. I knew Jesus and received Him as my Lord and Savior when I was 12. I heard Him call my name when a message was given to our church by a traveling evangelist. It was unusual for an evangelist to be at our church, but there he was. I do not know what he said, but I do know Jesus met me there and called my name. I went forward and have never been the same. But having Jesus does not mean fear does not visit me.

All I ever wanted to be was a great wife and mother. I was afraid of not being able to be a mother because infertility plagued my husband and me for five years. Then by my husbands leading we adopted our daughter and 3 years later adopted our son, then 3 years later gave birth to a son. I was beginning to learn to rely on the Lord in my life.

But fear visited me again as that daughter became rebellious and continually ran away. I was afraid that she would be hurt or killed. I did not know what to do so I looked everywhere for an answer. I looked at God's Word, but did not know it like I know it today. I needed Jesus with flesh on. I received great counsel and not so great counsel from God's people who I thought could show me what to do. Being a perfectionist and a people pleaser I knew I could do it. It almost killed me. I woke up everyday for 5 years looking at our daughter and in my mind asking, "How is today going to be? Are you going to cooperate and be a part of our family or are you going to do things that hurt our family and yourself?" Drugs were involved and eventually our daughter reaped what she had sown and we received that call that all parents fear saying that she was being rushed to the hospital with an apparent drug overdose. The doctors said that she may not make it through the night, but by God's mercy, He allowed her to live. She lived for 24 days in intensive care, having grand mal epileptic seizures every 2 minutes. The doctors were able to give her medication to calm the visual effect of the seizures, but they were still going on in her brain. She was in a coma most of the time. We were in an unusual intensive care unit which allowed us to be with her all the time. We had a room to ourselves. I feared she would die.

In those days of being with her and still being Mom and Dad to two boys, we struggled with many fears, but there was a peace that passes all understanding. We just dealt with the moment and got into a routine of one of us being at the hospital and the other going through the motions of making life go on for our boys.

The doctors said her brain was not working, but I prayed for a sign that it was and she came out of the coma to say a simple sentence: "Wait just a minute." We were so excited. Her brain was working.

Over the 5 years leading up to this moment I had learned about forgiveness through God's word. So as she slipped back into the coma, my husband and I stood by her side and asked her to forgive us for anything we had ever done to hurt her. We told her that we forgave her for anything she had done to hurt us and for bringing drugs into our lives. Most importantly we told her that God did not see her as guilty, but that all our sins Jesus had died for and that even though she could not reach up in her body, she could in her spirit and receive the forgiveness God had for her in Jesus. Tears flowed out of her closed eyes and we told her that we knew she had heard us. Several days later as her condition worsened, we turned off the respirator and watched our daughter die.

I wanted to die. I was afraid of the pain of loosing someone else I loved so dearly. I was mad at the world, and at God for I knew He could have healed her. Much later, as I sat with Him and His Word, I realized that He had healed her and taken her home.

The path I walked with my husband, our sons and our Lord since that day 21 years ago has been one of struggle and of victory. Have I been afraid in the last 21 years? Sure I have, but fear does not stay for when fear comes, the Word of God is the sword I now use to break the power of fear in my life. As I learned more of God's word and wrote it on my heart and spoke it out of my mouth fear had to leave me. Now I do not live in fear of anything. In fact things, circumstances and the evil one had better get out of my way because I am coming through with God's word. 2 Timothy 1:7 reads: "**For God did not give us a spirit of timidity, but a spirit of power, of love and of self-discipline**" NIV. I know who I am and who my family is: we are children of God, victorious, forgiving, laughing, loved unconditionally by our Father who cares for every detail of our lives. It sets us free to work, to play, to laugh, to cry, to hope, to dream, to love unconditionally as children play in the safety of the watchful eye of a loving Father.

I learned much in the story of The Father (some people call it the Prodigal Son). I call it the story of The Father. If I had it to do over again, I would still deal with the drug problem by getting her help, as we did. I would let our daughter know how much she was loved, as we did. I would assure her that she had a warm safe place to stay, but that she could not bring drugs into our home and that we had rules in our family, as we did. But if she still wanted to leave, I would help her pack and let her go with the knowledge that the door is always open. And if and when she came home, I would welcome her with open arms celebrating that our daughter was home and alive. I would not talk about past horrible times. Yes, she might go again. I cannot control that. I can just trust my loving Father to be true to His promise that my husband's and my faith sanctifies our children. I can rest in His arms, for He carries me and them and He will not loose us.

I realize now that the decision to be a part of a family rests on each member of that family. I can only do my part. God has no grandchildren only children and He created His children with free will.

Everyday I offer myself as a living sacrifice, holy and acceptable unto God which is my reasonable service. I will not be conformed to this world, but I will be transformed by the renewing of my mind that I may prove what is that good, acceptable and perfect will of God.

I will not think more highly of myself than I ought to think, but I will think soberly for God has given to every man the measure of faith. Romans 12:1-3 says, **"Therefore, I urge you, brothers, in view of God's mercy, to offer your bodies as living sacrifices, holy and pleasing to God-this is your spiritual act of worship. Do not conform any longer to the pattern of this world, but be transformed by the renewing of your mind. Then you will be able to test and approve what God's will is-his good, pleasing and perfect will. For by the grace given me I say to every one of you: Do not think of yourself more highly than you ought, but rather think of yourself with sober judgment, in accordance with the measure of faith God has given you."** NIV.

In His grasp,

Judy Standridge

The Appendix of "Transforming Emotions in a Leader's Heart" contains additional testimonies by my friends who experienced one of the emotions discussed in this curriculum, with their insights from God's Word. If you are teaching the material from this book, please note that the format of this book offers you a way to personalize the material and serves as a tool for you to build authentic friendships and community. This book is available in bound format for your personal use or in a loose leaf binder format so you can easily insert pages with your own testimony and with testimonies from those in your community.

In the section titled "Personalize this curriculum to build authentic friendships and community" I have included a sample letter of invitation for you to invite your friends to write their testimonies. You may invite them to pick one of the emotions covered in this curriculum that is most relevant to their lives: Loneliness, rejection, or fear.

By drawing them in to be a part of this personalized leadership material, you are affirming their presence in your community and helping other Believers see themselves as ministers of God's hope in their communities. When all the segments of your personalized curriculum are assembled, you will have created a personalized keepsake that captures the lives of those God sent into your midst for a time of mutual growth and encouragement.

I pray you will let God transform your emotions with His mighty Word in order to fulfill His purpose. May we learn the royal ways as one who is a child of the King of Kings! We are royal family so let us exhibit royal emotions fitting for a child of the King of Kings!

Walking as a daughter of the King with you,

Anita Carman